The Cross, the Candle, and the Crown

MERCER UNIVERSITY PRESS

Endowed by

TOM WATSON BROWN

and

THE WATSON-BROWN FOUNDATION, INC.

The Cross, the Candle, and the Crown

A NARRATIVE HISTORY OF MOREHOUSE COLLEGE, 1867–2021

Marcellus Chandler Barksdale

MERCER UNIVERSITY PRESS
MACON, GEORGIA

MUP/ H1053

Published by Mercer University Press
1501 Mercer University Drive
Macon, Georgia 31207

29 28 27 26 25 5 4 3 2 1

Books published by Mercer University Press are printed on acid-free paper that meets the requirements of the American National Standard for Information Sciences—Permanence of Paper for Printed Library Materials.

Printed and bound in Canada.

This book is set in Adobe Garamond.

Cover/jacket design by Burt&Burt.

ISBN 978-0-88146-967-7
Cataloging-in-Publication Data is available from the Library of Congress

This book is dedicated to

Julia and Andrew; Mary and Frank;

Robyn and Frank;

Mattie, Wendell, Clarence, and Lawrence

and Jon.

Contents

Acknowledgments

In relation to the more than a decade that I labored, with love, on *The Cross, the Candle, and the Crown: A Narrative History of Morehouse College, 1867–2021*, one person must be recognized above all others: Robert Michael Franklin Jr., tenth president of Morehouse College, who, in 2010, asked me to update the school's history to commemorate its sesquicentennial in 2017. I was honored to work on this history, which was last documented during the school's centennial in 1967. With a generous grant from the Arthur Vining Davis Foundations, the research got underway. Dr. Willis Sheftall Jr., provost and senior vice president at the time, gave me a reduced teaching schedule to devote time to the project. The research team consisted of several individuals, including Trenton Bailey, my office manager, who collaborated with me until the manuscript was finished. Trenton, a graduate of Morehouse with a doctorate from Clark-Atlanta University, is also a published author. Daron Calhoun, the administrative assistant for the sesquicentennial project, was invaluable in planning research trips, making appointments, booking hotel rooms, and reserving transportation. Daron now works for the Avery Institute and the College of Charleston, where he earned a master's degree. Khari Ford was the other Morehouse student whose indefatigable work moved the research forward. Khari served as an officer in the United States Marines and now has a law degree. It must be noted that Margaret Bryant, my administrative assistant in the African American Studies program, proved valuable in editing the manuscript as she typed its first iteration.

Valuable input was provided by Frederick Knight, Collie Burnett, Frank Sims, and Tobe Johnson, who read the manuscript and gave it their critical review. Critical insight was also given by Roy Hamilton as we talked about the manuscript over the years. His keen sense of proportion as an expert proposal writer was useful to me on many levels. Larry Carter, dean of the Martin Luther King Jr. International Chapel at Morehouse, encouraged me to stay the course and to submit the proposal to Mercer University Press. Hamilton reviewed my proposal and gave salient suggestions for its improvement.

The staff who worked at the various archives and libraries where research was conducted were very helpful in the discovery phase of the project. At the outset, I searched in the collections of the Georgia Archives and the National Archives of Atlanta (Southeast Region), both in Morrow, Georgia. First and foremost, however, I received key support from the personnel at the Robert W. Woodruff Library Corporation's archives in the Atlanta University Center, where papers and memorabilia associated with Morehouse are in abundance. Papers relevant to the American Baptist Home Mission Society and the Baptist denomination in general were examined in the collections available at the Mercer University archives in Macon and Atlanta, Georgia.

The collections at the Rockefeller Archive Center in Sleepy Hollow, New York, were invaluable, and the staff there was exceedingly helpful. As a matter of record, the center was so interested in the project that Daron Calhoun and I received additional funds from them which allowed us to make a second trip to the center to continue our work. The Moorland Spingarn Collection at Howard University in Washington, DC, was useful, as were the findings at the archives of Virginia Union University in Richmond, the Schomburg Library in New York, the Library of Congress in Washington, DC, and the Robert W. Woodruff Library at Emory University in Atlanta. Visits were also made to the archives at Duke University and the University of North Carolina at Chapel Hill. In addition, I am abundantly grateful for the enthusiastic assistance I was given at the Augusta (GA) Historical Society, the Auburn Avenue Research Library and Archives in Atlanta, the Atlanta History Center, and the archives at the University of Georgia in Athens. Our research team also visited an archaeological dig in rural Aiken, South Carolina, where the old Silver Bluff Baptist Church, regarded as the oldest organized Black church in the United States by the Department of the Interior, once stood. When this church dissolved, many of its members merged with Old Springfield Church.

Four churches are associated with the early years in the history of Morehouse: St. John Methodist, whose congregants gave the edifices for Old Springfield Baptist Church, where the first classes of the school were held; Old Springfield Baptist Church; Harmony Baptist Church, where the school moved in 1869; and Friendship Baptist Church in Atlanta, where Atlanta Baptist Seminary students were taught and tutored until the school occupied the new building at the corner of Elliott and Hunter Streets. Our team made several visits to these churches where we spoke with staff members and made physical observations at Old Springfield.

Lastly, for the encouragement, support, and diversion given by my best friend "Ben," I am eternally grateful.

Foreword

This is an American adventure story. It tells of a nation slowly overcoming the ravages of a long and costly civil war and how a variety of small colleges emerged to assist in national reconstruction. Among the many historically black colleges and universities that emerged at that time was a school that began to claim a unique role as a liberal arts leadership academy for young men.

This is a story comprised of multiple stories and threads that interwove to create a powerful tapestry of educational achievement and democratic promise. In time, this small college, which was animated by a moral ethos and by audacious leaders, produced a movement aimed at changing the world. They took this idea seriously. It was rooted in a conviction about the nature of the universe and the forces that shape and drive it. A mix of science, culture, and theology empowered them to believe that concerted human action could produce change in the minds, hearts, and the material and social relationships of black and white Americans. New ideas could contribute to a new world. And those new ideas would be communicated and energized through courageous action fostered by colleges like Morehouse. This book relates how institutions, individuals, and ideas came together for social transformation.

Educating students to become Renaissance men with social consciences and global perspectives became the Morehouse mission and its particular way of making an impact on the larger world. Morehouse was a school planted in the soil of Augusta and later transplanted and nurtured in the red clay of Atlanta. It worked to prepare its graduates to risk becoming pioneers in various vocations and communities around the country aimed at dismantling a society built on the abuse of power and racial hatred, thereby initiating change that resulted in better people in better institutions resulting in a better society.

In his classic essay *The Gift of Black Folk*, W. E. B. Du Bois wrote that during its first hundred years, America made few advances toward creating an authentic and inclusive democracy until African Americans led the struggle to do so. "It was the black man that raised a vision of democracy in America such as neither Americans nor Europeans conceived in the eighteenth century and such as they have not even accepted in the twentieth; and yet a conception which every clear-sighted man knows is true and inevitable."[1] Yet most Americans do not know that heroic story, in part because it has been suppressed, distorted, and ignored. But, as William Cullen Bryant declared, truth crushed to the earth will ultimately rise.

In light of Du Bois's insight, one could say that the history of America's reluctant, complicated democratic narrative is interwoven with the history of institutions like Morehouse. And reading through this text, one comes to see how profoundly this one school and its alumni transformed the nation. The Martin Luther King Jr. Memorial in the nation's capital offers visible evidence of this point. This book captures the sacrifices, hopes, triumphs, tragedies, and the joys that one small school in the American South undertook for the common good.

The author, Marcellus Barksdale, is a distinguished historian who brings to this work a lifetime of teaching, research, and devoted service to the field of higher education, in general, and to Morehouse, his alma mater, in particular. He has sifted thoughtfully and critically through more than 150 years of events, ideas, individuals, and dramas to craft a fascinating perspective on higher education in the service of common and lasting values. Barksdale also reminds us of the power of dreams and the movements of common people to do uncommon things. Helen Vendler, the eminent professor of literature at Harvard, has observed that the vocation of educators is to teach students to love what they have loved. I think that she captures precisely Barksdale's achievement to illustrate how the early Morehouse founders taught their students to love what they have loved: truth, justice, liberty, goodness, and beauty. Morehouse has succeeded in keeping this noble practice robust among subsequent generations.

---

[1] W. E. B. Du Bois, *The Gift of Black Folks*, 65.

This will be a compelling study for people who know little about and have no relationship to this particular college. But given the crisis in our democracy today, this is a story we all need to hear. It may inspire more of us to light candles in the dark.

—Robert M. Franklin, PhD

Preface

When Dr. Robert Michael Franklin Jr., tenth president of Morehouse College, asked me to update the school's history since the publication of Edward A. Jones's *A Candle in the Dark: A History of Morehouse College* (1969), I humbly agreed. The year was 2010. The new history of the college was to help commemorate the sesquicentennial of Morehouse in 2017. As the research got underway, I decided not just to update the previous history but to retell the history of Morehouse from its establishment in 1867 to 2017. The central theme of the story of Morehouse College is about an idea that the founders had that black men, two years after the Civil War, could be educated for service to their communities. At some points in the narrative, the story may take the form of report-writing as I allow the voices of the people who played important roles in the development of the college or writers on the subject to be heard. I was disappointed by the absence of the documents my predecessors used to write their books. Nevertheless, I used their narratives to help write the first one hundred years of the Morehouse story and enlarged it with new evidence uncovered in the research process. The story after 1968 is based on new discoveries. In writing the narrative, I have taken agency as it is based on my voice. This is not the story of all historically black colleges and universities (HBCUs), which were not designated as such until Title III of the Higher Education Act of 1965. At that time, Congress defined HBCUs as those schools of higher learning accredited and established before 1964 whose main mission was the education of black students. Prior to this, these school saw themselves as colleges like other American schools of higher learning but were segregated because of Jim Crow laws. The curriculums and standards were similar to those of white schools, but like white schools, they varied because of missions and endowments. For many years, leadership positions and faculties at black colleges were held by white men who had been educated at traditionally white colleges and universities. They brought their learning to bear on how they taught the students at the black schools.

It is generally known that before the end of the Civil War there were only three black institutions of higher learning in America: Cheyney University (PA), Lincoln University (PA), and Wilberforce University (OH). Shortly after the war, there was an explosion of schools for black students, largely because the black community saw the power in learning and people were eager to become literate. But there was also a desire on the part of the white citizenry to acculturate black men and women into a way of thinking, particularly on the part of white missionary groups like the National Theological Institute, American Baptist Home Mission Society, American Missionary Association, and Christian Methodist Episcopal Church. The exception to this were the schools established by the African Methodist Episcopal Church. After its establishment by the National Theological Institute, for more than sixty years Morehouse operated under the authority of the American Baptist Home Mission Society. For most of the early history of Morehouse, its norming schools were others black colleges. That changed after 1965. I identify Morehouse College as an American institution of higher learning whose mission is to educate men, especially black men, for lives of stewardship and service.

Old Springfield Baptist Church, Augusta, Georgia, ca. 1867.

Harmony Baptist Church, ca. 1869, was the second home of the Augusta Theological Institute.

Atlanta Baptist Seminary, original campus
at Elliott and Hunter Streets, ca. 1879.

Historic Samuel T. Graves House,
first building on permanent campus, ca. 1889.

Morehouse College campus today
with Graves House shown in the background.

Aerial photo showing the early Morehouse College campus.

Henry Lyman Morehouse (1833–1917),
namesake of Morehouse College.

Historic Samuel T. Graves House, showing the bell in the bell tower, was constructed in Atlanta, Georgia, 1889.

Morehouse students in the legendary chapel.

The funeral march for Martin Luther King, Jr. in Atlanta on April 9, 1968. The march began at Ebenezer Baptist Church and ended at Morehouse College.

The mourners at the funeral of Martin Luther King, Jr. on the Morehouse College campus, April 9, 1968.

Benjamin Elijah Mays delivers eulogy at the funeral of Martin Luther King, Jr. at Morehouse College, April 9, 1968.

New student orientation, a Morehouse tradition.

Commencement at Morehouse College.

Introduction

The Cross, the Candle, and the Crown: A Narrative History of Morehouse College is the inspirational story about how members of a church in Augusta, Georgia, had the idea that black men, just two years after the end of slavery, could be educated for service to their communities. With a strong faith and a sincere hope, they established a school for young men that would produce literate preachers and teachers. The school faced financial exigencies and housing challenges in its early years but survived to become one of America's leading institutions of higher education. In 1866, this idea was fostered by three men, Edmund Turney, Richard Coulter, and William White, who believed that African American men—some free, others just out of bondage; some literate, many others illiterate—could be educated to serve their people. The idea came to fruition in 1867 when Augusta Theological Institute was opened in the sanctuary and balcony of Springfield Baptist Church. The school met the challenges of the late nineteenth century and the first decade of the twentieth century and was eventually named Morehouse College in 1913. This is the story of Morehouse College, which still fosters the idea that black men can be educated for stewardship and service not only to their communities but to the world. The beliefs and dreams of the founders of Augusta Theological Institute in 1867 have developed into a world-class institution of higher education primarily for black men in keeping with its original mission but which is also open to men of all races and ethnicities.

Historical writing is based on available sources and the evaluation and interpretation of these sources. However, the acceptance of "what really is/was or what is only believed depends upon the culture, learned behavior, under study"[1] The Morehouse culture is often cloaked in some degree of mystery and myth, and the story of Morehouse College is heavily veiled in what is called the "Morehouse Mystique." Previous histories of Morehouse, such as Benjamin G. Brawley's *History of Morehouse College* (1917) and Edward A. Jones's *A Candle in the Dark: A History of*

---

[1] Robert F. Berkhofer Jr., *A Behavioral Approach to Historical Analysis* (New York: Free Press, 1969) 22.

Morehouse College (1968), told the story of the school based on the lived experiences of the writers and the evidence available to them at the time. Like these writers, the present author writes his narrative based, in part, on lived experiences. Encrusted beliefs about Morehouse notwithstanding, the story of this institution of higher education is as engrossing as it is intriguing. At the heart of the Morehouse experience are hidebound traditions that undergird the Morehouse Mystique but which also support the idea that black men can be educated and become leaders in their chosen professions.

Morehouse College is located in the South, in Atlanta, Georgia, but it is also part of the history of education in the United States. Morehouse did not develop in isolation but in conjunction with other colleges. Since 1965, when the Higher Education Act became law, Morehouse has been identified as an HBCU—a historically black college and university. Bobby Lovett's *America's Historically Black Colleges and Universities* does an excellent job narrating the story of these American institutions of higher education from 1837 to 2009. Lovett's book devotes fourteen pages to Morehouse, but the school's history is so compelling and impactful that its story warrants its own book. In telling this story, three emblems are used to represent milestones in the history of Morehouse College: the cross, the candle, and the crown.

The cross represents the founding of the institution by the National Theological Institute and University, which soon came under the authority of the American Baptist Home Mission Society. Both were Christian organizations whose mission was the training of Negro preachers and teachers who would help uplift other members of their race. The original name of the school made clear its religious mission: Augusta Theological Institute. The founders of the school were members of Springfield Baptist Church, where the first classes were held. The first teachers at the theological institute were three women who worked as teachers for the American Missionary Association, yet another Christian connection to the founding of the school. The first three presidents of the institution were ministers—Joseph T. Robert, Samuel T. Graves, and George Sale—and later, three other ministers also became presidents of the college: Benjamin Mays, Robert Michael Franklin Jr., and John Silvanus Wilson Jr. Until the late 1950s, the Morehouse School of Religion, which is now at the

Interdenominational Theological Center (ITC), was a part of the college. And although Morehouse is nonsectarian, it still has strong ties with the Baptist denomination. Affixed to the front wall of the Martin Luther King Jr. International Chapel, just above its name, is a symbolic Christian cross, which identifies the fundamental work of this celebrated building.

The candle was adopted as a symbol for Morehouse College around 1967, when Edward Jones was inspired by words from an old Chinese aphorism: "It is better to light a candle than to curse the darkness." Jones modified this sentiment to reflect the centennial work of Morehouse in dispelling ignorance, like "a candle in the dark," for the title of his book on the history of the college. The Morehouse motto, *Et Facta Est Lux*—"And there was light"—speaks to the idea of the candle. It may also be said that thousands of Morehouse men, by their deeds and "daily walks," are like candles in the dark in places where provincial attitudes and actions exist. The work of civil rights leader Dr. Martin Luther King Jr., a Morehouse Man, is one of the best representatives of a candle in the dark. And although the school's Candle in the Dark Gala annually awards the "Bennie" (honoring Dr. Benjamin Mays) to a Morehouse Man for his accomplishments and the "Candle" to a non-Morehouse man for his achievements, they all shine like candles in the dark.

The crown, which is often spoken of at Morehouse nowadays, was inspired by a statement made by Dr. Howard W. Thurmond, who graduated from the college in 1923 and who said, "Over the heads of her students, Morehouse holds a crown that she challenges them to grow tall enough to wear." Dr. Benjamin Elijah Mays, the sixth president of the college, put the idea of the crown another way when he addressed the graduating class of 1961, saying, "There is an air of expectancy at Morehouse. It is expected that when you wear the insignia of a Morehouse Man, you will do well in all your pursuits." Dr. Robert Michael Franklin Jr., the tenth president of the college, was also thinking about the crown when he encapsulated the "Five (now Six) Wells" of a Morehouse Man: well-read, well-spoken, well-dressed, well-traveled, and well-balanced, and well-written. As the old saying goes, "You can always tell a Morehouse Man, but you can't tell him much." Wearing the insignia of Morehouse Men, thousands of graduates strive to be the best in their professions, occupations, and personal endeavors. For more than 150 years, thousands of black men and others have proven the founders' idea that they could be educated to serve their communities. This is the story I have told using the sources available to me and personal, firsthand knowledge of many of the events in the history of Morehouse as an alumnus and a member of the faculty for many years.

Chapter 1

"The Cross in the Sanctuary": Augusta Theological Institute

On a cold winter's evening in February 1867, a group of men affiliated with Springfield Baptist Church in Augusta, Georgia, met in the home of Jonas Singleton, a deacon at the church, to finalize the list of names of the men who would become the first students of Augusta Theological Institute. The deacons were responding to a letter from the Reverend Doctor Edmund Turney, founder and president of the National Baptist Theological Institute and University in Washington, DC, to organize a branch of the institute south of Richmond, Virginia. The letter had been delivered by Richard Coulter and given to William Jefferson White. Among the men at the February 14th meeting were Rev. Henry Watts, pastor at Springfield Baptist Church; Deacon Jesse Jones, who kept the minutes of their deliberations; and William Jefferson White, who presided at the meeting. Also attending the meeting were John T. Shuften, editor of *The Colored American*, Augusta's first black newspaper; Robert Harper, a skilled piano tuner and musician; Simeon Beard, a Union Army officer; Thomas Beard, who became a state legislator; and, of course, Richard C. Coulter, a graduate of the National Theological Institute.[1] The list of names was sent to Reverend Turney and once the names were approved, Mr. White "approached a friend, Captain Charles H. Prince," who secured the support of the American Missionary Association, a Congregationalist organization in New England, which sent three teachers to get the institute started.[2]

Augusta is the second oldest city in Georgia. It was founded three years after Gen. James Oglethorpe received a royal charter from the crown

---

[1] Edward J. Cashin, *Old Springfield: Race and Religion in Augusta* (Augusta, GA: Springfield Park Foundation, 1995) 53.

[2] Edward A. Jones, *A Candle in the Dark: A History of Morehouse College* (Valley Forge, PA: Judson Press, 1967) 25. Unrecorded conversation with Dr. Samuel M. Nabrit, a 1926 graduate of Morehouse.

of England to establish a thirteenth English colony in America for the poor and destitute. By 1865, a sizable black population lived in Augusta, most of whom lived in the Third Ward. Springfield Baptist Church was in the Fourth Ward. Springfield Baptist Church began as a "brush arbor" church near the Savannah River. However, in 1844, St. John Methodist Church, a white congregation, gave its old New England-style edifice to the Springfield congregation; the building was moved to its present site on logs. It was in this meetinghouse that the first classes of Augusta Theological Institute were held in February 1867.

The National Theological Institute was founded in Washington, DC, in December 1864. By 1867, the first branch of the institute had been organized in Richmond, the former capital of the Confederate States of America, and then the second branch was organized in Augusta. The mission of the National Theological Institute was twofold: to proselytize the freedmen and convert them to the Baptist denomination and to educate the newly freed African Americans for uplift and citizenship. In other words, the school worked to educate black men to become stewards in service to their communities. Richard Coulter, a former Georgia slave, left Washington in the fall of 1866, perhaps traveling on the Atlantic and Gulf Railroad, with a letter from Dr. Turney "authorizing him to establish a school in Augusta or at some other location in the South which he might choose."[3] Coulter chose Augusta, the place of his birth and early life. He was thirty-three years old when he presented the letter to William Jefferson White, a prominent member of the black community. During the Civil War, Coulter left Augusta in the service of his slaveholder as a valet, like thousands of other black men who worked for the Confederate Army in support service to white military garrisons. Also, like many other black people, in military service or otherwise, Coulter was determined to be free. He first fled to Washington, but as the theater of war moved northward toward the nation's capital, Coulter fled to Philadelphia. When the Civil War ended, he was intent on returning to his native Augusta, where he felt his talents and training were sorely needed and where he believed he could be effective in improving the lives of his people.

On his journey back to Augusta, Richard Coulter stopped in

[3] Ibid., 171.

Washington, DC, where he took jobs to earn money to help finance his trip. He also took classes at the fledging National Theological Institute, where he met Dr. Edmund Turney. The fortuitous Coulter-Turney encounter would soon give birth to the idea of a school in the South that would, in less than fifty years, be named Morehouse College. Although Turney had the idea for the school and Coulter delivered the letter, it was William Jefferson White wo played the critical role in the establishment of the school and is often identified as its founder.

The Reverend White recalled his first meeting with Richard Coulter, whom he had not known during slavery before the Civil War. It was late in the fall of 1866, after Coulter's return to Augusta, when he, a fine young man of perhaps thirty years of age, called at the large furniture house of Platt Brothers and asked for W. J. White.[4] Coulter was directed to the "coffin room" on the third floor of the manufacturing company, which is where he found White, the firm's "undertaker" who was in charge of the coffin department. White did not make coffins but supervised a staff of a dozen men.

Coulter knew that his years of absence from Augusta and the South would make it difficult for him to open a school there, but he knew of Rev. White's prominence in the city, so he turned over his letter to him, saying, "Brother White, Dr. Turney put this letter into my hand when I was leaving Washington, but I find that I can do nothing with it, and so I have come to turn it over to you; if anybody can do anything with it, you can." White read the letter carefully, then sat down at his desk right there in the coffin room and wrote Dr. Turney, informing him of his willingness to offer any assistance he could to help establish a school in Augusta. This opened up correspondence between White and Turney, and in a short while it was agreed that if White would secure sufficient students, the National Theological Institute would supply a teacher without cost to the school.[5] Richard Coulter, "a bright young man," remained in Augusta but his relationship to Augusta Theological Institute is a mystery. He did not join the congregation at Springfield Baptist Church but

---

[4] Jones, Candle in the Dark.

[5] William J. White, "The Founding of Atlanta Baptist College," in the Atlanta University Presidential Records: John Hope, Box 72, Folder 2, Archives Research Center, Robert W. Woodruff Library and Archives, Atlanta University Center.

became a member of the Central Baptist Church pastored by "the honored old veteran" the Reverend Henry Jackson, who also taught at the Walker Street School in Augusta. Coulter was soon licensed to preach and "was quite useful in his church and community."[6]

William Jefferson White was one of Augusta's prominent black individuals in 1867. He "identified himself proudly with the Negroes despite his non-Negro parentage"[7] According to the 1870 US Census Report, White was a mulatto, the progeny of one black parent and one white parent. If the census report is to be accepted, then it must be asserted that William Jefferson White's mother was black and his father was white. He was a member of Springfield Baptist Church, the most prominent black church in town at that time, and most of his associations were among members of the black community in Augusta. When he agreed to take the lead in the venture that resulted in the founding of Augusta Theological Institute, White discussed the matter with the Reverend Henry Watts, Springfield's pastor, and with the deacons of the church. Emboldened by their deliberations and by the actions of Rev. Watts, efforts were made "to recruit students for the bold enterprise, promising to use the church as the schoolhouse."[8] The founding committee had planned to meet at the church, but no fire had been started to heat the cavernous building, so they moved the meeting to Deacon Singleton's house, which was not far from the church.[9] The founders "enrolled deacons, preachers, and young men aspiring to the ministry. No females, nor other than the above, were enrolled. 'It was to me one of the most inspiring experiences of his life,' White said. A majority of the men enrolled were older than White, but with them it appeared to make no difference."[10] Along with the list of students that was sent to Turney in Washington, DC, was a request for a teacher.

The request for a teacher at the incipient Augusta Theological Institute was not immediately granted. Dr. Turney commissioned William

---

[6] Kenneth Coleman, ed., *A History of Georgia* (Athens: University of Georgia Press, 1991).

[7] Ibid.

[8] Jones, Candle in the Dark, 25.

[9] Samuel Nabrit, '25, on Marcellus Barksdale.

[10] White, "Founding of Atlanta Baptist College."

Jefferson White to assume this role until such time as a teacher could be supplied, so Augusta Theological Institute did not begin classes right away. "Of the thirty-seven students who applied, almost all were literate as a result of having attended [Rev.] White's 'blockade schools'"[11] that he had organized in the 1850s. And although Williams Jefferson White had been commissioned to assume instructional duties at the new institute, he was already gainfully employed and not seeking employment. Reverend Henry Watts, pastor at Springfield Baptist Church, was also asked to be the school's first teacher, but he too declined, although he vigorously recruited students for the daring enterprise and offered the church as its first campus. With no teacher, White realized that too much effort had been invested in this bold venture to be wasted; he could not abandon the fledgling project at its incipiency. He thought the enterprise was too important to be taken over by persons who were less capable and not as devoted to the project as he was, so in order to keep the idea alive, he became the first teacher at Augusta Theological Institute.

While White was deciding whether or not to accept these duties, he received a communiqué from Gen. Oliver Otis Howard, commissioner of the Bureau of Refugees, Freedmen and Abandoned Lands (Freedmen's Bureau) in Washington, DC, informing him that he had been appointed a field agent of the bureau in Georgia with the duties of traveling across the state, monitoring and supervising the work of the bureau among African Americans. White had to decide whether to teach or become an agent for the bureau. The bureau work was very attractive and carried a certain prestige, and in his heart of hearts, White wanted to take this plum assignment. But the first class of students at the school were eager to begin their studies. As he wrestled with his conscience about which path to take, White decided to consult with Capt. Charles H. Prince, who oversaw Augusta schools that were supported by the American Missionary Association (AMA). Prince agreed to help White by securing the services of teachers for Augusta Theological Institute. Three white women who were already teaching at AMA schools, where their workloads were already demanding, agreed to provide part-time instruction in the evenings at the "theological" school. Miss. Julia A. Sherman, a Baptist from C. H.

---

[11] Ibid.

Spurgeon's Tabernacle Church in London, Miss Sarah Burt, a Congregationalist from Binghamton, New York, and Miss Mary Welch, from the western region of the United States, became the first faculty members, after Reverend White, at Augusta Theological Institute.

William Jefferson White was born in 1831 in South Carolina. He was the son of a black mother and a white father, and the census records identify him as a mulatto. He was not considered a slave but was socially marginalized. White's mother had married a black man, which drew the objection of a local white man who abducted her, taking her to Ohio, where William Jefferson was eventually born. This white man was William Jefferson White's father. His mother eventually escaped from her captor and returned to her black husband in Augusta, but she kept the boy's father's surname—White—for her son. When he was ten years old, William Jefferson's white father took him from his mother and situated him with a man named "Uncle Dennis," a peddler or hawker. A clerk in Uncle Dennis's store took the boy to live with members of his family who lived a short distance from Augusta, where he grew into his manhood.

White's mother had taught him to read with the help of the widely used *Blue Black Speller*. Because he could read, he spent most of his leisure time reading the books he found in the home of Uncle Dennis. When the White family moved to South Carolina, they took William with them. He stayed with the family until he was nineteen years old, at which time he left the family to find work and his independence. Eventually, he returned to Augusta, where he learned the trade of cabinetmaker. He was thrifty and temperate and saved his money while preparing for marriage and family life, finding employment with the Goodrich Furniture Manufacturing Company owned by the ancestors of the of the Goodrich rubber dynasty.

White soon met and married a black woman who was a bondsperson and a seamstress. When the couple married, they lived in the house of his wife's slaveholder, and it was there that the first of their four children were born.[12] According to an account from Mary Bouyer White Blocker, when the Civil War started, William Jefferson White Sr. drilled with the Confederate soldiers in downtown Augusta with the intention of joining the

[12] Jones, Candle in the Dark.

Confederate Army and deserting when his regiment fought in the North. However, the love he had for his wife and family caused him to abandon his plans. He continued to work hard and save money, and when the Civil War ended in 1865, William rented a house, had it furnished, and moved his family out of the house of his wife's former slaveholder. An enterprising man, he eventually built a two-story house for his family on the corner of Campbell (now 9th) and Gwinnett Streets.

Having been ordained as a Baptist minister in his early years, perhaps in his late teens, William Jefferson White was a man of strong religious convictions. He affiliated with Springfield Baptist Church but became the first pastor at Harmony Baptist Church, where he served until his death in 1913, the year Atlanta Baptist College was named Morehouse College. White also founded *The Georgia Baptist*, the official organ of the black Baptist in the state. His sons helped him publish the well-edited and widely read publication. He was not an ordinary man: although equipped with a minimum of formal education, he was almost totally self-taught and was endowed with a rare combination of innate gifts—intelligence, ambition, self-reliance, integrity, foresight, and courage. William Jefferson White was a born teacher, preacher, and leader.[13]

Although the official founding date for Augusta Theological Institute is February 14, 1867, it was not until May 1867 that the Reverend J. W. Parker, DD, of Massachusetts, arrived in Augusta "under the auspices of the National Theological Institute, to locate the school for the training of preachers and teachers for the colored [*sic*] people."[14] The school's instability at this time is reflected in the changes of leadership that occurred over the next two years. J. Mason Rice took charge of the fledging school when Reverend Doctor J. W. Parker took ill and had to return North. Rice was followed in November of the same year by Rev. Charles H. Corey and his wife, who kept the school in a rented room, and mostly at night. Corey wrote, "The times, politically, were unsettled. Prejudices were strong, and with but few facilities, not very much was accomplished. I had some warnings from the Ku Klux Klan, and on a few occasions the

[13] Ibid.

[14] Leroy Davis, A Clashing of the Soul: John Hope and the Dilemma of African American Leadership and Higher Education in the Early Twentieth Century (Athens: University of Georgia Press) 7.

city authorities, unsolicited by me, sent some policemen to protect our evening school." The Black Horse Cavalry, Jayhawkers, and Regulators were among other terrorist groups that sprang up in Georgia and across the South. Made up of ex-Confederate soldiers, these mobs "beat, mutilated, and murdered freedmen, sometimes drove them from plantations to avoid paying wages, and often practiced simple brigandage. These bands were later absorbed into the Ku Klux Klan."[15] In the face of these adverse forces, there was still a strong desire to maintain an institution of higher learning reserved exclusively for the education of the "colored young men of the city," although girls and young women also attended some of the school's earliest classes. Although long-term security was tenuous at best, five months after the founding of Augusta Theological, an announcement appeared in *The Daily Loyal Georgia*,[16] a local African American newspaper, on July 19, 1867. "Many of the colored young men of this city wanted an evening school that would teach the rudimentary branches of education, and be started *exclusively* for themselves." At this time, the school was struggling to attract students, especially males. So, a group of young black men called on their peers to come to a meeting: "To encourage so commendable a desire, and test the practicability of the enterprise, a meeting will be held at Springfield Church, this evening, at precisely eight o'clock. Let every young man come and bring along with him his comrades. If a sufficient number can be obtained for the class, the school will be formed." The school was meant exclusively for the young men. The specific outcome of this meeting is unknown, but due to the strong desire to keep the idea of a school for black men alive, the fledgling institute survived. In the long scheme of things, Morehouse College survived. Much credit for its survival must be given to William Jefferson White and to the three women who worked with him in Augusta under auspices of the American Missionary Association: Julia Sherman, Mary Welch, and Sarah Burt.

Julia A. Sherman took the lead in managing the affairs of Augusta Theological Institute. For instance, in her letter in November 1867 to

---

[15] Donald L. Grant, ed., *The Way It Was in the South: The Black Experience in Georgia* (New York: Carol Publishing Group, 1993) 97.

[16] University of Georgia Archives, Athens, Georgia.

Rev. E. P. Smith, she told of the difficulty she and the other teachers had getting from their boardinghouse to the school. It was more than two miles, so she requested funds to pay for a carriage to drive them to the school. By November 1867, Sherman, Welch, and Burt were joined by two black teachers from Augusta—W. L. Chaddous and Robert Hankerson.[17] Of note in her teacher's monthly report, though, Miss Sherman claimed "there is a lack of interest among the colored people in education." Whether there was a lack of interest in education or an urgent need to provide a livelihood for themselves and their families is a matter of conjecture. The extant evidence, however, tells us that there was great interest among African Americans in achieving some level of education in the region that once comprised the Confederate States. Sarah Burt had a different perspective. In her April 6, 1867, letter to Rev. Smith, who was a Congregational minister, secretary of the Christian commission, and field secretary of the AMA, and which was written less than two months after the school's opening, Burt said that she taught at the "Theological School three nights per week" and that she enjoyed her work there very much. She reported that "the young men are so anxious to learn, so respectful and kind to us, we feel it a great privilege to assist them." She went on to talk about the sewing class that was held for girls every Wednesday evening and that while the girls were at work they learned songs, had social talk, and closed with prayer.[18] The need for more staff suggests that Burt's observation was more credible than Sherman's when it came to the desire of the black population to gain literacy.

By May 1868, enrollment at the theological institute had reached about sixty students, of whom seventeen were studying for the ministry. When Reverend Corey's mission at Augusta ended in July 1868, he transferred to the Richmond Theological Institute and was replaced in Augusta by the Reverend Lucian C. Hayden, DD, the following winter. When the Reverend W. D. Siegfried arrived to head the school on November 15, 1869, it was agreed that a more permanent location for the school was needed. An eligible lot measuring 180-by-180 feet was purchased on

---

[17] Sarah Burt to Rev. E. P. Smith, April 6, 1867. In the American Missionary Association Archives, Auburn Avenue Library and Archives, Atlanta.

[18] Ibid.

Telfair Street for $5,700. But the conditions of the old building on the property and the racial climate in the city forced Reverend Siegfried to leave the city and the state, and the school was discontinued for a while.[19] The idea almost died. Fortunately, the work of Augusta Theological Institute was continued at Harmony Baptist Church, which had recently been founded by Reverend William Jefferson White. Because of his strong voice on behalf of education for members of the black community in Augusta and for African Americans in general, White was almost lynched. It was this outspoken stand against racist forces that his membership at Springfield became tenuous at best. At worst, he was encouraged to quiet his voice or leave the congregation among whom Augusta Theological Institute had been founded. Soon White was given a letter of dismissal from Springfield.

On "May 10, 1868, Mr. White and Deacon Thomas, Brother Jacob McKinley, Sister Brown and daughter, and Deacon Ceasar Johnson, with Deacon Horace Hughes and six others became the founding members of a new congregation."[20] "With letters of demission from Springfield Church, the former members organized and constituted 'The Harmony Baptist Church' on a lot adjoining McKinley's grove, a part of which had been given by Mrs. McKinley and a part bought from her."[21] The name of the new church—Harmony—is intriguing, to say the least. The first Harmony Baptist was a brush arbor church. The work done at Springfield was continued at the Harmony Baptist brush arbor school. A brush arbor school is a post-and-beam construction without walls which uses branches and brush for the roof. Courses in reading, writing, arithmetic, cursive, and religion were among the first classes offered by Augusta Theological Institute. As temperament and etiquette were important facets of the curriculum and pedagogy in the nineteenth century, they, too, were directly and indirectly imbued in the students. In May 1869, the work of the National Theological Institute transferred to the Baptist Home Mission Society, headquartered in New York City. Thereafter, the work of Augusta Theological Institute was included in the contract. Dr. James W. Parker

---

[19] Ibid., 101.

[20] Jones, Candle in the Dark, 24.

[21] *Our Baptist Ministers*, American Baptist Historical Society Papers, Mercer University Archives, 531–32.

was sent down to Augusta to make an evaluation, and he gave a flattering report to the Society indicating that he found the school in full operation. Before leaving Augusta, Dr. Parker took steps to identify and secure a permanent location for the school. A petition to the city for land was quickly honored and two lots on the corner of Center and Taylor Streets were granted for use by the school. Unfortunately, the property was never used and the lots eventually reverted back to the city.[22]

Struggling against mounting odds, the 1870s were not the best years for Augusta Theological Institute. On the recommendation of the all-white Georgia Baptist Church Convention, and endorsed by the all-black Georgia Baptist Missionary Convention, which had been organized at Central Baptist Church in Augusta on May 13, 1870, with eighty-six delegates attending, the Reverend Joseph T. Robert, LLD, a white Georgian, was appointed by the Home Mission Board to lead the school. Robert began his work on April 1, 1871, and for the next eight years, he kept the school open against many difficulties and challenges. Enrollment fluctuated, the campus was not ideal, funds were uncertain, and the racial climate in Augusta was charged with violence, hatred, anger and fear. But "the candle in the dark" remained lit; the idea was too strong to die. Those involved with Augusta Theological Institute kept the "cross in the sanctuary" as they established the foundation for Morehouse College. If Augusta Theological Institute had discontinued, we would have no Morehouse.

Writing in *The Journal of Negro Education* in 1958, history professor Glenn Sisk of the Georgia Institute of Technology described the conditions at Augusta Theological Institute at the turn of the 1870s as precarious and unpromising; the whole project was looked upon with "extreme disfavor" by most of the white people in the community. "Actual odium" was associated with it. The buildings were dilapidated and in need of extensive repair. Not an article of furniture belonged to the school. A few nails in the walls and a few books on a bench represented the entire equipment.[23] This was the state of Augusta Theological Institute in the 1870s during President Robert's tenure.

---

[22] Benjamin Brawley, *A History of Morehouse College*, New York: The John F. Slater Fund, 1923.

[23] Glen Sisk, "Section D: Morehouse College," *The Journal of Negro History* (Spring 1958) 201.

After briefly holding classes at the original site of Harmony Baptist Church "in the southern part of town in a grove,"[24] the school moved to a building that had been used by the Medical College of Georgia on Telfair Street. In the meantime, a frame building was quickly erected to house the growing Harmony congregation and the theological institute, but challenges continued to face the school at every turn. There was no sustained leadership, there was competition with Freedmen's Bureau schools for students, there was little financial support, and the physical plant barely existed. Joseph Robert had many challenges when he took charge of the school in 1871, but Augusta Theological Institute survived under his leadership, and within a few decades, and with two intervening names changes, it eventually became Morehouse College. The idea that black men could be educated for stewardship also survived and was transferred to Morehouse. Dr. Joseph Thomas Robert is considered the first president of Morehouse College.

---

[24] "Proclamation in Recognition of Harmony Baptist Church," Office of Mayor Deke Copenhaver, May 11, 2008.

Chapter 2

"Surveying the Wondrous Cross": The Augusta Institute and the Atlanta Seminary

By 1871, Augusta Theological Institute, or the Institute, as it was commonly called, had captured the attention of both the black and white communities in Augusta and its environs. It was of great interest to black men who had a strong desire to become leaders in their community as preachers and teachers. In addition, there were a few white individuals in the area who supported providing the basic elements of literacy to black people, but most of the white community saw the school as a violation of the culture of white supremacy. This was a time when most of the black population in Augusta and beyond was struggling to survive in the postbellum period. They did not have the financial resources to support the Institute, and because there was little to no financial support from the white community, the situation at Augusta Theological Institute was so dire that the school faced permanent closure. It had nothing but the proverbial "wing and a prayer." The Reverend James Dixon, pastor of First Baptist Church, a white congregation in Augusta, and a friend of Rev. William Jefferson White, was moved to see what could be done to save the situation. Reverend Dixon and Rev. Joseph Robert were friends, and he persuaded Robert to take charge of the struggling Institute. Reverend Dixon's efforts paid off, and in 1871, the Reverend Joseph T. Robert, LLD, was entrusted with the management of the fledging school. He was endorsed by the Georgia Baptist Missionary Convention, comprised of black Baptists, and the all-white Georgia Baptist Convention. The official appointment of Robert as head of the school came from the New York-based American Baptist Home Mission Board. It was generally accepted that white men would take charge of schools for black students, and in the acts of proselytizing them, their moral philosophies and ethics could be instilled in the black preachers and teachers, which they would then pass on to their congregants and pupils. Thus, "surveying the wonderous cross" was done through the lens of a white worldview at the Institute and other black schools. Perhaps this did not happen as conspicuously at African Methodist Episcopal (AME) schools such as Morris Brown College, Paul Quinn College, and Allen University.

Joseph Thomas Robert was born on November 28, 1807, in Robertville, South Carolina, "the second son of Charlotte Ann Lawton Robert and James Jehu Robert, a longtime deacon and pastor of Black Swamp Baptist Church. His paternal lineage could be traced back to Pierre Robert, a native of Switzerland, who was the first pastor of the French Huguenot colony on the Santee River in 1685. On his mother's side, Robert was descended from Captain William Lawton, a prosperous rice and indigo planter from Edisto Island, South Carolina."[1] He was baptized at age fifteen, in 1822, and in 1825, at the age of eighteen, Robert entered Columbian Seminary in Washington, DC. He eventually enrolled at Brown University in Providence, Rhode Island, where he graduated with honors in 1828. Aspiring for a career in medicine, Robert spent two years (1829 and 1830) as a resident graduate student at the Yale University Medical School. However, he left Yale and returned to South Carolina, where he received his medical doctor's degree from the South Carolina Medical College in 1831. Shortly after he returned to the Palmetto State, Joseph Robert married Adeline Elizabeth Lawton, his first cousin and the daughter of Alexander J. and Martha Moses Lawton.[2] But Dr. Robert was not as enthusiastic about a career in medicine as he was about the ministry, so he began to pursue his inner ambition, and in 1832, Robert was licensed to preach by the Robertville church where he had been baptized seventeen years earlier.

After being licensed to preach, Robert spent two years in study at the Furman Theological Seminary in Greenville, South Carolina. Following his theological studies, Robert held pastorates in several locations: in 1834, he was ordained pastor of the church in Robertville; in 1839, he moved to Covington, Kentucky, to take charge of the Baptist Church in that Ohio River city; and in 1841, he moved to the pastorate of a Baptist

[1] R. Frank Saunders Jr., "Joseph Thomas Robert and the Wages of Conscience," *Georgia Historical Quarterly* 88 (Spring 2002) 2.

[2] Ibid., 3.

church in Lebanon, Kentucky. In 1848, Rev. Joseph T. Robert accepted the invitation to lead the First Baptist Church of Savannah, Georgia. However, he soon decided to move to the North to shield his family from a society that was informed by slavery and white supremacy in all layers of life. He left the Savannah Baptist church in 1850, the same year Congress passed the Compromise of 1850, in order to take the pastorate of a church in Portsmouth, Ohio, where he remained until he accepted a professorship of mathematics and natural sciences at Burlington University in Iowa.

The Civil War, the war that brought emancipation to more than four million enslaved and marginalized African Americans, divided the United States in general and families in particular, affecting them physically, socially, politically, economically, and mentally. Robert and his family were living in Iowa at the onset of the war, and it was here that he began to express his antipathy to slavery. Adeline, Robert's wife, on the other hand, "retained strong southern sympathies in spite of her husband's disapproval. She was distraught when her second son, Henry, chose to remain in the Union Army."[3] In 1864, Dr. Robert became professor of languages at Iowa State University, and in 1869, he was offered the presidency of Burlington University. Two years later, he returned to the South to head Augusta Theological Institute. President Robert was committed to the idea that black men could be educated for stewardship, and his indefatigable leadership and vision are why the Institute survived. The survival of the Institute meant the survival of Morehouse College and the ideals on which it stands.

When he took the helm of Augusta Theological Institute on August 1, 1871, Dr. Robert was not only the president of the school, he was also its faculty and staff. He conducted the school for four years without an assistant, during a time when the average annual enrollment was fifty-two students, resulting in a student-teacher ratio of 52 to 1. There were no student or administrative records, its facilities were in disrepair, and there was an extreme shortage of funds. President Robert not only gave his time and knowledge to the students, he also gave financial support to keep the Institute open. He strongly believed in the mission of the school, and his

[3] Ibid., 8.

deep religious beliefs prompted him to "survey the wonderous cross" as he instilled his beliefs and precepts in his pupils.

Shortly after he assumed his role as head of the school, Dr. Robert reported to the American Baptist Home Mission Society (ABHMS) that "a few nails in the walls and a few books on a bench constituted its entire equipment." Robert's efforts at the Institute attracted more attention from the ABHMS. At first, little support was forthcoming from white Augustans, but eventually local black Baptists and a few white individuals raised enough money to put a new roof over the building on Telfair Street used by the school in 1871. The Shiloh Missionary Baptist Association and Harmony Baptist Church, two black organizations, contributed the most support to the Institute. At this point, Springfield Baptist Church, where Augusta Theological Institute had been founded in 1867, no longer a sponsored the school. It should be remembered that William Jefferson White had been dismissed from Springfield by then, and the school had come under the care of Harmony Baptist Church.

The American Baptist Home Mission Society worked to proselytize and evangelize Americans, including African Americans, Native Americans, and Mexican Americans, in the tenets and precepts of its faith. Before the Civil War and shortly thereafter, members of the black community had been converted and baptized by white ministers. But the ABHMS and Dr. Robert were convinced that the conversion of black individuals and their public affirmations of the faith should be conducted by black ministers. There was an underlying educational philosophy associated with this notion: "Since unlettered freedmen could not read, education was difficult. They had to learn how to read and write and these educated black ministers would serve as their teachers. Thus, by educating black ministers, the Baptists would be able to reach the uneducated masses and mold their social and spiritual lives. Robert observed that many whites thought that ex-slaves could not be roused mentally, but he felt that he had proved otherwise."[4] Between 1871 and 1878, the year before the Institute moved to Atlanta, "245 men enrolled, 150 of these being ministerial students." No women attended the school after President Robert took charge, and no males under the age of sixteen were enrolled. "Before 1871

---

[4] Ibid.

only residents of Augusta attended the school. In 1874 thirty-one out of fifty-six [students] were from other places, and in 1877, sixty-four out of ninety-two."[5] The students who enrolled at the Institute in its early years were not yet prepared to do real college work, so the academic offerings of the curriculum were limited to the fundamentals of literacy and biblical studies—surveying the wonderous cross.

By 1879, President Robert had done a masterful job keeping the theological institute open, but it was tough going in Augusta. Because of the adverse racial climate in the city, and at the invitation of the Reverend Frank Quarles of Atlanta's Friendship Baptist Church, Augusta Theological Institute moved to the capital city of Georgia. The transition was not complicated. Joseph T. Robert and his associates took the Georgia railroad from Augusta to Atlanta. Leaving Richmond County, the trip of about 150 miles took them through the present-day counties of Warren, Hancock, Green, Morgan, Newton, Rockdale, DeKalb, and Fulton. The move from Augusta to Atlanta was met with mixed feelings by the black and white communities. Paine College, another historically black college, would be established in Augusta in 1882 but was not a replacement for Augusta Theological Institute.

To give the school a new branding, the name of the Institute was changed to Atlanta Baptist Seminary, reflecting the support it now received from the American Baptist Home Mission Society. Members of the ABHMS board of trustees petitioned the incorporation to the state of Georgia 1879, and it read in part, "The objects of the said corporation are to promote education among the colored people of the South, especially by the training of preachers and teachers of the colored race, and to this end, to better accomplish its objects the corporation will establish and maintain such schools, colleges, and universities as it deems necessary."[6] The petition was accepted and Atlanta Baptist Seminary was officially incorporated.

The Reverend Joseph Robert moved to Atlanta and continued in his role as the president of the seminary. A July 30, 1881, report was issued from the Office of the President of the Missionary Baptist Convention of

[5] Sisk, "Morehouse College," 201–202.

[6] Grant, The Way It Was in the South, 88.

Georgia, the black Baptist organization, to all Baptists and the general public, emphasizing that for ten years they had labored without intermission for the establishment of a school for young men who could take their place when they had gone to their "long rest." "In this we have succeeded and today we have the Atlanta Baptist Seminary." Missionary Baptist Convention members were confident that the young men studying at Atlanta Baptist Seminary were "sound in the faith" and would one day become "giants in the gospel." They committed to praying for their success and provided them with the financial aid that would allow them to stay at the seminary until graduation. The president of the Missionary Baptist Convention emphasized the organization's commitment to the seminary, saying that "the school must be nursed and nurtured year by year, and made stronger as time rolls on, so that its grand, its glorious mission may be fully accomplished, and abundant fruit borne to the honor of God."[7] The Missionary Baptist Convention and Dr. Robert promulgated the idea that black men could be educated for scholarship and stewardship and also "survey the cross."

The first classes of the new Atlanta Baptist Seminary were taught in the basement of Friendship Baptist Church, but this was also where female students were already being taught. Because the seminary was still committed to exclusively enrolling only male students, the Missionary Baptist Convention's president called for the erection of a building to accommodate the young women. Assurances were made that at least $5,000 would be raised for that purpose by black Baptists in Georgia, and an all-girls dormitory was proposed near West Hunter and Elliott Street. Without this plan, female students could have been considered students of Atlanta Baptist Seminary, thereby making the school coeducational. Fortunately for the sake of the original mission, the recommendation for an alternate school for female students was realized when, on January 21, 1881, the American Baptist Home Mission Society created Atlanta Baptist Female Seminary, which became Spelman Seminary and eventually Spelman College.

For the first few months of the academic year 1879 to 1880, classes

---

[7] "Minutes of the Middle Georgia Baptist Association Meeting," Springfield Baptist Church, Hawkinsville, GA, September 2–5, 1881, Office of the President, Missionary Baptist Convention in Georgia, 4.

for the Atlanta Baptist Seminary were held at Friendship Baptist Church, where the Reverend Frank Quarles was the pastor. A new edifice for this historic church had recently been built on Mitchell Street, just a few blocks from downtown Atlanta. Atlanta was now the capital of the state of Georgia, after having moved from its Civil War location in Milledgeville in 1868, and the black population of the city had grown noticeably in the decade since then. One of the reasons the school was moved to Atlanta was due to the city's role as the capital of the state; the region was rapidly becoming the central location of the "New South." Atlanta was growing, and there was a vision was that it would one day "become the major educational, cultural, and financial center of the Southeast. Indeed, it was to be one of the most important cities in the nation."

Friendship Baptist Church was established in 1862 during the early months of the Civil War and then independently organized in 1866 in the months after the end of the war. The Reverend Frank Quarles was Friendship's founding pastor (1866–1881), and in its early years, the congregation met in a boxcar that had been sent to Atlanta from Chattanooga, Tennessee. It was in this boxcar that Atlanta University, a sister institution to Morehouse College, was founded in 1865. As people began to return to Atlanta after its decimation during William Tecumseh Sherman's "March to the Sea," the city's boundaries had grown to three miles in diameter by 1866. The *Constitution* newspaper was started in 1868, the Union railroad depot was constructed in 1871, the public school system opened in January 1872, and a new city charter was ratified in February 1874.[8] Atlanta Baptist Seminary was purposely situated in an environment where education had been prized for more than a decade. "The City Assessor's report of May 9, 1867, to [the city] Council indicated that 'there were in Atlanta twenty-three schools, four of which were for colored children.'"[9] As the debate over the place of African Americans in mainstream American life and thought intensified during the early years of

[8] "Atlanta in 1890: The Gate City," *Atlanta Historical Society* (Macon, GA: Mercer University Press, 1986) 17.

[9] Alexa Wynelle Benson, "Race Relations in Atlanta, As Seen in a Critical Analysis of City Council Proceedings and Other Works, 1865–1877," thesis submitted to the faculty of Atlanta University in partial fulfillment of the requirements of the degree of master of arts, Department of History, Atlanta, August 1966, 24.

Reconstruction, "some of the people of the South thought that 'since emancipation was a fact, the wisest policy for the South was to educate the negro [*sic*] so as to make him able to live up to that state of freedom into which it had pleased the North to call him.'"

By the time the Institute moved to Atlanta, a respect for education among the African American population in the city was apparent in their commitment to the establishment of primary, secondary, and higher educational institutions. In addition to public schools, black students had access to private primary and secondary education. The Atlanta Baptist Seminary joined Atlanta University (1865, chartered in 1867), Clark College (1869), and Gammon School of Theological (1872) to choose from, creating a hub of black excellence that could not be found anywhere else in the world. In 1881, Morris Brown College and Spelman College joined the seminary and the other schools in the area. "It was felt by many throughout the South that Atlanta was making the most of the Negro situation and not only provided rudimentary education for Negro children in public schools but had six institutions of higher learning elaborately equipped and liberally endowed."[10] Defining the role Atlanta Baptist Seminary would take in the rich educational environment that was Atlanta in 1879 was the task before President Joseph Robert, the Reverend Frank Quarles, the Reverend William White, James Tate, and all who were stakeholders in the noble enterprise—the "Idea." Their strongly committed efforts to keep the candle in the dark burning were successful, and Atlanta Baptist Seminary survived and grew in the capital city. The circumstances and dynamics that contributed to its next phase, its change from Atlanta Baptist Seminary to Atlanta Baptist College, in 1897, are another chapter in the story of the evolution of this tenacious and purposeful commitment to the "Idea."

From the very beginning, it was understood that the seminary could not and would not remain in the basement of Friendship Baptist Church forever, so land in Atlanta was eventually purchased for $600. Interestingly, the original 1879 charter of Atlanta Baptist Seminary does not explicitly state that the school was meant for men only. To wit, it states the following: "The objects of said corporation are to promote education

---

[10] Brawley, Morehouse College, 32.

among the colored people of the South, especially by the training of preachers and teachers of the colored race, and to this end, and to better accomplish its objects, the corporation will establish and maintain such schools, colleges, and universities as it deems necessary."[11]

Friendship Baptist Church had been a welcoming refuge for the fledging Atlanta Baptist Seminary before it moved to a four-acre lot at the corner of West Hunter (now Martin Luther King Jr. Drive) and Elliott Streets. The land was purchased from Richard Peters for $2,500, and the $7,500 was spent to construct the school's new brick building, which was situated one block west of the Atlanta Terminal Railroad Station, where the Richard Russell Federal Building is located today. Before the move to Atlanta, the Missionary Baptist Convention of Georgia, where the Reverend Frank Quarles served as president (1871–1881), purchased land for a theological institute in May 1878 for $600. Funds for the Elliott Street building's construction came from the sale of Augusta Theological Institute's property for $5,000 plus cash and pledges totaling $2,000. This gave the Missionary Baptist Convention $7,000 toward the $10,000 needed to build the school.

The original site proposed for the school was at the edge of the city, but this location was deemed unacceptable when both the black Baptists and their white advisers decided that "a more central location was desirable." Thus, the original land that had been purchased for $600 was sold and put toward the purchase of the West Hunter and Elliott Streets property. An executive board made up of black and white Georgians was created to oversee the seminary.[12]

The Atlanta Baptist Seminary edifice was a two-story brick structure measuring 45-by-60 feet that was designed by New York architect W. A. Purdy. Occupying half of the first floor was a schoolroom, and a second room took up another quarter of the floor space. Sliding doors separated the rooms, and when the doors were opened, enough space was available to serve as an auditorium or a chapel seating 200 to 250 people. The remainder of the space on the first floor was divided into the president's office, a library, and a hat-and-coat closet. Five classrooms and a room for

---

[11] Ibid.

[12] Ibid.

a tutor were located on the second floor.[13]

The dream of the Missionary Baptists Convention was realized when Atlanta Baptist Seminary opened the doors of its new building for convocation on December 18, 1879. The program began at 10 A.M. and lasted for three hours, ending at 1 P.M. The auditorium-like space was filled to capacity and featured a number of dignitaries, including the Reverend Frank Quarles, representing the Missionary Baptist Convention of Georgia, Georgia governor A. H. Colquitt, and school commissioner G. S. Orr. The superintendent of public schools, the Reverend J. H. DeVotie of the State Mission Board, and Sidney Root, the official delegate of the American Baptist Home Mission Society, were also on the program. And, of course, the Reverend Joseph T. Robert, president of the seminary, was present. One can only imagine his pride in what had been achieved in such a short time. The formal and definitive organization of Atlanta Baptist Seminary had only been received on July 18, 1879, at a meeting of the board of trustees at the office of the American Baptist Home Mission Society in the Astor House in New York City. The board of the seminary retained its twelve-member makeup, and Henry Lyman Morehouse was elected secretary. This is the first reference to the name Morehouse in conjunction with the school. Additional members of the board included Joseph B. Hoyt, president, and Joseph Brokaw, treasurer, along with the Reverend William J. White of Georgia, S. S. Constant of New York, the Reverend Doctor E. Lathrop of Connecticut, W. A. Cauldwell of New York, I. G. Johnson of New York, the Reverend J. S. Lawton, MD, of Georgia, and the Reverend William H. Tilman of Georgia. Two vacancies on the board were yet to be filled, and the board passed, by vote, bylaws for its operations. One of the board's first actions was the approval of the Reverend Doctor D. Shaver and W. E. Holmes as assistant teachers at the seminary. The school now had a faculty.

Just a few years after the seminary began classes in its new building, the site became unsuitable because a railroad had been built nearby. The noise from the trains and the growing human presence in the area made it difficult to conduct classes that had a heavy reliance upon recitation. The Baptist Home Mission Society decided to sell the property and

[13] Ibid.

purchase a more suitable site for the seminary to "erect suitable buildings for the education of men and women."[14] But as the sale of the West Hunter and Elliott Streets property began and plans were being developed to accommodate both men and women in the new setting, Sophia B. Packard and Harriet E. Giles, representatives of the Woman's American Baptist Home Mission Society, weighed in and urged the board to make separate arrangements for the exclusive education of the girls. "They disagreed with the proposed co-educational scheme because it was their experience that in co-educational schools the courses were planned primarily for men, and training for women received only secondary consideration. They also believed that the special education which women required could best be accomplished apart from the distractions caused by constant companionship with men."[15] Miss Packard and Miss Giles are recognized as the founders of Spelman College, but it must be remembered that the idea from the American Baptist Home Mission Society for the education of black women came at a January 21, 1881, board meeting of Atlanta Baptist Seminary, now Morehouse College. The "companionship" of Morehouse Men and Spelman Women was formed at that time and continues to this day.

After nearly fifteen years of devoted and tireless service to the institute/seminary and to the idea that black men could be educated to become stewards in their communities, President Joseph Thomas Robert died in Atlanta on March 5, 1884. He left Atlanta Baptist Seminary on solid footing for its second president. The school had a growing enrollment, an attractive edifice, and a committed faculty. In fewer than thirty years, the seminary would become Morehouse College, but in 1884, the search for its second president was at hand. This search would bring the Reverend Doctor Samuel T. Graves to Atlanta to lead the all-male school.

---

[14] Ibid.

[15] Beverly Guy-Sheftall and Jo Moore Stewart, "Spelman Centennial Celebration, 1881–1981" (Atlanta: Spelman College, 1881) 23.

Chapter 3

"Bearing the Cross": A New Leader and a New Campus

For several months after the death of Joseph Robert, the search continued for the next president of Atlanta Baptist Seminary. In the meanwhile, David Foster Estes, a member of the faculty, served as acting president. Dr. Robert had preserved the idea, conceived by the founders, that black men could be educated to be stewards to their people as preachers and teachers. These men would be imbued with moral ethics, as the white Baptist believed, and would convert black men and women to this faith. The search was for a leader who would continue the accomplished work of President Robert, which included the transition from Augusta to Atlanta, the commitment to accepting only male students, the construction of a school building, and increased the enrollment. The board of trustees eventually selected Samuel Graves as the second president of Atlanta Baptist Seminary in 1885.

Samuel T. Graves was born in Ackworth, New Hampshire, on March 15, 1820. He earned degrees from the Hamilton Literary and Theological Institute in New York (Madison University, now Colgate University) and two years later from the theological seminary. Just like his predecessors, Graves was a minister, and after a short stint as a tutor at the theological seminary, he accepted a pastorate in Ann Arbor, Michigan. But his work as a tutor had excited in him a passion for education, so, in 1851, at the age of thirty-one, he accepted the chair of Greek language and literature at Kalamazoo College in the city by the same name in Michigan. He held this position for eight years and "distinguished himself as a dedicated and competent teacher."[1] While he distinguished himself as an educator, Graves still had a yearning for the pulpit. In 1859, he became the pastor of a Baptist church in Norwich, Connecticut, where he served for ten years. In 1869, he moved to the Fountain Street Baptist Church

[1] Jones, Candle in the Dark, 48.

in Grand Rapids, Michigan, where he began his work on January 1, 1870. His work at Fountain Street Baptist Church was productive, but after fifteen years of service, he resigned the pastorate in May 1885 to assume the presidency of Atlanta Baptist Seminary, "an institution for the education of colored boys in theology and the liberal arts."[2] Why did he do this? How was he elected president of the seminary? Why did Samuel Graves want to "bear the cross" in Atlanta?

Dr. Samuel Graves was married to Mary Baldwin, who had been born in New Jersey, and the couple had four children: Eliza, Mary, Schuyler, and Willie. Dr. Graves is described as "a man of singular beauty and dignity of character, adding to sterling manliness, fervent piety, tender sympathy for the needs of others, and a fine appreciation of the beautiful in literature and art, and a genuine enthusiasm that was a most important factor in his success as the head of Atlanta Baptist Seminary."[3] By the time Graves became the seminary's second president, the school was offering a liberal arts education alongside its traditional theological studies. But due to logistical issues and physical-plant constraints at the Elliott and Hunter Streets location, plans were made for a new campus soon after his arrival. At a called meeting of the students, Graves shared his immediate plans for relief of these conditions and solicited their prayers in his efforts. Because of his unflagging zeal, unremitting toil, and unshakable faith, together with voluminous correspondence in the winter and travel in summer, President Graves was able to finalize his plans for the new building.

Architectural renderings for the new building were produced, and construction began on a new tract of land west of downtown Atlanta. The property upon which the new building was built was acquired in April 1888 at a cost of $7,500. The original tract of land comprised fourteen acres on what proved to be a most historic spot during the Civil War. Confederate soldiers had staged there some of their most stubborn resistance to Union forces during the memorable siege of Atlanta. At this time the land was bought, the site was still marked by the earthworks erected by the Confederate soldiers, and when the land was cleared and

---

[2] www.migenweb.net/kent/baxter1891/13churches.htmal

[3] Jones, Candle in the Dark, 49.

graded for the new campus, many skulls were reportedly dug up. Edward A. Jones observed the irony of the construction of the new facility on the "spot which was one of the focal points of the fratricidal struggle waged largely over the issue of slavery [that] was to serve thereafter as the locale for the intellectual and moral betterment of the descendants of slaves."[4] In 1889, the building was completed, and on the recommendation of the board of trustees, the building was eventually named Graves Hall in honor of the president of the seminary at that time. With a strong aesthetic sense, President Graves knew that there is a subtle tie between the physical, the intellectual, and the moral. These dynamics react and interact with each other, for better or for worse, and the "Main Building," as it was originally called, testified to the interest with which these properties were viewed by the Christian intelligentsia of the late nineteenth century.[5] Graves Hall was an attractive building that conveyed the seriousness of the work it represented. This was Atlanta Baptist Seminary, whose reputation was being cemented by the accomplishments of its graduates. In the face of almost daunting challenges—racism, economic proscriptions, social disadvantages, and political restrictions, the leadership and the students at the seminary bore the cross and moved forward. The founders' idea was alive and well, and the seminary was producing men who lived up to the precepts of the Baptist faith and the liberal arts.

The move from the site at Elliott and West Hunter Streets to a location contiguous to an affluent and historic, overwhelmingly white West End community begs the question, Why? Why did the American Baptist Home Mission Society opt to position the campus farther west of downtown Atlanta and at a greater distance from the east side of the city, including the Fourth Ward, a district where many of Atlanta's black leaders resided? Some quick answers to this question are that the new campus was now closer to Friendship Baptist Church on Mitchell Street, it was just a short distance from the Elliott-Hunter Streets campus, and it afforded a larger land acquisition. Given the increasing racial hostilities in the South at that time, reflected in the attitudes of many members of Atlanta's white

[4] National Register of Historic Places, NPS Form 10-900a, United States Department of the Interior, National Park Service, Atlanta History Center Collections.

[5] Jones, Candle in the Dark, 50.

community, it seems that it would have been more prudent to locate the new Main Building in Summerhill or one of the other predominantly black enclaves. Nonetheless, the Main Building was completed and was an immediate success in the increased space it provided for the school and the increased enrollment it attracted.

The new campus was near the West End at the corner of Ashby and Fair Streets and was comprised of fourteen acres on a hilltop on the site of Fort Whitehall. It is likely that the building's architect was W. A. Purdy, who had designed the Elliott Street structure. The design for the iconic building was in the Victorian-Gothic style commonly found on college campuses in the late nineteenth century. It rose to four stories and was sheathed in red brick with a granite basement. The structure was capped with a bell tower under a pyramidal roof that accentuated a central bay. The entry stoop featured a heavy, rusticated stone arch supported by truncated Romanesque columns, and double front doors opened onto an abbreviated lobby or vestibule. The beautiful building contained sixty rooms, with forty-five set aside as dormitory rooms for the students. It also had a space for administrative offices, a chapel, the English preparatory school, a dining hall, kitchen, laundry room, printing office, and the president's residence.

Construction funds were raised among white Northerners and by black Georgia Baptists. The Main Building was completed on November 1, 1889, on schedule and at a cost of $27,000. On May 25, 1889, Commencement Day, the cornerstone was laid during the annual meeting of the Georgia Baptist Missionary Baptist Association, the organization of African American Baptists in the state. Six thousand dollars more was needed to equip the building with a steam heating system and more money was needed to furnish the dormitory spaces, the kitchen, the dining hall, and the multi-purpose hall, bringing the total cost to construct the Main Building to $40,000.

The Main Building was the only building on campus until 1898, when Quarles Hall was dedicated. Also in 1898, the majestic edifice of the Main Building was rededicated and renamed Graves Hall in honor of the school's second president. It was in Graves Hall that black men, many coming from impoverished backgrounds, were transformed into self-assured, knowledgeable, articulate, and ethical graduates. These men largely came to the school from the Southeast and then dispersed to towns and cities in Georgia, South Carolina, Alabama, and beyond. In the five-year period that Samuel T. Graves served the seminary, the construction of the now-historic Main Building is notable. Graves bore the cross and elevated the work of the seminary as he changed the lives of many individuals who embraced a new way of living, proving that black men could be educated and return to their communities or settle in new ones where they would be stewards in service to their people. President Samuel T. Graves left the seminary in good order when he retired in 1889.

Entreaty

"The Man Who Wanted to Bear the Cross": Henry Lyman Morehouse

As the corresponding secretary at the American Baptist Home Mission Society, Henry Lyman Morehouse was familiar with the search for the third president of Atlanta Baptist Seminary, and he wanted the job. As a result, he made his desire known to John Davison Rockefeller Sr. The philanthropist Rockefeller was an ardent Baptist, and Henry Morehouse needed the oil tycoon's support. So, in a June 13, 1890, letter, Morehouse asked for his endorsement. He had given eleven years of service to the American Baptist Home Mission Society (ABHMS) and was feeling the strain brought on by his workload. He did not know how much longer he could continue there, and he told Rockefeller of his desire to retire and "take charge of one of our schools for colored people." More specifically, Morehouse said,

> I am attracted [to] Atlanta. A president is needed for Atlanta Baptist Seminary—the school for young men. A good building (Graves Hall) is completed at a cost of about $35,000. Another will soon be needed. If I were at Atlanta, as a Trustee of Spelman Seminary, I could devote consider able attention to its affairs as circumstances might require. It is not likely that Miss Packard will long be able to do what she has done, & when a change in administration comes, there will be a need for much care.

Morehouse wanted Rockefeller's "special support to some extent for about five years." And if everything went according to his plans, he would "make the boy's school one of the very best in the South." After stating that he wanted an annual salary of no less than $2,500, which was $1,500 less than his salary as ABHMS corresponding secretary, Morehouse believed there were "lines of work for the colored people which I am confident I can develop successfully in many ways, but will refrain from particulars. To these my vocation would be largely devoted, though in not so exacting a way as here in my present position." Henry Morehouse was willing to travel to Cleveland, Ohio, to talk with Rockefeller if necessary. But if Rockefeller were not "not so disposed, Morehouse would pursue the subject no further unless to answer inquiries, but would turn his attention to some other field—perhaps Mexico."[1] The ABHMS was also working among Mexicans and First Nation people.

Six days later, Rockefeller responded to the letter from Dr. Morehouse, praising his work. The philanthropist wrote, "I am in receipt of your favor, of the 13th ins. I have known for a long time you were doing very hard work, and much more than you could do in justice to your health; but I do not like to think of your making a change. You have done an invaluable work for the Baptist Home Mission Society, and it is appreciated by a multitude of people." Although Rockefeller praised his work at the ABHMS, he refused to endorse Dr. Morehouse for the presidency of Atlanta Baptist Seminary. "In respect to the Atlanta [Baptist] Seminary to which you refer, I do not know and could not say out of hand. This much however, I can say, that with the confidence I have in you, if you were engaged in that work and I felt it to be the most important place to put money, nothing would give me greater pleasure." So, no endorsement from Rockefeller was forthcoming, but the philanthropist was willing to receive a five-year plan of the requirements of Atlanta Baptist Seminary. He told Morehouse that "if I have time I would be glad to have a few words with you before I leave the [New York] city on Friday evening, but fear I will not have time."[2]

John D. Rockefeller Sr.'s response to Morehouse's proposal was not affirmative, so in a June 19, 1890, letter, using a much more formal salutation, Morehouse immediately wrote again to Mr. Rockefeller: "Your highly esteemed favor of this date is at hand. I thank you for the kind expressions concerning my service to the Home Mission Society." But, he continued, Morehouse felt that his work at the ABHMS was "practically done" and that "another could handle it." He thought that "another work somewhere is to be done" and that "Atlanta and its possibilities grow upon

---

[1] Henry Lyman Morehouse to John D. Rockefeller, June 13, 1890, Rockefeller Archive Center, Sleepy Hollow, NY, Box 28, Folder 2.

[2] John D. Rockefeller to Henry Lyman Morehouse, July 19, 1890, Rockefeller Archive Center, Sleepy Hollow, NY.

me and become more and more an attraction." Thanking Rockefeller for his "generous support of the American Baptist Education Society," Dr. Morehouse closed by saying, "you are making a new era in our educational work. My soul grows big with thoughts of the possibilities of the society if it can be properly sustained. I love the Home Mission Society; I love the Education Society. I love you."[3] Dr. Henry Lyman Morehouse never became president of Atlanta Baptist Seminary, for in July 1890, a month after he wrote to Rockefeller, the Reverend George Sale was called to bear the cross as the president of the seminary while he was conducting meetings in Toronto, Canada. Reverend Sale had been recommended to the board of trustees by Dr. Malcolm MacVicar, superintendent of education for the American Baptist Home Mission Society.

By the end of his ten years of service to the Home Mission Society, Dr. Morehouse's record was commendable. "The total receipts for the ten years reached $3,700,000 or $200,000 more than for the preceding forty-seven years. During this decade, the number of ABHMS schools grew from eight to twenty, and six hundred and eighty-seven church edifices were built; more than twice as many as in the previous history of the Society. This great advance did not just happen; it was brought about by patient, intelligent, and unremitting toil."[4] Physically and mentally exhausted, and disappointed by his failure to get support for his proposal to become president of Atlanta Baptist Seminary, "the Executive Board [of the American Baptist Home Mission Society] voted Doctor Morehouse a leave of absence for three months, which he spent in European travel."[5] Tired and worn, Morehouse was glad to have the opportunity to get some rest. In a letter of appreciation to the board, he revealed his state of mind: "Ten years' arduous and almost incessant service had allowed so little opportunity for recreation, that in all these years the Secretary had not had the benefit, at any time in one year, of three weeks' absolute respite from toil, while some years have witnessed hardly a break in the service."[6] He kept a diary of this of his experiences while abroad and "in his letters to

[3] Morehouse to Rockefeller.

[4] Lathan A. Crandall. *Henry Layman Morehouse: A Biography* (New York: American Baptist Society, 1919) 65.

[5] Ibid., 66.

[6] Ibid.

his mother—of which there were many—he wrote of increasing vigor.

Henry Lyman Morehouse was not the only person with ambitions to the presidency of Atlanta Baptist Seminary. William E. Holmes, a graduate of Augusta Theological Institute, also had ambitions for the presidency of the school. When Sterling Gardner, a teacher at the seminary, died on December 8, 1877, two of his best students worked with his students in the lower grades, although they recited daily to President Robert. Holmes and another student named Collins H. Lyons had entered the Institute with a good academic preparation and done limited teaching in his first year as a student-tutor. In 1881, Holmes became a full-time member of the faculty and served the Institute and Atlanta Baptist Seminary for twenty years. Holmes left the seminary in 1899 to become the president of the newly organized Central City College (CCC) in Macon, Georgia, but earlier, in 1889, when the American Baptist Home Mission Board was looking for a successor to President Graves, Holmes wanted the presidency.

William Holmes's departure from his teaching post at Atlanta Baptist Seminary was not without controversy and acrimony. When President Sale heard that Holmes was being considered for the presidency of the soon-to-be-opened Central City College in Macon, he wrote to ask him to state in writing whether he would accept the presidency. Clearly, the CCC would compete with Atlanta Baptist College for students, support, and recognition, and since it had the backing of the black Baptists in Georgia, Holmes's defection was seen by the ABHMS as an act of defiance and ingratitude. Holmes, in what appears to be a spirit of decency, agreed to work out his contract and finish the academic year 1898 to 1899 at the Baptist seminary, but when President Sale asked him to take a public stand against CCC, he refused. Sale wrote, "I have no words to say against the proposed college at Macon, but the spirit in which the movement to establish that college was born, and its attitude toward the work of the Home Mission Society are such that a man cannot be wholly in sympathy with both. I must therefore ask you for an unequivocal statement of your position."[7] The position taken by Sale prompted Holmes to resign from

---

[7] Adele Oltman, Sacred Mission, Worldly Ambition: Black Christian Nationalism in the Age of Jim Crow (Athens: University of Georgia Press, 2012) 126–27.

the seminary and assume the presidency of CCC. "In view of the fact that my loyalty to the work is questioned, I return my commission and with it tender my resignation to take effect."[8] With his resignation from Atlanta Baptist College in 1899 and acceptance of the helm of the new Central City College in Macon, William Holmes became the first in a long line of future Morehouse Men to serve as a college president. An element of race figured in this controversy as Holmes was black and the ABHMS, through its board of trustees, did not think the time was right for a black seminary president.

Many prominent black Baptist ministers in the state, however, continued to support Atlanta Baptist College, which the seminary had become by 1899. The Reverend Frank Quarles, for whom a building on the campus had been named, and the Reverend William Jefferson White were among those who maintained fealty to Atlanta Baptist College. But by 1906, Macon's Central City College had 175 students enrolled in all departments, property valued at $25,000, and $4,000 in expenditures for that year. In contrast, in 1910, Atlanta Baptist College was listed among the "First Grade Colored Colleges" with fourteen or more units of entrance requirements and more than twenty students of college rank. Other colleges in this grade were Howard, Fisk, Atlanta University, Wiley, Leland, Virginia Union, Clark, Knoxville, Spelman, and Claflin. CCC had graduated only three male students by 1910 while Atlanta Baptist College had forty-two alumni.[9] Nevertheless, CCC represented the initiative and work of many black individuals in Georgia who demonstrated that they could take care of the education of their people. It foreshadowed the early twentieth-century debate about the qualifications and preparation of black people to assume leadership of the colleges that had been established for them by white religious organizations. White leadership of some of these schools continued until the middle of the twentieth century. Florence Matilda Read, a white woman, was the president of Spelman College until 1952. George Sale, a white Canadian, became the fourth president of Atlanta Baptist Seminary in 1890.

---

[8] Du Bois, "Economic Co-Operation Among Negro Americans," Atlanta University Publications 12 (New York: Russell & Russell, 1907) 84.

[9] Ibid, 47.

Chapter 4

"The Cross and the Candle on a Red Hill in Atlanta": Atlanta Baptist College

Henry Lyman Morehouse's failed bid for the presidency of Atlanta Baptist Seminary might have surprised his contemporary colleagues. He was as qualified as the school's former president and its next president because he had firsthand knowledge about the school and he knew how to raise money. In addition, Morehouse was a Baptist minister and a friend of John D. Rockefeller. Nevertheless, because he had done so well as corresponding secretary for the American Baptist Home Mission Society, the seminary board thought that he should continue in that job. In 1889, when the board was searching for a new president, Atlanta Baptist Seminary was on a solid footing on the west side of Atlanta. After searching for a new leader for the school, one who could bear the cross and light the candle in the dark, George Sale was selected.

George Sale was born in Toronto, Canada, on September 13, 1856, to Julian and Mary Ann Tomlin Sale. He received his early education in Toronto, and in 1876, just before his twentieth birthday, he enrolled at the Canadian Literary Institute (Woodstock College) in order to prepare himself for the Christian ministry. Sale studied there for four years, preaching at churches in the area during the school term and as the pastor of a church during his vacations. His studies at Woodstock instilled in Reverend Sale a rich background in the Scriptures, and after graduating from Woodstock in 1880, he entered Toronto University, where he pursued the course in the arts, specializing in metaphysics. He graduated from the university in 1884 and was honored with a silver medal for distinction in metaphysics. Reverend Sale spent the next two years in theological training at McMaster Theological Seminary refining and deepening his knowledge in this field. When this phase of his education was completed, Reverend Sale accepted the pastorate of First Baptist Church in Montreal, Canada. He also had a partnership, with his older brother in the Julian

Sale Leather Goods Company in Toronto.[1]

Eventually, though, the intellectual and professional strain of his work as pastor of First Baptist Church in Montreal weighed heavily on Reverend Sale, and he resigned from the pastorate in 1885. He spent much of the next five years on St. Joseph Island in Georgia Bay, Canada, where he led an outdoor life designed to regain his physical vigor.[2] The extent to which Atlanta Baptist Seminary's board of trustees was aware of Reverend Sale's loss of physical vitality is unknown, but the year before he was called to lead the school, he married Clara Goble.

The Reverend George and Clara Sale took over the helm of Atlanta Baptist Seminary in 1890, a critical time in African American history. In that year, eighty-five black individuals were lynched, and the "Mississippi Plan," which employed all sorts of schemes to disenfranchise black citizens to eliminate them as voters, was adopted by other Southern states. Jim Crow was in full effect.

In 1890, when the Reverend George Sale assumed the presidency of Atlanta Baptist Seminary, it is estimated that 1,205 African Americans had earned bachelor's degrees, twelve had been awarded master's degrees, and a black student, Edward Alexander Bouchet, earned his PhD in physics from Yale University in 1876.[3] In seven years, Atlanta Baptist Seminary would confer its first bachelor's degrees on three of its students. In the meantime, as an incorporated institution under the authority of the American Baptist Home Mission Society, the board of trustees of Atlanta Baptist Seminary was composed of members from the Society. The endowment, small as it was, was held by the Society in an absolute trust, and the Society, having accepted the trust, was "bound to administer it according to the wishes of the donors, and if at any time in the future it should be deemed best to convey to the respective institution the amounts thus held for its benefit, the Society might encounter legal difficulties in making the transfer."[4] The Home Mission Board was only the custodian of the

---

[1] Jones, Candle in the Dark, 54.

[2] Ibid., 54–55.

[3] Rayford Logan, The Negro Thought in American Life and Thought—The Nadir, 1877–1901 (New York: Dial Press, 1954).

[4] "1884 Report of the Board, American Baptist Home Mission Society," Rockefeller Archive Center, Morehouse, H. L. Collection, Record Group I, Box 28, Folder 1.

endowment and understood that the Society "shall be at liberty and have the right, at its discretion, to transfer these funds to the care of the respective Boards of Trustees of such institutions, with proper and sufficient guarantees, in the transfer, as to the investment of such funds and the purpose to which the income shall be applied."[5] Make no mistake, Atlanta Baptist Seminary was an American Baptist Home Mission Society School.

George Sale served as president of Atlanta Baptist Seminary (which changed its name to Atlanta Baptist College during his tenure) from 1890 to 1906. Graves Hall's construction freed President Sale from the problems related to physical-plant expansion as the magnificent new building provided space for classrooms, administrative offices, dining facilities, a library, chapel, dormitory rooms, and apartments for the president and faculty. But he faced other administrative problems having to do with organizational structure, conservation of resources, and planning and guiding for the future. The faculty was growing and "needed to be welded together and given cohesion and esprit de corps." This was the first time the school had a boarding department, and it needed polices and direction. In addition, "an unstable" course of study needed definite form. And then there were "problems relating to full cooperation between the American Baptist Home Mission Society and the Negro Baptists of Georgia, since the school's future depended on such cooperation." These imperatives had to be addressed. In order to solve these problems, President Sale "needed above all other qualities, tact, organizational ability, sympathetic understanding, patience, and a temperament conducive to optimum efforts on the part of teachers, students, trustees, and Baptist supporters."[6] Sale was up to the challenges the school faced in the 1890s, and it was in this decade that the seminary became a college.

The construction of Graves Hall and the move of Atlanta Baptist Seminary from its Hunter and Elliott Streets location to its site on Fair Street near the West End, resulted in an unprecedented increase in enrollment. So many students were enrolled that the dormitory space in the all-purpose Graves Hall could not accommodate them all. It was suggested that the building at Hunter and Elliott be converted into living quarters

---

[5] Jones, Candle in the Dark, 55.

[6] Ibid.

for the overflow, but Sale rejected this idea "on the reasoning that the old building was too far from the seminary to make its use practical."[7] The facility was in a deplorable state of dilapidation and not fit for habitation. And the fact that the dormitory would not be close to the new campus would make it difficult to maintain discipline.

Potential disciplinary problems notwithstanding, the economic depression of the 1890s and questions about educational policy in the social, economic, and political climate that existed in the South and in the North at this time commanded much of President Sale's attention. He had to walk a fine line between the two regions and at the same time work with African Americans who supported the school through their monetary contributions and enrollment. The so-called "Negro problem" was a major point of contention among the white community, with some recommending removal or genocide. The author of a column called "The Rambler" wrote a strident criticism of Southern missionary schools based on an experience he had had with one poorly equipped student, the product of one of these schools. In response to this negative assessment, President Sale wrote, on May 11, 1895,

> I think the references to the matter of Negro education wholly unfair to the Southern mission schools. A few questions suggest themselves in connection therewith. Why take a poor fellow who had an imperfection in his speech and cannot read correctly as a sample of the kind of work done in these schools, when you might find hundreds of young men who would pass an examination in every way creditable?

He then argued a fact that would be true of any group of college students, then and now. "Let it be granted that it is not 'of the slightest use' to teach the majority of our young Negro aspirants geometry, astronomy, logic, Greek, church history, etc.; is there any reason why the minority who show aptitude for these studies should not be taught to them? And if these studies have value for white students, why should they not have the same value for Negroes?"[8]

The Atlanta-based *Christian Index* published a series of letters in

---

[7] Ibid.

[8] Ibid.

1894 discussing the value of educating black citizens in the South. In response, and using the same forthrightness, diplomacy, tact, logic, and conviction that were the hallmark of his administration, President Sale wrote a letter to the editor dated April 25, 1894. After mentioning instances of support and cooperation offered by individual Southerners, he pointed out that there was little sympathy for the school among white Georgia Baptists many from the Northern white population. The faculty and staff at Atlanta Baptist Seminary did their work and lived their lives apart from the general Atlanta population. And while some in the white community had taken an interest in the Baptist Seminary, President Sale asked, "Is this separation necessary? Must it ever be so?"[9]

The core issue, it seems, was the social and political status of the African American, especially in the South. And President Sale disavowed "any political mission in his work among the Negroes." But by contradiction, the work of Atlanta Baptist Seminary/College was doing exactly that: it was preparing generations of seminary graduates for scholarship and stewardship. These men would bear the cross as ministers, pastors, and preachers but also as scholars. The educated black man is a politicized man as demonstrated by legions of Morehouse Men.

The debate over the brand of education that best suited African Americans intensified after Booker T. Washington made his controversial September 18, 1895, "Atlanta Compromise Speech" and replaced Frederick Douglass as the titular leader of the black community in America. Once again, President Sale responded in a letter, on March 26, 1896 and accepted an invitation to speak about his work at a convention of ministers in early April of the same year. The invitation came after a resolution had been passed commending the work of the Baptist in Georgia, including the work President Sale had done at Morehouse.[10]

Perhaps the most cogent response to Washington and his supporters was made by Henry Lyman Morehouse in an essay published in *The Independent* under the title "The Talented Tenth" in 1896. With his intimate knowledge of the success of the graduates of Atlanta Baptist Seminary, it is highly likely that Dr. Morehouse was referencing them when

[9] Ibid., 56.

[10] Ibid., 57.

wrote, "It is this talented tenth man of our colleges that in after years reflects more honor on his *alma mater* than the other nine; it is this tenth man that is the recognized leader in his profession and the leader of public opinion. To him, rather than to the other nine, the many look for suggestion and advice in important matters." Then, in a profound affirmation, Dr. Morehouse declared that "this being true, I repeat that not to make proper provision for the high education of the talented tenth man of the colored people is a prodigious mistake." Morehouse correctly surmised that "the powers of the talented tenth man are often latent" and may not be suspected by his possessor. Therefore, he entreated, "in our educational work for the colored people, proper provision should be made for the talent tenth." Assuredly, W. E. B. Du Bois read this article; and so did President Sale.

With a strong vision to guide the policies of the seminary, Sale had a more difficult go of it with the African American Baptists in Georgia. It was in this highly charged social and political climate that William E. Holmes left the college for the presidency of Central City College in Macon. By 1893, the black Baptists in the state had divided into the old Missionary Baptist Convention and the new General State Baptist Convention. President Sale was caught in the middle of this divide and had to call on wisdom and diplomacy in his work with the two organizations. In a letter to William Jefferson White, editor of *The Georgia Baptist,* Sale revealed his tenacity and willingness to act with a spirit of good will. "I have taken no part whatever in the divisions of the black Baptist in the state. When separation was made, I thought it unwise. As opportunity came to me, I discouraged it. But the division was made, and the separate conventions exist. It numbers among its adherents some of our very best men, graduates of this school and of other schools, men whom I respect and who bear an excellent reputation for character and intelligence." President Sale made the position of the seminary clear when he said, "Lest any misunderstanding of the position should remain, let me say distinctly that so far as the attitude of the school is influenced by me, it will not ally itself to either convention to the exclusion of the other, unless it is forced to do so by the exclusiveness of the conventions. It will continue to keep out of the discussion of the points of difference, and to do its best for the Baptist family, irrespective of dividing lines."[11]

In the late nineteenth and early twentieth centuries, many students spent eight years at the school: four years in the academy and four years at the college. Because of the different levels of preparation students had before entering the seminary, the 1880s presented a great problem: how to reconcile the pedagogical goals of the high-minded teachers, most of whom were trained at schools in the North, with the lessons to be taught. What would classically trained teachers teach to grown men who desired an elemental education while also attending classes with bright young men who were eager to acquire the more advanced knowledge? The solution was to offer different levels of education. The Normal Course was a three-year grammar school; the Academy Course was equivalent to a high school curriculum; and, of course, there was the Theological Course. This was the design of the curriculum in the academic ear 1881 to 1882. The next year, 1882 to 1883, the Theological Course was dropped and two years of grammar school and two years of high school work were added to the Normal Course. These changes were designed to move the seminary toward the rank of a college and heralded an ambitious projection of the seminary's curriculum—the introduction of a "Collegiate Department" consisting of a four-year Scientific Course and a Classical Course.

The Classical Course scheduled introductory Latin in the first year but offered altogether four years of Latin and three years of Greek along with courses in chemistry, geology, zoology, logic, trigonometry, astronomy, and political economy.[12] The new curriculum was put in place to give seminary students the kind of collegiate work that was available at other traditional liberal arts colleges. By doing this, the seminary could apply to the state of Georgia to be incorporated as a college.

The Academy Course continued to be very popular, and students enrolled in respectable numbers. Quarles Hall, named in honor of the Reverend Frank Quarles, was built in 1898 and Morehouse Academy was housed in the new facility.

The new classical curriculum "proved more idealistic than realistic for the time, but it set the target where the leaders of the school wanted—

[11] Ibid.

[12] Ibid., 59.

and were determined—to go. Not a single student completed the Classical Course before 1892." The Classical Course was premature and was reduced to four years in the academic year 1883 to 1884. This made it parallel to the Scientific Course. Most students, however, were planning to become teachers and were enrolled in the Normal Course, which became a prerequisite for the Scientific Course. In these early days of gearing the seminary toward a collegiate curriculum, only a few students pursued this course of study. From 1881 to 1884, only Nash B. Williamson of Athens, Georgia, enrolled in the Scientific Course. In the school year of 1884 to 1885, Jefferson D. Walker of Warrenton, Georgia, studied the Classical Course and Martin V. Russell of Augusta, Georgia, was pursuing the Scientific Course. The overwhelming majority of the students at Atlanta Baptist Seminary, though, continued to enroll in the Normal Course or in the theological department. One hundred and fifty-four students were enrolled at the seminary in the academic year of 1884 to 1885, of whom thirty-six were in the theological department and forty-four in the Normal Course. Between 1886 and 1888, the general trend remained unchanged and no students were enrolled in the Collegiate Department.[13]

Students enrolled in the Normal Course at Atlanta Baptist Seminary in the Academic Year 1884 to 1885 followed the prescribed curriculum of the time. During both semesters of the first year, they studied reading and language, intermediate arithmetic, elementary geography, and penmanship. In the second year, students studied a higher level of reading and language along with practical arithmetic, higher geography, and advanced grammar. In the third year, what is now called the junior year, Normal Course students took history of the United States, algebra, physiology and hygiene, and English analysis in the first term and history of the United States, algebra, rhetoric, and bookkeeping in the second term. In the senior, or fourth year, students studied natural philosophy, geometry, mental science and theory, and practice of teaching in the first term followed by civil government, English literature, moral science and theory, and practice of teaching in the second term. And while hundreds of young men took the Normal Course and studied theology, the seminary moved toward collegiate status. The 1879 charter for the seminary was

[13] Ibid., 42.

amended in 1897 accordingly: "That in the corporate name 'Atlanta Baptist Seminary' the word 'College' be substituted for the word 'Seminary.'" To reach this pivotal point, the institution had to admit students qualified to do college-level work and, of course, provide a college course of study. By 1897, during the presidency of George Sale, this important milestone was reached, but not without challenges on many fronts. The first graduates of Atlanta Baptist College (now Morehouse College) were Henry A. Bleach, John W. Hubert, and Major W. Reddick. These three men became principals of schools in Georgia and, no doubt, recruited many young men for their alma mater.

A source of frustration and embarrassment to the seminary at this time was the constant turnover of faculty personnel. Minor problems plagued the school commensurate with the usual problems faced by faculty and students. "Among others, cases of discipline and individual student programs occupied too much of the time of the faculty as a whole—an inevitable consequence of a too-limited teaching staff. The teachers frequently had to lend money to students to enable them to stay in school. And during the latter part of this period, school was dismissed at 1:30 P.M." Many of the seminary students were married and had families and were already preaching and the working as pastors of churches. Many of them were not the typical college student of today. And while they were "talented" adults, they often did not have the fundamental preparation necessary for college-level work. They were grown men and intelligent, but without adequate preparation. So, when teachers tried to impose a curfew, reprimand, punish, or otherwise control social behavior, these adult students pushed back, and disciplinary problems emerged. Many of the students were the same age or older than their teachers. The students at the seminary, adults and adolescents alike, began to privately and sometimes openly challenge the paternalism that had been the mindset of the founders and faculties of the schools for African Americans from their beginnings. Paternalism is "a system under which an authority undertakes to supply needs or regulate conduct of those under its control in matters affecting them as individuals as well as in their relations to authority and to each other."[14] To act out against the paternalism of the white

[14] *Webster's New Collegiate Dictionary* (Springfield, MA: G. & C. Merriam Co., 1974).

administrators and teachers at the seminary was viewed as an act of defiance and, therefore, as a disciplinary problem. When the formerly enslaved people were first recruited into the schools established by the Northern missionary societies and the Freedmen's Bureau, they were willing to submit to the authority of the all-white faculties and staffs. But consciousness develops in identifiable stages, and by the late nineteenth and early twentieth centuries, black students had come to see themselves in a different light. The students at Atlanta Baptist Seminary and Atlanta Baptist College saw themselves as men and wanted to be treated as such. Eventually, the consciousness of the students at Morehouse College reached the point where, in 1917, they "stage[d] a four-day strike against required attendance at study hall and the prohibition of evening study in dormitory rooms."[15]

Frustrated with the real and imagined internal issues of the seminary in the early years of the Sale presidency, the teachers also faced more serious external problems. Attitudes about race were very strong in Atlanta in the late nineteenth century, and persecution and proscription from the white community confronted the black and white teachers at the seminary. Black teachers were thought to be uppity and uncooperative when it came to following the rules of the culture of white supremacy, in which the white community was superior, and the black community inferior; and white teachers were accused of being "nigger lovers" for teaching black students and associating with their black colleagues and others on what was perceived as an equal social level. Teaching at a black school in the South in the late 1800s was not for the fainthearted. The depth of racial animosity in Atlanta would explode in the Atlanta Race Riot of 1906, which is discussed later in the narrative, but at this time, in the 1890s, Atlanta Baptist Seminary had the benefit of a strong leader in President George Sale.

From the very start, Augusta Theological Institute was fortunate to have some of the best instructors in the profession, including its first teachers—Julia Sherman, Sarah Burt, and Mary Welch. William E. Holmes remained at Atlanta Baptist Seminary and Atlanta Baptist College

---

[15] Raymond Wolters, *The New Negro on Campus: Black College Rebellion in the 1920s* (Princeton, NJ: Princeton University Press, 1975) 276.

for the first decade of George Sale's tenure, primarily teaching English and history. He also served as the secretary of the faculty and librarian. Professor William E. Marshall taught mathematics from 1890 to 1893, and Latin and Greek in the academic year 1897 to 1898, the first year of Atlanta Baptist College. Achilles T. Von Shultz joined the faculty in 1890 and was in charge of the natural sciences. The head of the Normal Practice School, later called the English Preparatory Department, was Carrie E. Bemus, a graduate of the West Chester (PA) Normal School and the Boston School of Expression. Frank A. Updyke served as teacher of Latin and Greek from 1893 to 1897; he later became a teacher at Dartmouth College in Hanover, New Hampshire. William Manguse replaced Von Shultz as head of the science department, and Emma L. Goble, from Woodstock, Ontario, Canada, was an assistant in the Normal Practical work. Other teachers in Sales's administration included George A. Goodwin, English and mathematics; Millie J. McCreary, assistant in the Normal Practical work; and Margaret McCreary, an assistant to Carrie Bemus. Some of the best students at Atlanta Baptist Seminary/College were engaged from time to time as assistants. Outstanding among these were John J. Mitchell, Major W. Reddick, Henry A. Bleach, John W. Hubert, Andrew Z. Kelsey, and John J. Starks, all of whom later distinguished themselves in education, with one eventually serving as a college president. David G. Gullins worked throughout this period as custodian and served the school in other ways as well.[16]

Understandably, most of the seminary's students came from Georgia, with men from Atlanta and Augusta leading the list. But they came from other Georgia towns and cities too, such as Elberton, Athens, Waynesboro, Newnan, LaGrange, Greensboro, Rome, Thomasville, and Macon. They also hailed from Oak Bower, Eden Station, Bartow, Berzelia, Penfield, Pine Ridge, Eureka Mills, McBean, Double Branches, Pope Hill, Hephzibah, Senoia, Long Cane, and Vienna. Remember, Atlanta Baptist Seminary (soon to become Atlanta Baptist College) was partially under the authority of the Georgia Missionary Baptist Association, so the school was promoted among its member churches by their pastors. A few students were recruited from South Carolina and Alabama.

---

[16] Jones, Candle in the Dark, 40.

There were no graduates of the institution before the year 1884, but students had been certified as having completed the Normal or Theological Course prior to then. William E. Holmes was noted as having completed the English, Normal, and Theological Course. He earned a master's degree from the University of Chicago in 1884 and awarded an honorary doctor of divinity degree from Lincoln University in 1910. Other graduates of the seminary earned advanced degrees from graduate schools at Chicago, Harvard, Howard, Rochester, and others, many of whom went on to become teachers, preachers, principals, businessmen, and lawyers.

The Atlanta Baptist Seminary and its students felt the battering waves in the wake of the social and political tsunami that came to be known as the "Age of Booker T. Washington" after his "Atlanta Compromise Speech." The Cotton States Exposition began on September 18, 1895, the day Washington gave his speech, and ended on December 31, 1895. By this time, Booker T. Washington had made a reputation for himself among many in the black community and some within the white community, so when the Cotton States Exposition was held in Atlanta in 1895, Washington was invited to speak in the main auditorium of the exposition, not in the Negro building. In a bold declaration that would have serious ramifications for Atlanta Baptist Seminary/College, and hence, Morehouse College, Booker T. Washington said, "No race can prosper till it learns that there is much dignity in tilling a field as in writing a poem. It is at the bottom of life we must begin, and not at the top."[17] For more than two and a half centuries, black individuals had been positioned at the bottom, in slavery or quasi-free conditions. In 1895, they were still at the bottom, but it was the goal of the board of the American Baptist Home Mission Society and the staff of Atlanta Baptist Seminary to help move African Americans toward the top. Indeed, it would be a struggle, but with the cross as their symbol and the candle to light their way, the men of the seminary continued to grow tall enough to try to wear the crown. It is certain that President George Sale heard Washington's speech, but how he responded to the rising influence of his colleague from Alabama is not known.

President Sale made sure that Atlanta Baptist Seminary was

---

[17] www.biography.com/articles/Booker-T-Washington-9524663?print

adequately represented at the exposition alongside other schools supported by the American Baptist Home Mission Society. Representatives from the seminary participated in the American Association of the Education of Colored Youth, and they most assuredly recruited students to come to the school. As a result of the exposition and the exhibits in the Negro building, African American schools "were given renewed support through legislative appropriations." As Washington began to wield great power over the distribution of funds and other support for black educational institutions, some began to court his favor. But in 1895, George Sale was busy keeping the candle lit as Atlanta Baptist Seminary moved toward full collegiate status. In the mid-1890s, there was a move by the American Baptist Home Mission Society "to discourage theological education at any [of its schools] but the Richmond Institute." After the death of President Graves, the task of teaching the Theological Course had fallen to President Sale and Professor William E. Holmes. Both men were already overworked, and theological education at the seminary suffered. From time to time, this area was infused with stimulating lectures sponsored by the Home Mission Board of the Southern Baptist Convention, and eventually, after the seminary became Atlanta Baptist College, the Theological Course was reinvigorated by the development of a more structured curriculum and the appointment of the Reverend Doctor C. C. Smith as director of the department. This was the beginning of the School of Religion.

It is interesting to note that before Booker T. Washington's advocacy for an industrial-agricultural "education" for African Americans became widely accepted and implemented, Atlanta Baptist Seminary, under the leadership of George Sale, attempted to establish an industrial department. Sale was "a very practical man and [was] sensitive to the dramatic need for skills beyond the scope of the 'liberal arts.'" In the early 1890s, he sought to "introduce training in carpentry, gardening, and shoemaking." While most of these efforts at industrial training did not succeed due to a lack of funds, President Sale was able to establish a printing office early in 1892 that was set up in Graves Hall. Sufficient type for a small press was acquired thanks to the generosity of friends, and *The Advance,* a seminary paper that had Sale as its editor, began publication in March 1892. Former president Samuel Graves and Professor William Holmes were regular contributors, and "from time-to-time students were encouraged to contribute brief articles on their work and other subjects of general interest." Articles by missionaries in Africa with ties to Atlanta Baptist Seminary and Spelman Seminary were also published in *The Advance*.

President Sale was interested in creating a beautiful campus, so he oversaw improvements to the grounds with included terraces and the cultivation of lawn grass. On December 22, 1894, twenty-four elm trees were planted in long rows along the main driveway, from Graves Hall to the entrance, transforming the bare hill of red clay over the years. These trees weathered the winds, rain, and occasional ice storms that are reminders of yesteryear. They link the present Morehouse place and family to its past. A diverse group of students were hired to do the work of beautifying the campus and other jobs, coming from different parts of the state of Georgia, the South, and the nation. The range in age of the school's students was relatively wide at this time. It was common for a twenty-five- or thirty-year-old man to be in a class with a fourteen-year-old teenager. But the wide difference in ages did not seem to dampen the spirit, the esprit de corps, of the student body or their sense of Christian brotherhood. "All were poor and worked for eight cents an hour out-of-doors, on the halls, in the newly established printing office, or in the laundry, in order to help defray the cost of room and board." This contributed to what came to be known as the "Morehouse Mystique," reflected in the sense of brotherhood forged by common economic problems, the quest for an education, and deep religious convictions along with countless hours of conversation, debate, argument, and discourse among the men at the college.

During the sixteen years that Dr. George Sale was president of the institution, several important developments took place. In addition to growing the student body, the Sales administration also established Morehouse Academy. Atlanta Baptist Seminary became Atlanta Baptist College when its charter was amended by order of Judge J. H. Lumpkin on March 10, 1897. The amended charter stated the following: "Whereas your petitioner in order to promote to better advantage the object for which it was made a body corporate, viz. the 'Education of the colored people of the South, especially the training of preachers and teachers of the colored race' and was approved in the Superior Court of Fulton County on May 28, 1879. That in the corporate name 'Atlanta Baptist Seminary' the word

'College' be substituted for the word 'Seminary.'" It was made clear that the "powers heretofore possessed by the said corporation are not in any way changed or affected" and that any trusts, endowment, or property which had been "procured, given or left by gift, bequest, or devised to" Atlanta Baptist Seminary would now be administered by Atlanta Baptist College.

The corporation had the power to offer courses of instruction in three areas: academic, professional, and technical. The school also now had the "power on the recommendation of the faculty of the said Atlanta Baptist College to confer such degrees or marks of literary or professional distinction as are usually conferred by institutions in the United States, possessing University powers." In recent years, there have been discussions about graduate school work at Morehouse, but to date, nothing has come from it.

The "Amended Charter of 1897" that changed Atlanta Baptist Seminary into Atlanta Baptist College did not radically change the curriculum or its personnel and physical plant. The American Baptist Home Mission Society and its board still had control over the institution, and the college's motto, which had appeared in the academic year 1895 to 1896, continued to be the watchwords for the school. "*Et Facta Est Lux*"—"And There Was Light"—was written in the college catalogue above the names of the members of the faculty. President Sale's name was not separated from the rest of the faculty, but was listed first on the list. His name was followed by the Reverend Jabez M. Brittain, DD, special lecturer in theology under the Southern Boards; the Reverend William E. Holmes, AM, English literature, history, elocution, and librarian; Miss Elizabeth V. Griffin, psychology, pedagogy, reading, and language methods; Miss Carrie E. Bemus, ME, superintendent of the practice school, and arithmetic methods; Miss Mille I. McCreary, drawing; Frank A. Updyke, AA, mathematics and science; William Manguse, BA, mathematics and science; George F. Browne, music; and Major W. Riddick, assistant in English. Among the student tutors were Henry A. Bleach, Andrew Z. Kelsey, John W. Hubert, and John J. Starks. Mrs. E. Kinney was the "matron" who taught etiquette and served as the chief hostess for the college, and the Reverend David G. Gullins was the custodian. These were the honored personnel who kept the "candle in the dark" burning brightly in order to guide students through the darks days of the nadir. Small as Atlanta Baptist College was—it featured only one building in 1897, Graves Hall (so named the following year)—it was an excellent school. It is interesting to note that while the heavy emphasis on religion, and the Baptist denomination in particular, was carried over from the seminary to the college, the Amended Charter of 1897 stated that "no religious test shall be made for admission to any department of the college." Nevertheless, the Baptist's parochial control of the college was made clear when the charter required

> that two-thirds of the Board of Trustees and the president of the college shall at all times be members in good standing in regular Baptist Churches; and so long as the college receives pecuniary help from the American Baptist Home Mission Society it shall be subject to visitation by the Superintendent of Education of the Society, and the teachers selected and appointed by said Board of Trustees shall be subject to approval by the Executive Board of said Society.

Except for African Methodist Episcopal schools, most black schools were controlled, to one extent or another, by white religious denominations. Atlanta University was governed by the American Missionary Association, Spelman was also under the control of the American Baptist Homes Mission Society, and Clark was controlled by the Christian Methodists. Morris Brown was an AME school.

When the seminary—"a Christian College operated by the American Baptist Home Mission Society, for the education of Negro young men, with special reference to the preparation of ministers and teachers"—became a college in 1897, its board was composed of the following members: the Reverend E. Lathrop, DD, from Connecticut (president); the Reverend William J. White, DD, from Georgia (secretary); the Reverend Henry L. Morehouse, DD, from New York; the Honorable B. F. Abbott from Georgia; Major Sidney Root from Georgia; the Reverend Joseph Elder, DD, from New York; the Reverend N. E. Wood, DD, from New York; the Reverend W. H. Tilman of Georgia; Mr. Joseph Brokaw, Esq., of New York; Mr. A. J. Robinson, Esq., of New York; and the Reverend W. C. P. Rhoades, DD, of New York. The Amended Charter of 1897 described the powers and structure of the board:

> That the affairs of the said corporation shall be managed by a Board of Trustees who shall have power to appoint and remove the president of said Atlanta Baptist College, and such professors, teachers, and other officers, agents or servants, as it may find necessary to employ, in carrying on the work of said College, and to determine the compensation for service of all its employees. The Board had the power to make and establish from time to time such rules and regulations as it may deem necessary to regulate the management of every department of said Atlanta Baptist College.

The board of trustees could have no more than eleven and not less than seven members, of whom the Society's corresponding secretary, for the time being, would be ex-officio, one of the number. The majority of the members of the board constituted a quorum for the transaction of business, and at the first meeting of the board, in order to assure that it would always have sitting members, it divided into three classes: "The first shall serve one year; the second class for two years; and the third class for three years." All succeeding board members were to be appointed for three-year terms and "vacancies on the board, whether caused by expiration of the term of office, or resignation, removal or death, shall be filled by the Board itself. Appointments to fill vacancies caused by resignation, removal, or death, shall be made only for the unexpired term of the office." Over the years, the size of the board of trustees would change, but its powers would be sustained. Atlanta Baptist College's board in 1897 was a good one that had the best interests of the school in mind and at heart, and they collaborated with President Sale in an effort to grow the college as the twentieth century was just on the horizon. Increasing the student enrollment, adding new members to the faculty, and making additions to the physical plant to accommodate the growing student population were their priorities. These priorities required greater financial resources and a larger endowment.

Quarles Memorial Hall was constructed and dedicated in 1898 to provided much-needed space. The new building was named for Rev. Frank Quarles, former pastor at Friendship Baptist Church. In addition to the plan to build Quarles Hall, the board also approved changing the name of the Main Building, erected under the presidency of Rev. Samuel Graves, to Graves Hall in recognition of President Graves's success in securing funds for construction of the building. Funds were also allocated for the endowment of the president's chair.

Graves Hall and Quarles Hall constituted the physical plant in 1898. Quarles Hall was a two-story brick structure that would serve the college well into the twentieth century. In 1902, on the recommendation of Dr. Malcolm MacVicar, superintendent of education for the American Baptist Home Mission Society and a member of the college's board of trustees, a commodious two-story home was built for the president of the college at a cost of around $5,000.[18] The new building was sited just a few yards from Graves Hall on the north side of the campus. Sheathed in red brick, this new building was architecturally in harmony with Graves and Quarles Halls. It would be nearly a century before a building would be constructed and named for William Jefferson White, one of the most prominent founders of the college. And no building or facility on the campus has honored Edmund Turney or Richard Coulter.

[18] Jones, Candle in the Dark, 70.

Chapter 5

"Seeking the Crown with the Cross and Candle": Atlanta Baptist College Becomes Morehouse College

President George Sale, just as his predecessors had done, served the school well. He oversaw the transition of Atlanta Baptist Seminary to Atlanta Baptist College, increased enrollment in all departments of the college, and supervised a beautification project that made the campus attractive to all who took pride in the college. President Sale served the college for sixteen years, and when he resigned to accept a job as superintendent for the schools under the authority of the American Baptist Home Mission Society, the search for the next president began.

Atlanta Baptist College had been operating for nine years at this point, not counting the years that the school had operated as Augusta Theological Institute and the Atlanta Baptist Seminary, and several hundred students had matriculated by then, many of whom had earned degrees and were working as successful teachers and preachers in communities in Georgia, South Carolina, Alabama, and beyond. Some graduates had gone on to earn master's, medical, and law degrees and were practicing their professions, mainly in locales in the Southeast. The reputation of the college was strong, as was its relationship with Spelman Seminary and Atlanta University, Clark University (Clark College), Gammon Seminary, and Morris Brown College. Atlanta Baptist College (ABC) also interacted with other black colleges through scholastic and sports activities.

The college had a solid faculty when President George Sale resigned in 1906. Among the members of its faculty was John Hope, who had come to ABC from Roger Williams College in Nashville, Tennessee, in 1898, and had made a name for himself as a teacher and leader. After deliberating on who would be the school's fourth president, the Baptist Home Mission Board extended the invitation to John Hope. The invitation was for a one-year probationary period, and Hope accepted, becoming one of the first African Americans to head a black college, other than the leaders of African Methodist Episcopal schools, in the early twentieth century. While this development is historically significant, it should be noted that John Hope looked like a white man.

John Hope was a native of Georgia, having been born in Augusta in 1868. After attending grade school in Augusta, he enrolled in Worcester Academy in Massachusetts, after which he attended Brown University. Shortly after graduating from Brown, Hope accepted a teaching position at Roger Williams University in Nashville. He joined the faculty at Atlanta Baptist College after receiving a letter from Malcolm MacVicar, the American Baptist Home Mission Society superintendent of education: "Your letter of June 4th was received on my return to the office last week," MacVicar wrote to Hope. "Our Board met yesterday and appointed teachers for the coming year. Your name was recommended both by the president of Roger Williams, and the president of Atlanta Baptist College; but in accordance with your expressed wish, you have been appointed to fill a vacancy in Atlanta." Apparently, Hope was interested in returning to his native state, and MacVicar optimistically predicted "may we not hope that in the near future you will become an important factor in promoting the educational interests of your people in Georgia." MacVicar informed Hope that he would officially notify President Sale of his appointment to the college and would also inform President James of Roger Williams that it was Hope's decision to come to Atlanta. "Indeed, had I your permission," MacVicar wrote, "I would mail him a copy of your last letter, which I think would be a satisfactory explanation of your course."[1] With this, John Hope became a member of the faculty at Atlanta Baptist College. Hope was well-educated and he carried his learning with him when he taught at Roger Williams and Atlanta Baptist College. The academic training and extracurricular activities he had experienced at Worcester and Brown influenced his leadership style.

John Hope had been a good student at Worcester who "could always be found in the newspaper room, digesting the most significant social and

---

[1] Malcolm MacVicar, superintendent of education, American Baptist Home Mission Board, New York, to John Hope, professor at Roger Williams University, Nashville, TN, June 14, 1898, John Hope Collection, Robert W. Woodruff Library and Archives, Atlanta University Center.

political news of the day."[2] He enjoyed sports, and while he was not an outstanding athlete, he "did make the second team in football and baseball." He was also a fair boxer. Hope's closest friends at Worcester were white, although his roommate for two years was John Harvey Wigginton, one of the few black students at the academy. In order to meet his financial obligation to the school, Hope washed dishes and waited tables in the dining hall and kept the academy's stoves loaded with firewood. He also worked in the hospitality industry at hotels and restaurants in the city.

John Hope had internalized much of the unyielding code of behavior demanded of him at Worcester, where smoking and card-playing were grounds for expulsion, and where other infractions, such as cursing and attending dances and variety shows in the city, brought stiff penalties. His respect for these codes of conduct informed his time at Atlanta Baptist College (eventually Morehouse).[3] After four years of intellectual and social growth at Worcester, John Hope graduated in 1890, the year George Sale became president of the seminary. He was accepted at Brown University, where he enrolled on September 17, 1890, at the age of twenty-two.

When he entered Brown University, John Hope intended to major in the classics to study the language, literature, and culture of the ancient Greeks and Romans. But he came under the sway of Elisha Benjamin Andrews, the president of Brown at the time, who taught "Moral and Intellectual Philosophy," after which Hope decided to major in philosophy. His grades were excellent, and in some cases stellar, and his studies at Brown became the foundation for his belief in the effectiveness and centrality of the liberal arts in higher education; he would come to join like-minded intellectuals in opposing Booker T. Washington's belief in the importance of industrial and agricultural training for African Americans.

The financial demands associated with attending Brown were more dire than they had been at Worcester, so once again Hope found work in the hospitality industry, working with caterers and in restaurants. Money continued to be a problem for him while he was a student at Brown, but as he continued to work in the hospitality industry, he found time to be active in student affairs. He worked for several newspapers as the Brown

---

[2] Ibid., 51.

[3] Jones, Candle in the Dark, 82–84.

correspondent and as a staff member of the *Brown Daily Herald.* He also served as both sophomore class treasurer and president of the Worcester Academy Club at Brown, played sandlot football, and continued to box. Hope eventually became the editor of the *Brown Daily Herald* and delivered the class oration in his senior year.[4]

The dilemma of racial identity was a constant choice for John Hope, and he confronted it head on. He insisted on identifying with the African American race but could have easily passed for white. He was medium in stature, around five foot seven inches in height, and weighed between 135 and 150 pounds. His Scottish DNA showed in his reddish hair, and his eyes were blue-gray. Hope's aristocratic presence was amplified by his conservative taste in dress and his sartorial preciseness. He appreciated things European, especially French foods.[5]

At a time when Hope embraced his maternal African American ancestry, thousands of other biracial Americans whose phenotype was more white than black crossed the color line to identify with their white forebears. But not only did John Hope embrace his blackness, he joined causes for the advancement of black people. Two events of national and international significance challenged John Hope in 1906, the year he became president of Atlanta Baptist College: the Niagara Movement and the Atlanta Race Riot. Each of these represents a major episode in American history, and John Hope was involved in both.

When John Hope first arrived at Atlanta Baptist College in the fall of 1898, he had recently married Lugenia Burns at Grace Presbyterian Church in Chicago on Wednesday, December 29, 1897. "It was a quiet wedding conducted without much fanfare and was over almost as soon as it began."[6] When Professor Hope and his wife moved to Atlanta, the school's campus was comprised of one building—Graves Hall—on fourteen acres about a mile from what was then the heart of Atlanta. Since housing for teachers was unavailable when the Hopes arrived on campus, President George and First Lady Clara Goble Sale offered them the hospitality of rooms in their Graves Hall apartment. Before the beginning of

---

[4] Davis, A Clashing of the Soul, 71–72.

[5] Ibid., 73.

[6] Davis, A Clashing of the Soul, 100.

the fall semester, later in September 1898, Hope met the other members of the faculty: William Holmes, Carrie Bemus, Waldo Truesdell, John Hubert, and Mary Hyde. President Sale, who taught religion and philosophy, rounded out the small but capable faculty. Unlike his assignment to teach science at Roger Williams, at Atlanta Baptist College, John Hope had been hired to teach the classics, the areas of his expertise and great interest.

While the structures located on the college's campus may have been in harmony at this time, the African American Baptists and the all-white American Baptist Home Mission Society were not. By the turn of the twentieth century, a new class of educated and articulate African Americans had emerged along with a new sense of race and class consciousness. Their credentials made them capable of assuming leadership roles at the institutions that had been established for black students and where most had received their undergraduate degrees: Morehouse, Fisk, Howard, Shaw, and Atlanta University are representative of this group. These professinoals were called "race men and women," and they were imbued with self-esteem and a vision for the black community: they were about uplifting the African American race. But this new attitude did not meet with acceptance by some of their white counterparts, even the white Baptists in Georgia who had been giving limited support to the Baptist seminary. Black Baptists had come to see Atlanta Baptist Seminary as their school, although it operated under the authority of the ABHMS, a white Baptist organization. These educated, articulate black Georgians knew they could seek the crown with the candle as well as the whites could do, but the white Baptists, however, thought it was unfortunate that "there had arisen among them an exaggerated notion of the importance of being independent.... Certain leaders have carried this assertion of independence to its extreme and advocated an entire breaking away from organic relations with their white friends."

Many white Baptists believed black professionals were not prepared for such action, arguing that not one of the schools under the control of black leaders was well-equipped and that no initiatives had been made for an endowment. In some cases, they were heavily burdened with debt. White Baptists believed that what was "needed for the present and for years to come is a cordial cooperation of all friends of the race in a fraternal united effort to establish and endow a few central institutions such as those at Richmond [Virginia Union], Raleigh [Shaw], Atlanta [Morehouse (1913) and Spelman], and Nashville [Roger Williams], and to foster such secondary schools as experience may show to be desirable." Arguing that school leadership should follow the money, and asserting that "the money for this stupendous task must come almost wholly from the capital accumulated by white Baptist [the Rockefellers and others], it follows almost of necessity that the chief control and general management of the schools endowed by them shall remain as it now is, in the hands of those who created these institutions."[7] Nevertheless, John Hope became the first African American president of an ABHMS school. Benedict, Shaw, Spelman, Virginia Union, and Roger Williams all had white presidents in 1906.

As the issue over control of African American schools was debated, tension between the black and white communities in Atlanta percolated. The racial climate in the city reached a volcanic level in the late summer of 1906, and on Saturday, September 22, the racist volcano erupted.

Due to political propaganda and vitriolic racist rhetoric, some within Atlanta's white population (and from surrounding communities) vented their hatred and fear of the black population in the most heinous acts of violence. John Hope, who participated in the first meeting of the Niagara Movement, whose mission was to fight for the civil rights of African Americans, had just assumed the office of president of Atlanta Baptist College when the white attack on black individuals and their businesses and institutions occurred. Hope, as the head of a visibly successful Southern institution meant for the education of black students, faced challenges similar to those faced by other black leaders. In 1905, the year before the Atlanta Race Riot, for example, Professor William B. Smith of Tulane University published *The Color Line*, a polemical book describing and celebrating the Negro's alleged failure in the struggle for existence. Smith claimed in his introduction that he was careful to guard "against the emotion of sympathy, of pity for the unfortunate race...which the unfeeling process of Nature demands in sacrifice on the altar of the evolution of

---

[7] Ibid, 71.

Humanity."[8] White people of all stripes agreed with Professor Smith: black people were inferior, they believed, and would eventually disappear in competition with the superior white race. Some white individuals were not willing to wait for the false theory to be realized and thought the extermination of the black race was the way to go.

While most of the white mob that participated in the Atlanta Race Riot of 1906 had not necessarily read Professor Smith's book, many of them had read the *Atlanta Constitution* newspaper and the incendiary reporting and racist propaganda it distributed to the public in the weeks leading up to the riot. Most of the headlines were fabricated stories about black men assaulting white women. One headline in the *Constitution* that "covered Dixie like the dew" claimed "NEGRO DIVES AND CLUBS ARE THE CAUSE OF FREQUENT ASSAULTS." A secondary headline said a "HALF CLAD NEGRO TRIES TO BREAK INTO HOUSE: BOUND OVER BY THE RECORDER."[9] Reports of alleged assaults, editorials, and cartoons aimed at portraying black men as animalistic brutes became the fuel for the firestorm that swept through the east side of the city from September 22 to 24 in 1906. Although Atlanta Baptist College was located on the west side of Atlanta, there was no less worry, fear, or trepidation among its administrators, faculty, staff, and students than on the other side of the city. There was no guarantee that the riot would not turn in its direction to teach the "uppity niggers" and white "nigger lovers" a lesson. As the members of the college prepared for the worst, the riot raged on in downtown Atlanta, on Decatur Street, and moved southeast down Pryor Street and Central Avenue toward Clark University and Gammon Theological Seminary. In the wave of racial violence, hundreds of black residents were assaulted and unfortunately as many as forty black people were killed. Fortunately for Atlanta Baptist College, the riot did not move to the west side of the city to vent its rage on the college or Atlanta University or Spelman Seminary. In 1905, Roger Williams University in Nashville had been burned to the ground under suspicious circumstances. This was the beginning of the end for that prominent

---

[8] George Fredrickson, *The Black Image in the White Mind* (New York: Harper & Row, 1971) 104.

[9] www.georgiaencyclopedia.org

ABHMS school.

The horrific energy of the riot spent, John Hope turned his focus to the Baptist college. He was on probation for a year, a status not applied to his predecessors. Nevertheless, Henry Lyman Morehouse, secretary of the ABHMS, in a letter to Hope recommended that he seek the counsel and advice of outgoing president George Sale. Hope was confident about his abilities and made this known by his independent actions on matters vital to the interest of the college.[10] And while he appealed to the white leadership of the ABHMS and other white liberals, he was also attractive to those in positions of black leadership in Georgia, especially the members of the Missionary Baptist Association. The student body at the college in 1906 was in such strong support of his presidency that they "agreed to do nothing that would in any way 'put a strain' on the 'trial' of the president."[11] John Hope's probationary period lasted for a year before he became permanent in 1907.

President Hope was the first of five consecutive presidents of the college who had worked as faculty members before becoming president. Unlike today, the inauguration of President John Hope was not filled with pomp and pageantry. His probationary period at an end, he transitioned to the office on a permanent basis with the unanimous approval of the American Baptist Home Mission Society, but with little fanfare. The ABHMS did not make a public event of the appointment of the first Negro to head one of its schools, and later, in the midst of a fundraising campaign, "the ABHMS did not mention in a circular that one of its most important schools was headed by an African American president."[12] Most American Baptist Home Mission Society and American Missionary Association schools were headed by white presidents, and most members of the faculties were white. Without a shadow of doubt, John Hope's white phenotype played a major role in his appointment to the office of president of Atlanta Baptist College.

John and his wife, Lugenia Burns Hope, and the first of their two sons, Edward Swain Hope, eventually moved into the recently

---

[10] Jones, Candle in the Dark, 87.

[11] Ibid.

[12] Davis, A Clashing of the Soul, 182.

constructed president's residence. The beauty and serenity of the campus quadrangle is at the core of what acclaimed American architect Robert A. M. Stern calls "pride of place," and students enrolled at ABC in the early 1900s began to take pride in the place where they pursued academic coursework and engaged in cocurricular, extracurricular, and social activities. As a student living in Graves Hall arose to meet the day, he could look out over the campus and be inspired by what he saw. The green lawn glistening with the morning dew as it was bathed by the sunlight emanating from the rising sun to the east, over Quarles Hall. He would see twenty-four elm trees with their leaves gently rustling in the cool morning breeze. And the campus building called him forth to begin his academic work of the day. A student could take pride in this place, now known as Atlanta Baptist College, and eventually Morehouse College (1913). Robert Stern believes that "the college campus is the representation of beliefs, of the specific character of a place, of a community, of an institution. It is the setting for the continually evolving interaction of people and ideas over time."[13] Indeed, this is true of Morehouse College. What we now call the "Century Campus" is the place created by President Sale, enhanced by President Hope and acting president Archer, and made sacred by President Mays. College campuses may be organized into three groups, according to Stern: "the Embedded Campus, those closely connected with the fabric of the cities and towns in which they sit; the Citadel Campus, those perched above and removed from the surroundings; and the Garden Campus, those whose buildings sit in a more casual configuration in the landscape."[14] The history of Morehouse College shows the evolution of the campus from the Citadel type to the Garden campus, and now the Embedded campus. Pride of place, as embraced at Morehouse, must be understood in the context of the incipient "Morehouse Mystique"; it is more than an abstraction or an idea. It is also about a real place, the place on a red clay hill in west Atlanta whose surrounding communities form the perimeter of the Morehouse campus. It is a place where ideas conceived in Augusta have been made real by thousands of black men as they bear the cross while lighting the candle in the dark. The Morehouse

---

[13] Books.google.com/books/about/Robert_A_M_Stern.html?id=keB1CpZp3-8C.
[14] Ibid.

Mystique is religious, as Moseley knew when he wrote the words to the college's hymn: "Holy Spirit, Holy Spirit, make us steadfast, honest true, to old Morehouse, and her ideals, and in all things that we do."

As the first African American president of American Baptist College, John Hope faced many challenges. There was the challenge of the racial climate in Atlanta and the South in the early years of the twentieth century. He had to deal with the racial divide between white philanthropists and their increasing support for vocational and agricultural trainings for Negroes, as advocated by Booker T. Washington, and the classical liberal arts education espoused by his friend W. E. B. Du Bois. Recruiting students over the reservations of parents after the Atlanta Race Riot, which had occurred just days before the opening of the fall semester in October 1906, also tested Hope's ability as an administrator. He also had to work with the Georgia Missionary Baptist Association and its growing calls for more input from the black community when it came to decision-making and these white-controlled schools that educated African American students; in 1906, the faculty at ABC was largely staffed by black professionals.[15]

John Hope found Atlanta Baptist College in good standing when he assumed the office of president. But like all African American institutions and organizations, then and now, there was a need to sustain the college through fundraising efforts. To one extent or another, President Hope modified his political position as he pursued financial support from the American Baptist Home Mission Society, the General Education Board, and the Missionary Baptist Association in Georgia. This was the main challenge he faced, and he would prove himself up to the job. President Hope was very familiar with Atlanta Baptist College on every level when he assumed the presidency of the college, which was only nine years old as a degree-granting institution. He had been a member of the school's faculty since 1898, had worked in administration for the institution, and knew the students well. Hope introduced football to the students at ABC and supported their interests in athletics. And although he was the first president of the college who was not a minister, he advocated for "rigid discipline, puritanical values, and religious indoctrination for all students

[15] Davis, A Clashing of the Soul, 106–107.

regardless of their age."[16] Published "rules" prescribed the conduct and actions of the students at ABC. The opening paragraph explained, "It is the aim of the faculty to govern by principles rather than by rules.... [A]ll regulations are based upon the Golden Rule: 'Whatsoever ye would that men should do to you, do ye even so them.'" Boarding students were required to be in the buildings during school hours and before 6 P.M. Absences during these hours were permitted only by special excuse. When not engaged in the classroom, students were to remain quiet in their rooms. Other rules were revealing on several levels, but what was the general purpose or goal of the rules, and how did the students respond to them? Students were required to be punctual for class and chapel exercises. A record was kept of attendance, and repeated absences could result in suspension or dismissal. Students were required to clean their rooms and have them ready for daily inspection. Each student had to work one hour a day as directed by the president. Firearms and other weapons were forbidden, and if such weapons were found in the possession of a student, faculty would confiscated them since they would be liable to arrest and imprisonment by city authorities in Atlanta. "Using "tobacco and intoxicating liquors" was forbidden. Understandably, the students were required to respect the faculty and staff. Unless they were attending a "Christian" service elsewhere, all students were required to attend Sunday services at the college and to remain on campus on Sundays except to participate in religious services off campus. "Breaches of discipline may be punished by suspension or dismission from school."[17] Some of these rules continued to be applied well into the twentieth century.

These rigid rules of conduct were consciously applied to alter or modify the behavior of the students at the college to create what came to be called the "Morehouse Man," the college-bred man, the man under the hovering crown. But because some of the students at the school were adults in their mid- to late twenties or early thirties, and in some cases married with families, such strict rules of behavior posed challenges to their sense of adulthood, manhood, and self-determination. Students were not allowed to play cards, smoke, dance, or engage in any activity deemed

---

[16] Atlanta Baptist College, 1899–1900.

[17] Ibid.

immoral by administrators. The application of strict disciplinary rules generally indicates that the group they are applied to has not been adhering to expected behaviors, and this was sometimes the situation at Atlanta Baptist College, as the suspension of Foster Wilson in 1908 illustrated. Apparently, Wilson left the grounds of the college and was gone for several hours, which was a violation of school policy. Where he was and what he did is unknown, but he was suspended. Writing to Wilson's mother regarding the suspension, President Hope made it clear that he did "not regard it safe to keep a boy like that and will have to ask you to send for him at once. That would relieve me of having to do so." Hope thought that if Foster left Atlanta Baptist College now and was "put to hard work he will have a better appreciation for his opportunities." Foster was from Montgomery, Alabama, and had been difficult to control, and President Hope believed that "nothing but severe discipline will save him." This had to be done "so that when he came back again, he would know how to behave himself. Save your admonition until you see him," President Hope advised, "but write for him at once and send me a letter at the same time."[18] There is no evidence to show that Wilson's behavior was representative of the actions of most of the students at ABC, though. As a matter of fact, it was common for students to write personal letters to Professor Hope, as he was called, even after he assumed the office of president, telling him everything from their arrival back home to deaths in their families. Professor-President Hope was well-liked by the students at Atlanta Baptist College, and they soon began calling him "Father John."

Wealthy white Atlantans were not in a giving mood when it came to black institutions in the early twentieth century, so Hope had to look outside of the city, state, and region for financial support. One of his first efforts, though very circuitous in form, proved fruitful. In 1909, Hope sought support from steel magnate Andrew Carnegie for a new building estimated to cost $40,000. Two years earlier, in 1907, shortly after becoming president, Hope had appealed to Carnegie for philanthropic support but to no avail. But this time, with hindsight and political savvy, he turned to his peer at Tuskegee, Booker T. Washington. An appeal was

[18] John Hope to Mrs. F. M. Wilson, Montgomery, AL, March 18, 1909, in the Hope Collection.

made to Carnegie with Washington's blessings, whereupon the philanthropist gave ABC $10,000, half of the amount Hope had requested. When the new building was constructed, it was named in honor of George Sale, not Andrew Carnegie; there is no Carnegie Hall on the Morehouse campus, but there is one at Tuskegee.

Sale Hall joined Graves and Quarles Halls and the president's residence to form a quadrangle to create a quintessential collegiate campus formation. The new addition to the campus was a three-story, red-brick building designed to bring it into consonance with the other buildings, constructed in 1910 at a cost of $40,000. Arguably one of the most attractive and utilitarian buildings on campus, Sale Hall contained administrative offices on the first floor, classrooms on all levels, and a 700-seat auditorium, fondly referred to as the "chapel," on the top floor. The Manual Training Department was located in the basement, which was later used for additional classrooms and a much-used library or reading room. In the original design, the Sale Hall basement was divided into two large rooms, one of which was dedicated to the Manual Training Department and the other equipped as a gymnasium with provisions for hot and cold showers. In the rear of the building was an annex that contained a heating plant that provided steam heat for all campus buildings. Later in the century, this space served as a classroom, bookstore, and purchasing department.

It cost $40,000 to build Sale Hale, and in addition to the $10,000 Carnegie gave, on the condition that the remaining $30,000 be raised, the American Baptist Home Mission Society advanced $20,000, the General Education Board promised $5,000, and the remaining $5,000 was raised among black Southerners. In this capital fundraising effort, President Hope proved his mettle and was respected for his work. Atlanta Baptist College was in good hands and the future seemed bright.

The social and political maneuvers behind the scenes that resulted in the funds for the construction of Sale Hall were not without compromises on the part of President Hope. He had to appease two opponents of the classical collegiate course of study for African Americans—Booker T. Washington and Andrew Carnegie. The two leaders "belonged to a mutual admiration society that knew no restraint,"[19] and Hope was caught between his need to expand the college with contributions that would come from Carnegie, with Washington's blessings, and his friendship with W. E. B. Du Bois, which he had cultivated after his arrival in Atlanta in 1898. Du Bois was on the faculty at Atlanta University. But his love for the institution transcended his philosophical bearings, so he put the college first: because Carnegie believed that an industrial/manual arts curriculum was best for African Americans, a manual arts shop was installed in the basement of Sale Hall. But the Manual Arts Department was short-lived as students enrolled at Atlanta Baptist College for the academic education ("Normal," or teacher preparation) and the theological training (preparation for the ministry), not the manual arts.

Between 1906, when John Hope assumed the office of the presidency of Atlanta Baptist College, and 1913, when the name was changed to Morehouse College, the school improved its status in every way. Seventy-seven men completed academic, theological, or collegiate courses of study and graduated. The faculty was strengthened, and in 1913, President Hope created, for the first time at the college, the office of the academic dean. He appointed Professor Benjamin Brawley, a son of the college who was then teaching at Howard University in Washington, DC, to the position of dean. Professor Brawley accepted the position and went on to establish a strong liberal arts curriculum at Morehouse. Brawley "was a sensitive, highly cultured man and an exacting and thorough scholar, who contributed to the tone of the institution."[20] He was a Harvard-educated scholar. So, with emphasis on religious training and morals, the cross continued to be borne; at the same time, the candle burned brightly as the veil of ignorance was pulled back through the heavy emphasis on the liberal arts. It was in this environment that the Morehouse Man emerged.

---

[19] Davis, A Clashing of the Soul.

[20] Jones, Candle in the Dark, 91.

Chapter 6

"The Brightly Burning Candle": The Morehouse Mystique Emerges

The metaphoric "candle" that was emblematic of Atlanta Baptist College was burning brightly when John Hope moved from the ranks of the faculty to become the fourth president of the college in 1906. Hope had been at the college for eight years and understood the organizational structure and culture of the school. The attractive campus was small, compact, and mostly isolated from the surrounding community. The president's residence, erected in 1902, not only provided living quarters for President Hope and his family, but also held an office that allowed the president to work from home. President and Mrs. Hope entertained guests at the president's residence, including students and faculty. Benjamin Brawley and Samuel Archer, as his top administrators, were frequently in the president's home. Brawley was academic dean, and Archer, who had joined the faculty a few years after Hope, was the president's "right hand man."[1] For the good of the college, these men were strong supporters of a vibrant student life at ABC.

Intramural and recreational sports were played at the school before the formation of the Athletic Association in 1896. Baseball was the main sport played by the students at Atlanta Baptist College. At this time, there were no coaches, so students themselves handled the selection, management, training, supervision, and promotion of their teams, which were sometimes composed of "outsiders" as well as students.[2] Atlanta Baptist College competed in baseball games against teams from Atlanta University, Clark University, and Morris Brown College, all of whom were members of the City Intercollegiate Baseball League. The CIBL disbanded early over the issue of playing "outsiders," or non-students, on member teams. ABC and Atlanta University were against fielding outsiders while

---

[1] Ibid, 123.

[2] Frank L. Forbes, Athletics at Morehouse College, 1896–1966, 33.

Clark and Morris Brown favored them. Soon the administration felt the need for more faculty supervision of the school's athletic program, so President Hope appointed Dr. Alfred D. Jones, a talented pitcher at the school in the 1890s, as the first regular athletic coach. Despite the controversy that led to the dissolution of the CIBL, the college continued to schedule games against Clark and Morris Brown, but only on an "exhibition" basis.[3] An attempt was made to reorganize the CIBL in 1901, but it failed over a dispute about whether Atlanta Baptist College or Clark, with identical season records, had won the league championship. ABC proposed a one-game playoff, but Morris Brown was willing to concede one game to Clark in order to give the school the title. After the CIBL disbanded, Atlanta Baptist College played as an independent collegiate team against local non-school teams. But in 1904, the city league reorganized, and in 1905 ABC won the championship with a record of four (4) wins and one (1) loss. Some of the outstanding players during this era were S. L. Young, S. E. Allen, H. P. McClendon, Judson Kilpatrick, E. R. Mattison, Wanza Davis, M. E. Morton, J. H. Young, and A. M. Jackson.

Baseball continued to be a popular sport at Atlanta Baptist College under the auspices of the institution and the rules of the City Intercollegiate Baseball League. This all changed with the formation of the Southern Intercollegiate Athletic Conference (SIAC) in 1913; the CIBL disbanded as the regulations of the SIAC prevailed. New eligibility rules were put in place, and in 1917, the legendary Burrell T. Harvey, a graduate of Colgate University, was appointed the coach of the ABC's baseball team. Baseball continued to be an important extracurricular activity at the college in the twentieth century, and in 1966, Donn Clendenon, '56, who had been a top-notch player on the 1953 to 1956 team, was elected to the National Intercollegiate Athletic Association (NAIA) Baseball Hall of Fame. Martin Luther King Jr., a member of the celebrated class of 1948, volunteered to be Clendenon's "big brother" and helped him acclimate to college life at Morehouse.[4] After Morehouse, Clendenon played professionally with the Pittsburgh Pirates, Montreal Expos, New York Mets, and retired from the St. Louis Cardinals in 1972.

---

[3] Ibid.

[4] Ibid.

With the organization of the Southern Intercollegiate Athletic Conference, athletics became formally recognized by ABC's administration, and other teams were added within a few years. Football was the next sport to join baseball. Benjamin Griffith Brawley, a man described by E. A. Jones as "fastidious in taste and mannerisms, and studiedly correct in speech and manners," seemed an unlikely person to foster the sport at Atlanta Baptist College, but as president of the Student Athletic Association in 1900, he was the man who purchased the first football was used in intramural games on the campus quadrangle.

Basketball was first played at ABC as an interclass activity during the 1908 to 1909 academic year, and it became an intercollegiate sport the next year. Matthew W. Bullock, who was also a football coach, is credited with bringing intercollegiate basketball to Atlanta Baptist College.

Athletic teams had been formed before John Hope became president. In the late 1890s, in fact, when Hope was a member of the faculty, an athletic association was organized under the oversight of a faculty committee. The association focused its attention on outdoor sports of interest to the students. Football and baseball soon became staples among student activities, but religious, literary, and performance organizations were added as well. Most of the students at Augusta Theological Institute were preachers who were often called to be the pastor of a church. As a result, they were frequently invited to preach at other local congregations. This practice continued when the Institute moved to Atlanta, and in the 1880s, two societies were established at the seminary: the Missionary Society, which regularly met to promote home mission work, and the Ciceronian Lyceum, which met to practice extemporaneous speaking and parliamentary procedures. Remember, it was President Joseph T. Robert's son who wrote the famous rules for parliamentary procedures and protocols in his enduring *Robert's Rules of Order*. Prayer meetings were held every Wednesday evening, and a required religious service on Sundays was instituted later. As the two societies gained greater recognition among the students and the people of the community, the Missionary Society became the Young Men's Christian Association, the Ciceronian Lyceum was joined by the Young Men's Literary Society, and, in 1886, seminary students organized the Congo Mission Circle. These four organizations served the extracurricular needs of the students into the last decade of the nineteenth century.

In 1898, around the time that the athletic association was formed, Athenaeum Publishing Company was established by Timothy Williams and some advanced students at Atlanta Baptist College and Spelman Seminary for the purpose of regularly publishing a journal. John A. Mason was the first editor of *The Athenaeum*, and he set a high standard of excellence that also depended on the combined talents and cooperative efforts of the business manager and the foreman of the college printing office, who was also a student. Benjamin Brawley observed that "from time to time the *Athenaeum* had shown a tendency to publish articles that were too serious-minded in tone." But Professor Brawley also said that "more than once...[the publication's] reflection of college life had attained even unto brilliancy, and on the whole it is by virtue and merit that the periodical had continued to appear as the voice of student sentiment and ideals."[5] *The Maroon Tiger*, the voice of the student body, eventually replaced *The Athenaeum* and afforded the Men of Morehouse greater freedom of speech. The college-supported intercollegiate debating team was formally added in 1906, and its first contest was against Alabama's Talladega College. Knoxville College in Tennessee soon joined the two to form a debating triad.

Clubs, publications, and sports were not the only organizations fostered by the administration and faculty at Atlanta Baptist College. The college Glee Club formed in 1911 where it cultivated quality singing talent and strengthened its members' leadership skills. President Hope appointed Professor Kemper Harreld, a graduate of the Chicago Musical College and an accomplished concert violinist, to the faculty in that year. And although there was a Glee Club at the college before Professor Harreld arrived, it was he who created its strong foundation at the school. Harreld expanded the school's culture of music and became a major artistic and academic force at both Morehouse and Spelman and in venues around the city of Atlanta. Harreld developed the Morehouse Glee Club into a nationally acclaimed organization of tenors, baritones, and basses, all-male voices that traveled in the Northeast and Midwest, and organized a small collegiate orchestra that was comparable to orchestras at other

[5] Brawley, Morehouse College, 119.

colleges. Both the Glee Club and orchestra performed concerts locally. Harreld eventually formed additional influential musical ensembles, including the celebrated Morehouse Quartet; the Spelman Glee Club, an accomplished group of all-female sopranos and altos; the polished Atlanta-Morehouse-Spelman (AMS) Chorus; and the Kemper Harreld String Quartet. He trained the gifted voices and instrumentalists to perfection, and his influence was felt beyond the campus and the city of Atlanta; it was felt in the region and the nation. Professor Harreld founded the Fine Arts Study Club to foster an appreciation for good music and offered private music lessons for the people of Atlanta.[6]

Other student organizations began to emerge by the end of the first decade of the twentieth century. Student organizations have consistently had the support of the presidents of the college over the years, but the presidents have also kept the institution operating by leading its faculty and staff, maintaining financial solvency, and strengthening the brand of the institution. John Hope was mindful of this in the early years of his presidency as sports, musical groups, and other organizations were established. Mordecai Wyatt Johnson, '11, wrote one of the college's first songs, which was, and is, often sung with gusto at sporting events: "Morehouse College, bless her name!" Bless her name, indeed. Atlanta Baptist College's strong academic program and vibrant extracurricular activities all contributed to the love of the school exhibited by its students and graduates. It was during the administration of John Hope that the image of the Morehouse Man, enveloped in the Mystique, emerged. The esprit de corps generated by the involvement of students in an assortment of clubs and sports, with the support of the faculty, had much to do with this collegial mood.

This mood, or Mystique, was unique to ABC/Morehouse because of its demographics, faculty, and physical plant. Enrollment was consistently small, with most students coming from small towns and rural areas of the South. These men shared a common bond in their family backgrounds since many had been born on sharecropping farms. Many of the students

[6] Jones, Candle in the Dark, 186.

had attended Rosenwald Schools taught by Jeanes teachers,[7] while others had been students at Morehouse Academy. While there may have been a few Methodists, most of the students confessed the Baptist faith. The faculty was small but engaged in the students' academic and social lives. A few faculty members lived in dormitories on campus, while the others lived nearby, within walking distance of the campus. The president's residence was on campus and was one of the buildings that formed its quadrangle. The faculty, more often than not, attended or participated in all student activities. The campus and physical plant of ABC was small, and this compactness gave cohesion to the culture of the school. It was the tireless work of Hope's predecessors that brought the college to the emergence of the Mystique. But President Hope was more than just a supportive and involved college president; he was active in the work of important organizations that directly or indirectly affected the lives of African Americans.

John Hope, along with W. E. B. Du Bois, Alonzo Herndon, and others, was one of the founders of the Niagara Movement and the National Association for the Advancement of Colored People. He eventually turned his attention and energies to the Young Men's Christian Association (YMCA) as well. Hope had admired the work of the Y while at Worcester and Brown, and he "was particularly proud of black Atlanta's involvement in the YMCA that had come to the United State from Europe in 1851 as an organization dedicated to serving the spiritual and educational needs of young men and boys." There was no better fit for the work of the Y than Morehouse College and Academy, schools created to educate young men and boys. "John Hope became an avid support of the black YMCA branches on the ABC campus and in the city almost as soon as he arrived in Atlanta. By 1900 he had become the faculty adviser to the Y Club at A. B. C. and had delivered numerous speeches to the organization."[8] After he became president of the college, Hope still found time to give service to the Atlanta YMCA as a member of its management

[7] These schools were supported by funds from Anna T. Jeanes, a Philadelphia Quaker and philanthropist, and Julius Rosenwald, president of Sears Roebuck and philanthropist. They worked with Booker T. Washington and others to establish schools in African American communities across the South.

[8] Jones, Candle in the Dark, 92.

committee, "which was responsible for the overall direction of the local organization." In addition to his work with the Y, as an African American leader in the South, Hope supported the black branch of the Atlanta Anti-Tuberculosis Association, becoming its chairman in 1915, and he eventually came to serve as president of the National Association of Teachers in Colored Schools. Despite the tension between Hope's role as president of ABC and his commitment to various community organizations, which competed for his attention and time, he refused to slow down.

In the early years of the twentieth century, Atlanta Baptist College grew in size and prestige, due in large measure to its alumni and faculty. The college offered a challenging curriculum, and its code of conduct imposed high standards of deportment and comportment. The students were proud of their school and they exhibited it beyond the campus. The faculty, albeit a small one, was well-prepared and dedicated to the students and the mission, the idea of the school. And the school continued to have the support of Henry Lyman Morehouse.

To honor Dr. Morehouse, in 1913 the name of the institution was changed from Atlanta Baptist College to the appellation that is has today: Morehouse College. The rationale for the name change "was, therefore, particularly to honor an educational statesman who had done much for Negro education in general and for Atlanta Baptist College and its predecessors, Atlanta Baptist Seminary and Augusta Theological Institute, that Morehouse was so named."[9] But the story behind the renaming of ABC is more intriguing than this statement suggests. In his unpublished paper on the politics behind this historic event titled "The Politics of Philanthropy," Daron Calhoun II (College of Charleston and the Avery Institute) reveals the conversations and machinations that brought about the name change in April 1913.[10]

William Jefferson White, principal founder of the school when it began as Augusta Institute of Theology, died on April 17, 1913, just days before Atlanta Baptist College was renamed Morehouse College in honor of one of the school's most ardent supporters, Dr. Henry Lyman Morehouse. Calhoun tells us that in 1912, the board of trustees "began talks

[9] Ibid., 199.

[10] Daron Lee Calhoun II, research assistant, Morehouse Sesquicentennial Project.

about the renaming of the institution for the great friend of the Negro Education Movement." The facts reveal that on March 30, 1912, the board unanimously voted to change the name to Morehouse College and that this decision was met with the approval of the American Baptist Home Mission Society, although it took another nine months before the ABHMS officially approved it, and another five months for the petition to be filed with the Superior Court of Fulton County, Georgia. Why was the school named for Dr. Morehouse, an understandable choice, but there were other options: it could have been named for founder William Jefferson White or even John D. Rockefeller Sr., a major benefactor. Rockefeller College would have been the counterpart to Spelman College, which is named for Rockefeller's wife, Laura Spelman, and the two schools would have represented the husband-and-wife linkage.

The first class of students to graduate from the school that bore the name of Morehouse College entered in the fall semester 1910, when the school was still called Atlanta Baptist College. The reputation of ABC was strong, and its students had much pride in their alma mater. It would take some adjusting to the new name, and for years there was a mixture of living alumni who graduated under both names. Eventually, all alumni of Atlanta Baptist College accepted the Morehouse name and were "true forever" to it.

By 1913, John Hope's reputation had been solidly established as an educator, social activist, and articulate spokesman for Morehouse College. "Most significant, Hope imbued Morehouse College with a spirit of race leadership—of commitment, obligation, and personal responsibility. Whatever their chosen professions, Morehouse students were expected to be 'race men' who by their actions, demeanor, and character epitomized black America's finest."[11] In 1915, the year that marked the beginning of the African American diaspora, twelve students graduated from the college, but due to strong enrollment management and other reasons, there were twenty-three graduates in the class of 1916.[12] The idea that black men could be educated for scholarship and stewardship had been confirmed for more than fifty years by the students who had attended Augusta

[11] Davis, A Clashing of the Soul, 199.

[12] Brawley, appendices.

Theological Institute, Atlanta Baptist Seminary, and Atlanta Baptist College. There was no radical change in the mission of the school when the name was changed to Morehouse College in 1913. Shakespeare said a rose by any other name would smell just as sweet, and so it was that Atlanta Baptist College, which became Morehouse College, retained its excellence.

Chapter 7

"The Candle of Resilience": 1917 and Beyond: Fifty Years of Growth in Scholarship and Stewardship

The idea that had been conceived in the bedroom of a deacon at Springfield Baptist Church in Augusta, Georgia, on February 14, 1867, was fifty years old in 1917. The Institute, seminary, and college had demonstrated its resilience, and it was now time to commemorate and celebrate. The idea that black men could be educated for service to their communities as preachers and teachers had evolved into a college that awarded bachelor's degrees to students who completed its collegiate curriculum. [1] And so, on

[1] A random sampling of graduates of Atlanta Baptist Seminary, Atlanta Baptist College, and Morehouse College reveals some of the graduate and professional degrees they earned and the career paths they took. Hanes B. Adams, 1911, attended the University of Chicago; Clarence E. Allen, 1907, earned a dental degree from Howard University and practiced in Philadelphia; John H. Allen, 1914, was the pastor at First Baptist Church and principal of a public school in Commerce, Georgia; and Peter G. Appling, 1907, was the principal of Macedonia High School in Jackson, Georgia. Oscar A. Arnold, 1910, was a contractor in Atlanta; Joseph D. Avent, 1907, earned another bachelor's degree from the University of Chicago and was an assistant professor of English at Florida A&M in Tallahassee. Edward Birkstiner, 1916, was a principal of the public school in Barnesville, Georgia; William G. Bivins, 1907, was the pastor of St. John Baptist Church in Memphis, Tennessee; and Benjamin Brawley, 1901, earned a second BA degree from the University of Chicago in 1906, an MA from Harvard University in 1908, and became a dean and professor of English at Morehouse. A goodly number of the graduates of the college became affiliated with Morehouse as teachers, staffers, and administrators in the early twentieth century. P. James Bryant, 1903, was the pastor of Wheat Street Baptist Church in Atlanta; George S. Burruss, 1886, was a physician in Augusta; Edward R. Carter, 1884 and 1913, was pastor of historic Friendship Baptist Church; Garfield A. Curry, 1909, earned a master's degree from the University of Chicago in 1916 and was a high school teacher in Kansas City, Kansas; James H. Dixon, 1908, earned an MD degree at Meharry Medical College in 1912 and practiced medicine in Sparta, Georgia. James H. Ellison, 1913, was an undertaker in Jersey City, New Jersey; and Buck C. Franklin, 1902, was an attorney and postmaster in Rentiesville, Oklahoma. William J. Harvey Jr., 1906, earned a medical degree from Howard University in 1910 and was a physician in Oklahoma City. William H. Haynes, 1915, who earned another BA degree from the University of Chicago in 1916, was a probation officer for Negro juvenile delinquents in Atlanta and professor of economics and

February 14, 1917, Morehouse College marked the school's fiftieth anniversary with a restrained yet tasteful commemorative program. Although the anniversary was on February 14th, the commemoration covered three days and included two programs on Sunday, February 25, 1917. The first program was held in the Sale Hall chapel at three o'clock in the afternoon, with the Reverend John F. Purser, DD, president of the Morehouse Board of Trustees, presiding. After the doxology, invocation, and the singing of "The Rock and the Mountain Shall All Flee Away," a Negro spiritual, the Scripture was read by the Reverend Edward A. Carter, DD, alumnus and pastor of the historic Friendship Baptist Church in Atlanta. Dr. Carter was also the secretary on the Morehouse board. The assembled celebrants then sang "Anniversary Hymn," which had been written by Professor Benjamin Brawley, dean of the college, with music composed by Professor Kemper Harreld. The main address, or sermon, was delivered by the Reverend W. H. P. Faunce, DD, president of Brown University. Following the address, the anthem "Seek Ye the Lord" and the hymn "Spirit of God, Descend upon My Heart" were sung and the benediction was offered. This concluded the first program.

Considered representing his last "state paper," Dr. Henry Lyman Morehouse sent a letter to Morehouse College on the occasion of the commemoration and celebration of the school's fiftieth anniversary. Dr. Morehouse lived in St. Petersburg, Florida, at the time, and the message was dated February 20, 1917. He congratulated the college, writing, "The American Baptist Home Mission Society in the eighty-fifth year of its history extends to one of its children, Morehouse College, its greetings and congratulations upon the attainment of fifty years of its history." He concluded with praise for the school, its president, and the staff and by offering this statement:

---

sociology at Morehouse. James H. Hubert, 1906, was the executive secretary of the Brooklyn (New York) branch of the National Urban League; and one of the college's most distinguished graduates, Mordecai Wyatt Johnson, 1911, earned another BA degree from the University of Chicago, graduated from Rochester Theological Seminary in 1916, and was the international secretary in the student department of the Young Men's Christian Association in Washington, DC. David S. Klugh, 1890, did not attend the University of Chicago but earned an MA degree from Virginia Seminary and College in Lynchburg in 1904, a DD degree from Eckstein-Norton University in 1905, and served as pastor of Immanuel Baptist Church in New Haven, Connecticut.

> I cannot undertake full to estimate the values in many ways of such an institution as this. Doubtless others will ably discuss various aspects of the subject in their addresses on this occasion. Suffice it to say, in my judgment, the expenditures that have been made here are fully justified by results, and the record of the past is but a prophecy of better and larger things in the future, for fifty years in the life of such an institution cannot give adequate proof of its capabilities and possibilities.

Dr. Morehouse then projected the future with great accuracy when he stated, "The coming fifty years will undoubtedly bring a larger and richer harvest than in the first fifty years. May God's blessing richly rest upon the institution in the days to come."[2]

The second program, which was also conducted in Sale Hall, began at seven o'clock in the evening and featured the "president's Address and Platform Meeting" with the Reverend Charles L. White, DD, associate corresponding secretary of the American Baptist Home Mission Society, presiding. Hymns punctuated the program: "O Zion, Haste, Thy Mission High Fulfilling," "Now to Heaven Our Cry Ascending," and "The God of Abraham Praise." The spiritual ("Melody," as it was called) was "Study War No More," and the Scripture was read by the Reverend B. W. Valentine, AM, president of Benedict College, an ABHMS school in Columbia, South Carolina. The main address was delivered by President John Hope and was titled "Fifty Years of Negro Education and the Outlook." The speech looked at the past fifty years in the history of the college, highlighted its status at its golden anniversary, and projected a bright future for "the Greater Morehouse," which was his vision for the institution in the years ahead. The fiftieth-anniversary commencement exercise held on May 30, 1917, three months after the Semi-Centennial Founders' Week, culminated the commemoration and celebration of Morehouse College's golden anniversary. The "Candle of Resilience" would symbolize the college for its next hundred years. In good times and bad times, the candle in the dark would show its resilience and keep the flame burning. Most of the founders were deceased by 1917, but they would have been very proud to see the fulfillment of their dream. In 1867, the idea was but a pipe

---

[2] Letter from Dr. Henry Lyman Morehouse.

dream established on the proverbial "wing and a prayer.

As President John Hope's reputation garnered international attention, so did the reputation of Morehouse College as one of the quality institutions of higher education in the South. Booker T. Washington, who had positioned Tuskegee Institute at the top of the list of schools for black students, died on November 15, 1915, thereby ending the era associated with his name. Nonetheless, his influence continued to be felt in black society and the nation at large through the legions of Bookerites, his disciples, who had internalized his philosophy and vision and continued his work long after his death. At Tuskegee, Robert Russa Moton, a friend of John Hope's, succeeded Washington as president of the institution. But as these friendships were being forged, world events entangled Morehouse College in ways good and bad. World War I!

At Morehouse, "a major problem posed by the entry of the United States into the war was the acquisition by Morehouse of a Student Army Training Corps unit (S.A.T.C.), which permitted college students to remain in college and continue their studies while receiving basic army training on campus."[3] Established by the Committee on Education and Special Training of the War Department during World War I, the SATC was designed to train draftees in a variety of fields needed for the war plans that would be jointly administered by the college or university and the military. The Morehouse campus became one of the training grounds for students who drafted for military service but who remained enrolled at the college. Regardless of this status, many Morehouse students and alumni directly participated in World War I. In a letter to Mordecai Johnson, President Hope expressed concern, saying, "We have had among other burdens the worry that had come to some students and teachers because of the possible draft; we have had more than fifty of our finest fellows to be called into the Army and the end is not yet."[4]

The concern about the downturn in enrollment due to the military draft was of serious concern to President Hope and his administration and faculty. With a relatively small enrollment already, the summons of

---

[3] www.worldwar1.com

[4] John Hope to Mordecai W. Johnson, March 4, 1918, Mordecai Wyatt Johnson Papers, Moorland-Spingarn Collection, Howard University, Washington, DC.

college-age men to military service would be devastating to the college. Nevertheless, when called to duty, the Men of Morehouse and thousands of other African American young men provided military service to their country.

The Young Men's Christian Association contributed important "welfare" work to the servicemen in the theaters of battle during World War I. This work today is in the area of what is known as human services, but "its goals, however, are the same as they were during the First World War, to help develop the spiritual, mental, and physical strength of service men and women and military families." Services to address the needs of military personnel in these areas have been institutionalized with each military service command but were woefully inadequate in 1917. John Hope had long worked with the YMCA, so a branch of the organization was established on the campus. In September 1918, President Hope went to Paris to fulfill his assignment under the auspices of the YMCA to work with black soldiers. His initial assignment was educational and involved visiting with the African American soldiers and talking to them on academic and career topics. But he was soon asked to give social and psychological advice to the black soldiers "in tents, and he labored to alleviate their lot, for their participation was restricted, for the most part, to labor details."[5] In other words, they were servants to the white soldiers. The racism and discrimination against black men that was practiced in the United States continued overseas. But the work of the YMCA was critical to the war effort, for without it, the outcome might have been different. It was in this service that the president of Morehouse College, John Hope, took a leave of absence to work for his country but among his people. He had reluctantly and with reservations accepted the call by the YMCA to serve the cause, but after seeing firsthand the discrimination that black soldiers faced and the extreme conditions under which they worked and lived, on September 15, 1918, he wrote to Dr. Jesse E. Moorland, senior international secretary representing the Negro troops on the National War Work Council of the YMCA:

> If I had any question about being needed over here, that question is now settled. There are many jobs over here for men—and I am

[5] Jones, Candle in the Dark, 98–99.

> praying to God that I may be able to do a man's job.... There is so much over here to engage you that ordinary emotions find small place. Men talk in the simplest, off-hand manner about the most stupendous undertakings; and heroes are so numerous as hardly to attract attention.... I can now get an idea of what the Crusades must have meant.[6]

Among the Morehouse Men that President Hope met while serving the YMCA in France was Dr. Raymond Carter, class of 1903 and the son of Dr. Edward R. Carter. Dr. Raymond Carter was a physician attached to the Ninety-Second Division which consisted of black soldiers and non-commissioned officers. President Hope was assigned to this division during the early years of the Battle of the Argonne Forest, on September 26 to November 11, 1918. This campaign represented a concerted effort between the Allied Forces and the United States of America against the German forces and was fought on the Western Front in France and helped bring World War I to an end.

The end of the war did not mean an end to the services provided by the YMCA or the immediate return of President Hope to Morehouse College; he did not return to campus until late in the spring of 1919. While he was in service to his county and his people, Professor Samuel Howard Archer served as acting president of the school. Shortly before President Hope left for his international work with the YMCA, and after the appointment of Professor Archer as acting president by the American Baptist Home Mission Society's board, Professor Benjamin G. Brawley, the dean of the college, abruptly resigned. As dean, Brawley's authority was seen as second in line to the president, so he understandably felt slighted when he was not appointed acting president of the college while Hope was on military duty in Europe. Using his powers of persuasion, President Hope and others convinced Professor Brawley to stay for another academic year. But eventually Brawley joined the men and women of the literati and intelligentsia that created the cultural flowering that came to be called the Harlem Renaissance.

Benjamin Griffith Brawley ranks among the most intellectual men to graduate from Morehouse, and the scholarly fire was burning in him in

---

[6] Benjamin G. Brawley to John Hope, February 3, 1917, in the Hope Papers.

February 1917 when he expressed, in a letter to President Hope, the following:

> My Dear President Hope. In the rush of our work, I have for some weeks now deferred something that had been very much on my thought. It is a matter that we have discussed before and that we thought we had settled last September, but that like Banquo's ghost (*Macbeth*), will not [die] down. I refer to the possibility of my leaving for a year to continue my studies at Harvard University. Once more I appeal to your wisdom as well as your generosity and ask you to consider the whole question on its merits.

Then in clear words, Professor Brawley asked, "Is it possible for us to arrange for me to go? Any consideration that you may give to this communication will be greatly appreciated; and I shall be doubly grateful for an early reply." Closing with "very truly yours," he signed the letter "B. G. Brawley."[7] Benjamin Griffith Brawley would leave Morehouse to become a contributor to the cultural nationalist movement of the 1920s. The college, however, was in good hands as it operated under the leadership of Professor Samuel Howard Archer, the third acting president of the school after David Foster Estes and John Hope.

The First World War greatly affected the enrollment at Morehouse, forcing the college to delay ordering textbooks until the numbers for the fall semester 1918 were known. It was noted that the school would "probably be largely military in character this year" and that courses should be planned "so as to enable the government to use the school to the best possible advantage."[8] Morehouse students were on the mind of President Hope as he sailed for Europe. In a poignant letter, he revealed the love he had for the Morehouse administration and faculty and for the students he was leaving behind at the college. President Hope had already left the country by ship when he wrote an open letter to an "unknown" student. He said that he was sure he had taken the proper course and that the college would flourish in his absence, and he encouraged students to stay in school until such time as they might be called "for that supreme sacrifice at the front. You will be far less restless in college than away from it, and

---

[7] Jones, Candle in the Dark, 101.

[8] Ibid, 102.

our people least of all can stand for a man turning his back on learning simply because he thinks that he may not have an opportunity to use it." He called students who sat around waiting for the draft "a sort of slacker." Ending his personal message to the students, he wrote, "My dearest thoughts go out to you and our beloved College. Let the aim of you and me be to face each other again proud of the knowledge that we have a man's part in the trying hour of the world when individuals as well as nations are being 'sifted.' God help all of us Morehouse men to come through the fire clean and noble." President Hope closed with "your affectionate teacher," not your affectionate president.

On November 11, 1918, one month and eleven days after the beginning of the fall semester 1918, the Armistice was signed ending World War I. An eyewitness account tells how the news was brought to Morehouse students. A rally was being held in Howe Hall, the auditorium in Rockefeller Hall on the Spelman campus where acting president Archer had just delivered an eloquent, stirring oration in support of the war effort. A message was handed to Lucy Hale Tapley, president of Spelman, and in a choked voice, she rose to tell the students and all who were in the audience that the Allied forces and the Germans had signed the Armistice at 11 A.M. that day. The eyewitness recalled, "Hardly had she pronounced the last word of the historic message when all present burst into wild, uncontrolled shouts of rejoicing which put an end to the formal program of the occasion."[9] Rejoicing notwithstanding, the war had taken a toll on the enrollment at Morehouse, and only three men were awarded the bachelor of arts degree at the 1919 commencement. Three men also earned the bachelor of theology degree, and eight earned diplomas. Seventeen students graduated from Morehouse Academy that year.[10] But by the next year, 1920, enrollment had returned to normal. Twelve men graduated with the BA degree, six with the BTh degree, and twenty-four from the academy. The numbers continued to increase in the 1920s, the decade of the Roaring Twenties.

The lives of black Americans were once again the subject of attacks in their own country following World War I. The Ku Klux Klan had been

---

[9] Ibid.

[10] Ibid.

reactivated at Stone Mountain, Georgia, about fifteen miles from the Morehouse campus, and the vitriolic racism the KKK avowed strengthened as its membership grew by tens of thousands. All across the country, African Americans were the main targets of the discrimination and violence advocated by the KKK. Military service to their country did not shield black citizens from being targets of the actions of this terrorist organization. In 1920, fifty-nine black and five white people were lynched in the United States. The National Association for the Advancement of Colored People (NAACP), of which John Hope and other members of the Morehouse community were members, fought against the KKK in court, but as a secret society, the anti-American federation of violent chapters continued their oppressive deeds. The interracial faculty at Morehouse had to be on guard when they ventured beyond the perimeter of the campus.

The Committee on Interracial Cooperation (CIC) was founded in Atlanta in 1919 not only to oppose the 1906 riot, but also in response to the lynchings of the Red Summer of 1919 that resulted from the explosion of violent confrontations between the black and white communities in Chicago, Illinois; Elaine, Arkansas; and Washington, DC. In addition to opposing lynching, the CIC also crusaded against mob violence and peonage, and the group mounted campaigns to inform and educate white Southerners about the most heinous aspects of racial abuse. While the organization kept its headquarters in Atlanta, branches of the CIC were formed in some 800 locations. John and Lugenia Hope, the president and first lady of Morehouse, were charter members of the commission that included in its leadership Will Alexander, executive director; Jessie Daniel Ames, director of woman's work; Robert B. Eleazer, director of education; and Arthur Raper, director of research. But despite the implication that it was an interracial organization, few African Americans were listed among its leaders. Robert Russa Moton, president of Tuskegee Institute, was the only African American listed among the key leaders of the CIC, and Moton and Bishop R. E. Jones, the only black bishop of the Methodist Episcopal Church, were invited to join several months before President Hope. Nonetheless, Hope's main focus was on the future of Morehouse College.

Two years after he left Morehouse, John Hope returned to the college and resumed his duties and responsibilities as president. The vision of a

"Greater Morehouse" was conceived by President Hope in response to the social and intellectual energy he perceived among African Americans in the early years of the twentieth century. The "Dusk of Dawn," or a renaissance—a renewal—was on the horizon for African American life and thought and would come about for a variety of reasons, including an increase in wealth and education among the black population, the great movement of the black population from the South to other regions, and an embrace of self-help, solidarity, and race pride.[11] A Greater Morehouse would involve expanding academic offerings, increasing enrollment, enlarging the faculty, and positioning the college to become one of the best in the South and the nation. A part of President Hope's plan for a Greater Morehouse rested on the recruitment of the Reverend Mordecai Wyatt Johnson, '11, who at the time was a minister in Charleston, West Virginia. Professor Brawley had by then accepted an offer to go to Liberia, and, like him, Reverend Johnson, too, was unpersuaded to accept a position at his alma mater. "Once more let me thank you heartily for giving me the opportunity to return to Morehouse," the Reverend Johnson wrote to President Hope. "I have considered your offer thoughtfully and prayerfully and with every favorable bias such as would naturally arise out of my affectionate attachment to my alma mater. At length, however, I have come to the conclusion that I cannot accept it." Rev. Johnson did not "feel free to inflict upon [his] present work the disarrangement of plans and the consequent loss of effectiveness which would result from a leave of absence for four months."[12] While President Hope's plans for a Greater Morehouse with Rev. Mordecai Wyatt Johnson by his side never materialized, Johnson's eventual role as the first African American president of Howard University would do much to strengthen the reputation of Morehouse College since this historic professional milestone had been achieved by a Morehouse Man. In the years ahead, tens of thousands of Morehouse Men would serve their alma mater not only by joining the faculty and staff, as many others would do, but by their service to their professions and communities in the nation and around the world. These graduates of

[11] August Meier, *Negro Thought in America*, 259; Nathan Huggins, *Harlem Renaissance*, 3; and W. E. B. Du Bois, *Dusk of Dawn*.

[12] Mordecai Johnson to John Hope.

Morehouse were like "candles of resilience," and their achievements were emblematic of the impact the college had on their lives. They were Morehouse Men instilled with and inspired by the Morehouse Mystique.

John Hope never earned a doctoral degree, but in 1920, Howard University conferred upon him an honorary doctor of laws degree. And as Dr. Hope moved forward with his vision of a Greater Morehouse, two secretaries of the General Education Board—Wallace Buttrick and Trevor Arnett—took note and helped the college receive its first significant financial gift of $165,000 from the board. This was supplemented by a gift of $5,000 from black citizens through the Missionary Baptist Association of Georgia. These gifts were used to construct the last building on the campus during Hope's administration, the science building now known as Hope Hall. It was a three-story structure designed to be architecturally harmonious with Sale and Robert Halls, and the new building provided laboratories and additional classrooms for the school as well as offices for the biology, chemistry, and physics teachers.[13]

The Greater Morehouse idea was further made real when the General Education Board made an endowment of $200,000 to the college and the American Baptist Home Mission Society provided an additional $100,000. The creation of a reputable liberal arts college for African American men in the South was the core mission behind the idea of a Greater Morehouse, and this had been true since the idea was first conceived in Augusta in 1867. But to secure future grants from foundations, the college had to mount fundraising campaigns for matching gifts. President Hope first appointed Albert Dent, class of 1926, and then Maynard H. Jackson Sr., class of 1914, to serve as public relations and fundraising officials for their alma mater. It worked.

The essence of a Greater Morehouse, according to one account, was partially reflected in the decade of 1920 to 1930, which was a spectacular period in the history of the college. Every facet of college life was proving more successful than previous decades in terms of academic life, cultural events, student activities, and faculty growth. Intellectual life at the college was particularly vibrant and active during this decade. Drawing its students primarily from Morehouse Academy, which provided a thorough

---

[13] Jones, Candle in the Dark, 105.

grounding in the classics with its emphasis on Latin and Greek, the academic atmosphere was conducive to excellence, and the literary level of the college students was high. Cocurricular activities, ancillary to academic performance yet also symptomatic of it, were everywhere more in evidence: debating, concerts, dramatics, literary contests, lectures, and so forth. The Morehouse yearbook, the *Torch*, was published, Shakespearean plays performed (*Julius Caesar*, *Twelfth Night*, *Hamlet*, *Othello)*, and debates conducted, including against teams from England's Oxford and Cambridge Universities. The marvelous musical performances given by the Glee Club and orchestra featured some of the greatest African American, American, and European composers, and were performed under the capable direction of Professor Kemper Harreld. These performances were enjoyed not only by those affiliated with Morehouse, Spelman, and Atlanta University, but also by the community at large. Periodically, internationally acclaimed artists such as tenor Roland Hayes and pianist Hazel Harrison were featured, as was Professor Harreld himself, as a violinist. During the holiday season, Professor Harreld began a musical tradition that continues today, the always popular and well-attended Christmas Carol Concert.

In the summer of 1921, John Hope went to Chicago to meet with Benjamin Elijah Mays, who was then enrolled at the University of Chicago, and invited him to teach college mathematics and high school algebra at Morehouse. President Hope tempted Mays by offering him the "lucrative" salary of $1,200 to teach for eight months, beginning in September of that year, but Mays was not interested in teaching mathematics since he and his first wife, Ellen, had agreed that it was in the field of religion that he would make his career. President Hope did not press Mays for an immediate answer, giving him time to reflect on the proposition, and the more Mays thought about the salary, the more attractive the offer became. This was his first job offer since graduating from Bates College, and he began to consider how the teaching position at Morehouse would allow him to continue his graduate work at the University of Chicago. After weighing his options and the challenges the offer presented—including having to leave his wife at Morris College, where she worked, in Sumter, South Carolina—Mays decided to accept President Hope's offer after all, where he made history by teaching the first course in calculus ever offered at Morehouse.[14]

The Atlanta that Benjamin Mays encountered in 1921 was "grim" and "ugly," with its "closed doors, the barriers, the ever-present threat of physical harm, the strangling miasma of emotional assault, or spiritual attack." How did the administrators and faculty at Morehouse respond to "the injustices that bore down upon them every minute of every hour, every hour in the day, and every month in the year"? Dr. Mays remembers the Morehouse response to the Atlanta culture of white supremacy in the 1920s:

> Morehouse certainly did not teach students to accept, let alone gloss over the environment as they found it. Though no one at Morehouse taught submission, neither did anyone encourage Morehouse students to attempt by force to overthrow or change the system.... However, judging from the harvest, she must have—however indirectly—planted good seeds, and the field was unquestionably fertile. For many Morehouse men of this period made...valiant, and frequently successful, efforts to change the ugly world in which they were born.

This was a reflection of the Morehouse culture, then and now, and foreshadowed the idea of "the crown" over the head of Morehouse Men that Howard Thurmond orated and which has been popularized in recent years.

> The Morehouse tradition is a proud and honorable one that evoked the best from its students, one that provided a lifelong goal. At Morehouse, the A. B. [BA] had never been considered a terminal degree. The Morehouse man learned well that "a man's reach should exceed his grasp" and never accept the idea that the ceiling was the limit of his striving. Rather, the sky was his goal, even though, all too often, his wings were clipped at the ceiling level.[15]

This culture of white supremacy that Mays described resulted in the deaths of two Morehouse students in the 1930s. By the 1920s, thousands

---

[14] Benjamin E. Mays, *Born to Rebel: An Autobiography* (New York: Charles Scribner's Sons, 1971) 66–67.

[15] Ibid., 89–91.

of African Americans had been denied due process and were lynched. The numbers vary, but Georgia ranked number two behind Mississippi in the number of black individuals killed by the lynch mob, the outlaws who committed extralegal acts of jurisprudence.

In spite of the oppressive culture of white supremacy found everywhere in Atlanta, Morehouse nevertheless thrived in the 1920s and graduated some of its now-legendary men, including Walter Chivers, '19; Nathaniel Tillman, '20; Claude Dansby, '22; Samuel Nabrit, '25; Edward Jones, '26; Brailsford Brazeal, '27; and Frank Forbes, '28. All of these Morehouse Men served their alma mater in very important roles in the years after graduating from the college. The prestige of Morehouse was such that W. E. B. Du Bois, writing in the *American Mercury* in October 1924 under the title "The Dilemma of the Negro," and with a nod to his friend President Hope, shared this opinion of the college: "Morehouse changed from a white president to a colored president, but the church which opened the school took a man of scholarship and character and unusual executive ability, it gave him increased appropriations, and he is building one of the finest institutions in the whole South, white or black." Furthermore, Du Bois believed that "in it colored people see a colored institution with a colored faculty where their sons are getting sympathetic attention and first-class training, and they are beginning to yearn for more schools of that kind."[16] To paraphrase the Negro spiritual by Morehouse composer Uzee Brown, President John Hope and his administrators, faculty, and staff were "building a home, one that would not soon decay"; one that would survive the vicissitudes of racial hatred and violence; one that would challenge the belief in the innate inferiority of African Americans; a home, a Morehouse home, that would produce men who would lead and serve their college, the city of Atlanta, the state of Georgia, and the entire nation in many important ways; and a home of higher education that would hold a crown over the heads of its graduates, challenging them to grown tall enough to wear it.

Professor Mays had come to Morehouse to stay for one year and then return to the University of Chicago to continue graduate studies. Despite the confrontation he had with President Hope, he was asked to stay on

[16] Jones, Candle in the Dark, 109.

for two more years. Professor Mays believed that Hope "had equal respect for him, as a teacher who believed that students came to college to get an education. The academic discipline Mays had received at Bates had become a part of him, he tried to apply this discipline of thoroughness to his Morehouse students."

While Professor Mays wanted his students to do well in his classes and to pass, many of them failed. "I was considered hard," he wrote, "but, I think, never unfair. I believe John Hope understood this." The respect Hope had for Mays was seen in his appointment of him as acting dean for the academic year 1923 to 1924, when his salary was increased by fifty percent, from $1,200 to $1,800. This was Benjamin Mays's first experience in an administrative capacity, and it would serve as a learning experience for his later work as dean of the School of Religion at Howard University and, of course, as the sixth president of Morehouse College. In 1924, the "May era" of Morehouse College was still sixteen years away. Yet Mays still had work to do to prepare: he left Morehouse that year to return to his graduate work at the University of Chicago. Some of his colleagues at Morehouse at this time were Samuel H. Archer, Claude B. Dansby, E. Franklin Frazier, Burrell T. Harvey, Kemper Harrell, Charles Hubert, and Nathaniel Tillman. By 1925, Morehouse had a quality faculty and was recruiting capable and talented students.

The Southern Intercollegiate Athletic Association was ten years old in 1923 while Professor Mays was still at Morehouse, who reported that as acting dean, he did not deserve the reputation he had of being against intercollegiate sports: "I was against students who, though failing in their work, went on a basketball tour for two or three weeks. And I did insist that the men who played football should be up in their studies. This reputation persisted throughout the twenty-seven years of my presidency at Morehouse because we didn't buy players and didn't produce championship teams."[17] Basketball and football were just two of the sports played at the college. Morehouse had teams for baseball, track, and field as well, and some of the teams were pretty good. Samuel Archer had been the coach of many of the Morehouse teams until 1915 when he was replaced by head coach Burrell T. Harvey, who was in charge when Mays was a

---

[17] Mays, *Born to Rebel,* 92–93.

member of the teaching staff and acting dean. Contrary to what Dr. Mays remembered, during the period 1920 to 1924, the football team had a record of twenty-eight victories, eight losses, and two ties, "suggesting that outstanding players were no exception at Morehouse" during those years.[18] But football victories at Morehouse faltered in the late 1920s in the last years of Harvey's coaching. This was attributed to several factors, including the fact that Morehouse did not have the kind of recruitment and subsidy programs that were being adopted by other schools at this time. In addition, Morehouse Academy began losing students to Booker T. Washington High School, which opened in 1924, causing Morehouse College to lose talented young players for their college teams. While the emergence of recruitment and subsidy programs had its disadvantages, it was the elimination of the high school program that perhaps dealt the more serious blow for the Tigers' athletic teams, particularly football. Since the beginning of its competition in athletics, Morehouse, along with most—if not all—of the institutions appearing on its athletic schedules had followed the practice of allowing students from their high school departments to participate in varsity sports. This practice not only provided a longer developmental period for potential athletes, it also made it possible for some to participate for as many as seven, eight, or even nine years.[19]

Among the graduates of Morehouse College who brought national recognition to the school was the Reverend Mordecai Wyatt Johnson. The Reverend Johnson came to Morehouse from Paris, Tennessee, and participated in many student activities, including as a member of the debate team, Glee Club, and the football team. Graduating in 1911, Johnson went on to earn graduate degrees from the University of Chicago, Rochester Theological Institute, and Harvard Divinity School. As described earlier, in 1917, the Reverend Johnson accepted the pastorate at the First Baptist Church in Charleston, West Virginia, where he served until he was elected the first African American president of Howard University, in the nation's capital, in 1926. Johnson served as president for thirty-four years before retiring in 1960, and it was under his leadership that Howard University assembled one of the finest university faculties in the country

[18] Forbes, Athletics at Morehouse, 43.

[19] Ibid.

and brought international recognition to the institution. Rev. Johnson inspired another Morehouse alumnus who also achieved international prominence. Howard Thurman, class of 1923, met the Reverend Johnson in 1919 while attending a Christian student leadership conference in the spring of his senior year, and Thurman was impressed by how articulate, well-dressed, and well-educated Johnson was.[20]

Howard Thurman was born in Daytona, Florida, and became the first African American to earn a high school diploma in that city. He became the valedictorian of his graduating class at Morehouse and was ordained a minister in the Baptist denomination in 1925. He earned graduate degrees at Colgate Rochester Theological Seminary and studied philosophy at Haverford College. The Reverend Thurman pastored the Mount Zion Baptist Church in Oberlin, Ohio, from 1925 to 1928, served as dean of the Rankin Chapel at Howard University (while Mordecai Johnson was president), and eventually became dean of the Marsh Chapel at Boston University, where he served from 1953 to 1965. In 1944, Thurman was instrumental in the founding of the Church for the Fellowship of All People in San Francisco, and during his career he authored twenty-one books, wrote numerous sermons and speeches, and published other introspective works. The Reverend Howard Thurman ranks among America's great thinkers and most prolific writers of the twentieth century.

The Nabrit brothers, James and Samuel, were contemporaries of Howard Thurman at Morehouse. James Nabrit, class of 1923, went on to graduate from the School of Law at Northwestern University and to work with Charles Hamilton Houston and Thurgood Marshall at Howard University (while Mordecai Johnson was president) in the 1930s. Significantly, James Nabrit was on the legal team that won the landmark United States Supreme Court case of *Brown v. Board of Education of Topeka, Kansas* (1954). After serving as dean of the Howard University School of Law from 1958 to 1960, James Nabrit was elected to succeed Mordecai Johnson as the second African American president of Howard. He served from 1960 to 1965, and again from 1968 to 1969. Samuel Nabrit, James's younger brother, graduated from Morehouse in 1925, earned a master of

[20] John Eaves, The Morehouse Mystique, 33.

science degree from Brown University in 1928, and the doctor of philosophy degree in biology from Brown in 1932, making him the first Morehouse graduate to earn a PhD. Many more would follow his lead. And while we remember and celebrate the achievements of Johnson, Thurman, and the Nabrit brothers, in the 1920s, many other Morehouse Men were making their marks as educators, lawyers, physicians, pastors, and more.

By the mid-1920s, the structure of the curriculum at Morehouse College, which would continue with few changes for the rest of the twentieth century, was established. The concept of the "academic major" had been introduced at Harvard University in 1910 by Abbott Lawrence Lowell, Harvard's president at that time. "It required students to complete courses not only in a specialized discipline, but also in other subjects (the core curriculum)."[21] Today the academic major is definitive among tertiary schools (colleges, as differentiated from secondary schools or high schools). As Morehouse students began to declare majors, admission standards were raised. The Office of Admissions, housed in the registrar's office, began to require the Scholastic Aptitude Test, the SAT, as one of the standards for admission to the college. Historically black colleges and universities were not admitted to full membership in the Southern Association of Colleges and Schools (SACS) until 1957, perhaps as a Southern response to the landmark Supreme Court decision from 1954. Dr. Mays, as president of Morehouse, fought for full membership for black schools.

The vision, rhetoric, relationships, and facilities were good and getting better at Morehouse College when disaster struck the nation in the final year of the 1920s. Between October 24 and 29, 1929, the Stock Exchange saw millions of shares of stocks change hands, resulting in the loss of billions of dollars in capital value. Unfortunately, the newly established Atlanta University Affiliation was one of many casualties of the crash, which occurred just a few months into the first full semester of cooperation that now existed between Atlanta University (now a graduate school) and Morehouse and Spelman. The collapse of the stock market and the resulting Great Depression brought on one of the lowest periods in the history of Morehouse, as it did for the rest of the nation and the world. This nadir almost brought Morehouse to the brink of extinction. The

[21] http:/en.wikipedia.org/wiki/Academic_major.

candle flickered, but the institution survived, and for good reasons. But what happened to put the school on tenuous grounds?

Morehouse College was sixty-two years old in 1929, and on April 1st of that year, the official document forming the Atlanta University Affiliation (AUA) was signed. Since their founding (Atlanta University in 1865, Morehouse in 1867, and Spelman in 1881), the three schools forming the AUA had existed independently of one another, even though their campuses were contiguous. The affiliation redefined the formerly coed undergraduate Atlanta University as a graduate and professional school with Morehouse and Spelman as the undergraduate colleges. This historic event took place on the Spelman campus in the office of Florence M. Read, president of the all-female college. The "Agreement of Affiliation" was officially signed on April 11, 1929, by presidents John Hope of Morehouse, Florence Read of Spelman, and Myron Adams of Atlanta University, thus creating the new Atlanta University Affiliation.

President Hope, whose head was now crowned with snow-white hair, was nearly sixty-two years old at the signing. As president of the new graduate school, he was expected to bring to fruition "the blueprint for its future that included schools of business, law, and medicine, and a community service component (a nod to Mrs. Lugenia Burns Hope) unmatched anywhere in black America."[22] There is no doubt that the men and women involved in the formation of the Atlanta University Affiliation had been influenced by the Howard University model and wanted a similar, perhaps stronger, university for African Americans in the mid-South. But, as history has often shown, while certain coalitions, alliances, cooperatives, mergers, or affiliations could be successful, sometimes, too, they could fail. Clarence A. Bacote's history of Atlanta University argues that while the vision for the university was not fully realized—no law or medical schools were established—the affiliation did work. However, there had to be adjustments for it to work, as we will see during the presidency of Dr. Benjamin E. Mays.

The language of the contract of affiliation reveals much about the construction of the new arrangement among the three schools, including the nature of their collective and independent authority. After the opening

---

[22] Davis, A Clashing of the Soul, 297.

paragraph stating that the three corporations held charters from the state of Georgia and that each operated separately from the other, the contract described their intention to formulate certain principles relative to a cooperative educational arrangement in the nature of a University Foundation. Further, "said corporations desire in the meantime to cooperate in the advancement of college education and university training, both undergraduate and graduate, for colored people and also desire to readjust the scope of their individual activities so as to increase the efficiency of all in the work they are doing and desire hereafter to do, the three corporations in consideration of the premises and of one dollar in hand paid by each to the others the receipt of which is hereby acknowledged and in further consideration of the common advantages to each do hereby agree as follows."

The Atlanta University Board of Trustees changed its name to the University Board while Morehouse and Spelman retained their boards, officers, and directing bodies. Atlanta University would no longer accept freshmen and would discontinue undergraduate work in three years. Conversely, Morehouse and Spelman agreed not to offer graduate or professional instruction. Graduate work would begin at AU as soon as it could be offered at a high level, and one professor was to be appointed to the graduate faculty during the academic year 1929 to 1930. Graduate work offered by the graduate faculty could be supplemented by graduate courses taught by members of the college faculties. In July 1930, Clarence A. Bacote, a graduate of the University of Kansas with a master's degree in history, was appointed the first professor in the graduate school.[23] One of the reasons for the creation of the AUA was to streamline the work of the three schools and to maximize their financial resources. The affiliation agreement stipulated that the University Board would cooperate with Morehouse and Spelman in securing funds and that no capital funds campaign could be undertaken by either of the undergraduate schools without previous consultation with the University Board. The presidents of the undergraduate colleges also had to consult with the university president before making faculty appointments.

The idea of this type of affiliation for the African American colleges

[23] Clarence Bacote, The Story of Atlanta University.

in Atlanta had been envisioned for many years, since the late nineteenth century, in fact. The men and money behind those earlier merger proposals were all white and were associated with the schools for African Americans—Edward Ware at AU and Gilbert Haven at Clark—or the boards and funds that supported them—Wallace Buttrick of the General Education Board, George Sale of the American Baptist Home Mission Society, and George Dickerman of the Slater Fund. In 1908, they proposed developing Atlanta Baptist College and Spelman Seminary as strong preparatory academies or high schools with AU serving as the college department. The proposal was rejected. In 1914, the year after Atlanta Baptist Seminary became Morehouse College, another proposal was pitched to Atlanta University, an American Missionary Association school, for a merger with Fisk University, also an AMA school, in Nashville, Tennessee. AU rejected this far-fetched suggestion. As the schools of higher education for African Americans in Atlanta continued their work into the second decade of the twentieth century after World War I, the thought of supporting so many schools became a source of great concern to educators, philanthropic board members, and businessmen. At the June 1921 Atlanta University commencement, Jackson Davis, general field agent for the General Education Board, was the keynote speaker, and he reflected the sentiments of the white philanthropic and foundation community when he said the changes that had occurred in recent years placed the denominational and independent colleges in a different light. They had begun in a missionary appeal and it was important to conserve the "fine moral earnestness" that had entered into their foundations, but that moral earnestness must be supplemented by "sound scholarship and common sense." The merit of these colleges had to correspond with universal standards, and the quality of the scholarship of the black colleges was being questioned.

With little support from alumni, it was difficult to raise money to keep the schools operating and to increase their meager endowments. The disparity between the endowments of Morehouse and Spelman was significant. In the academic year 1930 to 1931, the Morehouse endowment was only $324,000 while Spelman's endowment was $2,930,000, almost ten times that of Morehouse. The AU endowment was $329,000 when the affiliation was formed.[24] With "visions of hope" for the improved education for African Americans in Atlanta, the first entreaty was made by the General Education Board through Trevor Arnett, its president. He pitched the idea to John Hope for the construction, equipment, and maintenance of a common library for the black colleges in Atlanta. Very soon, Florence Read, the recently elected president of Spelman, was brought into the conversation. Arguably, John Hope was the most dynamic president of the black colleges in Atlanta at that time, and at the 1928 National Interracial Conference held in Washington, DC, in December, he delivered an address on the "Educational Achievements and Need," as they applied to African Americans. While the speech was not profound, it did make an impression on the audience, especially Beardsley Ruml, director of the Laura Spelman Rockefeller Fund; Jackson Davis of the General Education Board; Edwin Embree, president of the Julius Rosenwald Fund; and Will Alexander, director of the Commission on Interracial Co-operation. In the weeks leading up to the formation of the AUA, John Hope, then president of Morehouse College, was actively recruited to head the newly configured Atlanta University as a graduate school.

In the initial agreement, John Hope would continue as Morehouse president until his replacement was named and had assumed office. Without "Father John," as Hope was often called, agreeing to head the graduate school, the whole AUA would have stymied and failed. The men of money made it abundantly clear that Hope was their choice and that their philanthropy was based on him taking the job. However, the venture was not without controversy even before it was put in place. This was especially true with respect to the alumni and students at Morehouse and Atlanta University, the undergraduate school. It came down to a matter of school pride: Morehouse did not want to be subordinate to the more "prestigious" graduate school, and the students at AU did not want to finish their work elsewhere, at Morehouse, for instance, and lose the fierce rivalry it had relished over the years. Morehouse and Atlanta University were football rivals in the early years of the twentieth century, and both schools were involved in the formation of the Southern Intercollegiate Athletic

[24] Ibid., 258.

Conference. Just as Morehouse and Spelman students had memorable undergraduate experiences for the first three decades of the twentieth century, the men and women at AU, the undergraduate school, had enjoyed the same. But in order to make the AUA work and benefit from the millions of dollars earmarked for it, the undergraduate school had to go away.[25] At dinner on the evening following John Hope's address at the interracial conference in Washington, and with Hope's talk still ringing in their ears, Davis said, "We're tired of giving out little dots of money first to one college, then to another in Atlanta. There ought to be some way to bring them together." Ruml then suggested that Alexander, who was also on the Atlanta University Board of Trustees, take the lead in bringing about a merger of the schools. The next day, Alexander, in a conversation with Clark Foreman, a Southern liberal and the nephew of Clark Howell, editor of the *Atlanta Constitution*, brought up the idea of a merger of the three schools, and Foreman recommended John Hope as president of Atlanta University while remaining head of Morehouse College. In other words, a merger could be effected through by Hope serving two schools. James Weldon Johnson, an alumnus of Atlanta University and a friend of John Hope, was apprised of the strategy and recruited to get the AU alumni onboard. Florence Matilda Read, a graduate of Mount Holyoke, had been elected president of Spelman effective July 1, 1927.

John Hope had long supported the idea of some sort of cooperative work among the schools. Earlier in the century, he suggested the following possibilities: Morehouse becoming a school of technology; Gammon offering interdenominational theological departments; Clark developing into a school of biology and agriculture; Spelman continuing to provide undergraduate education for women; Morris Brown focusing on collegiate work, perhaps for men; and Atlanta University offering graduate studies. But, later, when the 1929 prospect of a cooperative arrangement among Morehouse, Spelman, and Atlanta University seemed hopeful, John Hope demurred. It was not until June 1929 that he accepted the presidency of Atlanta University, the graduate school, thus cementing the creation of the Atlanta University Affiliation. Within a few months, the money began to flow into the graduate school.

---

[25] Jones, Candle in the Dark, 151.

Trevor Arnett Library was the first building constructed for the AUA and was completed early in 1932 at a cost of under a half million dollars, including land and books. The General Education Board contributed $600,000 toward the endowment of the library. But this was just the beginning of the money-stream into the AUA, mostly for the graduate school. Hope proposed a six-year development plan for Atlanta University and Morehouse with a price tag of $6,400,000 for buildings, equipment, and endowment: $5.4 million for AU and $1 million for Morehouse. But proposals were just that—requests. And while funds were allocated from many sources for the construction of Harkness Hall (the administration building used by both schools), a residence for the president of AU on Beckwith Street, new dormitories (Ware and Bumstead Halls), an athletic field, and Dean Sage Hall (a classroom and auditorium building), things stagnated and went dormant at Morehouse. John Hope, who was sixty-one when he assumed the presidency of AU while continuing as head of Morehouse, ended up devoting much of his limited energy to bringing about the success of the graduate school. At the very beginning of the AUA, Morehouse was the odd man out in the arrangement.

As money poured in to help get the graduate school started, Morehouse's financial situation deteriorated. While Spelman's endowment continued to grow pass the $3 million mark, Morehouse found it necessary to dip into its meager endowment to merely survive. Spelman continued to have the support of the Rockefeller family; Morehouse had no such benefactor.[26] And it may be conjectured that because of the race of the leaders of the schools, this is why Morehouse was odd man out. Florence Read was the white president of Spelman, Myron Adams was the outgoing white president of Atlanta University, and John Hope was the biracial president of Morehouse, who left to head AU.

After July 1931, Samuel Howard Archer, the progeny of two black parents, became the fifth president of Morehouse College. "Big Boy Archer," as he was lovingly called by all who knew him, was unmistakably black. It is important to remember that the 1930s was a time when members of the black community became more empowered and vocally assertive. Miraculously, at a time when it seemed as though "hope unborn had

---

[26] Bacote, Story of Atlanta University, 262.

died," the men and women of Morehouse—several dozen females enrolled in the late 1920s and early 1930s—kept their vision of hope alive with the indefatigable commitment of President Archer and acting president Charles Hubert.[27]

In the years of the Great Depression, especially the first half of the 1930s, Morehouse's enrollment declined and tuition income dwindled, as did the earnings from the endowment. Faculty salaries were always late in payment, sometimes they went unpaid, and more frequently were paid only in part. All salaries were reduced by 10 percent and called "loans" to the college, which were never repaid. And to exacerbate the crisis at Morehouse, John Hope, the first president of Atlanta University as a graduate school, was the "part time" president of the college. After serving the two schools for two years, Hope stepped down from the presidency at Morehouse in 1931, and Samuel Howard Archer became the college's fifth president.

John Hope had long dreamed of a cooperative arrangement among the schools of higher education for African Americans in Atlanta. By the time of his death in 1936, this was becoming a reality as Clark College, Gammon Seminary, and Morris Brown College had moved their campuses contiguous to those in the affiliation. Interestingly, Morris Brown occupied the buildings on the old Atlanta University campus while Clark College moved across Chestnut and Greensferry Streets, separating it from Morehouse and Spelman. The cooperation among the schools did not materialize exactly as he had blueprinted or prophesied. For many years, cooperation among the Atlanta schools had been encouraged by philanthropic foundations, and this motivated the colleges to make a move toward greater association with one another.

By 1929, Morehouse had a strong reputation as a respected liberal arts college with a unique institutional spirit and personality. The students and alumni of the college were proud of their traditions, and they loved their school. J. O. B. Moseley immortalized this love of "Dear Old Morehouse" in the beloved hymn that is the school's alma mater, and which has been sung by thousands of Morehouse Men, Men of Morehouse, and

---

[27] Mays was building his reputation as a scholar, intellectual, and academician in the 1930s.

friends of the college. "Dear old Morehouse; dear old Morehouse. We have pledged our lives to thee. And we'll ever, yea forever, give ourselves in loyalty." This love of Morehouse was, perhaps, the main reason why the alumni were vehemently opposed to any loss of identity in the formation of the affiliation. This sentiment was also shared by the alumni of Atlanta University and alumnae of Spelman College.

"For years, Atlanta University had been a 'status' undergraduate college where the sons and daughters of many upper-class Negroes were educated. Dr. Hope's half-brother, Madison Newton, had been a student there not long after its founding."[28] But in the years immediately preceding the affiliation, Atlanta University was in financial straits and might have ceased to exist had it not been for the cooperative venture among the three schools in the AUA. Atlanta University survived, but as a graduate school whose reputation grew to international respect. Spelman fared very well with the support of members of the Rockefeller family. It was Morehouse that had to struggle to survive in the new arrangement. Samuel H. Archer, while a very capable leader, did not have the clout and connections that John Hope had, and Morehouse suffered through much of the 1930s. Nevertheless, the Atlanta University Affiliation was seen as a step in the right direction for African American education in the capital of the New South, especially the graduate component of the cooperative venture. A little more than two years after the document of affiliation had been signed by the appropriate authorities, President Herbert Hoover sent a letter of endorsement of the AUA to John Hope.

> July 16, 1931
>
> My dear Dr. Hope:
>
> The constant improvement of the relations between the white and Negro races deeply affects the national welfare. Further progress can be made by the cooperation of intelligent, well-informed and educated leaders from both the white and colored people.
>
> The plan to build up Atlanta University and the affiliated colleges into an institution capable of offering education of the highest type to adequately qualified young Negroes so as to prepare them for

[28] Bacote, Story of Atlanta University.

such leadership of their people will add more strength to the forces already set in motion by the institutions. It should bear fruit in the furtherance of better understanding and improved relations between the races for generations to come.

Yours faithfully
Herbert Hoover

Dr. John Hope
President, Atlanta University
Atlanta, Georgia[29]

With support from the president of the United States, the Rockefeller's General Education Board, and other white philanthropists, the new Atlanta University was destined to succeed. And the tireless work of its first president, John Hope, assured it would live up to the expectations many had for the emerging graduate university for African Americans in the Deep South.

But the decade after the crash of the stock market and the years of the Great Depression took an enormous toll on the Morehouse endowment campaign that was in full operating mode. Pledges to the campaign could not be met, and the college could not even pay the mounting expenses of the endowment fundraising effort. The small enrollment at Morehouse during this period forced the college to divert funds from the endowment campaign to cover debts incurred in operating the same. The American Baptist Home Mission Society had been expected to finance the endowment campaign, but, unfortunately, this expectation came at a time when the ABHMS was gradually moving away from its financial responsibility for Morehouse. Finally, in the midst of the struggle to survive, and thanks to Dr. Hope's unending solicitation on behalf of the college, Northern Baptists donated $100,000 to Morehouse, enabling the college to claim promised matching funds. With this turn of good fortune, John Hope could now give up the presidency of Morehouse and devote his attention and energies to moving Atlanta University forward. Dr. Hope had served as president of Morehouse for twenty-five years, from 1906 to

[29] Jones, Candle in the Dark, 166

1931, and his affinity for the college was still strong. But the college had a new president now, the fifth in its storied history, and as the school struggled to survive, it faced the economic and social challenges of the Depression years with resolve. The 1930s were a decade like no other in the history of the college, and President Hope's utopian vision for a "Greater Morehouse" became President's Archer dystopian experience of a "Lesser Morehouse."

Chapter 8

"The Flickering Candle": Morehouse during the 1930s

When John Hope finally gave up the presidency of Morehouse, in 1931, after heading both the college and the new Atlanta University, he handpicked Samuel Howard Archer as his successor. Archer had been Hope's right-hand man for almost three decades, and he had occupied the office of the president in 1917 while Hope was advising black soldiers during World War I. Benjamin Griffith Brawley, a member of the literati, had abandoned his ambition to head his alma mater and went on to accept professorial positions at Shaw University in Raleigh, North Carolina, and Howard University in Washington, DC, instead.

By the time John Hope relinquished the reins of authority at Morehouse to Archer, though, the very existence of the school was in jeopardy: enrollment was declining, the endowment was small, and the financial health of the college was weak. Despite this tenuous state of affairs, sixty-year-old Archer accepted the position as the fifth president of Morehouse College.

Samuel Howard Archer was an imposing man of over six feet in height with an athlete's physique. A graduate of Colgate University who, like John Hope, had taught at Roger Williams University in Nashville, President Archer had been Hope's number one lieutenant for many years. Dr. Archer was "a dynamic man, with a heart as big as his towering frame. Professor Archer's direct manner and booming voice have been known to strike terror in the timid student on first contact; but this terror was short-lived, and soon gave way to admiration and devotion, for he was everybody's friend. Great warmth and understanding lay behind his blustering exterior."

Archer had a contagious sense of humor but "as a teacher, Professor Archer was exacting, devoted, and effective—one of the truly great teachers in the history of the college. As a coach, he was no less successful, and in 1964, he was elected posthumously to the college's Athletic Hall of

Fame."[1] President Archer was a good man and a capable leader during a very difficult time. The difficulties facing Morehouse at this time were reminiscent of the founding years of Augusta Theological Institute in the 1860s, but the economic challenges President Archer faced in the six years he served as the college's chief executive were different. They were similar to those faced by institutions worldwide.

By this time, Professor Archer had worked at the college for twenty-five years as a mathematics teacher, dean, vice president, and football coach. Known by the sobriquet "Big Boy," Samuel Howard Archer was born in Chesterfield, Virginia, on December 23, 1870, the son of Nelson and Keziah Howe Archer. He began his education at the Peabody Public School in Petersburg, Virginia, and the Wayland Normal School in Washington, DC, a school under the auspices of the National Theological Institute, the founding organization of Augusta Theological Institute. At the age of seventeen, in 1887, he became a teacher in rural Virginia. He earned his bachelor of arts degree from Colgate University in 1902, where he studied logic, ethics, and the teachings of Jesus, the New Testaments, and church history. While at Colgate, Archer was the first black man to play on the football team, but he was also distinguished for his oratorical talent and scholarly depth. Three years after graduation, Archer married Annie Courtney Johnson, and their union resulted in four children—Samuel Howard Jr., Rosalind, Nelson, and Leonard.

Archer came to Morehouse as a teacher the year before John Hope assumed the duties of the president of the college. Recognized as a great American educator, as Marc Moreland tells us, "Dr. Archer had a rare talent for handling young men. Of impressive appearance and a wit as sharp as the fine edge of a seldom pleasure, he was to his boys, as much man as any of them and a scholar who could at once amuse and instruct. Here indeed was a teacher who won young men and influenced them for good."[2] There is a legendary story about Mr. Archer as dean that has been passed on through generations of Morehouse Men. And while we might find much amusement in the story, it speaks to the character of Samuel

[1] Ibid., 124.

[2] Marc Moreland, "Samuel Howard Archer: Portrait of a Teacher," *Phylon* (4th Quarter, 1949).

Howard Archer. One of the traits of a Morehouse Man is good character, so when Archer was president, students were required to be in their dormitory by eleven o'clock at night. But, as young men will do, some students violated the rule. One evening, finding the front entrance locked, they entered the dorm using the fire escape. President Archer, having been alerted ahead of time about an errant student, had entered the student's room, gotten into his bed, and waited for his return. When the student returned and turned on the light, he found the college president there. "As the boy stood in open-mouthed terror, Dean Archer said, 'Oh, I'm just keeping your bed warm for you, so.' Then followed a lecture and the prescribed punishment."[3]

The integrity and sense of fair play that characterized the presidency of Samuel Howard Archer was revealed early in his career at Morehouse when a football player he coached made a "dirty play," which the player tried to defend on the grounds that he was just trying to win the game for Morehouse. To this argument, Coach Archer replied, "with impatience and disgust, Son I'd rather lose the game through clean playing than to win it through dirty playing."[4] It was this frame of mind that carried President Archer through the difficult years of his administration.

Marc Moreland tells us "Samuel Howard Archer was more than the favorite teacher of several generations of Morehouse men; he was the great friend of youth everywhere. And many were they who in his time sought him out for his wit, his charm, and his kind and instructive wisdom. None that knew him could not but enjoy the bracing atmosphere in which he lived out his days and touch with wisdom and beauty the lives that touched his own."[5] At a time when the nation was beginning to feel the impact of the stock market crash and the economic crisis known as the Great Depression, racism, a pillar of the American social order, became more virulent through the numerous acts of discrimination and violence perpetrated against black Americans. The murders of two Morehouse students at the hands of lynch mobs revealed the pathology of white supremacy.

---

[3] Jones, Candle in the Dark, 124.

[4] Ibid.

[5] Moreland, "Samuel Howard Archer," 351.

In 1928, Thompson P. Barnes worked as a newspaper carrier to earn funds to support his pursuit of a Morehouse education. As a paperboy, it was his responsibility to collect payments from his customers, the subscribers to the newspaper. One of his customers, a café proprietor on Peters Street, about a mile from the campus, was overdue on his payment, so Barnes went to the eatery to collect the debt. The white subscriber, not liking the way Barnes spoke to him and that Barnes kept his hat on, killed the Morehouse student with a shot to the head. Barnes died as he staggered to the door, never making it to the street. The café owner argued that he killed Barnes to "teach him how to act when talking to a white man," and the all-white grand jury agreed with the proprietor, refusing to indict him for murder.[6] The murderous act committed by the café owner was demonstrative of the psyche of those who lived out the precepts and tenets of the received culture of white supremacy. This culture had its roots in the antebellum age of slavery and was maintained during the time of Jim Crow. Dr. Mays describes this oppressive proscriptive system: "Not only in major areas—the right to vote, the right to economic security, the right to education, the right to decent housing—was the Negro deprived. But these basic denials proliferated also in countless ways to guarantee that every Negro should be consistently subject to humiliating injustices and insults calculated to destroy his self-respect, his pride, and his sense of manhood."[7] Death was the lot of thousands of African Americans, like Barnes, who violated the etiquette of white supremacy. All black citizens "were equal and equally inferior, so far as the white man's law was concerned." Lynching was a staple among the tactics used by white supremacists, and, as Dr. Mays recalled, "the white press deliberately created the myth that lynching was necessary in order to protect white womanhood." Such was the fate of Dennis Hubert, another Morehouse student who met his death at the hands of a terrorist mob.

Dennis Hubert was an eighteen-year-old student at Morehouse and a member of the prominent Hubert family that included Charles D. Hubert, professor and future acting president of the college. The son of the Reverend Gaddus J. Hubert, a Baptist minister, Dennis had attended

---

[6] Jones, Candle in the Dark, 110.

[7] Mays, *Born to Rebel*, 75.

Sunday services on June 15, 1930, and was sitting in a park near the Crogman School, not far from the Morehouse campus, when a group of white men and women came upon the young man and accused him of speaking inappropriately to one of the white women in the group. An eyewitness to the confrontation between the black youth and the white men said the attack apparently resulted from a perceived insult Dennis made when he said, referring to the drunken white women, "You better take them women home." This was a clear violation of the etiquette of white supremacy, for a black person to tell a white person what to do. The white group left the scene, but returned with six other men, perhaps for a traditional lynching. But as Hubert was sighted, the white men, without warning, shot the Morehouse student in the back of the head, killing him instantly. In the aftermath of the murder of Dennis Hubert, the rabid mob, not yet satiated, began a reign of terror a week later in the African American community. The home of the father of the murdered student was burned to the ground; the family barely escaped with their lives. In the meantime, several white men were arrested, including the triggerman, T. L. Martin, and the city promised to bring them to trial. The decision to bring the criminals to justice "set off another round of violence, attributed to the Black Shirts, a KKK-like, terrorist group. Tear-gas bombs were tossed into Wheat Street Baptist Church, a black church on Auburn Avenue, during a rally to raise money to rebuild the Hubert home and help finance the prosecution." With blood in their eyes and hate in their hearts, "another group tried to abduct Charles D. Hubert and his son, relatives of the murdered student, from their home, but the elder Hubert fought them off. To further intimidate African Americans before the trial, night riders hurled stones and shattered the lamps on the Spelman College campus."[8]

John Hope knew Dennis Hubert and the Hubert family very well. Reverend Gaddus Hubert had attended Morehouse when Hope was president, and the Revered Charles D. Hubert, also a Morehouse graduate, was a professor of theology at the college at the time of the lynching of his nephew. Angry and exasperated, President Hope expressed the outrage of the African American community when he later wrote, "Must all

[8] Davis, A Clashing of the Soul, 313.

Morehouse students, must all the colored youth of Atlanta of Georgia, forever go about in terror of their lives?"[9] The administration at Morehouse took the lead in prosecuting Martin and was able to secure the legal services of William Schley Howard, one of Georgia's most famous criminal lawyers and a former representative of the United States Congress. African Americans, including President Hope and other members of the Morehouse community, filled the Jim Crowed courtroom as Attorney Howard persuasively prosecuted the case. The jury found Martin guilty, and his sentence was from twelve to fifteen years in prison. For several days and nights after the trial, black citizens stayed up all night with guns and other arms that they had bought on the black market (they could not legally purchase firearms) protecting their families and homes. Morehouse professors were among those who kept vigil, and one revealed to an interviewer years later that he still had his .25 automatic weapon. There were no acts of unwarranted retaliation, as the white citizens remained eerily quiet. Some might attribute the violence heaped upon the black community by those in the white to the bad economy of the 1930s, but the crusade to keep African Americans in a second- or third-class status had begun long before the Great Depression. The murders of Thompson Barnes and Dennis Hubert and countless other African Americans were indicative of an "American dilemma," a dilemma that would not be resolved during the twentieth century or the twentieth-first century: it worsened.

As a result of the lynchings of the Morehouse students, the Commission on Interracial Cooperation (CIC), which had been organized by forward-thinking citizens in the wake of the Atlanta Riot of 1906, ramped up its anti-lynching campaign. Professor Walter Chivers of the Department of Sociology at Morehouse was one of the leaders of a team that conducted a study of lynching and recommended ways to prevent these heinous murders. Arthur Raper, a graduate of Vanderbilt University, published the findings of this research in a massive volume titled *The Tragedy of Lynching* (1933) and argued that the crime of lynching "was rooted in economic competition between poor persons of both races rather than the customary explanations [rape and murder]."[10] But was this true?

---

[9] Ibid., 314.

[10] Ibid.

By the 1930s, after the lynching of Dennis Hubert but not directly because of it, the Commission on Interracial Cooperation began to shift its tactics away from moral suasion to a focus on the economic challenges that all Southerners faced during the Great Depression. Howard Odum, a sociologist at the University of North Carolina at Chapel Hill and president of the CIC, and Will Alexander supported the commission's change in direction, arguing that racial problems "could best be remedied through improving economic conditions for all southerners." But the depth of racism was so unfathomable that economic recommendations couldn't begin to stop it, and African Americans, in their persons and in their institutions, like Morehouse College, continued to suffer under the weight of racial discrimination and violence. In the 1930s, the college was on survival mode, and this was the challenge for President Archer and interim president Charles Hubert.

The Great Depression affected Morehouse College in several ways. The enrollment was drastically reduced. In the mid-1920s, the enrollment had averaged around 450 students in the college, academy, and school of religion. For the academic year 1929 to 1930, the same year the stock market crashed, enrollment was at 561, with 360 in the college, twenty-eight in the school of religion, thirty-four in the academy (its last year of operations), and 139 in the evening extension school (including women). The extension school had been established to help public schoolteachers improve the quality of their education and to earn a college degree. The enrollment was at its lowest in the academic year 1933 to 1934, when only 214 students enrolled in all departments at Morehouse: 208 in the college and six in the school of religion. By this time, the extension school had been discontinued, but Morehouse-Spelman Summer School, which began in 1927, had an enrollment of 354 in 1934. The enrollment gradually began to return to normal levels toward the end of the 1930s, but the involvement of the United States in World War II brought another period of crisis to the college.

Faculty salaries, always inadequate, were greatly affected by the economic crisis of the Great Depression. As described above, salaries were cut, paid late, or only partially paid. Public school teachers were paid in scrip, an emergency paper currency honored by local stores, but the college's teachers had to meet their expenses using whatever funds they were fortunate enough to receive. More often than not, grocery stores were understanding and cooperative and helped faculty members sustain themselves during the economic downturn. In the face of the economic depression, President Archer kept up the morale of the Morehouse faculty, preventing a deeper psychological depression from setting in among them. He used his well-known wit and great sense of humor to do this.

All was not focused on survival at Morehouse during the challenging years of the Great Depression. The Atlanta University Affiliation became the center of high artistic and literary culture for black Atlanta in the 1930s. And while the school was in an austerity mode, the human spirit and its creative needs were alive and well at Morehouse. Professor Harreld had been at the college for two decades by the 1930s, and among the many contributions he made to the artistic life of the AUA and the Atlanta community at large was the presentation of a "Christmas gift of music." The Christmas Carol Concert, which presented performances by the glee clubs of Morehouse and Spelman as well as a mixed chorus made up of voices from both singing groups and students from Atlanta University, was first presented in December 1927 in the newly built Sister Chapel on the Spelman campus. The concert was open to the general public without regard to race, and in the 1930s, it was a welcome respite from the vicissitudes and travails of the Depression. The concert continues to draw full-capacity audiences to hear traditional carols and compositions by celebrated composers. In addition to the Christmas Carol Concert and other vocal and instrumental performances, additional stimulating activities that broadened the cultural mindset of the student body were available. Debating, for example, continued to be a major student activity at the college. But as the college was holding on during the difficult years of the 1930s, sadness came to Morehouse, Atlanta University, the AUA, Atlanta, and the nation: the death of John Hope.

John Hope had devoted thirty-two years of his professional life to Morehouse College, with the remainder of his career to Roger Williams University and Atlanta University. In the last seven years of his life, he worked for the success of the Atlanta University Affiliation and to develop a spirit of cooperation among the historically black colleges of Atlanta. Championing the cause of black education in the 1930s was no easy task, and John Hope had traveled the country for that cause. Just days before he died, on February 5, 1936, he gave a speech to the Oklahoma State Teacher Association, where W. E. Anderson, one of his former students, was the president. And although he was no longer president of Morehouse, he still had a deep and abiding love for the college, and as a Morehouse Man, he continued to support initiatives for its survival and forward movement. But as he was returning to Atlanta from Oklahoma City, his high spirits were diminished by the onset of pneumonia. The first symptoms of illness were pains in his hands and feet that began on February 12, and the next day, he had the first indicators of a bad cold. Despite being sick, he kept a speaking engagement as part of Negro History Week at Oglethorpe School, not far from the Atlanta University campus, and after his presentation, he returned to his Atlanta University office to make plans for the summer school, which was several month away. But his condition deteriorated, and on February 14, Hope was taken to the MacVicar Hospital on the Spelman campus, where he was diagnosed with pneumonia. The pulmonary disease was so advanced that his prognosis was terminal. He would not recover, and on February 20, 1936, John Hope died, and with his death, so did an important era in education for the black population of Atlanta.

John Hope had lived for sixty-eight years. The board of trustees of Morehouse College and Atlanta University, after recalling Hope's life and reputation, memorialized him in their official minutes, stating, "John Hope's fame will rest upon his work and accomplishments in the field of education. He became president of Morehouse College when it was a weak and struggling institution. Under his administration it was developed into one of the outstanding colleges for Negro youth, it may be said that it became a mother of colleges." On Atlanta University, the minutes reflect that

> he undertook a task that called for balance and patience, perseverance and tact, faith and courage, wisdom and high statesmanship, and for the ability to work with black and white, North and South. All of these qualities he brought to that task. What he wrought at Morehouse and at Atlanta [University] gives him an assured place among the pre-eminent educators of his time. But he was far more than a prominent figure in education, he belonged to the rare company of great teachers.

Beyond Hope's work at Morehouse and Atlanta University, it was noted that

> even if there were not the monuments to his name at Morehouse and the new Atlanta [University], there would remain his sympathetic understanding of the student, his gift of imparting encouragement and stimulus, and the inspiration of his personal example. And so, he has an abiding monument in the hearts and lives of all youth that came under the touch of his influence, and that influence will be transmitted through them to other generations of youth. In a maximum degree he filled the triple capacity of educator, teacher, and friend.[11]

Several years before his death, President John Hope had dictated his wishes regarding his funeral arrangements to Constance Crocker Nabrit, his administrative assistant. He wanted no elaborate final rite, no sermon, no solos. He wanted a very plain casket that could be placed in a plain wooden box as it was lowered into his grave.[12] These funeral arrangements were to be executed in conjunction with the wishes of Lugenia Burns Hope, his wife, and Jane Hope Lyon, his sister. President Hope's funeral wishes were honored, and a brief and simple ritual was held in Sale Hall Chapel before an overflow gathering of mourners—family, friends, colleagues, and trustees. It is probable that the David T. Howard Funeral Home handled the final arrangements for the funeral. Mr. Howard, who had died in 1935, was counted among President Hope's friends, and Hope had appointed him to the University Home (Housing Project) Advisory Committee. Among the mourners was the eminent scholar and educator W. E. B. Du Bois, who was on the faculty at Atlanta University at the time. Hope and Du Bois had been lifelong friends, and one can only imagine the sadness in his heart as he joined the other mourners at the funeral.

Although President Hope had once been promised a burial plot in Lincoln Cemetery, one of Atlanta's prominent African American burial

---

[11] Ibid.

[12] "Instructions for the Funeral of John Hope and the Memorial Service," Hope Collection, Woodruff Library and Archives, Atlanta University Center.

parks on Simpson Road in Northwest Atlanta, his remains were interred on the common campus quadrangle between Morehouse and Atlanta University. His body was borne to its final resting place in sight of his offices at Morehouse and Atlanta University, where a simple but beautiful marble slab covers his grave, a hallowed grave where thousands of Men of Morehouse and Morehouse Men have paused in solemn reflection over the years.[13] A memorial fund was established in John Hope's name shortly after his death to endow a chair in his honor at Atlanta University. Du Bois remembered the fallen leader:

> The death of John Hope removed an unusual figure from American life. He was an American of Scotch [*sic*] descent who had somewhere among his ancestors a black man. From his physical appearance one would have never suspected this. Biologically, he belonged distinctly to the typical white American race, but by education and social heritage, he was just as typically a Negro. There was no inner soul dissension about this. He was at once white and glad to be black.[14]

And, further, it was shared that "in his premature dying, John Hope, above everything, left friends, not a great number, but a few persons who feel that with him, honest and unselfish devotion to duty has lost a beautiful exemplar, and that they have lost something inexpressibly near and absolutely irreplaceable."[15]

Three days after the funeral, the students of Morehouse College, Spelman College, and Atlanta University held a memorial service on Wednesday, February 26, 1936, in the Sale Hall Chapel at Morehouse at nine o'clock in the morning. It was a simple but dignified service that bespoke the sense and sensibility of the students of the Atlanta University Affiliation. The prelude was played by David M. Mells, after which the congregation sang "Morehouse College."

---

[13] "Order of Service" for the funeral of John Hope, *Atlanta University Bulletin* 4 (4th Quarter, July 1936): 6. Woodruff Library and Archives.

[14] "John Hope," *The Pittsburgh Courier* (March 28, 1936).

[15] Ibid.

> Morehouse College, Morehouse College, Morehouse College
> bless her name.
>
> Whether in defeat or victory, we are loyal just the same.
>
> And we'll cheer for Morehouse College, and for her we'll fight for
> fame.
>
> And we'll sing her praises loud in every land.
>
> Morehouse College, bless her name!

Drew S. Days then led the Pledge of Perpetuation:

> "We, the men of Morehouse College, do hereby pledge that we shall forever hold sacred and dear the ideals of this institution as conceived and taught by our beloved leader, Dr. John Hope."

This was followed by a responsive reading led by Lester A. McFall. Drew S. Days and B. Richard Durant played a violin duet, and a poem was read by John C. Long. John H. Young spoke before the "address," and the congregation sang a hymn. After the address was given, the congregation sang the "Negro National Anthem"—"Lift Ev'ry Voice and Sing"—which was followed by the recessional. Following the memorial service, a solemn and emotive wreath-laying ceremony was held at the grave. After singing the first verse of "O Son of Man," the wreath was laid, "Morehouse College" was slowly hummed, the pledge was repeated, and "Dear Old Morehouse" was sung.[16]

Russell Conwell Barbour asserted that "a college, like an individual, develops a character, possesses a spirit which distinguishes and identifies it." Barbour had been one of John Hope's students, and he crystallized the essence of what John Hope meant to Morehouse when he wrote, "John Hope was the life of Morehouse College. Throughout the years the educators of the Atlanta University system have placed less emphasis upon material equipment and more on that intangible and yet potent thing called college spirit. The most important thing about a college is not its Gothic architecture, with all it symbolizes, not rolling lawns and beautiful

---

[16] Ibid.

green trees, but spirit. John Hope gave Morehouse College—spirit."[17] But now President Hope was dead. One of the highest honors in African American life and thought was bestowed on Hope when he was awarded the Spingarn Medal posthumously, and Florence Matilda Read became acting president of Atlanta University after his death.

Within a few days of her husband's death, Lugenia Burns Hope moved out of the president's house on Beckwith Street. "At the insistence of Florence Read, president of Spelman and acting president of Atlanta University, she was required to vacate the premises earlier than she had expected, and she was not allowed to take any of her personal property."[18] Mrs. Hope moved out of the residence and into the apartment home of John and Elise Hope, her son and daughter-in-law, on Lee Street, not far from the Morehouse campus. After a few months she moved to New York City and into accommodations in the YWCA on 137th Street in Harlem.[19] After an extended illness, Mrs. Hope died on August 14, 1947. Her body was cremated and a funeral service was held in John Hope II's home in Nashville. Reflecting her love of Morehouse, but in accordance with her wishes not to be buried beside her husband, "several members of the Neighborhood Union, where she had been a prominent member, secretly climbed the tower of Graves Hall and scattered her cremains 'to the four wind' over the campus of 'the House'"[20] In November 1947, a memorial service for Mrs. Hope was held at Morehouse, with the Reverend Maynard H. Jackson Sr., pastor of Friendship Baptist Church, where she had been a member, presiding. Lloyd Lewis, the husband of her niece Emma, gave reflections and words of comfort on behalf of the family. Several colleagues and friends who had worked with Mrs. Hope over the years gave eulogies. They included Ira de Augustine Reid of Atlanta University; Walter Chivers of Morehouse; Charlotte Hawkins Brown, founder of the Palmer Institute in North Carolina; and Benjamin E. Mays, president of Morehouse College. The passing of Lugenia Burns Hope and John Hope marked the end of a significant era in the history of

---

[17] *National Baptist Voice*, the official organ of the National Baptist Convention of America (February 29, 1936).

[18] Rouse, Lugenia Burns Hope, 123.

[19] Ibid.

[20] Ibid.

Morehouse and the beginning of a new one. But the period of transition was not without its challenges. There was a sliver of light on the horizon, as the dim candle in the dark lit the way for the students and alumni of the college. The candle flickered on the day John Hope died, but it continued to burn. Professor Samuel Howard Archer held the candle aloft for another year, but the demands of the job and his age, coupled with declining health, prompted him to retired the next year, 1937. A year later, in 1938, the board of trustees of Morehouse named Samuel Howard Archer president emeritus. Charles DuBois Hubert, class of 1909, was named acting president of the college while a search for the sixth president got underway.

At this time, Professor Charles DuBois Hubert had served his alma mater as both teacher and as the director of the Morehouse School of Religion. He was a large man who topped the scale at more than three hundred pounds and was affectionately called "Colossus" by the Morehouse students and his friends. Professor Hubert was a capable administrator, but he was not interested in the presidency of Morehouse on a full-time basis. He was born in Hancock (Sparta) County, and following a family tradition, entered Morehouse Academy in the seventh grade. Hubert graduated from the academy (high school) in 1905, and, continuing his education at Morehouse College, earned the BA degree in 1909. Following the pattern of many Morehouse Men at that time, Hubert prepared for a career in Christian ministry and earned a bachelor of divinity degree from Rochester Theological Seminary in 1912. Morehouse conferred an honorary DD degree on Professor Hubert in 1923.

Dr. Hubert served as the pastor of several churches around the country, including Shiloh and Providence, two Baptist churches in Atlanta, and in 1914, while still serving as an Atlanta pastor, he became director of the school of religion at Morehouse. In all of his work, Dr. Hubert "exhibited the finest qualities of courageous, virile leadership in the noblest tradition of the Christian religion. The fighting spirit which he had shown as varsity half-back during his college days was everywhere evident in his attacks on the social ills which afflict the modern world."[21]

Although Dr. Hubert was a capable administrator and a good man,

---

[21] Jones, Candle in the Dark, 131.

not much was accomplished during his acting presidency: he had no authority to implement programs as more control over Morehouse shifted to Atlanta University and Spelman College. For a short while, Florence Read, president of Spelman, was acting president of Atlanta University. More importantly, she was the treasurer of the Atlanta University Affiliation, and in this role had authority over Morehouse's financial affairs. No purchases could be made by Morehouse personnel without the approval of Miss Read, and the salaries of Morehouse teachers had to be approved by Atlanta University and Spelman. Unfortunately, during the administration of interim president Hubert (1938 to 1940), the independent status of Morehouse was seriously threatened, and the college was on a path toward becoming an undergraduate school of Atlanta University.[22] But the search for the sixth president of Morehouse soon brought Dr. Benjamin Elijah Mays to the office, where he would go on to serve as the institution's chief executive officer for twenty-seven years. Mays accepted the position at a time when the college had both good students (although few in number) and a dedicated faculty, but which was admittedly weak in other ways. Presidents Archer and Hubert had borne the vicissitudes of the 1930s and kept the flickering candle burning. The school was beginning its seventy-third year of existence when Benjamin Elijah Mays and Sadie Gray Mays agreed to become the president and first lady of Morehouse College in 1940.

---

[22] Ibid.

Chapter 9

"The Candle Becomes the Torch": The Great Schoolmaster Builds Men

The 1930s had not been kind to Morehouse College. Enrollment had declined, funding and finances were weakened, and while the leadership of the college had been dedicated, it was tenuous at best. The new Atlanta University and Spelman College had more authority over Morehouse than the college had over itself, and there was talk of attaching Morehouse to Atlanta University, the new graduate school, as an undergraduate school. There were also rumblings of reducing Morehouse to junior college status. Because philanthropists had supported the creation of Atlanta University, with John Hope's blessings, it received more financial donations than Morehouse received. For two years, 1930 and 1931, John Hope was president of both Morehouse and Atlanta University, and by the time he turned over his Morehouse responsibilities to Samuel Archer, Archer's health was already in decline. Following Archer, Charles Hubert held things together for two years, but Hubert made clear he was not interested in a permanent appointment. Faculty salaries were low or nonexistent at times. Generally speaking, morale was low. Overarching all of this was the Great Depression. But thanks to its strong alumni base and committed faculty, Morehouse managed to survive the challenges of the 1930s, and soon the search was on for the sixth president of the college.

The process of searching for college presidents was not done then as they are done now. Essentially, the board of trustees constituted the search committee and identified persons who were qualified and might accept the job. So it was that Trevor Arnett, philanthropist and member of the board of trustees for Morehouse and the Atlanta University Affiliation, eventually called Dr. Benjamin E. Mays at his home in Washington, DC, on May 10, 1940, and informed him that he had been elected sixth president of Morehouse College.

Earlier in 1940, as the search for the new president was conducted in earnest, John Wheeler, another member of the board of trustees, and president of Mechanic and Farmers Bank of Durham, North Carolina, had already interviewed Dr. Mays and his wife, Sadie Gray Mays, who had, "with a woman's intuition," correctly predicted that her husband would be offered the job. Dr. Mays told Mr. Arnett that he would consider the offer, but first needed to have a conversation with Dr. Mordecai W. Johnson, the president of Howard University, the school where Mays was the current dean of the school of religion. Dr. Mays considered the offer for three weeks before he made the decision to accept the presidency. Salary was an important factor as he pondered the offer, but it was not a major impediment. "To tackle a big job that needs to be done and succeed in doing it is for me the essence of happiness," Dr. Mays professed. During his decision-making process, Dr. Mays also spoke with President Rufus Clement, John Hope's successor at Atlanta University; Florence Read at Spelman; Kendall Weisiger, chairman of the Morehouse Board of Trustees; Trevor Arnett; John Wheeler; Morehouse acting president Charles Hubert; President Emeritus Samuel Archer; members of the Morehouse faculty; and Will W. Alexander, another member of the board. Finally, after studying the physical plant and the financial affairs of the institution, on May 31, 1940, Dr. Mays accepted the presidency of Morehouse College effective August 1, 1940. This began a true love affair for the college that would be predicated on service to "the Lord." Not only was Dr. Mays a scholar and an educator, he was also a Christian and a preacher.

Having studied the situation at Morehouse, Dr. Mays made his assessment clear in advance, allowing the board to reconsider its offer, if it chose to do so. After informing the board of his and his wife's commitment to give a sabbatical year serving the Bantu people of South Africa, he informed them that he did not consider the initial salary offer "adequate and static." Further, he asserted that faculty salaries were too low and that he believed Morehouse must have equal status in the Atlanta University system. In his judgement, it was "unsound administrative policy to have the treasurer of Morehouse College outside of the administration of Morehouse." Mays was "convinced that it would make for better working relationships and that the cause of Morehouse would be better served if the treasurer were within the administration of Morehouse."[1]

---

[1] Mays, *Born to Rebel*, 170–72,

Kendall Weisiger, speaking on behalf of the board, stated that all points could be met in time to Dr. Mays's satisfaction.

Several factors influenced Mays's decision to accept the presidency. First, word had leaked to the press that he had been elected, so there was a concern that declining the offer might be viewed as "wishy-washy," as if he had made a commitment and then reneged on it. Second, he believed he had the support of the Morehouse faculty, trustees, alumni, and friends and that he could move the college forward. Third, his first teaching job had been at Morehouse, so he knew many of the graduates of the college who were making their marks in the world. And fourth, there was an intangible quality at Morehouse that instilled in its students a belief that they could accomplish whatever they set out to do.[2] It is this fourth factor that is the essence of the Morehouse Mystique, the core of the Morehouse Man. While Benjamin Mays was familiar with the college and its alumni, he knew his job was nonetheless fraught with challenges: enrollment was unstable, financing was not constant, business matters were not institutionalized, and the brand, while strong, was not on a solid foundation. Dr. Mays met the challenges directly, and the great teacher and leader set about building Morehouse Men.

In the sixteen years that had passed since Dr. Mays had been on the faculty and had served, for a brief time, as acting dean, from 1920 to 1924, his star had risen, so to speak. After leaving Morehouse, Mays once again enrolled at the University of Chicago in September 1924 to work toward the completion of his PhD. He decided to acquire a master's degree in New Testament in the process.

While at the University of Chicago, Mays experienced racism on and off the campus and surmised "that Indian students wore their turbans to make sure that they would not be mistaken for Negroes. In those days, a Negro wearing a turban could ride through the South unsegregated and unmolested."[3] While in Chicago, Mays was on leave from the pastorate of Shiloh Baptist Church in Atlanta, a church that he loved so well. Nevertheless, after earning his master's degree, Mays relinquished the pastorate and accepted an offer to teach English at South Carolina State College in

[2] Ibid.

[3] Ibid., 99.

Orangeburg beginning in the fall of 1925. He found Jim Crow to be as virulent as ever when he returned to the state of his birth. And just as he had met his first wife, Ellen (who died in 1923), at South Carolina State, Mays met Sadie Gray, his second and last wife, when he returned to the college in September 1925.

Benjamin and Sadie married in the summer of 1926 while they were conducting graduate work at the University of Chicago. Because her aged father's financial matters were dire, Mrs. Mays had assumed some responsibility as a good daughter ought. When Dr. Robert Shaw Wilkinson, president of South Carolina State College, would not make an exception to the practice of not allowing married couples to be employed, the Mayses accepted an invitation from Jesse O. Thomas, field director of the Nation Urban League, for employment as the executive secretary and as a case worker for the Tampa Urban League. They left Orangeburg, South Carolina, for Tampa, Florida, in September 1926, but their work there ended within two years, when, in 1928, Mays accepted a position as the student secretary of the national council of the YMCA and Mrs. Mays accepted a job with the Georgia Study of Negro Child Welfare. His journey toward a PhD (the presidency of Morehouse was not in his master plan) was again interrupted when the Institute for Social and Religious Research, funded by a Rockefeller agency, invited Mays to direct a study of Negro churches in the United States. He accepted the job, and, along with the Reverend Joseph W. Nicholson, a Colored (Christian) Methodist Episcopal minister, Mays worked for fourteen months collecting data, and then ten months writing a book that was published in 1933 under the title *The Negro's Church*. In this seminal work, the authors argued that its origin represented the most distinctive aspect of the black church: "The characteristic forces underlying Negro church's origins are thus seen to have been five: growing racial consciousness, individual initiative, splits and withdrawals, the migration, and missions of other churches."[4] Implicit in this pathfinding research, with its conclusions and publications, was the idea of "the Negro's God."

Sadie Gray Mays received a master's degree from the University of Chicago School of Social Service in August 1931, and the advanced degree

[4] Mays, *Born to Rebel*, 147–48.

of PhD was conferred on Benjamin Mays in 1935. He was elected to Phi Beta Kappa by the Bates chapter of the society in that year. By the time he received his doctorate, Dr. Mays was already in residence as the dean of Howard University's School of Religion in Washington, DC, a position he had assumed in the fall of 1934. Dr. Mordecai Wyatt Johnson, a man whom Mays greatly admired, was the president of Howard when the Mayses arrived to begin their work. Persuasion, pressure, and persistence are required of every dean and department chair, Dr. Mays observed, and his work at Howard reflected these qualities. And while he thought administrators "treated the School of Religion as of minor importance," he felt that the university had been kind to him during his six years there. This, in essence, represents Dr. Benjamin Elijah Mays's professional, academic, and personal experiences between the time he left Morehouse in 1924 and his return as the sixth president of the college in 1940.

Called one of the great schoolmasters, Dr. Mays was an imposing man who possessed a mighty intellect. Samuel DuBois Cook, political scientist, college president, teacher, and mentor, reminds us that Mays "was a theologian, philosopher, and prophet. He was a defender of the Christian faith, transcendent humanism, democracy, education, freedom, responsibility, the common good, justice, the ordinary man or woman, the intrinsic dignity and value of the human person, the woman or man farthest down, the 'least of these,' the fatherhood of God, the brotherhood of man, humility, and the Beloved Community of all of God's children."[5]

Dr. Mays was a strikingly handsome man with gentlemanly comportment. Dr. Cook's description of the schoolmaster is vividly on the mark.

> Tall, handsome, and unflappable, with piercing eyes that cut through pretensions to penetrate and expose the naked, inescapable truth, Mays walked erect and briskly and talked with dignity, clarity, grace, authority, and majestic countenance. Before his hair turned entirely gray, his black hair was graced with a vivid, dramatic shock of white hair on the left side of his head. He was an

[5] Samuel DuBois Cook, *Benjamin E. Mays: His Life, Contributions, and Legacy* (Franklin, TN: Providence House Publishers, 2009) 18.

> impressive figure who had magic about him. He had genuine charisma, which lit up the place, situation, or conversation.[6]

Dr. Mays had a dark complexion, square head, and a slender physique. His gait was measured and his attire impeccable. His presence did not drive back visitors but invited them into a presence that offered genuine respect and hospitality. Self-assured and strong-willed, Dr. Mays was the model for the Morehouse Man. This was the countenance and manner of the man who became the sixth president of the college in 1940. For the next twenty-seven years, he would tirelessly work to build Morehouse Men.

In the 1940s, African American college presidents, and black leaders in general, often had to compromise their integrity in order to advance the institutions and organizations that they led. Largely dependent of philanthropy and charity from white citizens, they acted—feigned—deferentially and presented themselves as sycophants. Ralph Ellison brilliantly describes such a black principal, as African American college presidents were often called, in the early years of their leadership in his acclaimed *Invisible Man.*

> Hadn't I seen him approach white visitors too often with his hat in hand, bowing humbly and respectfully? Hadn't he refused to eat in the dining hall with white guests of the school, entering only after they had finished and then refusing to sit down, but remaining standing, his hat in his hand, while he addressed them eloquently, then leaving with a humble bow? Hadn't he, *hadn't he?* I had seen him too often as I peeped through the door between the dining room and the kitchen, I myself.[7]

Ellison had attended Tuskegee Institute in Alabama, and his fictionalized remembrances of what he observed as a student driver for visiting dignitaries is as poignant as it is pathological. Dr. Mays contradicted this notion of the "usual" black leader, be it teacher or principal, as a subservient, second-rate minstrel. Mays believed in the self-worth of African Americans and challenged them to be the very best they could be. Even before

---

[6] Ibid., 20.

[7] Ralph Ellison, *Invisible Man* (New York: Random House, 1952) 82.

he brought this philosophy to Morehouse, he had made his belief in the potential of the black community abundantly clear in a speech he gave to "the Negro Older Boys' Conference at Benedict College on February 26, 1926" while serving on the faculty of South Carolina State College. His words would resonate and register with thousands of Morehouse Men in the years ahead. In this speech, Dr. Mays said, "Were I white and held a professor's chair in the University of South Carolina, were you white and represented the best white schools of this commonwealth, my task would not be so difficult. We would then be clothed in that skin that gives perpetual protection. We would represent that group that presumes to hold the destiny of this nation in its hand, and to whom the doors of opportunity are never closed." Pausing, he continued. "Were this true, I would define the goal without limitations. I would recommend that you aspire to be governor of your native state. I would point the way to the president's chair. As it is, Americans though we be, I must speak to you not as an American to Americans but as a Negro to Negroes." He continued:

> It is this regrettable fact that makes the goal most difficult for me to define.... Young men, you must strive to be an agriculturist, not a Negro agriculturist—just an agriculturist! Strive to be a doctor, not a Negro doctor—just a doctor! Seek to serve your state, not as a Negro, but as a man. Aspire to be great—not among Negroes, but among men! God knows I want to be a great teacher, not a Negro teacher—just a great teacher. I want no racial adjective modifying it. I want to preach the gospel of peace, good will, justice, and brotherhood—not to Negroes, but to men and for men. I want to act so that each tomorrow will find us farther than today—not the Negro race, the human race. It seems to me that this is our goal.[8]

Dr. Mays came to Morehouse to build men, not Negro men—but men. He wanted the graduates of Morehouse to stand shoulder to shoulder with men, not just black men. Soon after Dr. Mays assumed the leadership of Morehouse, the faculty and staff began to create a culture that transformed the unpolished, unsophisticated young men who enrolled at the college into confident, cosmopolitan graduates.

---

[8] Mays, *Born to Rebel*, 104.

Dr. Benjamin Elijah Mays was forty-six years old when he became the president of Morehouse College in 1940. He was seventy-three years old when he retired, twenty-seven years later, in 1967. In those nearly three decades of leadership and service, Morehouse was transformed into a citadel of academic exceptionalism, producing thousands of graduates, men who became leaders, not Negro, Afro-American, black, or African American leaders—*just leaders*! How did he do it, and what role did other administrators, faculty, students, alumni, the board of trustees, benefactors, and friends of the college contribute in the creation of an institution—Morehouse—that was in the business of building men? What are the realities and abstractions that produce the Morehouse Man?

Having been born into poverty on a sharecropper's farm not far from the town of Ninety Six, South Carolina, Mays could identify with his students, and they had a paternalistic feeling for him. He was not called "Father Ben," as Hope had been called "Father John," but Mays was clearly embraced as a father figure. The young men of Morehouse were inspired by Dr. Mays's personal journey from poverty to prominence and as a recognized leader in religion and education. Embodied in President Mays was the reality that black men could be educated for scholarship and stewardship. He had done it and he knew, beyond a shadow of a doubt, that others could do it too. He symbolized the cross since he was a religious scholar and preacher, and he was emblematic of the candle by virtue of his academic achievements and other accomplishments that brought to light knowledge about the black experience; this was the sixth president of Morehouse College.

In the 1940 United States presidential election, held on November 5th, President Franklin D. Roosevelt was reelected by an electoral vote of 449 to 82. The popular vote was 27,24,160 for Roosevelt and vice president Henry Wallace and 22,305,198 for Wendell Willkie and Charles McNary, the presidential and vice presidential candidates of the Republican Party. But while Benjamin Mays and many thousands of African Americans could exercise the franchise in national elections, they were denied the vote on the local level. This disfranchisement was because of various devices designed by white Southern politicos to strip black citizens of the right to vote. Dr. Mays recalled that African Americans were stripped of the ballot in South Carolina in 1895, the year after he was born:

> The Negro's loss of the ballot in 1895 meant that I was completely disfranchised until 1946 [at age fifty-two] when the white primary was declared unconstitutional [*Smith v. Allwright*, 1944] in Georgia. Since I was equally voteless during my six years in Washington, D.C. [1934 to 1940], for thirty-one years after I was twenty-one years of age I could not vote in any local, city and state elections—despite the fact that I was a college and university graduate and a college president.[9]

In the 1940s, the African American Civil Rights Movement was gaining momentum, and in 1944, four years after Dr. Mays assumed the presidency, a fifteen-year-old Martin Luther King Jr. enrolled as a freshman at Morehouse.

During the first four decades of the twentieth century, the state of Georgia made a little more effort on behalf of public education for its black citizens. In 1911, Georgia established the Division of Negro Education, a state agency that attempted to facilitate cooperation between public officials and private philanthropic foundations. Inherent in the establishment of this agency was an attempt to control the philanthropy directed to schools like Morehouse, but also to control the funds used to create grade schools for black students. By the 1920s, the number of black students attending public schools had increased sharply, rising to a total of 73 percent in that decade. The number of black secondary schools increased, and black teachers in city schools began receiving more formal training. For the black community, as for the white, a turning point in public education came in 1937 when the state provided free textbooks and a seven-month school term. Even after that, though, black schools continued to lag behind white schools. In 1940, black students had access to accredited four-year public highs school in only forty-eight of Georgia's 159 counties. By that time, the state's investment in buildings, grounds, and teaching aids for each black child stood at $35, compared to $142 for each white child. Though Georgia had begun to make a greater effort to educate her black children by 1940, white and black students did not

[9] Ibid.; Bennett, Before the Mayflower; Kull and Kull, An Encyclopedia of American History.

enjoy equal educational opportunities.[10] Many of the students who enrolled at Morehouse had earned a high school diploma in a county other than the one where their families lived. Dr. Brailsford Reese Brazeal, who became a legendary academic dean at Morehouse, for example, could only get an elementary school education in Dublin, Georgia, his hometown in the 1920s, so he attended Ballard Hudson in Macon, Georgia, before completing high school education at Morehouse Academy in 1923.

In the 1940s and '50s, most Morehouse students were from Georgia, where their high schools were more often than not considered inferior. Nevertheless, by 1952,

> Morehouse graduates had shown by their achievements that the type of education which they received at Morehouse had suited them peculiarly for successful participation in American life. Over and above the solid foundation in the arts and sciences which they acquired at Morehouse, they had also received an orientation and a perspective in which to view and appraise the human scene which one of the most distinguished sons of the college, President Mordecai W. Johnson of Howard University, aptly characterized as the "world view."[11]

Morehouse Men were educated to be "men of the world." Dr. Mays ramped up the work as he hit the ground running, so to speak, when he assumed the presidency in 1940. His first job was to get the administration of the college on an even keel so that the ship of the "House" would not founder in the waters of mediocrity and uncertainty.

When Dr. Mays arrived to begin his administration of Morehouse College, he moved into the office space designated for the president of the college in Harkness Hall. This hall was the administration building for Atlanta University, but 25 percent of the space was allotted to Morehouse at no cost to the college. This was a result of the agreement that forged the Atlanta University Affiliation, and in order to make the arrangement work between the three schools—Atlanta University, Morehouse, and

---

[10] Williams F. Holmes, "Social and Cultural Developments [in Georgia]," in Kenneth Coleman, ed., *A History of Georgia* (Athens: University of Georgia Press, 1991) 327.

[11] Morehouse College, "Student Life at Morehouse" (Atlanta: Morehouse, 1952). Rockefeller Archive Center.

Spelman—Morehouse had given more of itself than the other schools. Quarles Hall, a Morehouse building, was moved to make way for the new Harkness Hall, and it became the site for Atlanta University's School of Social Work. The president's office on the third floor of Harkness faced the quadrangle and was in sight of the president's residence on the north side of the campus. Because of this proximity, Dr. Mays often lunched with Mrs. Mays, and he could return to his office in the early evenings to do the work of the college. Decorated in the style of the time, it was comfortable, but not ostentatious. The dean's office was across the hall from the president's, and the registrar's space was on the second floor. Vaults for the three schools in the affiliation were in the basement, or first floor, of Harkness Hall, but there was no bursar's office or office for the Morehouse business manager. The business affairs for the college were at Spelman College, and this did not suit Dr. Mays at all. One of his first acts as president that would bode well for the college was to correct this shortsighted arrangement. For all of the twenty-seven years he led the college, Mays held the strong conviction that "the strength of one institution in the affiliation is the strength of all, and the weakness of one is the weakness of all."[12] Morehouse could not be subordinate to the Atlanta University and Spelman if it were to be a strong institution. It could not allow its financial affairs to be managed outside of the college's administration. And Miss Florence Matilda Read, treasurer of the affiliation, and an equal partner in the triumvirate, could not be allowed to continue to sign his paycheck. Dr. Mays took steps to remedy this inequity, and C. Everett Bacon, BS, assumed this administrative position on July 1, 1941, at the beginning of the new fiscal year.[13]

At the time Dr. Mays became president of Morehouse, the college no longer had an academic dean. Following Benjamin Brawley's departure, followed by Benjamin Mays's on exit in 1924, President Hope and his successors were not only the school's chief executive officials, they were also the principal academic administrators. In his first year as head of the college, Morehouse administration listed Dr. Mays as president, Charles

---

[12] Mays, Born to Rebel.

[13] Morehouse Bulletin Collection, Catalogue 1940–1941. Woodruff Library and Archives, Atlanta University Center.

DuBois Hubert as the director of the school of religion, Brailsford Reese Brazeal as "Dean of Men" (a questionable administrative position, given the fact that Morehouse enrolled only men), John Phillip Whittaker as registrar, Florence Matilda Read as treasurer (soon to be replaced by C. Everett Bacon), and Frederick Carrigon Gassett as assistant treasurer and bursar. Appointed as administrative assistants were Charles Hamilton Wardlaw, superintendent of buildings; Raymond H. Carter, MD, medical adviser; Ludie Andrews, RN, superintendent of the infirmary; Thomas Jackson Curry, secretary of the faculty; Mildred Lightbourne Burch, secretary to the president; Castella Janet Clark, secretary to the registrar; Richard Garland Martin, assistant to the bursar; Gerone Hendale Taylor, assistant to the bursar; Mary Demeris Slade, secretary to the bursar; Marjorie Elizabeth Greene, secretary to the dean of men; and Jeanette Brawley Stewart, hostess.[14]

In the academic year 1940 to 1941, the Morehouse faculty was constituted of members from Morehouse along with exchange teachers from Atlanta University and Spelman College. There were twenty-six Morehouse faculty members, sixteen from Atlanta University, and nineteen from Spelman. One exchange teacher was from Morris Brown College. Clearly, there were more exchange or adjunct teachers conducting classes at the college than full-time Morehouse faculty. Interestingly, Dr. Mays was a member of the faculty at Morehouse while his wife, Sadie Gray Mays, was on the faculty at Spelman, where she taught sociology. Benjamin Franklin Bullock taught "rural education," which was jointly offered to Atlanta University and Spelman students. Kemper Harreld jointly taught music at Spelman, Anna Margaret Cooke taught speech and dramatics to Morehouse Men, and Hale A. Woodruff, who became a celebrated artist, was an exchange teacher from Spelman. Clarence A. Bacote, history, and William E. B. Du Bois, sociology, were exchange teachers from Atlanta University. Curiously, Fred Douglas Maise was listed as a guest professor in "Scouting."[15]

Chapters from the four major African American fraternities had been installed at Morehouse before the arrival of the college's sixth president:

---

[14] Ibid.

[15] Ibid.

Kappa Alpha Psi, April 23, 1921; Omega Psi Phi, November 17, 1921; Alpha Phi Alpha, January 5, 1926; and Phi Beta Sigma, March 16, 1926. The fraternity committee in 1940 was made up of Claude B. Dansby, mathematics; Lloyd O. Lewis, religion; and Joseph L. Whiting, education. The other standing committees were advisory, debating, scholarship, program, and curriculum. Morehouse was organized into the college of arts and sciences and the school of religion. Summer school was conducted jointly with Atlanta University.

In the early history of Morehouse, the fall semester did not begin until after Labor Day, the first Monday in September. In 1940, Labor Day fell on September 2nd, and Freshman Week, as it was called then, began on Sunday, September 9th. Upperclassmen returned to the college on September 15th, with fall registration for classes taking place on September 16th and 17th. And so it was on September 18, 1940, a warm day at the end of the summer season, that President Benjamin Elijah Mays gave one of the most profound and meaningful speeches of his long and stellar career. On that Wednesday, Dr. Mays, the newly minted president of Morehouse College, gave the main address at the opening chapel service. After welcoming the returning students, faculty, and staff, and especially the new students, he reminded all "that Morehouse College is one of the outstanding institutions in the United States." He went on to say that while Morehouse had "achieved greatness primarily because of what its graduates have accomplished since the founding of the college in 1867," Dr. Mays made a point to say that standing on past achievements alone was not enough: "[for if we do,] nothing could be more damaging or demoralizing," he argued. "If Morehouse College is to continue to be great, it must continue to produce outstanding personalities."

Extolling the advantages of membership in the Atlanta University system, and enumerating his predecessors, Mays recalled his first association with Morehouse as a teacher in the 1920s. He revealed that although he was not a Morehouse graduate, "I am marked as a Morehouse man all over the country." Mays acted like a Morehouse Man, and Morehouse Men acted like Mays. President Mays knew that the founders of the college had the grand idea that black men could be educated and become stewards to their people. These "outstanding personalities" that had earned degrees from Morehouse were not only serving their people, but they were also making contributions that would help all people.

Dr. Mays continued, telling his audience what work lay ahead:

> When I realize what must be done for Morehouse College, the need of at least $1,000,000 more in endowment, the urgent physical needs such as homes for teachers, a new dormitory, chapel, academic building, and gymnasium, need of an increase in staff and raise in salaries, and the pressing need of scholarship for worthy students, I stand before you with fear and trembling because I know what a great responsibility it is to try to direct the thinking and to develop the character of young people.

The Reverend Doctor Mays sermonized, "It is serious enough when times are normal, but it is far more serious in times like these when the entire world seems to be going to pieces, when lying is a virtue, when the murder of women and children is right, and when hypocrisy is considered the normal procedure." Times were not "normal" in 1940, and they had not been that way for African Americans since 1619. Times were not normal when Morehouse was established in 1867. But against daunting odds, the college survived and had succeeded in producing graduates who had accomplished much in their chosen fields of endeavor.

In thinking about the primary responsibilities associated with the work he had to do, President Mays knew it was serious business to train young people in normal times, but that in times like these, it was enough to make a man shudder because the responsibilities of a college president were great. "I can choose what I say to you, what I do to you, and for you, but I can never choose the consequences of what I say or the consequences of what I do. I am talking to you this morning and the moment my words leave my lips they are beyond my control. I can only hope that what I say and do will be constructive." The sixth president of Morehouse made no fantastic promises, pointing out that his success depended not only upon himself, but upon factors beyond his control: he needed the confidence, moral support, and good will from the local and national public; financial and moral support from alumni and friends of the college; a positive attitude from the members of the board of trustees; the good will of the affiliated institutions; the support and loyalty of the faculty; and the cooperation of Morehouse students. In humble language that carried a powerful message, Dr. Mays said, "So I make you no fantastic promises as to what we will be able to do in this office. I am no miracle man. I am no magician. I am no trickster. I have no unusual, peculiar genius or power by which this job is to be done. I am only one of one hundred men that the Board of Trustees of Morehouse College might have chosen to do this job." Pointing out that he was "just a plain, ordinary, blunt man," Dr. Mays enraptured the audience with a closing declaration befitting one of the great theologians and preachers of his time. He declared,

> But I do promise you one thing as I close: I promise you before my Maker, before God, that I will give to Morehouse College all that I have. I will give to this institution and to you the best of my mind, heart and soul. I will give to this institution my money until it reaches the sacrificial point. In other words, I will serve you and I will serve this institution as if God Almighty sent me into the world for the specific purpose of being the sixth president of Morehouse College.

One might imagine that his rural South Carolina patois infused his learned oratory at this point. President Mays said he would not "work by the clock" and do more than "draw my breath and my salary." He would serve with the "same dignity and with the same pride that Franklin D. Roosevelt serves the people of the United States. This is all that I promise you. I will give you everything. I will be honest with you."

Dr. Mays closed his address to the students, faculty, and staff at Morehouse with words that represented the greatness of the man, saying, "When I reach the point where I cannot serve you this way, when the time comes when I cannot give you the best of my mind, soul, heart, time and energy, I will pass my resignation on to the members of the Board of Trustees. I pledge you this on the 18th day of September 1940, and, God helping me, I can do no other."[16] One can hear the audience as its members leapt to their feet in thunderous applause. Perhaps they felt a sense of the challenges of a brighter day in the history of Morehouse. But there is no doubt they felt that the right man had been chosen to lead them through whatever challenges would come in future years, which included

[16] "Opening Chapel Service," September 18, 1940, President Benjamin E. Mays, speaker. *Alumnus* 15 (February 1941): 6–8.

World War II, the continuing black struggle for freedom in America and abroad, and the turbulent "Searing Sixties." In 1940, Dr. Benjamin Elijah Mays began a twenty-seven-year presidency that by many accounts was one of the most successful and celebrated in the history of collegiate leadership.

As the first year of the presidency of Dr. Benjamin Elijah Mays got underway, classes began, the Glee Club and orchestra began rehearsals, and the football team began its 1940 season with practices on the lot at the corner of West Fair and Ashby Streets. It was also in the fall semester, due to the first official act by the sixth president of Morehouse, that Dr. Mays got the sobriquet by which he became affectionately known: "Buck Benny." At the beginning of his administration, Mays set a new policy on the collection of student debt. In 1940, "there was an accumulation of one hundred thousand dollars in unpaid bills."[17] Toward the collection of this debt, his office of business affairs sent letters to students with outstanding debt acquainting them with the new policy. A student owing a comparatively small sum was required to pay the debt in full before being allowed to register in September 1940. A student in debt for several hundred dollars had to reduce the amount before registering and had to pay the current fees for the academic year 1940 to 1941. The senior who owed the college $500 or $600 in September 1940 had to pay all bills for the current year and sign a note indicating when the rest would be paid before he could graduate. No transcripts would be issued until debts were settled.[18] The new policy worked so well that the college closed the academic year with only two to three thousand dollars outstanding, and much of this was collected over the summer. Some students were able to pay their debt to the college by working in tobacco fields. But the debt-collection policy earned Dr. Mays the name "Buck Benny" (as in the dollar—the buck), and, thereafter, anytime he gave a speech or performed an act that pleased the students, they would exclaim, "Buck Benny rides again,"[19] which came from a 1940 movie with the same refrain: *Buck Benny Rides Again* starred comedian Jack Benny, and one of his costars was the African

---

[17] Mays, *Born to Rebel*, 177.

[18] Ibid.

[19] Ibid.

American comedic actor Eddie "Rochester" Anderson. Morehouse students had seen the movie and adopted the title for their new president. Thereafter, Morehouse Men and friends of Dr. Mays lovingly and privately referred to him as "Buck Benny," with his approval.

The making of the Morehouse Man by Dr. Mays and the Morehouse faculty was the making of an American Man. It was the creation of a man with a cosmopolitan worldview. It was an actualization of the ideals of the "New Negro" movement of that era. The Morehouse Man that Dr. Mays molded was a man who moved effortlessly among the well-bred, tutored, and lettered assemblages of the world. This was social and cultural engineering at its best, it was telic. It was a continuation of the thrust of the black college rebellions of the 1920s toward integration into mainstream American society, not preparation for work in the skilled trades and vocations. But there was a paradox: how do you stay true to your black culture and at the same time embrace American cultures? The double consciousness that Du Bois posited at the turn of the twentieth century continued to plague African Americans and would continue to do so. Raymond Wolters argues persuasively that "the black colleges of the 1920s promoted the mainstream middle-class culture." This was the practice when Dr. Mays came to the presidency of Morehouse in the 1940s. Black youths were taught that the patois of the lower-class ghettoes and country fields was not proper English, and many folkways were deprecated as the unworthy legacy of an oppressive past. The colleges did not preserve folk culture and instead disseminated middle-class standards. Black students of the 1920s, like youths from other minority groups, were exposed to Anglo-Saxon norms and urged to become cosmopolitan Americans. Most black students of the 1920s surrendered their folkways in exchange for a liberal education.[20] This was, in part, the philosophy and practice of the Morehouse administration and faculty in the 1940s, 1950s, and for most of the 1960s until the "revolution" of 1969.

Although he set about building Morehouse students into men, not Negro men, Dr. Mays was a race man who would not bend his back, metaphorically. He stood straight as the proverbial arrow in posture and philosophy. He encouraged students, saying, "If I were you, I would stand

---

[20] Raymond Wolters, Black College Rebellions on Campus, 342–43.

for something, I would count for something, and no man would push me around because my skin is black, or his eyes are blue. I would stand for something. I would count." Exhorting the tenets that influenced a generation of Morehouse Men, mobilizing them to action for the cause of freedom and justice, Dr. Mays emboldened them when he said: I would not let my environment destroy me, beat me down, or make me accept what it said: that my family and my people were inferior to the White man. When a man accepts that designation of inferiority, he might as well die. He had nothing to live for. When he denies his inherent worth and denies that he is a person of infinite worth and value, he is dead even if he lives to be four score years and ten, or even a hundred.[21] Martin Luther King Jr. heard Dr. Mays's call to manhood when he matriculated at Morehouse in the mid-1940s. But in the first year of that decade, when Mays began his presidency, there were pressing matters that had to be addressed: enrollment, business affairs, salaries, facilities, and morale. It was within the context of capital improvements that Dr. Mays burnished the Morehouse brand, which had been developing for several decades, to a brilliant luster. Dr. Mays used the symbols, the spoken word, and images of campus life as he methodically committed himself and his faculty and staff to the task of making the Morehouse brand synonymous with academic exceptionalism and strong leadership capability. As he set about telling the Morehouse Story, the college continued to face challenges within the Atlanta University Affiliation.

The Atlanta University Affiliation, which was formed in 1929, was supposed to be an association of three institutions—Atlanta University, Morehouse, and Spelman—on an equal basis, but by 1940, when Dr. Mays came to the presidency of Morehouse, this was not the case. Morehouse had given up much to make the affiliation work but in return had not been treated as an equal partner in the Group of Three. Morehouse had deeded more than three acres of land facing Chestnut Street (now James P. Brawley Drive) on which Quarles Hall was located for the construction of Harkness Hall, the new administration building for Atlanta University. Quarles Hall became the Atlanta University's School of Social Work and was moved to property owned by Morehouse. In exchange for

---

[21] Cook, *Quotable Quotes of Benjamin Mays* (New York: Vantage Press, 1993) 11.

these major transfers of property, Morehouse was given 25 percent of the space in Harkness Hall for its administrative offices. The college had full access to Trevor Arnett Library, as did Spelman and the other schools that would become a part of the Atlanta University Center. The Morehouse infirmary was closed, and the MacVicar Clinic at Spelman was opened to the Morehouse students and faculty. The actions of Atlanta University and Spelman, the schools that had more philanthropic support than Morehouse, presaged Morehouse as a junior college in the affiliation. As Dr. Mays recalled, one colleague had said, "That isn't so bad" while another asserted, "It doesn't matter who does the teaching so long as it is good teaching."[22] But it did matter that Morehouse, a school that had already produced prominent leaders and professionals, was about to lose its identity, its brand. Dr. Mays did not accept this status quo of the affiliation, and he set about building a stronger and much-improved Morehouse. He had to end the authority, real or imagined, that Atlanta University and Spelman had over the faculty personnel at Morehouse, and he had to secure more financial resources, increase the size of the faculty, and improve the faculty by hiring teachers with stronger credentials. "A college is no stronger than its faculty," Dr Mays believed. "The buildings may be ever so fine, but if the faculty isn't strong, the college is weak."[23] Because there were so few of them, there was a challenge in securing the contracts of qualified African Americans to teach at Morehouse. There was keen competition for these scholars, and many chose to go to Howard University, a full-service university in the nation's capital. When celebrated marine biologist Ernest Everett Just graduated from Dartmouth in 1905, he was offered a job at Morehouse, but he chose to teach at Howard, where he would have the opportunity to do research. Nevertheless, Morehouse remained committed to the practice of hiring teachers with solid credentials in order to contribute to the Morehouse brand as the school worked to maintain its reputation for quality teaching, which reaped a great harvest in the success of its graduates.

The teaching staff at Morehouse in the 1940s, as it had been in the past, was very good despite the fact that only two members held earned

---

[22] Mays, Born to Rebel.

[23] Ibid., 178.

academic doctorates when Dr. Mays arrived. But an increase in the number of PhDs on the faculty would soon be realized as three members were on leave working toward their doctoral degrees at this time. Harold Finley was at the University of Wisconsin working toward his degree in biology, Nathaniel Tillman was also at Wisconsin completing the PhD in English, and Edward (E. B.) Williams was at Columbia University working on his doctorate in economics. The three men were Morehouse graduates, and they had the full support of President Mays, who secured fellowships for them from the General Education Board and the Rosenwald Foundation. He even provided partial salaries to help them defray expenses.[24] Dr. Mays also began a tradition of showing his appreciation to faculty members who were awarded doctoral degrees by honoring them at a post-commencement banquet. Showing appreciation, then and now, is an intangible reward that gives immeasurable benefits to both the giver and the receiver. It is important to faculty, students, and staff to know they are appreciated for the work they are doing. To oversee the academic division of the college, President Mays appointed Brailsford Reese Brazeal, professor of economics, as the academic dean. Dr. Brazeal, who held a PhD in economics from Columbia University, had been the dean of men, and over the next twenty-five years, he would become an institution at Morehouse as the dean of academic affairs.

Dean Brazeal, as he affectionately was called, was born in Dublin, Georgia, and attended high school at Savannah State College, Ballard Normal School in Macon, and Morehouse Academy, graduating in 1923. He subsequently graduated with honors from Morehouse College in 1927. Brazeal earned a master's degree in economics in 1928, and then a PhD in 1942 from Columbia University. His dissertation on the Brotherhood of Sleeping Car Porters pioneered the scholarly field on African American unionism, and his work was published as a book in 1946. As the academic dean at Morehouse, Dr. Brazeal was affiliated with a number of professional organizations in the field, and he at one time held the role of president of the Association of Colleges and Secondary Schools and the National Association of Collegiate Deans and Registrars. Dean Brazeal had been unanimously elected to the Delta Chapter of Phi Beta Kappa at

[24] Jones, Candle in the Dark, 143.

Columbia University in 1959, and he was a scholar and a gentleman and a legend in his own time. Just as there was a "triumvirate" in Hope, Brawley and Archer, the same might be said for Mays, Brazeal, and Hamilton (Henry Cook "Cookie," registrar).

While President Mays was undergirding the Morehouse structure by strengthening the faculty and staff, raising money, and freeing the college from the stranglehold Atlanta University and Spelman had on the institution, the student body was engaged in the usual activities that are the hallmarks of collegiate life. Student activities, however, were suspended on January 15, 1941, when the death of Samuel Howard Archer, fifth president of Morehouse, former professor, dean, and coach, was announced.

President Emeritus Archer was seventy-one years of age at his death, and his health had been in decline for several years. He was one of the architects of the modern Morehouse, which included President Hope, Dean Benjamin Brawley, and President Mays. The funeral was held on January 19, 1941, four days after his death. At 3.30 in the afternoon, two individuals each from the student body, the alumni, and the faculty carried the casket bearing his body into Sale Hall Chapel. There to comfort his family and pay tribute to the deceased leader were students, faculty, alumni, and friends. The thoughts of one spoke for all: "We were made more aware of our responsibility to help perpetuate the fine ideals which were so inextricably a part of the philosophy and life of Mr. Archer as we listened to several brief talks by those who had been privileged to know and work with him."[25]

> [President Archer] never sought recognition for his services, yet recognition came: Morehouse awarded him the honorary degree of Master of Arts in 1923. In 1932, his alma mater [Colgate] awarded him the Doctor of Divinity degree. In 1938, an award came from the Twenty-Seven Club of Atlanta in honor of his outstanding contribution as a citizen. Under Mr. Archer's administration during the challenging times of the 1930s, Morehouse received an "A" rating from the Southern Association of Colleges and Secondary Schools.

Dr. Archer had served the college in so many ways that students yet

---

[25] *Alumnus* 15 (February 1941): 2–3.

unborn would come to think of him as a Morehouse Man, and he was. He came to the institution in 1905 and remained for more than thirty years, from its early days as Atlanta Baptist College and including when it became Morehouse College in 1913. In addition to his role as the college's fifth president, Dr. Archer had also served as a professor of mathematics, a football coach, a dean, acting president, purchasing agent, and director of the Morehouse summer school.

Several prominent Atlanta University Affiliation leaders gave eulogies. Of Dr. Archer, President Benjamin E. Mays said, "I stand before you today in the presence of my God, expressing the conviction that Samuel Howard Archer was as free of selfishness as any man I have ever known." Dr. Mays concluded his commendatory remarks saying, "It must have been men like Samuel Howard Archer of whom [Ralph Waldo] Emerson spoke when he said 'see how the mass of men worry themselves into nameless graves when here and there a great, unselfish soul forgets himself into immortality.' Samuel Howard Archer forgot himself into immortality."[26]

Other members of the affiliation community gave remarks about the decedent before his remains were carried from Sale Hall Chapel to be interred in the South-View Cemetery on Jonesboro Road in southeast Atlanta. South-View was founded after Reconstruction, in 1886, in response to the disrespect African Americans faced when they were interred in segregated burial parks. Morehouse memorialized President Archer in 1957 when it named its new health and physical education building Samuel H. Archer Hall. Constructed at a cost of $835,000, Archer Hall "provide[d] facilities for a comprehensive health and physical education program, as well as some features of a student activity center."[27]

Under the leadership of President Mays, the candle burned so brightly that it looked like a torch. Every aspect of the student was the focus of a Morehouse education during his presidency. Not only were the young men who enrolled at the college at that time give a high-quality curriculum and an able faculty, they were also drilled in public speaking, proper attire, proper table manners, and proper greetings, including the handshake. The experience was quite holistic in that all members of the

---

[26] *Alumnus* (February 1941).

[27] *Morehouse Bulletin* 116 (May 1968): 31–32.

faculty and staff corrected the errant behavior of students. Professor Gladstone Lewis Chandler, one of the school's celebrated teachers, taught public speaking, which was required of all students. Attire was scrutinized in the classroom and on the campus, and wearing a tie and coat was required on Sundays. There were also a few occasions where full formal attire was de rigueur. Proper table etiquette was observed in the dining hall, and students were invited to banquets and formal dinners. To reinforce dining etiquette, a formal table was set at which students would dine under the watchful eye of a college matron who corrected flawed behavior. The handshake, grip, and eye contact were arbitrarily initiated by faculty and staff without warning. All of these practices and exposure to Western culture norms were a part of the "building of men." Dr. Mays knew it could be done because he had done it. He strongly believed that regardless of a student's socioeconomic background, by the time he graduated from Morehouse, he would have been transformed into a sophisticated, cosmopolitan man who would be comfortable in any social environment he might find himself as a professional. Building men meant creating upper-middle-class men. These men, proud graduates of Morehouse College, would be well-educated and have the social skills necessary to be stewards for their people and others.

Chapter 10

"A Candle in the Window": Beckoning Freedom Fighters Abroad and at Home

Early in the leadership of Dr. Mays, national and international events cast a pall over Morehouse and affected the school in several ways. To wit, World War II escalated as the United States entered the worldwide armed conflict in December 1941. African Americans, including many Morehouse students and alumni, would demonstrate their patriotism and contribute to the war effort in immeasurable ways. The ultimate act of bravery and sacrifice is to give your life for a cause for which you are fighting. World War II was fought to preserve the Four Freedoms—freedom of speech and religion and freedom from fear and want—and Morehouse Men died fighting for freedoms they did not always enjoy at home, in the United States. The sacrifice these men and many others made during World War II would change the course of American history in the second half of the twentieth century.

James A. Jackson, '40, a technical sergeant, was the first to die in August 1943. He succumbed to injuries received in a booby-trapped tank in North Africa, where he had participated in the successful campaign against Nazi general Rommel's Panzer units. Jackson had been trained in the 99th Fighter Squadron at Tuskegee, Alabama. William J. Faulkner Jr., '40, was commissioned as a second lieutenant at Tuskegee Airfield on April 28, 1943. Eight months later, he became a first lieutenant at Selfridge Field in Michigan and was commissioned a captain shortly before his death. A veteran of fifty-six missions, Faulkner was awarded the Air Medal and oak leaf clusters for heroic service. He was killed near Reichenfels, Austria. Walter D. Westmoreland, '40, lieutenant from Atlanta, was a member of the 332nd Fighter Squadron of the 302nd Group, Allied Command in Italy. He was reported lost over Italy in late 1944. Fred Funderburg, '40, lieutenant, from Monticello, Georgia, also a member of the 332nd Fighter Squadron, was reported missing over Germany on December 29, 1944. Aaron T. Govan, '26, private first class, from

Montgomery, Alabama, was a member of the 345th Quartermaster Truck Company. He died in France on October 13, 1944, from injuries received in a vehicle accident and was buried in Normandy on October 15, 1944. Logan Scott, from Atlanta, died in France from wounds he received in action on November 19, 1944. Charles W. Clemmons Jr., also from Atlanta, was killed in action in Italy on September 3, 1944, after only three months in military service.[1]

Other Morehouse Men who worked in the war effort include Robert E. Johnson, '48, a former editor of *The Maroon Tiger* who became the associate editor of *The Masthead*, the official Treasure Island Naval Station publication of the United States Navy. Johnson's military service disrupted his matriculation at Morehouse as a member of the class of 1945, but he returned to the college after the war and graduated in the class of 1948. Another Morehouse Man, Edward Swain Hope, '23, was the oldest son of President John Hope. He became the first African American to be commissioned a full lieutenant in the United States Naval Reserve, Civil Engineer Corp. Dr. Edward Hope, who held a master's degree in engineering from the Massachusetts Institute of Technology and an EdD from Columbia University, received his commission on May 20, 1941. On January 30, 1944, the Liberty ship *S.S. John Hope* was named for Edward Hope's father, the fourth president of Morehouse College. At the launching of the ship, the following sentiments were shared: "We hope this ship will hasten the day when liberty, justice, and peace reign over the entire world.... I know this would be John Hope's wish."[2] You must remember the valiant and courageous service president John Hope gave to the war effort during the First World War. Under the auspices of the YMCA, he had advised and counselled the black troops.

As World War II expanded and the United States became more engaged in the theaters of battle, young African American men were among those called to active duty, which had an impact on the enrollment at Morehouse. As a college for men, Morehouse was seriously affected by the war. Once again, President Mays had to handle a declining student body as he did when he assumed the presidency in 1940. By 1944, enrollment

---

[1] Jones, *Candle in the Dark*, 146–47.

[2] Ibid., 147.

had dropped to 345 students.[3] Not only was the student population drastically reduced, so too was the faculty as some members took government jobs. Hugh Gloster, professor of English, became a United Service Organization (USO) regional executive for services to black citizens in the Southern states, with headquarters in Atlanta. Professor E. B. Williams of the Department of Economics became an associate science analyst with the US Department of Agriculture in the Bureau of Economics, covering Georgia, Florida, Alabama, Mississippi, and South Carolina. Professor Frank Forbes of the Department of Physical Education worked as a USO director at Tuskegee Institute. Morehouse students enlisted in the 332nd Fighter Group that is celebrated as the "Tuskegee Airmen."[4] The important roles played by Morehouse Men in World War II and the impact the war had on the college notwithstanding, the doors of the college remained open.

As the Second World War raged on to preserve the Four Freedoms, African Americans and others began to call for the support of those same freedoms for all people in the United States of America. In the 1940s, the influence of Dr. Mays and Morehouse College was being recognized in the South and across the nation. On October 20, 1942, dozens of Southern African American leaders met in Durham, North Carolina, to consider the state of race relations in the South as they affected the black community. Dr. Mays was one of the conferees and a major architect of "A Statement by Southern Negroes," also known as the Durham Manifesto.[5] Of the eighty black Southerners invited to the conference, fifty-nine attended in person as the remaining twenty-one shared their positions through letters and telegrams. "The document spoke forthrightly against discrimination in politics and civil rights, industry and labor, service occupations, education, agriculture, military service, social welfare, and health."[6] The conference was held at the North Carolina College for Negros (North Carolina Central University), and no African Americans from the North were invited. Dr. Mays agreed with the decision not to invited black leaders from the North because "if Northern Negroes were invited

[3] Eaves, The Morehouse Mystique, 46.

[4] Jones, Candle in the Dark, 144.

[5] Mays, *Born to Rebel*, 216.

[6] Ibid.

the white South would have used that as an excuse to decline cooperation."[7]

Dr. Mays's position reflected the standard attitude of black leadership in the South before the psychological shift in the behavior of African Americans following World War II and into the 1950s and 1960s. This new way of thinking and behaving was soon reflected in the thoughts and actions of Martin Luther King Jr., Morehouse class of 1948, and other young Morehouse Men during the African American Civil Rights Movement, including Julian Bond, Amos Brown, and Lonnie King. But in the 1940s, black Southerners understood the received culture of white supremacy in the South (the culture of white supremacy in the North manifested itself in a different way) and they knew how to maneuver in it and manipulate it to their advantage. At the Durham conference, Dr. Mays carried his reputation and the Morehouse stature to the discussions. The idea of Mays and Morehouse became one and the same, inextricably and inseparably linked, having grown from the idea that had its origins in the establishment of Augusta Theological Institute in 1867 to educate black men for service to people everywhere.

The early years of the African American Civil Rights Movement depended on moral suasion to try to change white attitudes about black people in an effort to change laws that proscribed and circumscribed the life chances and conditions of one-third (the black population) of the twenty million (all) people living in the South at the time. The orientation of Morehouse students in the 1940s was geared toward proving their self-worth as good and loyal Americans in every way. The telic Morehouse Man was an American Man. The college put in place a machine of cultural engineering that turned many country boys into sophisticated, confident, and cosmopolitan professionals who had an impact on the leadership class of black Americans in untold ways. The Morehouse Man was (is) not an immutable, inflexible, rigid, fixed, or static entity. In the 1940s, as he had done before, and as he would do so later, the Morehouse Man used his sophistication, confidence, and cosmopolitan attitude to participate in and help bring about the great social and cultural changes of the fifties and sixties. The precursors for the "revolution" were being set in the 1940s

---

[7] Mays, Born to Rebel.

when, at the Durham conference, Dr. Mays "was the first to suggest that a drafting committee should be appointed to complete the document to be presented to the white South."[8] The committee decided to meet in Atlanta, Morehouse's home city.

Atlanta, Georgia, was the Southern city where the origins of the New South were well underway by the time Benjamin Mays took office as president of Morehouse. As the city developed strong business and corporate communities with links to the industrial Northeast and Midwest, pockets of great wealth began to accrue among a small class of white Atlantans. The Candler and Woodruff families and others garnered great wealth thanks to the monumental growth of the Coca-Cola Company. But the philanthropy that resulted from this wealth did not make its way to the African American colleges located in southwest Atlanta. Spelman, however, continued to have the support of the Rockefeller family and the philanthropic organizations that carried their name. Morehouse had no such single benefactor. In 1940, for instance, the Morehouse endowment was $1,114,688.16. It grew by only about $130,000 when, in four years, it stood at $1,245,530.06 in 1944.[9] This was the same year, however, that the United Negro College Fund (UNCF) was founded with the purpose of raising money nationally for the support of its member African American colleges. Morehouse College was a charter member of the UNCF.

The origins of the United Negro College Funds can be found in the financial exigencies brought on by the Great Depression and the changes in the philanthropic behavior of foundations and corporations. Years following the death of Booker T. Washington, the donations that Tuskegee had received while he was president had greatly declined. So, in 1943, in response to this critical situation, Frederick D. Patterson, then president of Tuskegee Institute, "crafted the idea of a united appeal for private black colleges carried out by an organization specifically created for fundraising."[10] There were thirty-three private black colleges in 1944, and eighteen of their presidents came to the first meeting of the UNCF at Tuskegee. Among the participants were Benjamin Mays, Florence Read, and Rufus

---

[8] Jones, Candle in the Dark, 159.

[9] Ibid., 146–47.

[10] Marybeth Gasman, *Envisioning Black Colleges: A History of the United Negro College Fund* (Baltimore, MD: Johns Hopkins University Press, 2007) 20.

Clement, presidents of the colleges in the Atlanta University Affiliation. The United Negro College Fund incorporated on April 25, 1944, and along with its purpose to raise funds for member colleges, it worked to promote better public understanding of and appreciation for the needs and problems of fundraising while setting an example of interracial cooperation in the organization's national campaign. Joining Morehouse, Spelman, and Atlanta University as charter members was Clark College, but not Morris Brown, a school that was still under the authority of the African Methodist Episcopal Church. Paine College, a Methodist Episcopal school in Augusta, Georgia, joined the UNCF in 1945, and the Interdenominational Theological Center became a member when it was established in 1958. During his presidency, Dr. Mays became one of the UNCF's strongest and most vocal supporters. While he led Morehouse to new plateaus of exceptionalism, he also advocated for the worth and value of all historically black colleges and universities. And by the 1950s, his words spoke volumes.

Five months after the founding of the United Negro College Fund, in September 1944, a fifteen-year-old teenager from Atlanta enrolled as an early-admission student at Morehouse and began his college career. He lived in the Old Fourth Ward, on Auburn Avenue, and had attended Booker T. Washington High School. He was a young man of average stature with the normal temperament that usually characterized boys in their mid-teenage years. He had been named Michael Luther at his birth, the same moniker his father had, but when his father eventually changed his name in 1935, so too his appellation changed. This first-year student of the class of 1948 was Martin Luther King Jr., who, without question, would become the college's most illustrious graduate. But for four years, 1944 to 1948, he was just another student at Morehouse. Dr. Mays, president of the college at the time, remembered that Martin "was just one freshman among many others. Only an omniscient God could have predicted his future."[11]

Martin Luther King Jr. was one of the first participants in the college's early-admissions initiative. Because Morehouse was an all-male school, World War II greatly affected the enrollment at the college. "Of

---

[11] Mays, *Born to Rebel*, 265.

all the Negro colleges in America, the war had hit and will hit Morehouse College hardest," President Mays said in 1944. He added that "on June 1, the closing day for the academic year 1942 to 1943, only 31 of the 400 men registered last September were under 18. We can expect practically none of the 400 to return in September of this year." He then announced plans for the early enrollment of students: "Our task is to recruit a student body of 16- and 17-year-olds, which is an almost impossible job because most Negro boys are 18 when they finish high school."[12] Age eighteen was also the age when young men were eligible for the draft into military service in the United States. In the 1940s, as now, young men from Georgia represented the largest group of students enrolled at Morehouse.

The early-admissions initiative at Morehouse was modeled after a similar program at the University of Chicago, President Mays's graduate alma mater, which was one of the first of its kind in the nation. The program at Morehouse was the first of its kind at an African American college, and while it "lasted less than four years," according to one account, "it was quite successful."[13] In 1952, another early-admissions program was started at the college, funded by the Ford Foundation. It, too, brought bright high school students onto campus who could handle a college curriculum, but unlike the previous participants, these students were housed separately, given special supervision, and awarded early-admission scholarships. The program also admitted younger students than the previous programs, with some students as young as fourteen years old. For these reasons, the previous group was much more readily accepted than the latter.[14] Maynard Holbrook Jackson Jr., the first African American mayor of Atlanta, was admitted to Morehouse in 1952 at the age of fourteen.

Early-admission scholarships were awarded to students not more than seventeen years of age who had completed at least two years of high school work and who could qualify for admission on the basis of superior academic achievement and test results on the Scholastic Aptitude Test. The scholarship was in the amount of $850 for the freshman year, which covered all costs, and which was renewable for each year if a B average was

---

[12] Ibid.

[13] Ibid., 145.

[14] Dereck J. Rovaris Sr., *Mays and Morehouse: How Benjamin E. Mays Developed Morehouse College 1940–1967* (Silver Spring, MD: Beckham House Publishers, 1968) 54.

maintained.[15] But in 1944, no scholarships were awarded to these students, except from the general scholarship program. The first program was implemented to boost enrollment and keep the college open during the dire circumstances created by World War II. Martin Luther King Jr. was not a scholarship student, just an early-admissions enrollee.

The program for the undergraduate college at the University of Chicago was adopted by Robert Maynard Hutchins. "Beginning in 1937, the University of Chicago's experimental, interdisciplinary College program admitted students beginning in the sophomore year of high school.... Early entrants were subject to five additional comprehensive examinations, but otherwise went through the same academic program as high school graduates."[16] The program at the University of Chicago was eventually abandoned, but it was adopted by other schools such as Morehouse and continues in one form or another to the present time. Support for early enrollment came from the Federal government during World War II when, "in 1942, the Educational Policies Commission made a formal recommendation that colleges admit academically skilled high school students after their junior year" in order to ensure recruits for military service were as well-educated as possible.[17]

World War II raged on for another three years, with many academically skilled African American high school students giving military service to their country. Many of these young men might have enrolled at Morehouse, but military service obligated them to temporarily set aside pursuits of higher education until a later time. When the war ended, many veterans did, in fact, enroll at Morehouse using the GI Bill to pay for their education. The period after World War II was a very important time in African American history and the history of Morehouse College. The war ended when President Harry S. Truman declared September 2, 1945, Victory over Japan Day, or V-J Day. Truman, the former vice president of the United States, had taken the oath of office as the thirty-third president of the United States when President Franklin D. Roosevelt died of a cerebral hemorrhage at Warm Springs, Georgia, on April 12, 1945. President

---

[15] Ibid.

[16] *Morehouse Catalogue, 1967–1968* 116 (Atlanta: Morehouse, 1968): 54.

[17] www.en.wikipedia.org/wiki/Early_entrance_to_college.

Roosevelt, who died at 4:35 P.M., was in his fourth term, making him the longest-serving president in the history of this country. Vice President Truman was sworn in as president at 7:09 P.M.[18]

After World War II ended, "the swollen postwar enrollments which characterized many American colleges, with Government footing the bill for the G. I.s, also happened at Morehouse. The total enrollment for the 1946–1947 Academic Year was 909 (905 in the College and four in the School of Religion). In the following years, the average enrollment was around 800 men. The College was bursting at the seams and hard put to accommodate so many students."

Enrollment remained high for the remainder of the 1940s, and to meet the needs of these students, three temporary frame buildings were constructed: one as a classroom structure and two as dormitories. The Sale Hall Annex, used for classrooms and faculty offices, is the only surviving building of these three. The United States government provided the money to build the Sale Hall Annex in 1954, and the building, located between Sale and Robert Halls, was given a brick-veneer face-lift in 1955, establishing it as a permanent hall on the campus. Sale Hall Annex accommodated 300 persons in several classrooms, and its construction made it possible for all Morehouse faculty to have offices for the first time.[19] While the classroom space was a welcome addition to the physical plant of the college, it was the exponential increase in the enrollment of veterans that changed the landscape of the student body at Morehouse.

The initials "G. I." could have several different applications when applied to military servicemen (and women), including general infantry, ground infantry, general inductee, and government inductee. But GI is most commonly known as "government issue," and the GI Bill provided financial support for "all who had served in uniform, whether or not they had fought on the front lines."[20] The Servicemen's Readjustment Act was signed into law by President Franklin D. Roosevelt on June 22, 1944, and was meant to atone for the ill treatment received by World War I veterans after they were discharged from military service, many of whom only

---

[18] Kull and Kull, An Encyclopedia of American History, 431–32.

[19] Jones, Candle in the Dark, 126.

[20] www.time.co,/time/magazine/article/0.9171.1891039.00html.

received $60 and a train ticket. The GI Bill of 1944 was the result of protest and pressure from many of these veterans, and it provided, among other things, an opportunity for those who served to resume their education or technical training after discharge. The government would pay tuition up to $500 per school year and provide a monthly living allowance for students pursuing their studies. Morehouse welcomed the men who had fought to preserve the Four Freedoms abroad just as it welcomed men who fought for justice and freedom at home. Morehouse put a "candle in the window" as a beacon for those who had fought in the war and those who were fighting for civil and human rights at home.

The GIs, or veterans, who were admitted to Morehouse after World War II were not your traditional eighteen-year-old college students. These men had experienced the rigors of military training, and some had participated in battle in the theaters of war in Europe, Asia, and the South Pacific. Even those who did not see combat and who had remained stateside were more experienced and hardened than the typical freshman from the past. Unlike many of the young men who had enrolled at Morehouse in the early 1940s, these veterans had been exposed to the diverse cultures of the United States and the world. Their worldviews were more cosmopolitan. And as men, they wanted to be treated accordingly. This issue came to a head in the late 1950s when the Men of Morehouse demanded to be addressed as men—as Mister—not as boys or by their given or forenames. In an article appearing in the January 16, 1960, issue of *The Saturday Evening Post* titled "The Difference between Black and White," Marcia M. Mathews, a white professor at Morehouse, said that her students objected to being called boys because "in some Southern communities a Negro man is a boy until he is sixty-five. After that he becomes 'uncle.'"[21] The faculty and staff agreed to address the Men of Morehouse as "Mr.," a tradition that continues to the present day.

Doctor Samuel Berry McKinney, class of 1949 and one of Morehouse's many distinguished graduates, is a shining example of a Morehouse Man who served his country in World War II. Dr. McKinney served as pastor of Mount Zion Baptist Church in Seattle, Washington, from 1958 until he retired in 1998. He was a civil rights activist who was

---

[21] Ibid., 161–63.

in the 1944 freshman class with Martin Luther King Jr., John T. Blassingame, Samuel DuBois Cook, William G. Pickens, Charles Vert Willie, and many other esteemed members of the class of 1948. The Reverend Doctor McKinney did not graduate with his class in 1948, though, because he was drafted into military service during his freshman year. Samuel McKinney was born in Flint, Michigan, but grew up in Cleveland, Ohio. His father was a member of the class of 1920. Sam McKinney was drafted into the army shortly after he turned eighteen, in December 1944, just three month into his first year at Morehouse. His uncle had strongly encouraged him to register for military service, as all eighteen-year-old male citizens were required to do, and he entered military service in the second semester of his freshman year, in 1945, as the war was winding down. McKinney served in the Army Air Corp, now a separate branch of the Air Force. The Armed Forces of the United States of America were separated by race at that time.

Sam McKinney reentered Morehouse in January 1947 (only former students who had served in the military were admitted in the middle of the academic year). Because he had only served in the army for a short while, McKinney had to plan how the benefits of the GI Bill could work in his favor. "As of Sept. 2, 1945, when World War II officially ended, you were given one year on the GI Bill. After that you had one month for each month you were in military service not to exceed 48 [months or] four years."[22] In order to finish his degree at Morehouse, McKinney enrolled in summer school in 1947 and 1948 (operated by Atlanta University) and took a full schedule of courses in the 1948 to 1949 academic year. He graduated with a major in history and political science, which operated as one department at that time, and a minor in sociology (the same major chosen by Martin Luther King Jr.). There was a common bond among the Morehouse students who had served their country in military service. The Reverend Doctor McKinney recalled the camaraderie on campus when he arrived in 1944. "Well, it was a good experience for about close to 400 freshmen who discovered there were about 50 upperclassmen on campus. Camaraderie was good, but some of us decided that since we

---

[22] Talk with Rev. Samuel Berry McKinney, '49, Greater Seattle Alumni Association (http://gsncaa.org/tigertalk/20-questions-with-reverend-samuel-berry-mckinney-49/).

outnumbered the upperclassmen there would be no hazing (a nationwide practice at that time) of freshmen. The camaraderie was good. But each month our ranks were thinned by those entering military service."[23] For student veterans, "Morehouse College made its facilities available as widely as possible to men returning from the various [military] services. The organization of the college permitted some flexibility in programs and adjusted itself to the needs of those seeking a broad background in the arts and sciences for a life career." Furthermore, "the College gave considerations where possible to the enrolled veterans without lowering the standards and impairing the prestige of the degrees for which these men [were] candidates. The College, of course, satisfied itself that the applicant was prepared to do the work of the proposed program, but allowed him to progress as fast as his abilities permit[ted]." Veterans could enter the college at three times during the year: in September, at the beginning of the first semester; in February, at the beginning of the second semester; or in June, at the start of summer school. "The Servicemen's Readjustment Act, approved June 22, 1944, and amended to include Korean [war] veterans, provides education training at government expense at an approved educational institution of the veteran's own selection for those who qualify under the regulations."[24] Morehouse College was one of the institutions approved for the training of veterans.

By 1945, the year World War II ended, more than 400 human relations committees, official and unofficial, had been established in American communities. Underneath the surface of the American nation there was a growing feeling that the race problem was deepening and was becoming dangerous.[25] But there was a new mood, a new consciousness, among black Americans, and they were not willing to go back to business as usual. The Morehouse community played a major role in the social and cultural sea changes that would occur over the next two decades. The black struggle for freedom, equality, and justice had been in effect for centuries. The Stono Rebellion happened in 1739, the Nat Turner Rebellion was activated in 1831, the Niagara Movement was organized in 1905, and

---

[23] Ibid.

[24] Morehouse College Catalogue, 1965–1966.

[25] Bennett, Before the Mayflower, 368.

the New Negro Movement was embedded in the Harlem Renaissance of the 1920s and 1930s, demonstrating organized efforts by the black community to remove the heavy burden of oppression and suppression from their existence. In addition to these documented acts in the black struggle for freedom, there were untold individual courageous acts of defiance against the unjust treatment they experienced. The heightened black consciousness that became visible after World War II had its antecedents in bygone years.

When World War II ended in 1945, Martin Luther King Jr. had just finished his freshman year at Morehouse. Julian Bond, Amos Brown, Lonnie King, and many future civil rights activists of the 1960s, were young children. But the seeds of discontent had been sown for score of years, and the sprouts were now bursting through the soil of racial discrimination and oppression. Morehouse graduate Lerone Bennett gauged the attitude of black Americans, who, "fearing another betrayal [like the betrayal that resulted from the 1877 Hayes-Tilden Compromise the ended black Reconstruction], fearing that they had once again wasted their blood reacted with fury." The postwar mood of the black community was revealed by a surprising act by the NAACP when, on October 23, 1947, they filed "An Appeal to the World" with the United Nations, asking that international body "to intervene in the domestic affairs of the United States on behalf of a suffering and persecuted minority. It was this pressure and the increasing militance of black activists that forced President Harry Truman to form a Civil Rights Committee. The Committee brought in a long and eloquent report, calling for economic, political and cultural action."[26] But like so many other efforts to deal with the American dilemma, the report did not reap much hay. It was essentially quoted, filed, and forgotten. But African Americans such as Asa Philip Randolph would not let the new consciousness among black Americans diminish. He and others continued to press for social change, and Morehouse became a major player in the intensified crusade for justice and human and civil rights for African Americans. Martin Luther King Jr. graduated from Morehouse in 1948.

Dr. Mays knew firsthand the indiscriminate nature of racial violence heaped upon African Americans. He had been almost mobbed on a

[26] Ibid.

Pullman car in Tennessee and again in a dining car in South Carolina. Unlike many other black men who had been killed when they encountered similar mobs bent on attacking them, Dr. Mays survived to tell his stories. Recalling the first harrowing incident, Dr. Mays said that in October 1944, he was en route to New York on the Southern Railway, not far from Greenville, South Carolina. He went into the dining car for lunch, where eleven of the twelve tables were occupied, including the one behind the curtain, supposedly reserved for Negroes. It was wartime, and most of the forty-four diners were soldiers. When he entered the diner, he stood momentarily, expecting the steward to seat him. When he failed to do so, Mays took a seat at the vacant table near the center of the car. Quick as a flash, the steward, a man named E. M. Hames, was there, protesting vociferously and insisting that he could not sit in that spot. Mays pointed out that if he did not wish for him to sit there, then it was his responsibility to move the four soldiers seated in the place reserved for Negroes. The steward refused and was becoming angrier by the second. Two passengers came rushing toward Dr. Mays with fists clenched, ready and eager to aid and abet the steward. Fearing to turn away from them, Dr. Mays walked backward out of the diner.[27]

The actions of the white mob, the steward, and the white men were the law. White people could defy the law and sit in the seats reserved for Negroes, but the steward could refuse to seat him at the only table vacant in the diner. The law was not made for white men to keep but for Negroes to obey. "I would have been a 'good nigger,'" Dr. Mays said, "if I had stood humbly and waited for the segregated table which white men were occupying."[28] Dr. Mays believed, and rightly so, that had he not backed out of the dining car, he would have been beaten and arrested upon his arrival in Greenville. He could have been set upon by a much larger mob of white men and teenagers, as was the custom in the South at the time, in an attempt to put him in his place. As troubling as the potential for mob violence was the fact that there were forty-four passengers and the steward in that diner—all white—and not one hand or voice was lifted in Dr. Mays's defense.

---

[27] Mays, *Born to Rebel*, 196.

[28] Ibid., 198.

There were many African Americans at that time who thought that black people should not make a fuss when they faced acts of discrimination and violence. Dr. Mays disagreed with those who believed any action he might take would be bad publicity for Morehouse and would militate against his efforts to raise money for the college. He could not in good conscience accept this position, and he had to do something about it, not just for himself alone but for the cause of justice. He knew that anyone who refused to give to Morehouse because of his actions would not have given to the college anyway. Dr. Mays moved forward with legal action against the Southern Railway Company through lawyers with the NAACP, including Thurgood Marshall, Spottswood Robinson, and Robert Carter. The lawyers took the case to the Interstate Commerce Commission (ICC), which reprimanded the Southern Railway, which, in a weak apology to Dr. Mays, promised it would not happen again, but the ICC rejected Dr. Mays's plea for $2,500 in damages. When all was said and done, though, what happened to Dr. Mays in 1944 pales in comparison to what happened to Hugh Morris Gloster, a member of the Morehouse faculty in 1941.

Jim Crow in public transportation in the South was the law in 1941.[29] When Hugh Gloster, who had recently joined the faculty at Morehouse, boarded the "Frisco" from Atlanta to Memphis, he took a set in the coach designated for black people. The coach had been configured in three parts, allowing white people to be seated in the space assigned to black customers if their coach became overcrowded. When the train arrived at Amory, Mississippi, a large number of black farmers and their families on their way to Tupelo to shop got on the train, causing the section designated for the black population to become overcrowded. All of the seats were taken, and many black men and women were standing, all while there were empty seats in the other sections because the conductor and baggage handler were sitting in the section closest to the one assigned to African Americans. The other section was completely unoccupied. The conductor and the baggage man were "engaged in their usual occupation of smoking, spitting, cursing and drinking." This meant that one-third of

[29] The United States struck down racial segregation commercial in state transportation (buses) in *Morgan v. Virginia* on June 3, 1946.

the coach was filled with black people, while two-thirds of the coach were occupied by two white men. After a short while, Gloster told the conductor about the reservations black customers had about sitting in seats where he and the baggage man were sitting, or choosing the section in front of them because doing so would violate the Jim Crow law and the learned behavior of black people in the South. The conductor's reply was to admonish Gloster, saying, "You have a seat, don't you? That's what's wrong now. Too many niggers trying to run the train." Gloster told the conductor he was not a nigger, and he was not trying to run the train. The conductor did not reply, but he did open up the unoccupied section to the black patrons. Knowing the racial culture of the South, Gloster knew he had violated the racial etiquette required for interaction between the black and white community. He told the man sitting next to him "that if anything happened to me to get in touch with Dr. Benjamin Mays, president of Morehouse College in Atlanta, or with Attorney A. A. Latting in Memphis, Tennessee." The unknown man did not think anything was going to happen, but Gloster knew otherwise.

When the trained reached Tupelo, the police, responding to a call from the conductor or his agent, came into the coach and demanded, "Where's the nigger who is trying to run the train?" None of the black men and women identified Gloster, so the conductor pushed his way through the crowded coach and pointed him out. When the police ordered him out of his seat, Gloster refused, telling the police he had paid a fare and had done nothing wrong. This act of defiance and courage caused the police to pull him out of his seat, kick him down the aisle, and throw him onto the platform at the train station. Then they beat Gloster and took him off to jail. The beating stop after they learned from his wallet that he was a teacher at Morehouse, but by this time, he was badly injured. Gloster "suffered the most excruciating agony when one of the brutish policemen put all of his two-hundred-pounds into a hard kick into [his] groin." He was then taken to jail. The jail cell had four bunks, and after finally figuring out how to pull down the top bunk, in a semiconscious state and without medical attention, he crawled into it, where he remained for the night.

Apparently, the man who was sitting next to Hugh Gloster on the train before all hell broke loose remembered to contact the persons the

Morehouse teacher had identified. Dr. Mays called the Tupelo authorities from Atlanta, NAACP officials called from New York City, and Gloster's family and Attorney Latting called from Memphis. As the news of his plight spread, Latting, Leo Zenn, and members of his wife's family in Atlanta came to Tupelo to rescue him from untold violence, even the possibility of death. The agent for the Frisco Train Company apologized, and, after suing the company, Gloster received limited compensation for the horrors and the "near-brush with death" he experienced "at the hands of Mississippi goon policemen."[30]

Stories such as these, told by persons intimately connected with the history of Morehouse in the twentieth century, tell as much about the history of the college as they do about the United States of America. But Morehouse was about building men who would challenge the status quo of white paternalism and racism. The lives of Morehouse students, faculty, alumni, administrators, and friends played out in many ways behind and in front of the veil of Jim Crow America. The right to vote is the foundation of American citizenship and is guaranteed by the Fifteenth Amendment, so in the early stages of the modern civil rights struggle, members of the black community thought this was the tactic to use. In the 1940s, most of the members of the Morehouse faculty, staff, and student body could not vote in the democratic or white primary elections in Georgia. Dr. Mays was fifty years old when he first voted in 1944. But there were other civil rights efforts mounted by Morehouse Men before the emergence of.Dr. Martin Luther King Jr.

In September 1950, Horace Taliaferro Ward applied to the University of Georgia's School of Law. Ward's application represented the first attempt by an African American to attend a historically white college and university (HWCU) in Georgia, and it was a test case. Ward had attended high school in LaGrange, Georgia, and was inspired to a career in law after seeing his first black lawyer, Austin T. Walden, a representative of the NAACP in Georgia. Born July 29, 1927, after finishing high school, Ward subsequently attended Morehouse College and graduated in the class of 1949. He majored in political science, and, as did many Morehouse graduates, he went on to earn a master's degree at Atlanta University

---

[30] Mays, *Born to Rebel*, 77–78.

in June 1950. It was in the fall of that year that he applied to the law school at the University of Georgia. In order to persuade Ward to attend a non-Southern law school, L. R. Seibert, executive secretary of the Georgia Board of Regents, offered him out-of-state tuition. Ward refused the offer, and nine months later, on June 7, 1951, he got a response to his application from William N. Danner, the registrar at the University of Georgia: "Mr. Ward, your application for admission has been received and is hereby denied."[31] O. C. Aderhold and other university officials insisted that Ward was not qualified for admission to the law school despite his excellent academic work at Morehouse and Atlanta University. It was self-evident that he was not accepted to the law school because he was black, so Mr. Ward and his legal counsel appealed the denial of his application, filing a discrimination lawsuit in federal court in 1952. The court date for his case was set for October 5, 1953, but was postponed after Ward was suspiciously drafted into military service. After serving his country for two years, including in the Korean War, Ward reactivated his lawsuit in 1955. After the lawyers for the University of Georgia and the state filed motions for dismissal, a court date was set for December 17, 1956, six years after Ward first applied for admission to the law school. "On February 12, 1957, Judge Frank A. Hooper dismissed Ward's lawsuit against UGA on the grounds that (1) Ward had refused to reapply to the law school under the new guidelines, which Ward's attorneys had argued was yet another ploy to keep Ward out, and (2) that Ward's enrollment at Northwestern University's law school had in effect rendered moot his application to UGA."[32] While his case was dragging through the courts of Georgia, Ward had been accepted to the Northwestern University School of Law in Evanston, Illinois, where he attended and earned the juris doctorate degree in 1959.

Dr. Benjamin E. Mays was involved in Ward's attempt to desegregate the law school at the University of Georgia, but he was not the one who selected the 1949 graduate of Morehouse to be the test case. The person who thought Horace T. Ward would be an excellent student to test the

---

[31] http://www.atlantamagazine.com.Channels/bestofatlantaprofiles/story.aspx?ID=116988870 and http://www.georgiaencyclopedia.org/nga/Article.isp?id=h-880

[32] Mays, *Born to Rebel*, 205.

Jim Crow laws governing Georgia schools was Dr. William H. Boyd, a professor of political science at Atlanta University. Dr. Boyd was also the head of the NAACP in Georgia at the time, and he had talked with Dr. Mays about Ward as the candidate to test the segregation waters. Dr. Mays remembered, "When Boyd talked to me about Ward, I agreed that he would be a good man. Ward did not ask my opinion, but had I been asked, I would have given my heartfelt approval."[33] But due to Dr. Mays's growing reputation, coupled with the fact that Ward was a Morehouse Man, it was naturally assumed that Dr. Mays was responsible for Ward filing the application for admission to the law school. Due to economic proscriptions and the power of the received culture of white supremacy, in 1950 it was difficult to find black people who were willing to put their lives and their livelihoods on the line for the sake of desegregation. Ward, an outstanding Morehouse graduate, was courageous in his willingness to be in the vanguard of the desegregation movement in Georgia.

Legends and myths are grounded in real or imagined beliefs, and it was the growing myths surrounding Dr. Mays that prompted a white man to come to his office to asked him to advise Ward to withdraw his suit against the University of Georgia and the state and to accept the offer of out-of-state aid. This man assured Mays that if his ploy were successful, money would be made available to build a law school for African Americans at Atlanta University. This was the initial effort by white individuals in Texas that led to the Supreme Court ruling in *Sweatt v. Painter* (1950), establishing that education encompasses more than just buildings and books. Responding with conviction, Dr. Mays "saw no honorable way he could persuade Mr. Ward to withdraw his application and accept out-of-state aid, and he would give further thought to his proposal and write him within a few days. In my letter, he reaffirmed his assertion that he could not be part of a scheme to get Ward to withdraw his application, and that it had long been his hope that the University of Georgia would open its doors to Negroes with federal mandate."[34] After earning a JD at Northwestern University, Horace Ward became a partner in the law firm of Hollowell and Ward, which would play a major role in the actual

[33] Ibid., 206.

[34] Ibid.

desegregation of the University of Georgia in 1961. A Man of Morehouse was involved in this historic event.

In 1953, Martin Luther King Jr. was nearing the completion of his studies at Boston University. The next year, 1954, the High Court rendered a monumental decision in *Brown v. the Board of Education of Topeka.* Martin Luther King Jr. moved to Montgomery, Alabama, to assume the pastorate of the historic Dexter Avenue Baptist Church, and he completed his doctoral dissertation in 1955. On December 1st of that year, Mrs. Rosa Park defied the Jim Crow seating arrangements on a bus in that Southern city, was arrested, and taken to jail. Edward D. Nixon, the president of the Montgomery branch of the NAACP, called Dr. King Jr., and after talking with leaders at Dexter Avenue Church, King agreed to join the movement in Montgomery. It was from the Montgomery Movement, organized by Joanne Robinson, E. D. Nixon, Ralph Abernathy, and other black leaders in Alabama's capital city, that Dr. Martin Luther King Jr.—a 1948 Morehouse College graduate with a bachelor's degree in sociology—emerged as the foremost leader in the black struggle for freedom in the United States.

Many members of both the white and black communities believed that with desegregation and integration, black schools would no longer have a purpose. Those who held the view that institutions created for or by African Americans were inherently inferior to those created for the white community believed that, in competition with white institutions, including schools, black institutions would eventually wither and die.

John H. Sengstacke, the editor and publisher of the *Chicago Defender*, one of black America's most respected newspapers at that time, claimed black schools were inferior and was challenged in his thinking by Dr. Mays. In an editorial, Mr. Sengstacke argued that black people did not have "sufficient intellectual baggage" to compete with white students at schools like Harvard and Yale. He want on to say, "Today, the Negro college, in the context of the quest for racial admixture, is an anachronism. For such an institution to insist on reserving its identity while the masses are striving to tear down the forbidding portals of segregation, is a confounding anomaly. Such an attitude amounts to a plea for perpetuating and financing segregation." He contended that "the Negro college would have much justification for survival if it were to engage into an active and genuine process of integration on both faculty and student level [*sic*]." Sengstacke was unaware of the origins of many black colleges that had white leaders and faculties. The practice of hiring white faculty was still strong at Morehouse. Dr. Mays, whom Lerone Bennett Jr. called the "Great Schoolmaster," agreed that only a few black students had been admitted to some of America's most prestigious colleges, perhaps due to racial discrimination, and responded to the claim that the "Negro college was an anachronism." Dr. Mays's stated, "The Negro college is also in quest for racial admixture. The Negro colleges, certainly those that seek funds through the UNCF, do not insist on preserving their identity while the masses are striving to tear down the forbidding portals of segregations." Mays then pointed out that

> the colleges that are now serving predominantly Negroes have been segregated institutions, but they have never been segregating institutions. Data from the New York headquarters of the UNCF reveal that there is nothing in the charter of the UNCF colleges that would exclude members of other racial or ethnic groups. The UNCF colleges are less segregated today than ever before. Students and faculties in the UNCF colleges have done much to break down the walls of segregation.

By their very longstanding existence, all institutions preserve their identities but at the same time they can be a part of a larger collective of similar institutions doing the same work. There was a telling paradox here. Commentators who thought black colleges and universities should change their identities or cease operations never thought the same about white schools. Why should Morehouse change its historical identity but not Harvard?

President Mays revealed that "twenty-eight percent of the faculty at Morehouse is Caucasian or White. Morehouse had always had a desegregated faculty and some of the so-called Negro colleges may have a higher percentage of desegregation in their faculties than Morehouse. We have had a few White students in our student body a long time." And then he editorialized: "The Negro colleges may not be, in every area, as good as the best of the colleges attached to Harvard, Yale, Princeton, and the University of Chicago, but they are better than most of us think they are." Dr. Mays pointed out that many black colleges were better than many white colleges, and that as white colleges were accepting black students, black colleges were accepting white students. The real goal of desegregation was not the disappearance of black institutions, but "these institutions will simply serve everybody and if they meet a need and if they are good, they will survive."[35]

Due to the work of its graduates, Morehouse's reputation was on solid ground in the 1950s. The student body was rapidly becoming more cosmopolitan. The Men of Morehouse came from more than thirty states and from the Bahamas, the Virgin Islands, the British West Indies, Nigeria, and Liberia.[36] Student life at Morehouse was robust, as seen in the myriad activities that engaged their bodies and minds, shaping them into Morehouse Men. However, events of the 1950s would usher in a new era of activism and cultural change at the college. The escalation of the decades-long civil rights crusade among African Americans in the 1960s involved Morehouse in significant ways. With Dr. King Jr. as a role model, Morehouse students in substantial numbers aspired to the pulpit and the pastorate, and their level of consciousness moved them to action. The struggle for freedom and justice was led by the middle class, and Morehouse prepared men to enter this stratum. In 1957, E. Franklin Frazier published his controversial book *Black Bourgeoisie*, "the book that brought the shock of self-revelation to middle-class blacks in America." The presence of Morehouse and other African American institutions of higher education in Atlanta contributed to the city having one of the largest black middle-class populations in the United States.

Writing about African American educational institutions, Frazier asserted that they "did not grow out of the traditional culture of the black folk." He argued that

> the schools maintained by the free Negroes before the Civil War were the result of the assimilation of European culture, while the schools built by the Negro religious organizations were imitations of culture patterns alien to the Negro's way of life. The Negro colleges and schools that were established by northern white

---

[35] *The Chicago Defender* (September 5–11, 1964) in Jones, *Candle in the Dark,* 373–74.

[36] "Student Life at Morehouse," Morehouse College, Robert W. Woodruff Library and Archives.

> missionaries represented an entirely alien conception of life and culture from the standpoint of the social heritage of the Negro masses.

Frazier then contended that "while the first generation of Negro teachers who gradually replaced the early white teachers enjoyed considerable prestige among the Negro masses, they too were, in a sense, representatives of the white man's way of life—and...they were dependent upon the whites who had provided their education." Therefore, Frazier opined, "From the beginning, the Negro intelligentsia [black leadership], or what DuBois [*sic*] called the 'Talented Tenth,' was created by philanthropic foundations supported by northern industrialists."[37] Black colleges and universities were a part of the American educational landscape, but he seemed not to remember that white colleges and universities did not represent the social heritage of the white masses. The essential question was whether American values were exclusively white values. The short answer to this salient question is no. The values that white Americans held dear were embraced by black Americans as well. Values such as equality, liberty, justice, democracy, unity, and family were important to black citizens. In fact, these were some of the values that undergirded the African American Civil Rights Movement. The demand for equality in bus transportation in Montgomery, Alabama, led to Martin Luther King Jr.'s emergence as a freedom fighter. Soon after, he became a national leader and led the Southern Christian Leadership Conference. With the Civil Rights Act of 1957 and the desegregation of Central High School in Little Rock, Arkansas, a renewed surge in the black struggle for freedom and justice began. By 1960, the new consciousness among college students, including those at Morehouse, began to challenge the perspectives of the older black leadership class. By the end of the decade, sweeping changes at the college would usher in a "new Morehouse."

---

[37] E. Franklin Frazier, *Black Bourgeoisie: The Rise of a New Middle Class in the United States* (London: Collier Books, Collier-Macmillan, 1969) 84.

Chapter 11

"We Shall Wear a Crown": Morehouse and the Civil Rights Era

The black struggle for freedom began on the shores of Africa, continued on the European ships that carried Africans into captivity in the Americas, and was evident as soon as the Africans were unloaded like cattle in the Americas. The early struggles took the form of running away, aggressive confrontation, and individual or mass suicide. Over the centuries of enslavement in the British colonies and the United States, black people held captive continued to resist their captivity by running away, engaging in surreptitious acts of resistance, or outright revolt. In the century before the renewed activation of the black struggle for freedom and justice in the 1960s, members of the black community protested by building an institutional infrastructure behind the veil of white surveillance and participation. The Niagara Movement, the NAACP, and Marcus Garvey's Universal Negro Improvement Association were visible protest organizations. Although there had been acts of direct protest before 1960, the activation of the "direct action" period of the black struggle for freedom and justice in the United States began in Greensboro, North Carolina, on February 1, 1960. On that day, four college students staged a protest against the racial discrimination policy at the lunch counter at the F. W. Woolworth Variety Store. The four young men were freshmen at North Carolina A & T, and these students—Ezell Blair, Franklin McCain, David Richmond, and Joseph McNeill—were soon joined by other students from A & T and Bennett College. A few white students also joined the sit-down protest as the movement spread to other North Carolina cities, including Durham (North Carolina College), Raleigh (Shaw University and St. Augustine College), Charlotte (Johnson C. Smith University), Fayetteville (Fayetteville State College), and Elizabeth City (Elizabeth City State College). Within days, sit-down protests spread across the Southeastern United States, especially in cities and towns where there was a black college(s) or a reasonably large high school. Nashville, Tennessee, the hometown of Fisk University, Tennessee State University, and Meharry Medical College, and Atlanta, the hometown of Morehouse, Spelman, Clark, and Morris Brown Colleges, Atlanta University, and the Interdenominational Theological Center (ITC), were in the vanguard of the new African American Civil Rights Movement. Howard Zinn, a professor at Spelman in the 1960s, called these student activists "The New Abolitionists"[1] as the students began to act independently of older civil rights activists. Activism was already stirring among Morehouse students when a rising junior agreed to be the desegregation tester at the University of Georgia in Athens. Hamilton H. Holmes Jr., an advanced sophomore at Morehouse, joined Charlayne Hunter as the first African Americans to be admitted, enrolled, and graduated from the state's flagship university. Holmes was a spring 1959 graduate of Atlanta's Henry McNeal Turner High School and entered Morehouse in the fall of that year. He withdrew from Morehouse in the fall of 1960 in order to be eligible to enroll at the University of Georgia in January 1961.

Some members of the Morehouse community, particularly those in leadership, were sorry to lose Hamilton to the University of Georgia because they, like President Mays,

> were not in favor of all of the best Negro students being drained away from Negro colleges. Mays was convinced that Morehouse could prepare Mr. Holmes for medical school as well as could the University of Georgia.... However, Mays and many others wanted to see the racial barriers at the university broken down, and they wanted a Morehouse student to be the first Negro male to do it.... So, President Mays strongly advised him to enter the University of Georgia, which he did in January 1961.[2]

White students and others rioted when Holmes and Hunter entered the University of Georgia, forcing the two black students to temporarily leave the school the first night because the UGA administration feared for their lives. After they left the university, 300 faculty members petitioned for their return.[3] While the University of Georgia was in a state of unrest due

---

[1] Howard Zinn, SNCC: The New Abolitionists (1964).

[2] Mays, *Born to Rebel*, 208.

[3] Ibid.

to the enrollment of two black students, Morehouse students were completing their first semester's work (the first semester ended in January). In a matter of days, students at Morehouse and the other Atlanta University Center (AUC) schools would resume the demonstrations and protests they had begun in 1960, leading to unrest in the city of Atlanta.

The Greensboro student movement began on February 1, 1960, but more than a month passed before AUC students mobilized. Nevertheless, on March 15, 1960, within a few weeks of the student sit-ins in Greensboro and other cities across North Carolina, the Atlanta Student Movement swung into action. Morehouse students and their comrades from the other AUC schools had been deliberating and planning for action soon after news of the events at Greensboro reached them. But the AUC presidents and other black leaders in Atlanta, the leadership class that was wedded to the Atlanta Way,[4] advised the students to move with caution. They counseled them to draw up a statement of their grievances, and Julian Bond, a Morehouse student, and Roslyn Pope, a Spelman student, drafted the document. "An Appeal for Human Rights" was the title of the activists' manifesto, and Rufus Clement, president of Atlanta University, arranged to have it appear as full-page ads in three local newspapers on March 9, 1960. "The Appeal" appeared in the Atlanta *Daily World*, the Atlanta *Constitution*, and the Atlanta *Journal*, and after receiving national attention, it appeared in *The New York Times.* True to the Atlanta Way, response to the Appeal ranged from disbelief to praise. Governor Earnest Vandiver did not believe African American students had the capacity to write such an outstanding document and attributed its authorship to forces outside of the United States (read Communist influences) while columnist Margaret Long found the Appeal intelligent and most moving, as she wrote in a column in the *Journal.* Mayor William B. Hartsfield thought the student manifesto was important to Atlanta as it "expressed 'the legitimate aspirations of young people throughout the nation and the entire world.'"[5] Hartsfield met with student leaders on the afternoon that the Appeal appeared in the local newspapers. The mayor and a group of

[4] The Atlanta Way had been in operation for years by the 1960s. Its goal was to bring black and white leaders together in order to achieve consensus and drive resolution and change.

[5] Mays, *Born to Rebel*, 290.

white ministers urged the students to meet with white business leaders before mobilizing their fellow student activists. But the students did not accept the recommendation of gradual change, and on March 15, 1960, several hundred college students from Morehouse, Spelman, Atlanta University, Clark, and Morris Brown began the Atlanta Movement by sitting-in at segregated lunch counters and eateries around the city.

"An Appeal for Human Rights," clearly stated the demands of the student activists and what needed to change in Atlanta. The manifesto opened with a preamble: "We, the students of the six affiliated institutions forming the Atlanta University Center—Clark, Morehouse, Morris Brown, and Spelman Colleges, Atlanta University, and the Interdenominational Theological Center—have joined our hearts, minds, and bodies in the cause of gaining those rights which are inherently ours as of the human race and as citizens of these United States." (The entirety of the famous document is available online.) The Appeal ended with a declaration:

> We, therefore, call upon all people in authority—State, County, and City officials, all leaders in civic life—ministers, teachers, and businessmen, and all people of good will to assert themselves and abolish these injustices. We must say in all candor that we plan to use every legal and non-violent means at our disposal to secure full citizenship rights as members of this great Democracy of ours.

The Appeal was signed by Willie Mays, president of Atlanta University's student council; James Felder, president of the Clark College's student government association (SGA); Marion D. Bennett, president of the Interdenominational Theological Center's student association; Don Clarke, Morehouse student body president; Mary Ann Smith, secretary of Morris Brown's SGA; and Roslyn Pope, president of Spelman's SGA.

Although the sit-down demonstrations did not have 100 percent participation from the Morehouse student body, it could be argued that 100 percent of the students at the college supported the movement philosophically and in spirit. The minds and souls of President Mays, other administrators and faculty members were challenged by the events unfolding on the campus and in the community. Calling the activists "young warriors," the leaders of Atlanta University schools supported the students in the struggle for freedom and justice. "The six presidents in the [Atlanta University] Center were in full sympathy with the students, and the Council of presidents never tried to over persuade, let alone dictate to them." The presidents asked the students activists to keep them informed and they were available to give them advice. Dr. Mays, who theoretically supported the students, made his position clear. "Each student should make up his own mind about participating in the sit-ins," he asserted, "and should be coerced by no one and once he had made up his mind to demonstrate, he should be prepared to take the consequences for violating the law, however unjust it surely was." President Mays made it clear to the Morehouse student activists that "time spent demonstrating and time spent in jail did not absolve them from meeting the academic requirements of the college."[6]

As Morehouse students took the lead in the AUC Student Movement, students were jailed and hauled into court. Lonnie King, who is generally recognized as the leader of the protests, was determined to bring down the barriers of segregation in Atlanta so he suspended his studies at Morehouse to serve as the chairman of the crusade. After the appearance of the Appeal, students met with their advisers for several days, and around midnight, on March 15, 1960, a group met at the Morehouse president's residence to inform Dr. Mays that they were going to march the next day. And march they did, staging sit-down protests at the Terminal Station, Union Station, the State Capitol, the Fulton County Courthouse, City Hall, the bus terminal, the Peachtree-Baker Building, the Peachtree-Seventh Building, and other places where Jim Crow policies were in place. Some 200 students participated in the first wave of demonstrations at white-only eateries, and the *Constitution* newspaper carried a front-page headline that read "77 Negroes Arrested in Student Sit-Downs at 10 Eating Places Here."

As the protesters had been trained, the sit-downs were orderly, quiet, and peaceful.[7] The sit-down protests were not spontaneously and randomly executed; rather, the demonstrations were planned during mass

---

[6] Ibid., 288.

[7] Ralph E. Luker, *Historical Dictionary of the Civil Rights Movement* (Lanham, MD: Scarecrow Press, 1997) 247.

meeting, usually held the evening before they took place. Leaders met with students in Sale Hall Chapel or at local community churches to instruct activists in nonviolent, civil disobedient tactics and to identify the Jim Crow establishments that were to be the targets of the demonstrations the next day. On the day of the sit-down protests, students from Morehouse, Spelman, and Clark would meet in the quadrangle in front of Trevor-Arnett Library. As they moved in pairs down Chestnut Street (now James P. Brawley) to Hunter Street (now Martin Luther King Jr. Drive), students from Atlanta University and ITC joined the march, and the students from Morris Brown would join the phalanx as it crested the hill moving east on Hunter Street and in the area of the campus bridge. The crusaders would continue on Hunter Street into the downtown Atlanta area, about a half mile to the east. They knew their assignments and would break away from the line to enter establishments and begin their protest demonstration.

There was praise for the Appeal before students moved into action, but attitudes changed once the protest demonstrations were underway. On March 16, 1960, the day after the first demonstrations, the *Journal* praised the nonviolent nature of the protests, the authorities, and the public in general, but also admonished the students, saying, "The protestors having made their point, the hope is that they now will leave well enough alone. When zeal and common sense are in conflict, the former too often prevails. But now is the time for common sense. Old customs and traditions are not changed by battering rams and dramatics but by time and attrition and with the help of good will."[8] The *Journal* did not consider the more than 200 years of slavery that did not come to an end by "time and attrition and with the help of good will." Slavery came to an end because of the battering rams and dramatic clashes of the Civil War. And so would the age of Jim Crow in the United States come to an end—because of the confrontations between black and white individuals. Reminding its readers that segregations was *de jure*—the law—an editorial in the *Constitution* chastised the students: "We repeat, the process of law have been started. These can be handled without any public interference by agitators bent on disorder. We are a nation which must continue to live by law,

---

[8] The Atlanta Journal (March 16, 1960).

and this is a good time to remember it. We all have too much at stake in the present and future of this city to besmirch it with violence or extreme action. Let none of us forget that important fact."[9] But the students did not heed the admonition of the editorialists, and the protests against segregations and discrimination in Atlanta continued for months. Lonnie King, who was a twenty-three-year-old student at Morehouse in 1960, was elected chairman of the Committee on Appeal for Human Rights (COAHR), a veteran of the United States Navy, a boxer, and a starting fullback on the Morehouse Maroon Tigers football team.

As the protest demonstrations were underway in Atlanta, the AUC presidents tried to meet with leading businessmen in the city to try to persuade them to end Jim Crow policies in restaurants and at lunch counters, but to no avail. The old "Atlanta way" was out of synch with the times, and the students continued their demonstrations. As the Student Movement continued across the Southeast and spread to other towns and cities, student activists, with vision and forethought, knew they needed an organization to coordinate regional movement. By April 1960, the student movement had become so strong, with protests in dozens of towns and cities, the sit-down or sit-in activists, on the advice of Ella Jo Baker, a member of Southern Christian Leadership Conference (SCLC) and a veteran of the Civil Rights Movement, decided to form an organization that would bring their indigenous struggles together for the common good of all. Because Jim Crow laws did not make public hotel facilities available for the proposed conference, Ms. Baker was able to persuade Shaw University, her alma mater, to open dormitories and the dining hall for the meeting during spring break of that year. When the call went out to student activists to attend, students from across the Southeast, eschewing their spring break respite, prepared to attend the Raleigh, North Carolina, meeting.

On April 15, 1960, several hundred students from fifty-eight colleges and universities met at Shaw, where they were inspired by talks given by Dr. Martin Luther King Jr. and James Lawson, both leaders in the SCLC. But on the advice of Ms. Baker, they decided to remain independent of the SCLC and form a "Temporary Student Nonviolent Coordinating

---

[9] Ibid.

Committee." Marion Barry, a leader in the Fisk University-Nashville movement, was chosen as chairman. By October 1960, after locating its national headquarters on Hunter Street in Atlanta, contiguous to the Atlanta University Center, the organization dropped the word "temporary" and was known as SNCC (pronounced "snick") for the Student Nonviolent Coordinating Committee.[10] Several Morehouse students were among the representatives from the Atlanta University Center present at the SNCC organizational meeting. As the Atlanta Student Movement took a hiatus during the summer break of 1960, Lonnie King, Julian Bond, and other activists had to decide about college and whether they should devote themselves fully to the cause or work part time in the struggle. The Atlanta Student Movement intensified in the fall when students returned to classes in September 1960. King and Bond decided to withdraw from the college and delay their graduations from Morehouse. King earned his degree in 1969 and Bond finished in 1971.

As the nonviolent protest continued, many students were incarcerated while others remained on the outside (e.g., Julian Bond) to retain legal aid, to keep the college administrators informed, and to keep the jailed students supplied with lecture notes, homework, and books. They also brought toiletries and clean clothing to their imprisoned comrades. The 1961 edition of the *Torch*, the Morehouse yearbook, dedicated two pages to "A Year of Protest." Congratulating the student activists, the editorial staff wrote, "In step with college students over the nation, the students of Atlanta joined in the wave of massive protest. Determined that the evil of segregation had existed too long, these students chose Dr. Martin Luther King, Jr.'s doctrine of massive nonviolent resistance. During the year nearly 90 students spent two weeks in jail as tangible proof of their sincerity and their willingness to pay the price of freedom." These brave students sacrificed classes, social privileges, and other activities associated with college life "in order to show the community, the nation and the world that the eradication of this evil was long over-due in our society. The *Torch* expresses sincere congratulation to them. In the interest of the worthy cause to which they have committed themselves, their

---

[10] Brisbane, *Black Activism*, 47.

contribution for the common good will remain invaluable."[11] Alongside the two-page spread were pictures showing the students and older adults (Dr. William Holmes Borders and others) during a protest picket, students leaving the jail, and white segregationists marching to maintain the old order. One picket sign read: "The PRESENCE of SEGREGATION Is The ABSENCE Of DEMOCRACY, JIM CROW MUST GO!" The sign worn by Dr. Borders, a Morehouse alum and pastor of Wheat Street Baptist Church, read "WEAR OLD CLOTHES with DIGNITY. DON'T BUY HERE!" One of the segregationists was outfitted in a Ku Klux Klan costume, but another was dressed casually, wearing a sign that read "SUPPORT THE MERCHANTS WHO SUPPORT SEGREGATION."[12]

A member of the faculty at Morehouse in the 1960s stated that, "believing as they do in the basic equality of all men, and having been nurtured in a college atmosphere that never accepted racial segregation even when law and custom forced surface conformity to local statutes and mores, Morehouse men could not remain aloof from the civil rights revolution which took place during the years 1960–1965."[13] The students had become dissatisfied with conformity to the laws of Jim Crow that had been the rule for generations, so they defied them by moving to topple the barriers that had kept African Americans out of downtown restaurants, hotels, cafeterias, drugstore- and department-store eating facilities, and any public accommodations that did not admit black patrons on an equal basis compared to how they admitted white patrons. This new black consciousness, and especially the new consciousness among college students in the 1960s, would not allow them to do otherwise. They stood up to the persistent culture of racial discrimination by sitting down. Morehouse students, along with other AUC students, were slow to act (six weeks after Greensboro) because, as Robert H. Brisbane, a Morehouse political science professor at the time, reminded us, "the city [Atlanta] had long prided itself in its reputation of good race relations, and this image acted initially as a restraint upon the potential activists on the black campuses." Nonetheless, once the movement in Atlanta got underway, it became one

---

[11] *The Torch* (Morehouse Yearbook) 1961, 104–105.

[12] Ibid.

[13] Jones, Candle in the Dark, 274.

of the major centers of activism.

In 1960, as the sit-down movement emerged, student life and college work continued at Morehouse. The 1961 *Torch* was dedicated to Professor Gladstone Lewis Chandler who, the dedication read, "had become almost eponymous with effective speech training and synonymous with impeccable English." The Maroon Tigers football team had a good season in 1960, defeating Tuskegee 13–6, Clark 16–0, and Fisk 38–0. Starring on the football team were such legendary players as Alfonso "Buddy" Crutch, Willie Jackson, Isaiah Coates, and Donald Dollar. Hamilton E. Holmes, who would transfer to the University of Georgia in January 1961, was also on the team. The Maroon Tigers basketball team was as successful as the football team. The hoopsters defeated Alabama State 74–62, Morris Brown 56–52, and Clark 56–42. The Morehouse Tiger Sharks swim team won its fourth consecutive Southern Intercollegiate Athletic Conference (SIAC) swimming and diving championship thanks to the skills of William Robinson, Edward Cooper, Carl Holsey, Robert Harris, Latimer Blount, and Benjamin Blackburn. Leroy Keith Jr., who would become the eighth president of Morehouse, was a senior swimmer and champion diver who had been diving for the team since its formation in 1957. Gwendolyn Ferrell, a Spelman senior, was named Miss Maroon and White, and Norma June Wilson and Marcia Beavers were her attendants. Rufus Stevenson, Calvin Grimes, William King, and Peter Lucas comprised the Morehouse Quartet under the very capable directions of Wendell Whalum, who also directed the Glee Club and the Morehouse Marching Band. Johnny Bullock was the president of the student government association, Marvin Anderson was the chief justice of the student court, and Waymon Wright was chairman of the social and cultural affairs committee. Debating the national debate topic "Resolved that the United States government should adopt a program of compulsory health insurance for all citizens" were Michael Davis, Willie Joe Wright, Charles "Chuck" Davis, and Charles Black. The debaters were coached by Dr. Brisbane. Charles Black was also the editor-in-chief of the *Maroon Tiger* newspaper and Willie Joe Wright was managing editor. Melvin Butler was the editor-in-chief of the *Torch*. In his closing message in the yearbook, Butler captured the sentiments of generations of Men of Morehouse when he wrote,

> In a larger sense, it is difficult—even impossible—to preserve many of the memorable events of the years because they are intangible. The tense atmosphere which permeated the campus during the first wave of student demonstrations, the subtle atmosphere or anxiety which hovered over the campus during final exams, the uncontrollable emotions at athletic events and many of the philosophically unsound and logically weak confabs of the dormitory "summits" are mere examples of college life.

And while Butler's epilogue rang true, a spirit of scholarship and stewardship continued to characterize the Men of Morehouse and Morehouse Men in the fall of 1960. Their efforts lifted them closer to wearing the crown that hovered above their heads.

The Atlanta Student Movement was two years old by 1963 and had brought about some changes in the culture of Jim Crow in Atlanta. But as Morehouse students returned to the campus after the 1962 Christmas holidays, submitted their semester papers, and took their final examinations, little did they know what an eventful and tragic year 1963 would be. Morehouse Men would feature prominently in the famous and infamous historical events of that year. In January 1963, a Morehouse Man brought positive attention to the college when he took his seat in the senate of the Georgia General Assembly: Leroy Johnson, a member of the class of 1949, assumed the office of senator from Fulton County, becoming the first African American in the state's assembly since Reconstruction. His election to the office in November 1962 came as the result of a court decision outlawing Georgia's "county unit system," thereby legalizing the doctrine of "one man, one vote." The ruling created a predominantly black senatorial district in Georgia's largest county by population.

Senator Johnson was born in Atlanta, attended Booker T. Washington High School, and entered Morehouse in 1945, a year after Martin Luther King Jr. enrolled. After Morehouse, Johnson attained a master's degree from Atlanta University, and, after teaching social studies in the Atlanta School System for four years (1950–1954), he entered the law school at North Carolina Central University, earning his JD in 1957. Johnson was the first African American hired by the Fulton County Office of the District Attorney, then called the solicitor general's office. Encouraged by the black political machine in Atlanta, and by the new activism in the city, he decided to run for the state senate. Johnson's arrival was met with hostility and resistance. "In his first days there," according to one account, "he was a lonely man. Few white senators would speak to him, and he had little or no chance to be effective. But Johnson quietly and shrewdly...won the confidence of enough influential senators to get into 'the club.'" On key, close votes, Johnson would withhold his support or opposition until he could win concessions, and would boast of his influence among black voters in certain senatorial districts. "Johnson obtained a reputation as a 'wheeler-dealer,' a 'politician's politician.' 'Old Leroy,' as some of the white senators affectionately called him, became a power broker of the first order, a force to be reckoned with, in the Georgia Senate."[14] Leroy Johnson, one of "Bennie's Boys," made the venerable schoolmaster proud by his academic and political accomplishments. The Morehouse community took ownership of the historic election of one of its graduates and swelled with pride in its significance. In the meantime, life at the college continued to function as usual.

David Satcher—who would go on to an exceptionally distinguished career as the future director of the Centers for Disease Control and Prevention, president of Meharry Medical School, and the sixteenth US Surgeon General and assistant secretary of Health and Human Services as well as professor and administrator at the Morehouse School of Medicine—was in the second semester of his tenure as president of the Morehouse student body in January 1963 when Leroy Johnson took his seat as a state senator. Satcher was elected to serve the Morehouse student body in spring 1962, at the end of his junior year. Born in Anniston, Alabama, on March 2, 1941, he had enrolled at Morehouse in 1959, and at the beginning of the second semester in 1963, he was looking toward graduation in June and graduate studies the following fall. Satcher was a member of the Psi chapter of Omega Psi Phi, and the 1963 *Torch* said of him, "Leading the student body is President David Satcher, who also comes from the ranks of *Psi* and had done a notable job maintaining a good student government, *Omega* is well represented on the council."[15]

One of the memorable campus events held during the second

---

[14] Hornsby, A Short History of Black Atlanta, 85.

[15] *The Torch*, 1963, 120.

semester of 1963 was the opening of Mays Hall and the Lane Dining Hall on February 3rd. After decades of taking their meals in the "dining hall" in the basement of Robert Hall, the new dining facility was a welcome addition to the Morehouse physical plant. Reflecting on the old dining room, and with a touch of sarcasm, the *Torch* said, "We stood patiently in rain, snow...waiting to get inside the building. Once inside, it was a nice trip up to the third floor, down to the first, and finally to the beautiful basement, where the line curved around the busy Housemen, already fortunate enough to have obtained food. After a short ten-minute delay, the line moved again, and we received our vittles. We miss 'old faithful' because 'it takes an awful lot of living to make a house a home.'"[16]

The construction of the Alvin H. Lane Dining Hall and Benjamin E. Mays Hall, which included the Sadie G. Mays Lounge, established a pattern for the future design of the Morehouse campus. Until the erection of the Thomas Kilgore Campus Center and dormitory, all of the buildings—Dansby Hall, Brawley Hall, Wheeler Hall, Du Bois Hall, Thurman Hall, Hubert Hall, White Hall, and King Chapel—followed the architectural look of Mays Hall, which displayed light-colored bricks and, with the exception of the dormitories, featured a wing. Architect Edward C. Miller designed Mays Hall, and the dormitory was the first building on what is now known as the "new campus." Rectangular in shape, the building featured four floors with a study room on the second level. There were three guest rooms and two furnished apartments. Each dormitory room was appointed with two beds, double closets and dressers, and a desk for each occupant. As the college did not have a policy of coed visitation, women could only visit on "open house" days. One of those days was the day Mays Hall opened. It was not unusual, however, for Spelman and Clark women to be escorted into the Lane Dining Hall. This was especially true when fraternities were honoring their queens. Ann Ashmore was named Miss Maroon and White during that year, 1962 to 1963.

The usual college culture prevailed at Morehouse in 1963. The football team, led by Isaiah Coates, crushed Howard University (28–6) and Clark (20–12) in the fall semester. The basketball team was "successful on the hardwood," and the "Walker Boys," Arthur and David (not related),

---

[16] Ibid., 13.

led the track and field team in several events championships. Unfortunately, the heretofore-first-placed Tiger Sharks finished second in the SIAC swimming championship. The Morehouse Glee Club continued to represent the college well during its Northern tour, which took the accomplished chorus to several cities across the country. By the time the Glee Club returned to campus after its spring break tour, the African American Civil Rights Movement was agitating in ways that would capture worldwide attention. The Birmingham Movement was about to explode on the world stage, and a sizeable number of Morehouse students had come from Birmingham and its environs, and even more from other parts of Alabama.

Dr. Martin Luther King Jr., unquestionably the most prominent figure in the African American Civil Rights Movement, had graduated from Morehouse nearly fifteen years earlier by the beginning of the year, and what a year it would be for him. His reputation had already been cemented by the events of 1955 and 1957, but in 1963, Dr. King Jr. would lead the Birmingham Crusade, pen his famous "Letter from Birmingham Jail," and give his electrifying "I Have a Dream" speech at the March on Washington. The national movement got a boost on February 25th when the United States Supreme Court reversed the conviction of 187 African Americans who had been arrested for protesting against Jim Crow in Columbia, South Carolina. Less than a week later, on April 3rd, Morehouse graduate Dr. King Jr., along with members of the Southern Christian Leadership Conference and local leaders such as Rev. Fred Shuttlesworth, issued the "Birmingham Manifesto" calling for an end to Jim Crow at all businesses and in all public facilities in Alabama's largest city. They demonstrated their sincerity by sitting-in at businesses in downtown Birmingham. The segregationists were successful in getting a state court injunction banning demonstrations, but King Jr., Shuttlesworth, and Ralph Abernathy defied the order and marched on City Hall on Good Friday. The black leaders were arrested, and King Jr. was held in solitary confinement. It was while he was in jail, isolated from other inmates, that he penned his most literary and powerful missive. "Letter from Birmingham Jail," delivered on April 16th, explicates why African Americans could no longer use a gradual approach in their struggle for freedom. Much like Du Bois's *The Souls of Black Folk*, Claude McKay's "If We Must Die," and the Atlanta Student Movement's "An Appeal for Human Rights," "Letter From Birmingham Jail" is an intellectual masterpiece on the struggle for African Americans to find their place in American life and thought. More than any other written piece, it explained why black folks were marching, sitting-in, getting arrested, and doing it all over again.

Perhaps Paul T. Walker, Morehouse SGA president (1963–1964), was reflecting on "Letter From Birmingham Jail" when he wrote for the 1964 *Torch*: "We are reminded by Lillian E. Watson in an introduction to her book *Light from Many Lamps* that 'today when we face what is probably the greatest challenge history had ever known, today when millions of people are troubled, uncertain, and confused, the rich deposits of inspiration left by preceding generations take on a new and vital significance.'" Addressing his comments directly to his schoolmates, Walker took a conciliatory tone, entreating his schoolmates to "respect the rights of the faculty, administration, and fellow students." He asked them to "be cognizant of and comply with the regulations pertaining to the educational policies that govern this institution." Furthermore, he declared, "We must always uphold the academic integrity of Morehouse College. For we are Morehouse, and we can be proud of a rich heritage. We are the salt of Morehouse, if we shall have lost our savor, wherein shall Morehouse be salted?"[17]

The Morehouse community joined the outrage that was felt by others near and far but who were determined to keep the momentum of the movement from slowing. They joined thousands of Americans on the Mall between the nation's capital and the Lincoln Memorial on August 28, 1963, as demonstrators in the March on Washington, just five days after the death of the great intellectual and activist Dr. W. E. B. Du Bois in Accra, Ghana. As the media recorded his words, a Morehouse Man gave the greatest speech of the twentieth century. "I Have a Dream" was delivered toward the end of the great event and is the only speech from that day that is generally remembered today. Dr. Martin Luther King Jr. gave the speech and the world listened. Morehouse family members listened as they stood on the Mall in Washington, DC, or watched the mass assemblage of demonstrators on live television. Dr. King ended the speech of

[17] Ibid.

with the sermonic "Free at last! Free at last! Thank God Almighty, we are free at last!" Then, after making edifying remarks, Bayard Rustin, the architect of the march, said, "We have finished this great demonstration. Now I want to introduce for the Benediction, a distinguished leader of the church and education. President of Morehouse, Dr. Benjamin E. Mays will give the benediction." As Dr. Mays moved to the podium, there was applause from the crowd. And in his uniquely distinctive voice and oratorical style, he began by imploring "God of history" to pour down benedictions upon America, its leaders and institutions, and especially on "Congress, who need wisdom, courage, a sense of justice, deep faith in democracy and an abiding faith in their God to enact legislation that will further implement American dreams." The Reverend Doctor President Mays blessed the departing assemblage petitioning the Divine Being, saying,

> Here we are, God, one hundred-eighty million people, one hundred years after Lincoln freed the slaves, ninety-eight years after the close of a bloody civil war, fought to preserve one nation under God, indivisible. One hundred eighty-seven years after [Thomas] Jefferson declared that all men are created equal, that they are endowed by their creator with certain inalienable rights that among these are life, liberty and the pursuit of happiness.

Dr. Mays reminded the Almighty that black people in the United States were "confused, baffled, floundering, afraid, faithless, debating whether the Congress of the United States should pass legislation guaranteeing to every American the equal protection of the law. Debating whether its businesses should have the right to discriminate against a man because thou, oh God, made him black." Closing his benediction speech, President Mays said,

> In peace and in war thou had blessed America as the nations of the earth look to the United States for moral and democratic leadership. May we not fail them, nor thee. Please God, in this moment of crisis and indecision give the United States wisdom, give her courage, give her faith to meet the challenge of this hour. Guide, teach, sustain and bless the United States, and help the weary travelers to overcome, someday soon, Amen.

The crowd plaintively responded "Amen," as thoughts of the assassination of Medgar Evers in June 1963 were on their minds. Less than a month later, another horror would stun the world when fourteen-year-old Addie Mae Collins, eleven-year-old Denise McNair, fourteen-year-old Carole Robertson, and fourteen-year-old Cynthia Wesley were killed in the bombing of the Sixteenth Street Baptist Church in Birmingham. The Morehouse community cursed, cussed, and wept.

The usual college traditions unfolded as the 1963 fall semester began. Classes, concerts, competitions, and courting settled in for the next three months. In order to qualify for the bachelor of arts degree, students had to satisfactorily complete courses in the General Studies Program and in a major discipline. Required in the General Studies Program were four semesters of English composition and two semesters in reading, four semesters in humanities, six hours in history, and six hours from either economics, political science, or sociology, "unless specific provision was granted to the contrary." History 151-152 had to be taken in the freshman year, and the second social science course selected by the student taken in the sophomore. If a student majored or minored in one of the required courses, six hours were accepted as his required social science course. Morehouse students were also required to complete two years of a modern foreign language, one year of mathematics, one semester of biology, one semester of physical science, four semesters of physical education, and a course in "Personal Hygiene," also called "Personal Living." Additionally, two semesters of religion and two semesters of philosophy were required, general psychology, public speaking, and English fundamentals. And, of course, depending on the academic department, twenty-six to forty-eight hours in a major had to be completed. Including free electives, a total of 124 hours were required for graduation from Morehouse in the mid-1960s. By a vote of the faculty, beginning in 1962 each candidate for a bachelor's degree from Morehouse College had to pass a comprehensive examination within his major concentration in the second semester of his senior year. Failing the "comp" prevented the student from graduating with his class. The prospective graduate also had to pass the English Fundamental Examination in order to earn his degree. The college also awarded the bachelor of science degree, and with a few requirements relevant to science disciplines and career tracks, students pursuing their BS degree took many of the same courses as those pursuing the BA. Science majors took chemistry, physics, one semester of religion, one in philosophy, three hours in history, and one in the philosophy of science. If a student started out in a science major but later changed programs, he had to fulfill the requirements listed for the BA degree. Biology majors were automatically required to minor in chemistry.

All major concentration fields had to be completed with a quality point average of 2 and no grade below C in any course in the discipline, including perquisites. The election of the major was subject to the approval of the major's department and had to be certified by the dean (Dean Brazeal, in the mid-sixties), and it had to be declared by the beginning of the sophomore year. Each student was also required to choose a minor that complemented the major, and he took courses in this field over two or three years. The quality point average and grade requirements also applied to minors. Majors were available in biology, chemistry, economic and business administration, education and psychology, English, history, political science, mathematics, modern foreign languages, music, philosophy, physical education, physics, religion, and sociology. All first-year students had to complete two semesters of freshmen lectures. Daily chapel programs were required of all students, and Sunday morning religious services were required for all residential students, regardless of their faiths. Attendance at "Chapel" was assiduously recorded, and too many absences without prior permission would jeopardize a student's graduation.

Because Chapel is well remembered by so many Morehouse Men, and because it has morphed into what today is known as "crown forum," it requires a bit of musing on its structure and nature. Calling the gathering of Morehouse Men "chapel" is a tad misleading. Yes, there were the usual hymns, Scriptures, and prayers, along with the wonderful organ renditions by Wendell Whalum, but for all intents and purpose, Chapel was an assembly program that lasted thirty-five minutes, from 9 to 9:35 A.M., Monday through Friday. Tuesdays were generally reserved for President Mays, and when he was in town, he, more often than not, gave talks and lectures. Seats were assigned according to your academic class. Seniors up front, then the juniors and sophomores. Freshmen occupied the remaining seats, including those in the balcony. Seats were assigned to allow Professor Claude B. "Pop" Dansby to check attendance, which was required.

This was serious business. And while Chapel might have been viewed as a burden the Morehouse student had to bear, it had an immeasurable and lasting effect on generations of Morehouse Men. Not only were students privy to the sage pearls of wisdom from Dr. Mays and the periodic talks given by Mrs. Sadie G. Mays, the first lady of the college, but they also heard other noted scholars and prominent personages.

All clubs were expected to present programs during the year, including the Glee Club, the band, fraternities, the classes, and the student government association. There was a need to schedule a program each day, five days a week, for two semesters that ran twelve to thirteen weeks each. But it was the prominent men (many of them alumni) and women who gave lectures, sermons, and talks at Chapel that had a decided effect on the minds and hearts of many Morehouse students and which carried over into their personal lives and careers. Speakers such as Howard Thurman, Robert Weaver, Martin Luther King Jr., Martin Luther King Sr., Charles Merrill, and many other luminaries and notables were presented from the stage of the chapel.

Hope-Archer Day was one of the traditional Chapel programs that was highly anticipated each year since it featured orations in homage to President John Hope and President Samuel Archer. The orators were chosen from the best student speakers, and while the audience often did not long remember what they said, they remembered how they said it. Great oratory, public speaking, and preaching skills are intimately identified with the Morehouse Man. Morehouse College's tenth president, Dr. Robert Franklin, recognized this attribute when he included "well-spoken" in his telic imagery of the Morehouse Man as a Renaissance man. Morehouse students had many opportunities to hone their speaking skills: in the classroom, on the debating team, and in the "verse choir." The latter was made up of a group of about ten Morehouse students with the occasional member from Spelman. Directed by Professor Elnora P. Chesterman, the group recited prose and poetry in rhythmic time, phrasing, intonation, voice inflection, and range of volume. Verse choir was very popular in the early 1960s but disappeared as the culture at the college changed in the 1970s.

In late 1963, as the first semester was well underway, a tragic event with international implications occurred that shook the Morehouse community. On Friday, November 22, at 12:30 P.M. Central Standard Time, as his motorcade neared the book repository in Dallas, Texas, John Fitzgerald Kennedy, the thirty-fifth president of the United States, was shot by Lee Harvey Oswald, according to the Warren Commission. Virtually all news media—television and radio—preempted their regular programming to carry the news of the national tragedy. The news of the president's assassination hit the Morehouse campus like a bomb, and a pall settled over the students, faculty, and staff. The Christmas holidays in 1963 were dampened by the tragedies of that year as Morehouse students returned home to write semester papers and prepare for their final examinations, which would be taken in January 1964.

Returning to the college to end the first semester and begin the second, the events of the previous year continued to weigh heavily on the hearts and minds of those in the Morehouse community, and this was reflected in a resolve to see changes in American society. In his first State of the Union address as president, delivered on January 8, 1964, Lyndon Baines Johnson vowed to end racial discrimination, poverty, and the threats of war from foreign enemies, real and imagined. Demonstrating his position against racial discrimination, On January 21, President Johnson appointed Carl Rowan, the respected Pulitzer prize-winning journalist and author, director of the United States Information Agency. President Kennedy had supported new civil rights legislation that would give all Americans the right to be served at all facilities that served the public. Kennedy had also advocated equality in voting for all citizens. The origins of the Civil Rights Act of 1964 began in June 1963 when President Kennedy proposed it. It gained more traction after his death as Americans mourned the loss of their chief executive. President Lyndon Johnson, sworn in after Kennedy's death, reinforced its importance in a speech before a joint session of Congress five days after the assassination in Dallas: "No memorial oration or eulogy could more eloquently honor President Kennedy's memory than the earliest possible passage of the civil rights bill for which he fought so long."

Despite filibustering and resistance from Southern Democrats, and as the spring semester ended with the graduation of the Morehouse class of 1964, the Civil Rights Bill moved forward. And so, on June 10, 1964, by a vote of 71 to 29, the United States Senate passed the legislation, that included, among other things, eleven entitlements relating to public accommodations and fair employment practices. President Johnson signed the bill into law on July 2, 1964, as Morehouse was in recess for the summer. But as the signing was televised, it was watched by the Morehouse family around the country. Indeed, Morehouse was represented by Dr. Martin Luther King Jr. in the East Room of the White House as President Johnson used seventy-five pens to sign the bill into law. Dr. King Jr. was one of the many invited guests to receive one of these pens as a memento.

The following fall, the Morehouse students who had been civil rights protesters, demonstrators, or freedom fighters returned and became civil rights "testers," persons who requested service at public accommodations to see if the law would be followed. There was some resistance, but most businesses obeyed the law. Some of the first public accommodations tests were conducted in the West End business district, less than a mile from the campus. And while some businesses properly served students, others chose to ignore the black customers without any physical efforts to remove the testers. The West End featured a variety of public accommodations: a movie theater, grocery stores, restaurants, banks, dry goods stores, drugstores (with lunch counters), a newsstand, a library, churches, a department store (Sears), garages, service stations, and more. Although the West End was part of Atlanta by 1964, it was also like a town unto itself.

As Jim Crow died all across the city and beyond, Morehouse captured the attention and imagination of the world on December 10, 1964, when the Nobel Peace Prize was awarded to Dr. Martin Luther King Jr. in an elaborately formal ceremony in Oslo, Norway. The Morehouse community took great pride in this significant honor, and they rejoiced in it. One observer was in the first semester of his senior year and remembered the time well. Dr. Mays, who was scheduled to retire with the class of 1965 after serving as president of Morehouse for twenty-five years, broke the news to the student body during the dinner hour on October 14, 1964, shortly after the winner of that coveted prize had been announced to the world. As students sat in the Lane Dining Hall, with its wall of windows facing Lee Street, they saw Dr. Mays approaching the Mays Hall complex. Immediately, they began to question what some recalcitrant Morehouse brother might have done to warrant a personal visit from the president and, possibly, a rebuke. But as the president came closer, they could see the countenance of his classically chiseled face, and the lineaments did not carry disdain, but, rather, they reflected joy. He entered Lane Dining Hall, where the beloved Clinton "Pop" Warner maintained watch as a sentinel, allowing ingress only to those who followed the rules and qualified to move inside. After entering the room, in his distinctive, somewhat raspy baritone, Dr. Mays made the great announcement. The Norwegian Nobel Committee had awarded the 1964 Nobel Peace Prize to Dr. Martin Luther King Jr., making him only the third black man to be so honored, preceded only by Ralph Bunche and John Luthuli. Hearing the announcement, Lane Dining Hall erupted in applause and other celebratory acts: hugs, hoots, hollers, and handshakes. The celebration continued long after the dinner hour and well into the evening.

Dr. Mays, a forward-thinking leader, immediately began planning how Morehouse College, the alma mater of the newly minted Peace Prize winner, would honor Dr. King. The prize is awarded to those who have "done the most or the best work for fraternity between nations, for the abolition or reduction of standing armies and for the holding and promotion of peace congresses." The committee, appointed by the Norwegian Parliament, accepts nominations and bases their decisions on recommendations from a panel of advisors. The peace prize is now awarded in a ceremony held at the Oslo, Norway, City Hall, and is the only Nobel Prize not presented in Stockholm, Sweden, but when Dr. King Jr. received his Nobel, it was awarded in the atrium of the University of Oslo Faculty of Law. Dr. King Jr.'s entourage included his wife, Coretta Scott King; his administrative assistant, Dora McDonald; his sister, Christian Farris King; and others. As they all left Atlanta for Oslo, members of the Morehouse Glee Club and many other well-wishers gathered at the old Atlanta Airport to send them off. The singers led the crowd in song, including the moving hymn "Dear Old Morehouse."

The ceremony for Dr. King was very formal, and the laureate wore morning dress. Back in Atlanta at Morehouse, Dr. Mays was preparing for the return of the college's most celebrated graduate and making plans to honor this esteemed member of the class of 1948. Mays was determined to see that Morehouse was the first to honor Dr. King Jr. and to make sure the city of Atlanta, his hometown, did the same. The first plan was a slam dunk, but the second objective would take some doing. Dr. Mays opined that "Atlanta had never been entirely happy over his leadership. Some considered him too radical, forever shaking the foundations of the status quo. Not only white Atlanta voiced this opposition—many Negro leaders were jealous of the man's tremendous power, his stature, his leadership, others sincerely believed that he was stirring up trouble."[18]

The Morehouse convocation honoring Dr. King Jr. was held in Samuel Archer Hall—the old gym—on January 21, 1965. The hall was packed to capacity, and the mostly black audience witnessed the presentation of citations from the student body and faculty. The Glee Club sang "Behold Man" by Ron Nelson among other selections to honor the former member of the acclaimed men's chorus. In his address, Dr. King Jr. spoke about the state of civil rights in the United States. Meanwhile, preparations were underway for a dinner sponsored by Atlanta's black and white leaders. Led by Dr. Mays, a committee was formed consisting of Ralph McGill, Rabbi Jacob Rothschild, and Archbishop Paul J. Hallinan "to get things going." Then a larger group was organized with representatives of the Atlanta Christian Council, the Conference of Christians and Jews, the Southern Christian Leadership Conference, the National Association for the Advancement of Colored People, and various Negro ministerial groups. Dr. Mays recalled, "We formed a small committee. Then a larger group was called together.... We wanted the celebration in the heart of Atlanta, downtown, not in the black community. The State of Georgia and the city of Atlanta had never produced a Nobel Peace Prize winner, so why shouldn't Atlanta rise to the occasion, welcome the opportunity to expand its image in the nation and the world?"[19] Plans for the dinner got off to a slow start, but after *The New York Times* carried an article criticizing Atlanta for being slow to finalize its plans for the event, and after Mayor Ivan Allen Jr. garnered strong support for it, plans were implemented for the first large integrated event in the history of the city.

The dinner was held at the Dinkler Plaza Hotel on Forsyth Street in downtown Atlanta on January 27, 1965, at seven o'clock in the evening. Eight hundred guests were expected, but thirteen hundred people were packed into the ballroom of the hotel. One firsthand attendee described

---

[18] Mays, Born to Rebel, 270.

[19] Ibid., 271–73.

the event. The cover of the dinner program read: A RECOGNITION DINNER *honoring* Dr. Martin Luther King, Jr. Winner of the 1964 NOBEL PEACE PRIZE, *Sponsored by* CITIZENS OF ATLANTA. A list of the previous American winners of the prize included Theodore Roosevelt, Elihu Root, Woodrow Wilson, Ralph Bunche, and General George Marshall. The program followed this order: Greetings were given by Rabbi Rothschild, followed by the singing of the National Anthem, an invocation by the Reverend Samuel Williams, the introduction of the dais, and then dinner was served. Mayor Ivan Allen Jr., Bishop Ernest L. Hickman, Rev. Edward A. Driscoll, Senator Leroy Johnson, and Archbishop Hallinan all gave tributes.

The honoree was introduced by Dr. Mays, and in his renowned oratorical style, Dr. King Jr. gave a powerful address. In part, he said,

> I must confess that I have enjoyed being on this mountain-top, and I am tempted to want to stay here and retreat to a more quiet and serene life. But something within reminds me that the valley calls me in spite of all of its agonies, dangers and frustrating moments. I must return to the valley. Something tells me that the ultimate test of a man is not where he stands in moments of comfort and the moments of convenience, but where he stands in moments of challenge and moments of controversy.

Making it clear why the civil rights struggle had to continue, Dr. King said he "must return to the valley—a valley filled at the same time with little Negro boys and girls who grow up with ominous clouds of inferiority forming in their little mental skies, a valley filled with millions of people who, because of economic deprivation and social isolation, have lost hope, and see life as a long and desolate corridor with no exit sign." Indicating the inhumanity of those who tried to stop the movement and the pressing need to eliminate poverty, he said,

> I must return to the valley—a valley filled with literally thousands of Negros in Alabama and Mississippi who are brutalized, intimidated and sometimes killed when they seek to register and vote. I must return to the valley all over the South and in the big cities of the North—a valley filled with millions of our white and Negro

> bothers who are smothering in an air-tight cage of poverty in the midst of an affluent society.[20]

The speech was well received, and the audience gave Dr. King Jr. a thunderous ovation before all—black, white, Protestants, Catholics, Jews, politicians, businessmen, professors, students, and citizens in general—joined hands and sang "We Shall Overcome, Someday."

The dinner ended with the presentation of gifts and a benediction given by the Reverend Ralph D. Abernathy. The fairly largely Morehouse presence at the dinner left with a feeling of pride and a determination to sustain the image and reputation that were underscored by the honor bestowed on its most prominent alumnus. Among the Morehouse students who attended the dinner were David Walker, president of the SGA; Glee Club member Robert Davidson, who would later be elected chairman of the Morehouse Board of Trustees; and future congressman Sanford Bishop.

Although Dr. King Jr. was acclaimed around the world, not all who served on the Morehouse Board of Trustees unanimously endorsed him or his work. It took a while before he would join his father, Dr. Martin Luther King Sr., on the board. Some members felt that his presence would bring honor and prestige to the board, but others bitterly opposed his election. "It was rumored that one trustee would not sit in the same room with Dr. King."[21] Despite the open racism exhibited by one member, most of the other members of the largely white Morehouse board were supportive of the idea that black men could be educated to be stewards in service to their communities. By the mid-1960s, Morehouse Men were being recognized for giving service to a wider swath of Americans. Charles Merrill, the financier from Boston who was the chairman of the board, was a major benefactor to Morehouse. Nonetheless, the mostly white board harkened back to a time when the school was under the authority of the American Baptist Home Mission Society and its all-white board which governed the Morehouse. After much wrangling, the board finally elected Dr. King Jr. to the board in 1966, and he served until tragedy struck in 1968. As the board of trustees of Morehouse College were

---

[20] Ibid.

[21] Ibid.

arguing over the election of Dr. King Jr. to membership, the tides of change were rising and roiling all over the country, and Morehouse was not isolated from the effects of the tsunamic aftermath.

The march from Selma to Montgomery, the Voting Rights Act, and the Watts Riot were among the major sociopolitical events that troubled the waters of the American culture. In February 1965, just weeks before the events at the Edmund Pettus Bridge in Selma, Alabama, sparked widespread criticism of the United States, Morehouse College celebrated its 98th Founders' Day. The featured speaker was the Reverend Harry S. Wright, who reminded the audience that the continuation of Morehouse was not guaranteed, and that the future of the college depended on the support it received from alumni and friends. It would take money to continue to produce graduates who would become stewards to society.

David Walker, student body president, agreed with Reverend Wright, pointing out that education was the answer that might avoid a potential World War III. Two weeks after the founders' commemoration at the college, on February 25, 1965, Malcolm X, also known as El-Hajj Malik El-Shabazz, was assassinated while addressing an audience of followers at the Audubon Ballroom in New York City. The self-defense philosophy was embraced by some members of the Morehouse community and was gaining more believers in 1966 with the emergence of the Black Panther Party and the Black Power Movement. The Civil Rights Movement formerly led by Dr. King continued to protest and demonstrate. Success had come the year before, in 1964, with the enshrinement of the Civil Rights Act, and in 1965, the struggle continued for the right to vote without favor of person and impediments. Those who participated in the march from Selma to Montgomery, Alabama, were motivated by the killing of Jimmie Lee Jackson, an activist who had been shot just days before the demonstration. The marchers faced violence and death, most notably during "Bloody Sunday," when Alabama State Troopers brutally attacked them, but the marchers eventually completed their journey.

The conscience of United States Congress was enlightened by the March from Selma to Montgomery, the May 2nd Children's March in Birmingham, and the June 12th assassination of Medgar Evers. Congress passed the Voting Rights Bill, and on August 6th, President Lyndon Johnson signed the bill into law as the Voting Rights Act of 1965. Georgia was among the states affected by the Voting Rights Act of 1965, as were most of the states in the Old Confederacy. By the end of that year, thousands of voters in Georgia were among the 250,000 African Americans whose names had been added to the voter registration rolls. "The passage of the Voting Rights Act of 1965 marked the end of the first phase of the black revolution," says Robert Brisbane. "It also marked the beginning of the eclipse of Martin Luther King and his brand of leadership. The 'mood' podium of the nation's black population was changing. From here on it would be black power, black nationalism, the black experience—just so it was black."[22]

The Black Power Movement and the Black Studies Movement were just months away when the Voting Rights Act of 1965 went into effect. Morehouse College and its constituents would fit prominently in these movements as its students strove to wear the crown. The shift in the philosophy of black Americana did not shift the mission of Morehouse College. The college continued to educate men, who were developing a new sense of black consciousness, for service to their communities. The upper middle-class culture that had been the hallmark of a Morehouse education began to change, but not fast enough for some constituents. As the consciousness of black Americans, including students and faculty at Morehouse College, was evolving, a change in leadership at the esteemed institution was also imminent: President Benjamin Elijah Mays was retiring.

---

[22] Brisbane, *Black Activism,* 103–104.

Chapter 12

"The Crown of Love": The End of the Era of the Great Schoolmaster

At the end of the spring semester in 1965, Dr. Benjamin Elijah Mays had served as the president of Morehouse College for twenty-five years, but he had been associated with the college for twenty-eight, counting the three years he served the school in the 1920s. Officially, June 30, 1965, marked his twenty-fifth anniversary.

During this period, the college witnessed dramatic growth in all areas, including the student body, faculty, administration, and campus footprint. But it was the branding of Morehouse College as a distinctive, exceptional institution that educated black men for stewardship that saw the most spectacular recognition across the nation and the world. The college paid tribute to Dr. and Mrs. Mays at the ninety-eighth commencement banquet with words of honor.

> When Benjamin Elijah Mays gave up the deanship of the Howard University School of Religion in 1940 to become Morehouse's sixth president,...Morehouse College was financially insecure, tiny, but already a respectable image of educational vitality on the world scene. The faculty for the first of these twenty-five years had only four persons, including the president, with earned doctorates. At the end of the twenty-five years, thirty persons on the Morehouse faculty had doctorates.

With regard to the school's graduates, the most important representation of the success of any school, "[of] 117 Morehouse men who had earned the highest academic degree, 43 (40%) of these received their baccalaureate degrees since 1940." In terms of faculty compensation and the endowment, "in 1940, the average faculty salary was $1,780.72. At the end of twenty-five years the average salary is $8,211. The endowment in 1940 was $1,114,688.16. In twenty-five years it had grown to $3,677,623.47." During the Mays presidency, "a total of $15,000,000 had been raised by the president for endowment, land, renovation of old buildings, construction of new buildings, faculty salaries, scholarships, grants, and special projects." Eighteen new buildings, including faculty housing, had been constructed, and six and a half acres had been purchased from Urban Renewal for the expansion of the footprint of the college. The college's early-admission program, pre-college programs, special reading programs for enrichment, and its remedial reading program were cited as "daring initiatives" taken during the Mays era[1]. All of these gains and development were made with the persistent idea that black men could be educated and, as graduates, be of service to their country and the world. To do this, Morehouse wanted to keep a quality faculty and provide a good living and learning environment for its students.

Morehouse was still financially insecure, though, with a limited endowment, and considered small compared with larger universities, with their tens of thousands of students. But under the far-reaching leadership of Benjamin E. Mays, Morehouse College had gone beyond mere academic respectability. Morehouse's "bigness" was not in student population or financial resources but in the quality of the educational program that had led to its earned recognition as a leading liberal arts college.

Dr. Mays was asked to remain at the college until 1967, when Morehouse would celebrate its centennial, and he accepted. Emerging in the mid-sixties, the Free Speech Movement (University of California at Berkeley, 1964), the Black Power Movement (Oakland, California, 1966), and the Black Studies Movement (San Francisco, 1966) took their cues from the black Civil Rights Movement. By the end of the 1960s, these three significant social and political movements would find expression among the students of Morehouse. But social behavior (culture) does not necessarily change without confrontation, conflict, concession, and consensus. Such was the case at Morehouse between 1969 and 1971.

Sociologist and author E. Franklin Frazier began noticing changes in the entire orientation and aim of higher education for black students in the 1950s. "It was natural that as the result of the revolt against missionary education, these institutions would lose much of their piety.... Only in the smaller and isolated schools did the tradition of piety linger." Regarding

[1] *Alumnus*, Commencement Issue, 1965.

respectability, Frazier asserted that it was "more a matter of external marks of high standard" and "less a question of morals and manners." Frazier had made keen observations and found that "as the children of the Negro masses have flooded the colleges, it was inevitable that the traditional standards of morals and manners would have to give way.... A chance for a college education represented for them the chief means of achieving social and economic mobility. The colleges had to make concessions to their poor educational and social backgrounds."[2] Social and cultural changes were afoot at Morehouse in the late 1960s, but many of the old traditions survived. Chapel attendance, with its emphasis on piety, morals, and manners, was one of the survivors. All of these actions were part of the making of the Morehouse Man, the whole man.

The Black Power Movement and the Black Studies Movement were beginning to capture national attention as the Morehouse Centennial Committee began its work. "The Black Power Movement ushered in a new dialog about the relations of power in society and the university, the pervasive character of racism, and the need for struggle to overturn the established order and create a more just society." Morehouse students who embraced the philosophy of black power "stressed the importance of self-determination—cultural, political and economic, and the need for power in achieving and maintaining it. They also argued for a relevant education, an education that was meaningful for the students, useful to the community, and reflective of the realities of society and the world."[3] And so, by the time Morehouse celebrated one hundred years of successes and failures, the light of a new age in the history of the college was dawning. The line of demarcation would occur in 1969. In 1967, however, Dr. Mays and the enshrined traditions were still in place, and Morehouse was Morehouse: a place where men were developed. As the candle in the dark burned brightly, the centennial year was at hand.

Morehouse's "centennial class" entered the college in the fall of 1963 and included among its members Robert Claude Davidson Jr., who would become chairman of the school's board of trustees in 2011. Once the

---

[2] Frazier, *Black Bourgeoisie*, 73–74.

[3] Maulana Karenga, *Introduction to Black Studies* (Los Angeles: University of Sankore Press, 2010) 11.

Morehouse Centennial Committee's work was completed, the college began its celebrations in January 1967, but the principal events took place during Founders' Week, February 12th to the 18th, 1967. On February 14th, Morehouse College was officially one hundred years old. A century of service to mankind, building leaders for the professional, social, and political life of this country, is no small achievement for an educational institution established in the wake of Emancipation. Founded to train former slaves and their descendants, the school was nurtured in a hostile environment that it had to cope with and ultimately transform through its impact. As Morehouse assessed its past—fraught with some failures but marked by an overall record of achievement—and its promising present, it began a second century with an assurance and confidence born from its meritorious past. A fitting way to recognize the "building of men for leadership" was the election of Hugh Morris Gloster, '31, as the seventh president of Morehouse, the school's first alumnus to be so honored.[4]

The commemoration began in November 1966 with a convocation at which Dr. Martin Luther King Jr., class of '48, was the keynote speaker. Founders' Week events began a few months later, opening on Wednesday, February 15, 1967, when the Glee Club was presented in concert with the Atlanta Symphony Orchestra. Wendell Phillips Whalum, '52, directed the men's chorus while Robert Mann, associate conductor, led the orchestra. Elizabeth Allen of Louisiana State University was the guest soloist. The concert was held in Samuel Howard Archer Hall, the college's largest venue at the time, before a packed and appreciative audience that expressed "its enthusiastic reaction in several standing ovations." Herald I. Starks, Whalum's former professor at the University of Iowa, was the guest conductor for the concert. The Glee Club and orchestra performed Requiem in D Minor by Luigi Cherubini, and Allen, soprano, sang Rhapsodie, Op. 53 by Johannes Brahms. Post-concert socials notwithstanding, the second event of the celebratory week took place the next morning in Sale Hall Auditorium.

A panel discussion on "Morehouse in Its Second Century" was moderated by Dr. Robert H. Brisbane, professor of political science, and featured Dr. Jeannette Hume of the Department of English, Dr. Henry C.

---

[4] *Alumnus* (Spring 1967).

McBay of the Department of Chemistry, De. Samuel W. Williams of the Department of Philosophy, Roswell Jackson Jr., president of the student government association, and Samuel Kelton Roberts and Richard Thomas White, members of the centennial class of 1967. According to one voice that was not on the panel, but a strong presence at the time, "Among the top priorities of the college's second century is a fully integrated student body drawn from all races and cultures."[5] One white student from Hesston, Kansas, graduated in the class of 1966. Howard T. Zehr Jr. graduated with a 4.0 grade point average and was one of four Morehouse graduates to be awarded the prized Woodrow Wilson Fellowship. And in the tradition of thousands of other Morehouse graduates, Zehr earned advanced degrees—a master's at the University of Chicago and a doctorate at Rutgers. Zehr was a Morehouse Man. The mission of the college to educate black men for scholarship and stewardship was changing.

At eleven o'clock on Friday morning, February 17th, the physics, mathematics, and foreign languages building was dedicated in honor of legendary math professor Claude B. Dansby. That evening, the night before the centennial convocation, the anniversary banquet was held in the convention hall of the Biltmore Hotel in downtown Atlanta. The event was historic not only for what it celebrated, but also because it was held at a public facility heretofore restricted to white patrons only. The banquet hall was filled to the corners with Morehouse Men and their wives from across the country who paid $10 per plate to attend the dinner. Dr. Howard Washington Thurman, '23, dean emeritus of Marsh Chapel at Boston University, and one of America's greatest preachers, was the principal speaker for the occasion. Dr. John W. Davis, '11, president emeritus of West Virginia State College, was the toastmaster for the banquet, which opened with an invocation delivered by Dr. Thomas Kilgore Jr., '35, pastor of Second Baptist Church in Los Angeles. The evening ended with the benediction by Dr. James Hudson, '26, chaplain at Florida A&M University in Tallahassee. The Morehouse Quartet (Ronald Garcia, '68, James Reed, '67, Herman Cain, '67, and Johnny Hamilton, '68) sang two selections, and Clarence Render Jr., '50, professor of music at Grambling College in Louisiana, accompanied by Herman Taylor, played two violin

---

[5] Ibid., 1.

solos: Romance in F Major by Ludwig van Beethoven and Tzigane by Joseph Maurice Ravel. The centennial banquet menu consisted of

Coupe of Fresh Fruit Hawaienne, Celery Hearts, Queen Olives
Broiled Sirloin Steak Maitre d'Hotel
Delmonico Potatoes, Green Beans a la Francaise
Salade Chiffonade, French Dressing
Bombe Voile with Melba Sauce, Petit Fours Glaces, Coffee.

Before the keynote speaker was presented, reports were presented by Morehouse alumni clubs from across the nation, and a roll call of alumni participants in the audience was made. Then the eminent Dr. Thurman began his address by reading from his *Inward Journey*. He then spoke on "The Private Value of an Education," pointing out that the most important thing in life was the development of the self, to actualize the potential of the self, and to follow it all the way to some end, to experience oneself as a human being.[6] Following Dr. Thurman's "characteristically moving spiritual message," President Mays presented Dr. Gloster and Mrs. Beulah Gloster, the seventh president and new first lady of Morehouse, to a standing ovation. The centennial banquet, by all accounts, was a great success. In the midst of a heightened esprit de corps, thousands of dollars were contributed to the college to advance its educational programs. Like its students, Morehouse was "chasing the crown," trying to grow tall enough to wear it.

The centennial convocation was convoked at three o'clock in the afternoon on Saturday, February 18, 1967, as the second in a series of four assemblies to be held during the hundredth anniversary of Morehouse College. As the participants in what was described as "the most brilliant, colorful, and impressive affair ever held at Morehouse" gathered on the quadrangle to join the processional, onlookers were captivated by the rainbow of colors in the academic regalia worn by the delegates. Seven hundred or more persons in full academic regalia participated in the long processional that included the Morehouse senior class, the Morehouse faculty, 337 official delegates of colleges and universities, including

[6] Ibid., 6.

Harvard, as the oldest (founded in 1636), leading the group, with an additional thirty-seven delegates from learned societies and professional organizations, twenty-four delegates from foundations, corporations, and governmental agencies, and one hundred or so Morehouse alumni from the professions of business, education, dentistry, law, medicine, and more. "Greetings and citations, many of them bound in leather cases, were received from several hundred American colleges and universities, from 24 foreign universities, from 26 foundations and corporations, from 12 learned societies, from 8 government agencies, from 8 government officials (national and state), from civic organizations and the news media, including N.B.C. and *Life* magazine."[7]

The long but impressive procession entered Samuel Howard Archer Hall to "The Centennial March" (based on the melody of the *Morehouse College Hymn*), which had been composed for the occasion by Frederick Tillis of Grambling State College. President Mays presided over the convocation. Once the delegates and those on the dais were seated, Isaac Watts's "O God, Our Help in Ages Past," a Morehouse standard, was sung. The Right Reverend Paul J. Hallinan, Archbishop of the Catholic Diocese of Atlanta, gave the invocation, and Dr. Mays gave the occasion. Greetings were expressed by Ivan Allen Jr., mayor of the city of Atlanta, after which comments on the future of Morehouse were made by Calvin Anderson Brown Jr., '52, president of the Morehouse Alumni Association, and Roswell Francis Jackson Jr., '67, president of the Morehouse Student Government Association. The Glee Club then performed "Laudate Dominum" by Frederick S. Converse. "Praise ye the Lord, for it is good to sing unto our God." Following this beautiful performance, Dr. Mays introduced Dr. James McNaughton Hester, president of New York University, who gave the centennial convocation address. Dr. Hester began his speech by saying, "This celebration has great significance, and it is a high honor to participate in it. The Centennial of Morehouse College is significant because it is the occasion to celebrate the achievements of the century since 1867. This celebration is also significant because it invites us to consider the course of Morehouse during the century ahead." President Hester closed his address with these thoughts: "If Morehouse can continue to

[7] Ibid., 9.

demonstrate exceptional ability for realizing the values of liberal education by preparing young people with unusual personal motivation, breadth of knowledge and high ideals, it will, in my opinion, move into the twenty-first century and beyond as one of the most highly prized assets of Atlanta, of the South and of our country."[8] After the applause for Dr. Hester's insightful remarks, the audience sang "God of Our Father," the hymn by Daniel C. Roberts. It was then time for the awarding of honorary degrees. Five honorary degrees were conferred: Francis Stephenson Hutchins, doctor of laws; James Wesley Silver, doctor of humane letters; Lorimer D. Milton, doctor of laws; James McNaughton Hester, doctor of laws; and John Hervey Wheeler, doctor of humane letters. Immediately preceding the benediction, given by the Reverend Roland Smith, '26, former pastor of First Baptist Church of Little Rock, Arkansas, the audience was conducted in the singing of the college's hymn, "Dear Old Morehouse," by its composer, James Orville Brown Moseley, class of 1929. The recessional concluded the convocation, marking the final event.

The Morehouse College Centennial Commencement program held on May 30, 1967, was the third convocation commemorating and celebrating the college's one hundred years of existence. It began at 10:30 A.M. in Samuel Howard Archer Hall gymnasium. After what was described as a "colorful procession of seniors, faculty, and alumni, proceeding from mid-campus with pomp and pageantry," the exercises began. Charles Merrill, chairman of the Morehouse Board of Trustees, presided at the centennial commencement, which processed into the hall to Henry Purcell's "Trumpet Tune" and Floor Peters's "Entrata Festiva," played by Dr. Wendell P. Whalum, organist.

President Mays, who was soon to retire (June 30), was the principal speaker, and his address was titled "Twenty-Seven Years of Success and Failure at Morehouse." After historically recalling the notions of black inferiority, Dr. Mays reminded the commencement audience of the pledges he made when he assumed the presidency of Morehouse College in 1940, and, in a cursory assessment, said, "I have no regrets in retiring from the presidency of Morehouse at this juncture in history. I regret, however, that what had been accomplished in these 27 years trails so far behind my

[8] Ibid., 14–16.

dreams for the college and so far behind what I had aspired for Morehouse to be that I feel a sense of failure. I wish I could tell you today that the future of Morehouse was guaranteed in the stars." All—alumni, faculty, trustees, students, friends, and Dr. Mays himself—must share the blame for the failures of the college, he asserted. The school had become an equal partner in the Atlanta University Affiliation, enrollment had increased from 358 to 962, the number of graduates who went on to graduate and professional schools had risen—in fact, 118 Morehouse Men had earned the PhD degree—and the quality and quantity of the faculty had improved, based on his belief that "there is no virtue in an academically weak faculty." The physical plant, too, had grown during his tenure as president. But the endowment had not grown as he had expected, having only gone from a book value of $1,114,00 in 1940 to $4,500,000 in 1967.[9] And yet the college had seen much success in its graduates due, in part, he argued "to the philosophy drilled into them that the Morehouse man can succeed in the world despite crippling circumstances under which he had to live." Still, though, the Great Schoolmaster was not satisfied. "The College had done well in recent decades, but not well enough." Soon-to-be President Emeritus Mays was speaking about the "crown of love" Morehouse Men had for their alma mater, which motivated them to succeed. When a graduate wore the insignia of a Morehouse Man, he was expected to succeed. He was expected to continue his education and do well in his chosen profession.

Looking toward the future for his beloved college, Dr. Mays said that "one fact is clear: Morehouse cannot live on its past reputation." Reflecting on education for African Americans during slavery and segregation, he said, "The power structure in politics, economics, and education, never intended to make schools for Negroes first-rate.... Desegregation, won through court decision, congressional legislation, and demonstration, had not changed this basic philosophy of inequality." The future of Morehouse and other historically black colleges and universities was not assured, the great educator argued. The "battle for justice and equality in the future," Dr. Mays said, "will not be against the [George] Wallaces, the [Ross] Barnetts, and the [Lester] Maddoxes, but against the subtlety of

---

[9] Ibid., 30.

our 'liberal friends' who will wine and dine with us in the swankiest hotels, work with us, and still discriminate against us when it comes to money and power." He was of the opinion that a seismic shift in the economic, political, and philanthropic terrain should be "the first order of the day." Morehouse, therefore, must attract funding "to 'buy' intellectually talented students just as many of the predominantly white institutions are able to do with finances given for that purpose." Morehouse's record and reputation had been built on the success of its alumni in the best post-baccalaureate schools. "If this record is diminished," Mays asserted, "we will be reduced to a role of mediocrity." The message was clear: alumni needed to give more to their beloved "Dear Old Morehouse." Dr. Mays pointed out that "Yale, Columbia, Harvard, Princeton, and Chicago will survive because their graduates will see to it that they do. Morehouse men have not accumulated millions, but if they really cared, they could contribute to the college $100,000 a year, and in time, $500,000." It was his hope that if Morehouse Men gave more, corporations and foundation and friends would do the same, potentially contributing millions of dollars to the college. "This is my final plea to the Morehouse alumni. If you really care, the future of Morehouse is secure. If you do not care, its future is precarious."[10]

Before Dr. Mays took his seat to enthusiastic applause and adulation, the members of the senior class rose to their feet at his request. He said to them, "What you have done, poorly or well, can never be erased. What you should have done and neglected to do cannot now be done. Not even an omnipotent God can blot out the deeds of history." Quoting the beautiful verse of Omar Khayyam, the renowned Persian polymath who was a philosopher, mathematician, astronomer, and poet, Dr. Mays, the accomplished preacher, sermonized that "the Moving Finger writes, and having writ, Moves on, nor all your piety nor Wit, Shall lure it back to cancel half a line, Nor all your Tears wash out a Word of it." Recognizing the irrevocability of the past, Mays advised the class of 1967 "to look to the future with courage and confidence." And in a poignant voice that caused the hearts of many in the audience to quiver, Dr. Mays said,

[10] Ibid.

> Twenty-five years from today it is more than likely that my days will long since have passed and you will be about 47 years old. I hope you will return in 1992 to celebrate your twenty-fifth anniversary. I trust you will return economically secure in houses and land, stocks and bonds, cars and bank accounts, intellectually secure in the constant pursuit of knowledge, and affectionately secure with fine wives and handsome children.

The seniors were encouraged to be the very best at whatever careers they pursued. The eminent sixth president of Morehouse College closed his valedictory address with a petition:

> My dear young friends, I do not know what happiness is and I do not think it is important that you be happy. But it is important that you find your work and do it as if you were sent into the world at this precise moment in history to do your job. If happiness can be achieved, it will be found in a job well done and in giving and not in receiving. May the years ahead be motivating, challenging, and inspiring years, and may they be gracious and kind to you and bring success in all the good things you do. *Leben Sie wohl!* Farewell!

As Dr. Mays returned to his seat, the capacity audience leapt to their feet in thunderous applause for the Great Schoolmaster and for his insightful, candid, and poignant words. It was a fitting tribute to the man who had devoted the last twenty-seven years of his life to Morehouse College. As the applause subsided, the Glee Club, featuring baritone soloist Henry Gore, sang "I Will Praise Thee, O Lord," by Heath.

Prizes were awarded by Dean Brailsford Brazeal, tenor Thomas Kimball led the singing of the traditional spiritual "Mt. Zion," and then Dr. Mays conferred degrees on the members of the centennial class. After they had been awarded their baccalaureate degrees, the new graduates, the members of the Glee Club, the dignitaries on the dais, and the entire audience sang "Dear Old Morehouse." The benediction was delivered by the Reverence L. Venchael Booth, pastor of Zion Baptist Church in Cincinnati and executive secretary of the Progressive National Baptist Convention. The recessional music was Purcell's "Trumpet Voluntary," and the line of march was instructed to end at the grave of President John

Hope, where the alumni held a brief service of remembrance. But this did not mark the end of the commemoration and celebration of the Morehouse College Centennial. Still to come was the "Testimonial Banquet for President Benjamin Elijah Mays," which was held on Wednesday evening, May 31, 1967, the next day. The banquet was a black-tie event hosted by the Morehouse Alumni Club of Atlanta at the Marriott Motor Hotel. This "most beautiful and memorable" dinner was attended by approximately one thousand enthusiastic and formally attired admirers who paid $10 per meal to honor the "great educational statesman."[11]

Dr. Albert W. Dent, a member of the Morehouse class of 1926 and president of Dillard University in New Orleans, was the presiding toastmaster. The principal speaker for the occasion was Dr. James Madison Nabrit Jr., class of 1923 and president of Howard University in Washington, DC. Other speakers were Ivan Allen Jr., the mayor of Atlanta; John Hervey Wheeler, class of 1929, who spoke for the Morehouse Board of Trustees; Professor Lucius M. Tobin, who represented the Morehouse faculty; Sanford Dixon Bishop Jr., president-elect of the Morehouse Student Government Association; Dr. Calvin A. Brown Jr., class of 1952 and president of the Morehouse National Alumni Association; Dr. Rufus E. Clement, president of Atlanta University; Dr. Stephen Wright, president of the United Negro College Fund; and George E. Meares, grand basileus (national president) of Omega Psi Phi Fraternity, Inc., of which Dr. Mays was a member.

Among the many legacies associated with the Mays era at Morehouse, none is greater than the establishment of a Phi Beta Kappa chapter at the college. "It took from 1953 (the years chapters of the Society were established at Fisk and Howard Universities) to 1966 to persuade representatives of Phi Beta Kappa to visit Morehouse to determine whether we qualified for membership," Dr. Mays reported. "In August 1966, the United Chapters of Phi Beta Kappa...voted to admit Morehouse College to membership. Only seven other institutions in the nation were selected that year."[12] The society considers the strengths and weaknesses of the institution in the development of liberally educated students, and attention was

---

[11] Ibid.

[12] Mays, *Born to Rebel*, 187.

paid as to whether the school

> recruits and retains good students and prepares them for graduate study, makes appropriate academic demands on those enrolled in its classes, including opportunities for honors studies for those who are especially capable, develops and maintains a faculty whose preparation and scholarly activity give evidence that they are able to establish and assess those demands, maintains financial resources sufficient to support the institutions' academic programs, and takes due precautions to prevent issues of governance, athletics, religion or politics from subverting the integrity of the institution's dedication to liberal education.[13]

At the time Morehouse applied to become the fourth institution of higher education in Georgia with a Phi Beta Kappa chapter (to join the University of Georgia, Emory University, and Agnes Scott College), seven members of the Morehouse faculty were members of society: Dr. Mays; Dr. Brailsford Brazeal, academic dean; Dr. Elnora Chesterman, English; Dr. Anna Grant, sociology; Dr. Jeannette Hume, English; Dr. Edward Jones, French; and Dr. Samuel H. Neff, physics. And so, after fourteen years of effort, on January 6, 1968, Delta of Georgia was established at Morehouse. The installment ceremony was impressive as it was witnessed by Phi Beta Kappa members from the other chapters in Georgia, the presidents of the Atlanta University Center institutions, trustees of the college, and outstanding students from the public schools in Atlanta. The first students initiated, on Friday, May 17, 1968, were Michael Lucius Lomax, English; Frederic Gordon Ransom, biology; Willie Frank Vann, biology; and Benjamin Frank Ward Jr., music, modern foreign languages, and philosophy. Dr. Mays recalled that since 1953, "Each triennium we had sent out credentials, and after each 'No" we worked harder for the academic excellence which would qualify us. Now the dream had come true." The "crown of love" resonated with the inductees and the guests as they heard Dr. Mays speak. It was evident that he loved Morehouse College as much as any Morehouse Man, and his name would be forever linked to it. He perfectly embodied the ideas—and ideals—expressed by the founders of the college: he was a man who came from dire circumstances who was

---

[13] www.pbk.org.

educated for scholarship and service to his people and the people of the world. Dr. Benjamin Elijah Mays was a living role model for the generation of "Bennie's Boys" who enrolled at Morehouse from 1940 to 1967. A legend in his own right, he left a lasting legacy.

Chapter 13

"Chasing the Crown": Tradition, Change, and Gloster

The age of Benjamin Elijah Mays at Morehouse officially came to an end on June 30, 1967, when Hugh Morris Gloster, a member of the Morehouse class of 1931, became the seventh president of the college. Although many consider the greatest period in the history of the college to have ended with the retirement of the Great Schoolmaster, Mays, the twenty years under Dr. Gloster's leadership were significant in many respects, as were the achievements of the five presidents who would follow him.

The beginning of the Gloster era was without controversy as he was inaugurated in Samuel Howard Archer Hall on Saturday, February 17, 1968. Gloster had been in the president's office for more than seven months by then, after having been presented to the Morehouse community as the school's future president during the centennial events held the previous year. The new president was well-received, and thing were looking up as the Morehouse community looked forward to this new administration and the advancements it would bring to the college.

Hugh Morris Gloster was born in Brownsville, Tennessee, a predominantly African American town about thirty miles northeast of Memphis, on May 11, 1911, the fourth child of John R. and Dora Gloster. He had two brothers, Clarence and Claudius, and one sister, Alice, who died in her teens. Although both had been born during slavery, Gloster's parents nevertheless became educators. John Gloster had attended Nashville's Roger Williams University, an American Baptist Home Mission Society school, and John Hope was a member of the faculty during this time. Roger Williams was the forerunner of LeMoyne-Owen College, where Hugh Gloster's father was a member of its board of trustees, and where he attended before enrolling at Morehouse in 1929. All three of the "Gloster boys"—Clarence, Claudius, and Hugh—graduated from Morehouse College: Clarence pursued a career in medicine, Claudius in music, and Hugh in higher education.

Two years after graduating from Morehouse and earning a master's degree at Atlanta University, Hugh began his teaching career at LeMoyne College in 1933. While at LeMoyne, he became the principal founder of the Association of Teachers of English in Negro Colleges that was the precursor of the College Language Association, the CLA. Gloster taught at Morehouse for several semesters under the presidency of Benjamin Mays before studying for a doctoral degree in English at New York University. During the Second World War, Gloster was an administrator with the United Service Organization (USO) and completed the requirements for the PhD in 1946. With his newly minted doctorate in hand, Dr. Gloster took a teaching position at Hampton Institute (now University) in Virginia, and in 1948 he published *Negro Voices in American Fiction*. During the twenty-one years he worked at Hampton, Gloster distinguished himself as a teacher, scholar, and administrator. It was at Hampton that he coedited with Helen O'Brien and Lillian Voorhees an anthology of student verse titled *The Brown Thrush*, and he wrote a college textbook called *My Life, My Country, My World* that is still in print today. Before his role as the seventh president of Morehouse, Dr. Gloster traveled and lectured in many parts of the world, including Hiroshima, Japan, where he was a Fulbright Fellow. So, Hugh Gloster was well-credentialed and highly qualified to be president of Morehouse College, but he did recall a Baptist minister at Hampton telling him, "Brother Gloster, trying to succeed Dr. Mays is almost like trying to succeed Jesus."

Dr. Gloster gave a speech to the college community in March 1967, less than three months before assuming the presidency of the college. Gloster regarded his return to his alma mater as a homecoming of sorts and recalled how, as a student there in the late 1920s, and in his remarks, he reflected on how he had at that time criticized the food and the daily chapel attendance requirement: "At the time of my graduation from Morehouse, I did not fully realize how much the college had done for me. I came to Morehouse as a boy, but I left as a man. I came as a student, but I left as a potential scholar. I came as a youth with vague vocational goals, but I left as a young man determined to earn the highest degree in my field and to make an excellent record as a graduate student and as a professional educator." Referencing his scholarly interests, he added, "I came with an interest in popular songs, movie stars, and athletic heroes, but I left with a respect for philosophy and religion, with the courage of my convictions, and with a sense of responsibility for the welfare of my own people and of other disadvantaged groups throughout the world." He shared that as a young man, he left Morehouse imbued with the ideals of the founders. After making some historical reflections, Gloster then turned his attention to the needs of the college as he saw them at its centennial. Morehouse needed money, he believed, and land, creative programs, a strong undergraduate curriculum, courageous leaders, and inspiring teachers. The president-elect called upon all who loved Morehouse to give their advice, help, cooperation, support, and encouragement as he began the job of running the school and advancing it into the future. Dr. Gloster called upon all in the Morehouse community to "strive and thrive" with him in guiding the great college into a many-splendored second century. He solicited their cooperation not only as a president-elect appealing to a student body, but also, most of all, as a Morehouse Man appealing to other Morehouse Men.

As he ended his first major speech to the Morehouse students, faculty, and staff, President-elect Gloster admonished them "to reject the battle cry of 'Burn, baby, burn.'" This was in reference to the times, when riots were occurring in many of urban areas, including the Detroit Riot of 1967. "Destruction and death are double-edged swords that inevitably turn and destroy those who wield them," Gloster asserted. "Furthermore, these weapons fertilize the fields of vituperation and violence, insuring a harvest of bitterness and brutality. Approach the problems of men with love in your hearts and logic in your minds, and you will never lose." Gloster then urged the students to embrace the concepts of "Learn, men, learn," "Earn, men, earn," and "Yearn, men, yearn." He believed that "education, if used wisely, can give you the information, the ideas, and the ideals that are so sorely needed to guide men aright in this confused and confusing world." It was pragmatic, the president-elect thought, to "make an honest living for yourself and your families but also to give generously to worthy causes" and to "yearn for a world of love, justice, and freedom—a world in which no man suffers because he is different from another in region, race, religion, or nationality." Before taking his seat to the applause of the those assembled in Sale Hall Chapel, President-elect Gloster taught the students to sing a song he had written for his alma mater titled "They

Must Be Morehouse Men." The actual singing of the song is lost to history, but the words brought to mind the chasing-the-crown behavior that was so valued by Morehouse students and alumni.

The new behavior exhibited by African Americans in the last half of the 1960s was due, in part, to a shift in consciousness. In 1968, the year Hugh Gloster was officially inaugurated as president of Morehouse, two black psychiatrists published a book that went on to become a classic in their field. The scholarship of William H. Grier and Price M. Cobbs, as reflected in *Black Rage*, told what was happening in black America at that time. In chapter 1, titled "Who's Angry," the psychiatrists posit,

> Aggression leaps from wounds inflicted and ambitions spiked. It grows out of oppression and capricious cruelty. It is logical and predictable if we know the soil from which it comes.... And of the things that need knowing, none is more important than that all blacks are angry. White Americans seem not to recognize it. They seem to think that all the trouble is caused by only a few "extremists." They ought to know better. We have talked to many Negroes under the most intimate of circumstances and we know better.[1]

And then the doctors explained why knowing the history of the black experience in America was critically important. "For if the black American is to be truly understood, his history must be made intelligible. It is a history that is interwoven with that of this country, although it is rarely reported with candor. In recent years superficial studies of Negroes have been made. For those few who truly search, the past of the black man is reflected in his daily life." The "black rage" that was sweeping the nation was evident, to one degree, in Dr. Mays's valedictory address at the centennial convocation. And it was evident in the Morehouse student uprising that occurred in less than a year after Hugh Gloster became president of the college. For just as there were grievances that had to be addressed in the black community, there were grievances that needed to be addressed on college campuses around the country. The student movement was well underway by the time Morehouse College celebrated it hundredth anniversary.

Dr. Gloster's inauguration was more elaborate, ceremonial, and

---

[1] Grier and Cobb, *Black Rage* (1968) 1–2.

multifaceted than any of the school's previous inaugurations. The day after the Glee Club's concert, an Inaugural Symposium was held in Sale Hall Auditorium on Friday, February 16, 1968. The theme for discussion was "The Negro College—What Next?," and the panel was composed of scholars and intellectuals, some of them Morehouse alumni. The evening after the symposium, the Morehouse community was in a festive mood, and an air of gaiety permeated the ballroom of the recently opened Hyatt-Regency Hotel in downtown Atlanta. Playwright and poet Raphael "Ray" McIver, '35, was the toastmaster, and the invocation was presented by the Reverend Doctor William Holmes Borders, '29, pastor of Atlanta's Wheat Street Baptist Church. The Morehouse Glee Club and Quartet performed several selections before Dr. John Hope II, '30, introduced Judge George W. Crockett, '31, of Detroit, who edified and electrified the more than one thousand guests with his address. After some levity and sobriety, with reference to his long friendship with Dr. Gloster, and some remarks about the struggles African Americans had endured in the quest for education and respect, Judge Crockett made a powerful statement when he said,

> Fifteen years ago a highly respected Michigan judge remark to me, "The future belongs to the colored man." Today I know that my friend, the late Judge Patrick O'Brien, was right. The future, which is today as well as tomorrow, belongs to the colored man—not because of his skin color but rather because he symbolizes the poor, the exploited and the meek of this earth, an earth which had become a veritable hell because of the selfishness, the exploitation, and the murderous wars of our white brothers.[2]

Judge Crockett then turned his attention to the theme "What I Want for Morehouse," a familiar topic to Morehouse alumni as they "chased the crown." One of the things he wanted was "that Morehouse should become dedicated to the idea of integrating Negroes and poor whites here in the deep South." He mentioned overhearing grumbling on the part of some of the black students at the symposium who were opposed to the idea of Morehouse becoming an integrated school. Judge Crockett argued that "the Negro is not going to be free until that poor white man over on the clay hills of Georgia is free also." He suggested that Morehouse "should

[2] *Alumnus* (Spring 1968): 20.

go out searching [recruiting] for them" and offer scholarships to deserving white students. The idea of a more integrated Morehouse would continue to be an ongoing conversation for the next fifty years, with many students speaking against it, as those students did that night, and ultimately, only a handful of white students would come to enroll at Morehouse from that time to the present day.

Judge Crockett shared that he thought too much emphasis was being put on science at Morehouse and that the emphasis should be on the humanities instead. He was "not so concerned about producing Negroes to go work for Dow Chemical Company and make napalm bombs, [he wanted Morehouse] to produce Negroes to come into the ghettoes and lead Negroes and whites." He also believed that the college should educate more African students for leadership roles in Africa, and that the faculty needed to encourage students to think and speak their thoughts. Judge Crockett was disturbed by the fact that he did not see more professors being quoted in the press, expressing themselves. To the professors in the audience, he said, "I get the feeling that you're just confining yourselves to the textbook when life is out there, outside the school." Before taking his seat to warm applause, Judge Crockett extended his congratulations to Dr. Gloster, saying, "I have no doubt that he will do a terrific job."[3]

Raphael McIver delivered a tribute he had penned for the occasion, "A Toast to President Gloster and to His Wondrous Wife," and after the Reverend Doctor Martin Luther King Sr., '30, pastor of Ebenezer Baptist Church, offered the benediction, the guests left the banquet, buoyed by what they had experienced and anxiously anticipating the great event that would take place the next afternoon—the inauguration of the seventh president of Morehouse College. This was the first time a president of the college would be installed with such ceremony, pomp, and pageantry.

At this time, Dr. Morris and his wife, Beulah, had already moved into the president's residence on the north side of the campus. Their residency in the house would not last long, though, as problems with the structure were soon discovered, prompting the construction of a new residence for the president and his family on tony Flamingo Drive in southwest Atlanta.

---

[3] Ibid., 20–21.

Inauguration Day was Saturday, February 17, 1968. The grand processional began on the Morehouse quadrangle in the early afternoon, minutes before the beginning of the program and ritual at three o'clock. College organist Dr. Wendell P. Whalum played "Fantasy and Fugue in G Minor" by Johann Sebastian Bach, a crowd pleaser, as the prelude, and the processional was Henry Purcell's "Westminster Suite." The processional marshal led the line of march and was followed by the Morehouse Glee Club, delegates from other colleges and universities, delegates from learned societies and professional organizations, and delegates from a variety of foundations, corporations, and governmental agencies. Then came the members of the Morehouse faculty, representatives of the Morehouse alumni, and the Morehouse senior class. The last group in the processional was the president's party, which included members of the Morehouse Board of Trustees. The convocation presided over by Charles Merrill, chairman of the board of trustees, who gave an opening statement. Then the audience joined the Glee Club in singing the hymn "Rise Up, O Men of God" and became prayerful during the invocation by the Reverend Samuel A. Owen, '11, pastor of Metropolitan Baptist Church in Memphis, Tennessee.

The convocation continued with greetings from Sam Massell, vice mayor for the city of Atlanta (Ivan Allen Jr. was the mayor); Bishop College (Dallas) President M. K. Curry, '32, who represented Stephen J. Wrights, the president of the United Negro College Fund who was unable to attend in person; Jerome H. Holland, president of Hampton Institute, where Dr. Gloster had worked for several decades; Albert E. Manley, president of Spelman College, who represented the Atlanta University Center; Calvin A. Brown, '52, president of the Morehouse Alumni Association; Sanford D. Bishop Jr., '68, president of the Morehouse Student Government Association; and academic dean Brailsford R. Brazeal, '27, who spoke on behalf of the Morehouse faculty. Then the students' representative, Sanford Dixon Bishop, whose legal and political career would eventually take him to the United States Congress, put the occasion in clear perspective with his remarks and this challenge to the new president. Bishop said that he believed that Morehouse should be judged not by the successes or failures of its alumni, but rather by the present status of its faculty, its administration, and its student body. While he knew this was an unconventional way to judge an entity, he argued that the college could "no longer be satisfied by the recital of impressive facts and statistics of the past." Morehouse had to move forward, and its failures, whatever they were, could not be justified by recalling successes from the past. The student body was prepared to work with the new president, he said, if President Gloster provided "powerful and dynamic leadership" to ensure the success of the college in the future. Traditions needed to be respected, but they were not sacred or inviolable. Looking to Dr. Gloster "for guidance as you steer Morehouse through the troubled waters of folly, ignorance, bigotry, injustice, and hatred," Bishop called on him to undertake "comprehensive transformation" at Morehouse as the school began its second century; its survival depended on it. Bishop then congratulated the new president and wished him "good luck and God's blessings." A little more than a year later, the students at Morehouse would take matters into their own hands and force a "comprehensive transformation" that would usher in a new age at the college. But this was Inauguration Day, and the program continued as Dean Brazeal greeted and saluted Dr. Gloster. He recognized the centrality of the faculty in molding the Morehouse Man, but also their irreplaceable roles in helping to think through and chart the school's academic development. There was a concern about the existence of Morehouse as the education landscape became more integrated and a fear that with integration, more top-ranked black male students would choose to attend traditionally white schools. In order to hedge against the possibility, Morehouse needed to generate more scholarship funds to be competitive in attracting academically prepared students. In addition, a good faculty was necessary in order to teach good students. The faculty, in the words of Dean Brazeal, expected Morehouse, under the leadership of Dr. Gloster, "to drive on to even more significant attainment."[4] Following Dean Brazeal's remarks, the Glee Club sang "Thy Will Be Done," by Paul Nelson, which seemed appropriate for the occasion. Following the performance, the official installation of the seventh president of Morehouse College was at hand.

Dr. Hugh Morris Gloster was presented for investiture by John H. Wheeler, '29, the secretary of the Morehouse Board of Trustees, and the

[4] Ibid., 32–35.

investiture was confirmed by Charles Merrill, board chairman. The seventh president subsequently gave his inaugural address. After reminding the audience of African American history, from the "inconsistency between the principles of the Declaration of Independence and...the bringing of slaves to Virginia in 1619," he discussed the significance of the creation of "a school founded for ex-slaves in Augusta, Georgia, in 1867." At this point, Dr. Gloster turned his attention to the present. He pointed out a stark reality. The new president was very much aware of the problems Morehouse faced. The old problems of race and money that challenged the school in her first one hundred years still plagued it as she began her second century. In the first one hundred years, Morehouse competed with black schools for students and funds. But the main task now, as Gloster saw it, "was to compete successfully with wealthier, predominantly white institutions for faculty, students, and support." As the college competed with the best American colleges in an integrated society, he knew that Morehouse had to be first class even in this company. Dr. Gloster elaborated on the issues of expanded competition, racism, and distortion made by non-black scholars and writers when he said, "At the beginning of her second century Morehouse had achieved not only academic respectability but impressive credentials as well." Further, he recited the strength of the college and the academic and professional achievements of many of its graduates. Closing his address, Dr. Gloster said that he realized that the presidency of Morehouse carried with it a heavy responsibility, but he promised to "apply the precepts of my inspiring professors by setting for myself unachievable aims and, in the process of striving to reach them, leave this school stronger and better than it was when I found it. In other words, I plan—along with the board, the Faculty, the Staff, the Student Body, the Alumni, and the friends of the college—'To dream the impossible dream.'"[5]

After the Glee Club sang the Wagner-Mead arrangement of "Prayer" from the opera *Lohengrin*, honorary degrees were awarded to Alvin H. Lane, '19, and Charles Merrill. "Dear Old Morehouse" was sung, and the benediction was delivered by Elder Blair T. Hunt, '12, of the Mississippi Boulevard Christian Church, in Memphis, Tennessee. Following the

[5] Ibid., 38–41.

recessional to William Walton's "Crown Imperial," the Morehouse College Inaugural Convocation was over. This marked the beginning of a new age in the history of the college, an age that would build on an idea conceived in 1867 that had been sustained and flourished over the years as Morehouse developed into a world-class institution of higher education. This was the beginning of new possibilities. But the start of this second century got off to a tragic and turbulent start. Just weeks after Dr. Gloster took office, Dr. Martin Luther King Jr., a member of the distinguished and celebrated class of 1948 and a member of the Morehouse Board of Trustees at the time, was gunned down by an assassin's bullet as he stood on the balcony of the Lorraine Motel in Memphis late in the afternoon on April 4, 1968. It was a tragic time in America, and a tragic and sad time at Morehouse.

Hugh Gloster's inauguration became the model for all future inaugurations at the college. The difference in future inaugurations would lie in the timing and circumstances surrounding the events. In 1968, Morehouse needed money, a constant necessity for the next fifty-three years. The idea of actively recruiting young white men to come to Morehouse, a school that had been founded on the idea that black men could be educated for scholarship and stewardship, posed a dilemma. Integrating whites students into the student body would change the mission of the college. That fact notwithstanding, though, for all intents and purposes, Morehouse has never denied admission to white students, although the school's early mission was the "education of the colored people of the South, especially the training of preachers and teachers." Eventually, a white student enrolled at and graduated from Morehouse, and the school's mission shifted from "training" preachers and teachers to operating as liberal arts college. Young men from Africa were recruited as well, and some did enroll at Morehouse. Martin Luther King Jr.'s inspirational statement that his children, and, by extrapolation, all people should not be judged by the color of their skin but by the content of their character would apply at his alma mater. But he did not live to see the changes that would take Morehouse into the twenty-first century.

On April 4, 1968, Dr. King Jr. was in Memphis to support protesting sanitation workers, who were calling for better pay, benefits, and working conditions. On this same day at Morehouse, students were looking forward to the end of the semester and preparing for examinations and SGA elections (soon after, Nelson Taylor was elected president of the student body). The weather in Atlanta on that fateful day was pleasant and conducive to leisure activities about the campus and at Spelman and the other schools in the area. But early that evening, as a dark cloud settled over the nation, people around the world reacted with shock and horror, sadness and outrage, as they joined the Morehouse Men who were devastated by the news of the assassination of their Morehouse brother. They would all remember where they were when they got the news that Dr. Martin Luther King Jr. had been shot by an assassin's bullet and was dead. He was only thirty-nine years old.

As the Morehouse community and the nation began an understandably long period of mourning, the R. S. Lewis Funeral Home prepared the body of Dr. King Jr. for a viewing in Memphis and for his return home to Atlanta. As the fallen leader lay in repose in a bronze casket, dressed in a black suit, hundreds of mourners viewed his body, many openly sobbing and crying. "Some kissed [Dr.] King's lips, others reverently touched his face. A few women threw their hands in the air and cried aloud in undulating agony."[6]

A deep sense of sadness and anger gripped the campus as reports on the death of Dr. King Jr. registered within the Morehouse community. Students were glued to the television sets in the communal areas of the campus, especially in the Sadie G. Mays Lounge in Mays Hall. They also kept their radios on stations that carried updates on the tragedy, WAOK in particular. Glenwood Ross, '71, was a freshman in 1968 and remembers "there was some anger over his death." He recalled that "there were a few burnings around the campus. So your first thought is that there must be some students involved, and there probably were. But I don't know directly. But there was a lot of anger, [and] the school did a lot to diffuse that anger." As students began to vent their rage, Ross recalled that "we were walking around campus, and for some reason they had us convene in Archer Hall, the old gym. I don't know where they found these

---

[6] http://askville.amazon.com/funeral-home-prepared-Dr-Martin-Luther-King-Jr-'s-body-vie.

speakers, but they had people come to speak to us, and girls from Spelman were there. We just stayed up all night to [hear] these speakers talking about Martin Luther King [Jr.] and how the struggle will go on. It was really inspirational."[7]

While most Morehouse students respected the philosophy and practices of Dr. King Jr., many were followers of Malcolm X and embraced his philosophy. They had read *The Autobiography of Malcolm X* and were familiar with his self-defense violence philosophy. The death of Dr. King Jr. was a call to arms for some of the students at Morehouse and the Atlanta University Centers schools. Joined by militant residents in the surrounding community, they began to express their anger by rioting. The maelstrom continued throughout the evening and into the early hours of Friday, April 5, 1968. In addition to bringing destruction to white-owned businesses near campus, the militant students began to demand that the school change its name from Morehouse to King College. Herbert Wheeler, a member of the class of 1968, remembers "thinking you can't do that. We put our time in, [had] done our work, and you're talking about closing the school [to change its name] and here we are a month and a half away from graduation. You have got to be out of your mind."[8] Neither Morehouse nor Atlanta University Center changed their names to honor the fallen civil rights leader, but classes were suspended until after the funeral, which was held on the Morehouse campus on April 9th, five days after Dr. King Jr. was murdered.

On April 7, 1968, two days before the funeral, President Gloster spoke to the student body, faculty, and staff at 2:15 P.M. in Sale Hall Chapel. Calling Dr. King Jr. "the greatest of all the sons of Morehouse," Dr. Gloster eulogized him, saying, "Today [our] alma mater is sad. Her head is bowed in grief and tears are in her eyes because her noblest son had fallen." Gloster then revealed that plans were being made for the construction of the Martin Luther King Jr. Memorial Chapel, which would "provide not only a much-needed chapel for Morehouse College but also an everlasting shrine to the memory of Dr. King." The president said that the chapel would "become a mecca for those who believe that love and

---

[7] Interview with Glenwood Ross II, '71, by Christopher Owoyemi.

[8] Interview with Herbert Wheeler, '68, by Elbert Byron Green.

nonviolence can solve the problems of mankind. In future years people from all over the world will come to this chapel at Morehouse College in order to gain strength and inspiration from his teachings."[9] And after challenging white America to make a decision between continuing "the old policies of division and distrust, of discrimination and prejudice, of hatred and segregation, of destruction and death" or "follow[ing] the teachings of Jesus Christ who counseled, 'Love thy neighbor as thyself,' and 'Do unto others as you would have them do unto you,,'" President Gloster closed his address to the Morehouse community by quoting from Dr. King Jr.'s "I Have a Dream Speech," calling its vision "a beautiful and attainable dream of a Morehouse Man who was certainly the greatest in achievement and fame and probably the deepest in love and loyalty of all our alumni." President Gloster then issued a challenge to the students.

> We are Morehouse men, and I challenge each of you and myself to help our fallen brother to realize the dream. The dream cannot be realized by the throwers of bricks at passing cars, by the smashers of windows or the looters of goods in stores, by the burners of homes and other buildings, of by the cowards who pull the triggers in the dark and then escape into the night. The dream will be attained by those who love their fellow men and who refuse to see other human beings denied the good life because of a difference in race, creed, color, class, or national origin. Men of Morehouse, we must not be a house divided. We must be a mighty army, united and unafraid. Our fallen leader had issued the call of love and nonviolence to a sick and sinking society and had painted for us his dream of peace and Brotherhood. Let us join hands and show the world that we can make a reality of the dream.

President Gloster, a member of the literati, ended his address by quoting from "Let America Be America Again," the powerful indictment of the American myth of equality by the renowned poet and author Langston Hughes. As the Morehouse assembly ended and the students, faculty, and staff filed down the steps of Sale Hall and onto the campus, some of them lingered to reflect on the touching words they had just heard and prepared their bodies, minds, and hearts for the hours and days ahead. The public

---

[9] *Alumnus* (Summer 1968): 12.

funeral for Dr. Martin Luther King Jr. on the Morehouse campus was just two days away. The college began to prepare the campus to accommodate the large assemblage of people who would come to the campus for the funeral.

As dawn broke on a day of contradictions, thousands of mourners had arrived in Atlanta from across the country and around the world to memorialize Dr. King Jr. It was a stunningly beautiful and sunny spring day in the South, but the heavy dark cloud of grief and anger still hung over the city. The remains of Dr. King Jr. had been returned to Atlanta on Sunday and lay in state in Sisters Chapel on the Spelman campus, an appropriate place since Morehouse had no chapel that suited the solemn occasion. Thousands of mourners viewed his body during the day and into the night. Hanley's Funeral Home on Bell Street was in charge of the funeral arrangement in Atlanta, and on the morning of the obsequies, the casket carrying his remains was borne to Ebenezer Baptist Church on Auburn Avenue in northeast Atlanta. This was Dr. King Jr.'s family's church, where he served as co-pastor with his father, Dr. Martin Luther King Sr., a member of the Morehouse class of 1930. Given the moderate size of Ebenezer, attendance at the first of the two rites was limited. Most of the seats were reserved for dignitaries who came to express their condolences to the King family and their friends and to honor the memory of the fallen leader. Vice President and Mrs. Hubert Humphrey were there, as were Governor and Mrs. Nelson Rockefeller of New York, Senator and Mrs. Eugene McCarthy of Wisconsin, Senator and Mrs. Robert F. Kennedy of New York, former first lady Mrs. John F. (Jacqueline) Kennedy, Richard M. Nixon, Governor and Mrs. George Romney of Michigan, Govern Ronald Reagan of California, Senator Edward Kennedy of Massachusetts, and Mayor John Lindsay of New York City.

Among the throng of activists and entertainers who came to mourn the death of a great Morehouse Man were Harry Belafonte, Sidney Poitier, Nipsey Russell, Eartha Kitt, and Sammy Davis Jr. They were all present in the sanctuary of the historic Ebenezer Baptist Church when Moneta Sleet, an award-winning photographer at *Ebony* magazine, snapped a picture of Mrs. Coretta Scott King cradling her youngest daughter, Bernice, in her arms and to her body. Sleet's photograph won a Pulitzer Prize. The more private obsequy at Ebenezer and the public funeral on the

Morehouse campus were officiated by the Reverend Doctor Ralph David Abernathy, Dr. King Jr.'s closest friend, comrade, and confidant. Among those also present at the church were US Attorney General Ramsey Clark, Secretary of Labor Willard Wirtz, Under Secretary of State Nichols Katzenbach, Secretary of Housing and Urban Development Robert C. Weaver, Massachusetts Senator Edward Brooke, Senator Wayne Morse, Senator Harrison Williams, San Francisco Mayor Joseph Alioto, United Nations Ambassador Arthur Goldberg, United Nations Under Secretary Ralph Bunche, and Atlanta Mayor Ivan Allen.

The funeral of Dr. Martin Luther King Jr. was the largest campus assembly of people in the history of the college. Thousands came from across the nation and waited on the campus quadrangle for hours for the processional to arrive from Ebenezer Baptist Church where a private, invitation-only last rite for the fallen hero was held. After the body of Dr. King Jr. was taken from the sanctuary of the church, the highly polished African mahogany casket was placed onto a wagon drawn by two mules and the march from Ebenezer to Morehouse began. The church service had lasted an hour longer than expected (not in keeping with Dr. King Jr.'s wishes), so by the time the three-and-a-half-mile march to Morehouse got underway, it was early afternoon. By this time, the sun was blazing overhead, and the slow pace of the march took a toll of many of the mourners. The marchers, whose numbers have been estimated at one hundred thousand, moved westward on Auburn Avenue to Courtland Avenue. Turning left on Courtland, the marchers moved toward the Georgia State Capitol, passed the imposing post-Civil War structure, and turned right on Mitchell Street, in front of City Hall, where the marches rested briefly. The mourners, now on the move again, proceeded to Hunter Street (now Martin Luther King Jr. Drive) and continued westward again. Leaving downtown Atlanta, the procession moved along Hunter Street pass historic Friendship Baptist Church, under the iconic bridge on the campus of Morris Brown College, past Paschal's Restaurant complex (where Dr. King Jr. held many meetings with Movement members and members of the Southern Christian Leadership Conference), continued to Ashby Street, and, turning left, processed up the hill on Ashby Street (now Joseph E. Lowery) to Fair Street (now Atlanta Student Movement Boulevard). Now in sight of the Morehouse campus, the phalanx continued eastward on Fair Street to the college's gate and onto the campus green where a pulpit had been constructed in front of Harkness Hall, the college's administration building. The casket was placed on the ground level as the waiting mourners began to weep and wail. By the time the people's procession reached the campus quadrangle, many of the marchers began to pass out. Many of the mourners who were waiting for the arrival of the body of Dr. King Jr., the marchers, and the dignitaries also withered in the heat of an unusually hot spring afternoon. Limousines carrying many of the family members and notables filled Fair Street between Ashby and Chestnut Streets. After the thousands squeezed into the limited space and spilled onto all available space near the campus quadrangle, the public funeral for Dr. Martin Luther King Jr. finally began on the campus of his beloved Morehouse College.

Dr. Wendell P. Whalum, '52, chairman of the Morehouse Department of Music and director of the Glee Club, was the organist for the funeral. He played, as a prelude, "Improvisation on Negro Spirituals" and "Improvisations on *We Shall Overcome*." The Reverend Doctor Ralph D. Abernathy, officiating, led the King family and the platform party as it processed to the pulpit to Dupre's "Cortege." Once the family and speakers were ready, they all joined the assembled throng in singing the standard hymn by Isaac Watts, "O God, Our Help in Ages Past." Prayer was invoked by the Revered Dr. Gardner C. Taylor, president of the Progressive National Baptist Convention. Rabbi Abraham Heschel, a professor at the Jewish Theological Seminary of America, read the Old Testament Scripture. The Morehouse College Glee Club then rose in unison and performed "Balm in Gilead" with emotion that touched the hearts of the mourners. Before the Ebenezer Baptist Church choir sang "Ain't Got Time to Die," another traditional Negro spiritual, the Reverend Franklin C. Frye, president of the National Council of Churches, read the New Testament Scripture.

Tributes to the fallen civil and human rights leader, and Morehouse Man, were given by the Honorable Ivan Allen Jr., mayor of Atlanta; Robert J. Collier, chairman of the board of deacons at Ebenezer; the Most Reverend John J. Wright, bishop of Pittsburgh, Pennsylvania; and Mrs. Rosa Parks, mother of the Montgomery Movement. The Reverend Joseph E. Lowery, chairman of the board of directors for the Southern Christian

Leadership Conference, and the Reverend Andrew J. Young, executive vice president of the SCLC, were on the program, but the crowd had grown weary, fatigued, and unsettled that they were not given their time at the rostrum. Ralph Abernathy described the situation as it unfolded on the Morehouse campus. "I had hoped to be able to start as soon as we arrived [on campus], but the crowd was milling around and talking as if they were at a lawn party rather than at a formal ceremony. When the family arrived, however, they surged around them, and we had chaotic shouting and screaming for about ten minutes." Abernathy continued,

> At that point I wasn't certain we would be able to hold the memorial service. I thought of the mob at Memphis on the first day when Martin had suddenly shouted "Call off the march!" I had that same sense of panic.... As I began to speak, Daddy King (as Dr. Martin Luther King Sr. was affectionately called) jumped to his feet and called out, "Ralph, you've got to get this over! People are dying!" The first time he said it I nodded and went right ahead, but he stood up again after about three minutes. In a voice filled with emotions, Dr. King Sr. jumped to his feet shouting, "We wanted him to live, but they killed him!" Then he turned to me. "You've got to cut it short, Ralph! You've got to cut it short!"

Dr. Abernathy remembered: "I thought things would calm down once we began the program, and several eminent clergy were waiting to speak, but before I got three words out Daddy King was on his feet again. 'Get Mays up there, Ralph, so we can end it!'" At that point Abernathy gave up and called on Dr. Benjamin E. Mays, president emeritus of Morehouse, to give the eulogy. Some of those cut from the speaking lineup included Joseph Lowery, who, Abernathy later opined, might never have quite forgiven him.[10]

Just before Dr. Mays came to the podium, the great gospel singer Mahalia Jackson gave a moving rendition of "Precious Lord, Take My Hand," arranged by Thomas Dorsey. Dr. Mays delivered his "Eulogy of Dr. Martin Luther King, Jr.," which is considered one of the Great Schoolmaster's most powerful speeches. The theological and educational

---

[10] Ralph David Abernathy, *And the Walls Came Tumbling Down* (New York: Harper and Row, Publishers, 1989) 463.

statesman began by recalling his relationship with Dr. King Jr. "To be honored by being requested to give the eulogy at the funeral of Dr. Martin Luther King, Jr., is like asking one to eulogize his deceased son—so close and so precious was he to me. Our friendship goes back to his student days at Morehouse College. It is not an easy task, nevertheless I accept it, with a sad heart and with full knowledge of my inadequacy to do justice to this man." The heart of the funeral speech spoke to the sufferings Dr. King Jr. endured and his steadfast belief in the philosophy of nonviolence "not only in solving the problems of race in the United States but in solving the problems of the world." Referencing some of the biblical prophets—Amos, Micah, Isaiah, Hosea, and Jesus—Dr. Mays preached that "if a prophet is one who interprets in clear and intelligible language the will of God, Martin Luther King, Jr., fits that designation. If a prophet is one who does not seek popular causes to espouse, but rather the causes he thinks are right, Martin Luther qualified on that score." Martin Luther King Jr. was not ahead of his time, Dr. Mays preached. "No man is ahead of his time. Every man is within his star, each in his time. Each man must respond to the call of God in his lifetime and not in somebody else's time."

Reverend Doctor Mays then recited a list of great leaders who died young but made their marks. And with prayers that Dr. King Jr.'s assassin would be apprehended and brought to justice, Dr. Mays gave a charge to the assembled throng. "If we love Martin Luther King, Jr., and respect him, as this crowd surely testifies, let us see to it that he did not die in vain: let us see to it that we do not dishonor his name by trying to solve our problems through rioting in the streets. Violence was foreign to his nature. He warned that continued riots could produce a Fascist state. But let us see to it also that the conditions that cause riots are promptly removed." The president emeritus brought the eulogy to a close, saying, "Morehouse College will never be the same because Martin Luther came by here, and the nation and the world will be indebted to him for centuries to come. It is natural, therefore, that we here at Morehouse and President Gloster would want to memorialize him to serve as an inspiration to all students who study in this Center." And just before the singing of "Dear Old Morehouse," the beautiful and moving song that Dr. King Jr. had sung so many times, Dr. Mays ended his eulogy: "I close by saying to you what Martin Luther King, Jr., believed. If physical death were the price he had to pay to rid America of prejudice and injustice, nothing could be more redemptive. And, to paraphrase the words of the immortal John Fitzgerald Kennedy, permit me to say that Martin Luther King, Jr.'s unfinished work on earth must truly be our own." With arms crossed and hands locked, the audience was led in the singing of the college's hymn and "We Shall Overcome," anthem of the black Civil Rights Movement. The service was concluded and the crowd of mourners began to disperse. Many rushed to their vehicles to join the cortege as it carried Dr. King Jr.'s body to its temporary resting place at South-View Cemetery.

The recessional, to Dvorak's "Largo," was challenged by the enormous crowd, the heat of the day, and the length of time it took to complete the two funerals. But the day of mourning for our slain Morehouse brother had not yet ended as the interment at South-View was yet to come. As the mourners recessed from the Morehouse quadrangle, the cortege, filled with family, dignitaries, and friends, left the north side of the campus on Fair Street. Led by a phalanx of police vehicles, the cortege moved east to Northside Drive, then to Stewart Avenue (now Metropolitan Avenue), turned left on University Avenue and proceeded to McDonough Boulevard, and, finally, to Jonesboro Road, where the historic cemetery is located. The interment service was short but sorrowful. It had taken several hours for the tens of thousands of mourners to vacate the campus for the surrounding communities where their cars, trucks, and buses were parked. The start of Morehouse's second century will be remembered for the untimely and tragic death of its most celebrated graduate, Dr. Martin Luther King Jr.

The day after the final rite for the most illustrious alumnus of the college, Morehouse reopened for business. Graduation was less than two months away, and, with the tragedy still resonating in their heads and reverberating around the campus, Morehouse students and faculty began to bring the year to a close. Commencement exercises were held in June. As fate would have it, the 1968 commencement season was also the twentieth reunion for the class of 1948, Martin Luther King Jr.'s class. There were 141 graduates in the class of 1968, and the commencement speaker was Dr. Stephen Junius Wright, president of the United Negro College Fund and former president of Fisk University. He was awarded an honorary degree, doctor of humane letters, along with Edward William

Brooke, senator from Massachusetts, doctor of laws, and the only African American serving in the United States Senate at that time.

President Gloster's "Charge to the Senior Class" was unique in that it was given indirectly to the graduates in the form of a letter to the late Dr. Martin Luther King Jr. Dr. Gloster began the letter saying, "Exactly twenty years ago you sat here as the seniors are doing today, and you received the usual exhortation to seek the best possible education in your professional field and to render the best possible service to mankind." After reciting Dr. King Jr.'s educational attainments and his social activism, Dr. Gloster said,

> Martin, in your brief earthly existence of 39 years you proved what Christ proved almost two thousand years ago—that the best life is one that is devoted to unselfish service to others and that love and nonviolence can win victories which are unattainable by hatred and distraction. In the midst of maddened men who called for division and destruction you call for peace and Brotherhood. I am sorry that you did not live to see people who were indifferent to you or opposed to you "rise up and call you blessed."[11]

President Gloster then summarized the class of 1968, suggesting that Dr. King Jr. would be proud of its members. "You would be interested to know that four members of this class were the first Morehouse students to enter our new Phi Beta Kappa chapter, Delta of Georgia. All in all, they are a fine group of fellows and—who knows?—one of them might become your worthy successor as a leader of our people."[12] Dr. Gloster then lamented, saying,

> Martin, it is very hard to give advice to young people at this time. The people of the world are divided by barriers of race, color, class, religion, and nationality.... But I do not think I can make a mistake in asking the members of this class to follow you in trying "to love and serve humanity." As a matter of fact, Martin, I believe that some members of this class would take this course even if I had not requested them to do so.

---

[11] *Morehouse Bulletin* (Summer 1968): 25.

[12] Ibid.

Closing his letter to the fallen leader, with its implications for the graduates, President Gloster said, "I am hoping to see you again someday."[13] In a postscript, he told Dr. King Jr. that scholarships had been reserved for Martin III and Dexter, the fallen Morehouse Man's sons, because "these two fine young boys may follow you, your brother, your father, and your maternal grandfather to Morehouse." Implicit in this imaginary letter to Dr. King Jr. was the founders' idea that black men could be educated for scholarship and service. Dr. King was a sterling example of the validity of this idea. And so it was that, following the post-commencement banquet honoring those faculty who had earned academic doctorates or honorary degrees, the school year ended. And what a memorable year it had been. Within a few months, social change brought "revolution" to Morehouse. But before then, the day after the commencement exercises, the nation was once again awash in grief when Democratic presidential candidate Senator Robert F. Kennedy was assassinated. National movements were unfolding that would influence the social and cultural activism at Morehouse and the Atlanta University Center in profound and significant ways. Men of Morehouse began to chase the crown in a different and profound way. What it meant to be educated took on new meaning, and the emphasis on service was amplified.

---

[13] Ibid.

Chapter 14

"Crown of Crowns": Protest Without Ignites Protest Within Africana '69

The academic year 1968 to 1969 began with the usual campus activities. The freshmen adjusted to the Morehouse culture and organizational offerings while the upperclassmen renewed old brotherhoods and made new friendships. The college was changing, the South was being transformed, the nation was in flux, and the world was watching. After two years of struggle, the first black studies program was established at San Francisco State College in the fall of 1968. This development did not go unnoticed at Morehouse, and students and faculty pondered the direction the college would take. After years of a traditional European (American) Studies curriculum, would Morehouse consider adding black studies as an option, in part or in whole?

In September 1968, the students were going about the normal life of the college. The Maroon Tiger football team was practicing on the field west of Archer Hall while the Glee Club practiced in Sale Hall Chapel, preparing for its annual trip to Bennett College in Greensboro, North Carolina, and for the annual Christmas Carol Concert in Sisters Chapel at Spelman. The football team lost to Clark College, 10–7, but was victorious over Howard University, 32–6. Nelson Taylor was the president of the student government association, and Lloyd Prysock was president of the senior class. Curtis Clark, Eddie Gaffney, and Samuel L. Jackson were in the junior class, Glenwood Ross, Gerald Truesdale, and Benjamin Woods were sophomores, and Uzee Brown, Collie Burnett, James Campbell, Alvin Darden, Paul Howard Jr., Dwight Jackson, Weldon Jackson, and Gordon Joyner were members of the oft-cited freshmen class. The total enrollment for the academic year of 1968 to 1969 was 1,083, with 195 seniors.

President Gloster retained Dr. Brailsford R. Brazeal as the academic dean for the first semester, and Dr. Ralph H. Lee, assistant to the president during the first semester, became the academic dean in the second semester. Julius A. Lockett continued as the bursar, and Dr. Henry C. Hamilton was registrar and director of admissions. Dr. Samuel J. Tucker was the director of personnel, William M. Nix was director of placement, and Nathaniel C. Veale Jr. was the director of development. Charles Merrill, the financier from Massachusetts, was the chairman of the board of trustees, These men represented the upper echelon of the Morehouse administration in 1968, the year before the revolt.

The Morehouse "revolution" was an indigenous campus revolt that was a part of an aggregated national movement among college students. Revolution, for this narrative, is defined as an act of fundamental systemic change. Revolutions are often long in the making, and generally have some act that triggers confrontation. The Morehouse revolution of 1969 was rooted in the history of the college, going back to the establishment of Augusta Theological Institute in 1867. In 1867, and for much of the history of the institution, paternalism and the absence of African and African American culture was built into the structure of the school's curriculum and culture. The question of whether Morehouse students were "men" or "boys" became an issue for dialogue in the late 1950s and into the 1960s, just a few years before the revolution. The presidents of the college were paternalistic, as were members of their administrations and staffs. This was especially the case with President John Hope, who was often called "Father John" by the students. Benjamin Mays, a towering father figure, emphasized a Eurocentric curriculum as part of his strategy in building the "Morehouse Man." In 1969, however, the Men of Morehouse, with the support of a few members of the faculty, revolted against the status quo at the college and dramatically changed the school's culture from what it had been for more than a hundred years. Morehouse protesters were seeking the "crown of crowns."

The Morehouse revolution unfolded in the context of an emerging new consciousness among college students nationwide. This new awareness had its origins in the African American Civil Rights Movement, which gave rise to the student movement in the early 1960s. At first, both the black Civil Rights Movement and the student movement were focused on inequities and improprieties beyond the campus culture. But as both social movements realized successes in their efforts, they began to see problems in the structures of their own academic institutions. Student unrest at Jackson State University in Mississippi and Texas Southern University in Houston in May 1967 led to the arrest of hundreds of students. The next year, Columbia University in New York City was the scene of campus violence by student demonstrators that led the university's leaders to close the campus on April 24th. Student demonstrators occupied campus buildings for five days but were eventually removed by the New York City police. One of the issues that prompted the campus demonstrations was the Vietnam War, which was losing support among young Americans as the horrors of the conflict were seen daily on the evening news. President Lyndon Johnson decided not to seek a second four-year term because of the criticism he received for how he was handling the war. As 1968 rumbled to a close, the Third World Liberation Front, a coalition of nonwhite student organizations at San Francisco State University, conducted a strike that lasted for 134 days.[1] The goal of the student demonstration at San Francisco State was the creation of an ethnic studies department. Morehouse students and faculty were well aware of the developments on college and university campuses elsewhere, and they discussed the pros and cons of the actions of the protesters. Morehouse students were divided along ideological lines on the topic, with some leaning liberal while others had a conservative bent. It should be remembered that not all Morehouse students participated in the protest marches against Jim Crow in Atlanta.

As 1969 began with the inauguration of Richard M. Nixon as the thirty-seventh president of the United States on January 20, student activists from around the country who had been on hiatus during the holidays once again began mounting protests. In February, student demonstrators clashed with police at Berkeley. In March, the National Guard was called to quell violence at the University of Illinois at Champaign. More than one hundred students were arrested at Harvard in April, and nearly a hundred armed African American students at Cornell University in Ithaca, New York, occupied administration buildings while protesting racism at the school and demanding the creation of a black studies program. These protests echoed across campuses nationwide, and it was in

[1] Sixties Chronicle, 394.

this context that four students interrupted a meeting of the Atlanta University Board of Trustees on April 17, 1969, and submitted a statement demanding that board members resign, and which the board rejected.[2]

For years, the board of trustees for the schools in the Atlanta University Affiliation (Atlanta University, Morehouse, and Spelman) were almost one and the same. When they refused to resign, the protesters, faculty, and students decided to force the issue by locking the doors to the boardroom in Harkness Hall.

Two months before the "lock-in," Morehouse had celebrated its 102nd Founders' Day with much success and publicity. Given the unrest on campuses across the land, at a Thursday evening meeting, on February 1, 1969, two weeks before Founders' Day, the Morehouse faculty endorsed a "Statement of Student Rights and Responsibilities" signed by the six presidents of the schools in the Atlanta University Center. This move by the Morehouse president and faculty was an attempt to prevent a strike at the college like those happening at San Francisco State and other institutions. The student activists believed, as Addison Gayle Jr. argued, "that the price of becoming an American was too high. It meant, at the least, to desert one's heritage and culture, at the most, to become part of all...that has been instrumental in wanton destruction of life, degradation of dignity, and contempt for the human spirit.'"[3] They believed, as Cheikh Anta Diop believed, in the African origins of civilization, and they had read John Hope Franklin's *From Slavery to Freedom* and Melville Herskovits's *The Myth of the Negro Past*. They questioned some of the canons of Western knowledge, and they demanded change. Morehouse, a traditionally black college, was not that much different in its curriculum and culture than historically white colleges in the United States. In the 1960s, it was common to hear people say that Morehouse was the Harvard of the South, and Dr. Mays had worked tirelessly to make this a reality. On the eve of the revolution, the Morehouse brand was well established, and the reputation of the college was at its apogee. But the heightened black consciousness that was growing among African Americans was also growing among

[2] *Alumnus* (Summer 1969): 25.

[3] Addison Gayle Jr., *The Black Aesthetic* (Garden City, NY: Doubleday & Co., 1972) xxi–xxii.

Morehouse students and faculty members. Thus, the preemptive "Statement on Student Rights and Responsibilities," whose opening appeared conciliatory: "The institutions of the Atlanta University Center endorse academic freedom—freedom to teach and freedom to learn, freedom to think, freedom to speak, freedom to write, and freedom to publish. These institutions also endorse our citizenship freedoms including freedom of peaceful assembly, freedom of the press, and freedom to petition for redress of grievance." Conceding that change was inevitable, the statement said that "the institutions of the Atlanta University Center seek constructive changes and will work with faculties and student government associations in order to make necessary revision in the program's procedures of our schools. They respect the right of student to criticize, dissent, and protest." Then the statement revealed its real purpose, which was to tamp down any efforts at "creative tension," an old Civil Rights Movement tactic. It stated, in part, that

> the Atlanta University Center institutions will tolerate the use of neither physical force nor physical obstruction which infringes upon the freedom of others, denies the opportunity for teachers to teach and for student to learn and interferes with the right of speakers to speak and listeners to listen...to seize and occupy school buildings, and to injure persons or to damage or destroy property.[4]

The statement ended with a warning that "students who use physical force and/or physical obstruction in an attempt to force their wills upon others will be held fully responsible, and discipline for such action will be prompt and sufficient to the cause."[5]

Three days before the statement was issued, at the Atlanta University Center convocation held on February 3, 1969, President Gloster had prayed for reconciliation: "Our Father, bless this world, bless this nation, bless this race, and bless each of us. And, Father, help us—whether we appear en masse or as individuals—to overcome the barriers that divide us, and to show our ultimate perfectibility by establishing in this life Thy Kingdom of peace, unity, love and justice."[6] This was the calm before the

---

[4] *Morehouse Bulletin* (Summer 1969): 39.

[5] Ibid.

[6] Ibid.

storm. The 102nd year in the history of Morehouse College was marked and celebrated on February 18, 1969, and it featured Dr. John Hope Franklin, the prominent scholar and professor from the University of Chicago, as the Founders' Day convocation speaker. Dr. Franklin's address spoke to the black revolution when he said, "One of the interesting consequences of the present mood is the great manifestation of interest in the past as a conscious search for its meaning and its significance. The demand for the study and the teaching of the history of Negro Americans is today unprecedented." Speaking to what he perceived as "the Black Revolution," Professor Franklin revealed that "Not a single day passes that I do not receive a request to lecture on some aspect of the subject or to provide a syllabus for a class and a bibliography for a would-be teacher or to consult with teachers and curriculum specialists in the matter of developing materials on the subject. This demand is a part of the black revolution and is a part of the search for an ideological basis for it."[7] John Hope Franklin had done significant research on the black experience and had published the seminal book *From Slavery to Freedom: A History of African Americans.* Like W. E. B. Du Bois, Franklin was a graduate of Fisk University and Harvard University. He had taught at the University Cambridge in England and was a professor at the University of Chicago.

Just as Carter G. Woodson had recognized the importance of the history of African Americans in the early years of the twentieth century, John Hope Franklin had known the value of studying his people in a systematic way when he was a graduate student at Harvard. His dissertation, and subsequently his first book, was on this subject: he published the first edition of *From Slavery to Freedom* in 1947. Two decades later, the book was widely read and receiving recognition anew. Following Dr. Franklin's speech, which was delivered to a capacity audience in the Sale Hall auditorium, ground was broken for two new dormitories and what is now known as Douglass Hall. The Founders' Day Banquet was held that evening at eight o'clock in the Lane Dining Hall, where Julian Bond, who had not yet earned his bachelor's degree from Morehouse, was the keynote speaker. Hinting at concerns about the kind of education students received at Morehouse, Mr. Bond said, "This does not mean that

---

[7] Ibid., 7.

Morehouse...ought to abandon its traditional role of preparing young black men for the professions. It does mean that Morehouse...ought in 1969 and the years ahead to carve out for themselves the kind of role and develop the kind of expertise in student and faculty that these times demand." In other words, Morehouse should continue to educate black men for scholarship but in a way that coincided with the times. The times were calling for an emphasis on the black experience to one extent or another. Maynard H. Jackson Jr. also spoke, giving a traditional pep talk to the audience and calling for all Morehouse Men to support their alma mater.

In the weeks that followed the anniversary celebration, the college returned to some semblance of business as usual. But clouds of change were gathering over Harkness Hall, the Morehouse administration building, as the storm of revolution approached. The Glee Club sang at the Second International Intercollegiate Choral Festival at Lincoln Center and performed at Town Hall, both events in New York City. Dr. Mays's new book, *Disturbed about Man*, was published in April, and plans were finalized for the "Marriage Institute" in to be held on April 23. Dr. Paul Weiss was scheduled to be the Phi Beta Kappa visiting lecturer at the college on April 21 and 22, but on the 17th, everything changed.

Charles Merrill, the chairman of the Morehouse board, was present at the board's afternoon session when the group of students from Morehouse and other schools in the Atlanta University Center (AUC) entered the room and made their demands. They wanted AUC institutions be consolidated as Martin Luther King Jr. University. Dr. Martin Luther King Sr., who was on the Morehouse board, made it clear that the King family disapproved of this tactic. However, the board agreed to meet with ten of the student activists the next day, at 9 A.M. Charles Merrill asked Morehouse Student Government Association members to attend the meeting on Friday morning, April 18. President Hugh Gloster, who had been on the job less than two years, was bothered by the desultory events that were occurring at the college. He would later threaten to resign. But on the evening of April 17, Morehouse students and others planned for the meeting the next day.[8]

The Morehouse College Board of Trustees met in the conference

---

[8] Morehouse Bulletin (Summer 1969).

room on the second floor of Harkness Hall, the administration building that had been shared by the college and Atlanta University since it was constructed in 1932. Harkness Hall was built on land once own by Morehouse, and on which Quarles Memorial Hall once sat. Designed in the Georgian colonial style, with columns and a cupola featuring a bell and a clock, Harkness housed the office of the Morehouse president as well as the dean, registrar, and bursar. The bookstore and post office, shared by the two schools, were also in the building. Entering Harkness Hall from the Morehouse quadrangle and ascending the stairs to the second floor, the conference room is located in the center of the building. In preparation of the April 18, 1969, meeting, the students, including members of the Morehouse Student Government Association—Nelson Taylor, president; Joseph Price, vice president; Emerson Godwin, secretary; Bill Gilbert, treasurer; Edward Wheeler, city-campus coordinator; and William McFarlin, program chairman—met on the eve of the meeting to discuss their thoughts on the impending crisis.

Nine students (three from Morehouse, four from Spelman, one from Clark, and one from Morris Brown) and one teacher appeared before the board at nine o'clock the next morning. Gerald McWhorter (Abdul Alkalimat) was the Spelman teacher who led the students, and he "once more demanded the Center institutions be consolidated and named after Martin Luther King Jr., and Dr. King Sr. once more objected to this action under pressure." Dr. King Sr. did not object to the idea, he objected to the way it was being proposed.

Under duress, the Atlanta University Board of Trustees adjourned, but by 11 A.M., the Morehouse Board of Trustees was in session in the same room in Harkness Hall. After the Morehouse Board convened, two teachers and approximately fifty students from Morehouse and the other Atlanta University schools locked the Morehouse College trustees and five Morehouse SGA representatives in the conference room of Harkness Hall and occupied the entire administration building. Among the "hostages" were Dr. King Sr. and Dr. Benjamin E. Mays, president-emeritus of Morehouse. In addition to the consolidation of the AUC schools and naming it Martin Luther King Jr. University, the protesters also wanted the white board members of all Atlanta University schools to yield their positions to black individuals. These demands were unacceptable to the faculties and administrations of the AUC schools, so the lock-in continued.

When Dr. Mays, Dr. King Sr., Morehouse board members, and the student government representatives were prevented from leaving the room by the protesters, a meeting was called by other Morehouse SGA members in Sale Hall Chapel, a venue about one hundred yards from Harkness Hall and visible from the board room. The SGA agreed to withdraw all proposals now before the board because the majority of the Morehouse students had not agreed on these demands. The SGA wanted time to discuss the proposal with the board and believed that continuing to hold them hostage was "morally wrong and unjust."[9] Following the meeting in Sale Hall, several hundred students gathered on the quadrangle in front of Harkness Hall and sang "Dear Old Morehouse," the college's plaintive hymn. And as the lock-in continued, several hundred students moved toward Harkness with confrontational and physical plans "to liberate the trustees and SGA representatives but were dissuaded because of possible injury to themselves and [the] students occupying the building."

By early evening April 18, the situation had reach a level of violability that Dr. Gloster "submitted his resignation as president of Morehouse College, effective on a date to be agreed upon by the board and himself, because he would not 'participate in a meeting in which members of the board of trustees are confined in the Conference Room by force and are subjected to insult and intimidation.'"[10] Declaring that he would not sign any document or vote on any motion made at the meeting, and would not be a party to concessions made under duress, Dr. Gloster read the letter to the board and then went to the balcony just outside the board room to read the letter to the crowd of students gathered on the quadrangle. The students were once again strongly advised not to enter the building by force. Around this time, and at the request of Dr. Gloster, Dr. Thomas Jarrett, president of Atlanta University, Dr. Albert Manley, president of Spelman, Dr. King Sr., and three other Morehouse board members were allowed to leave the board room because of age and/or illness.[11]

---

[9] Ibid., 30.

[10] Ibid.

[11] Ibid.

Gloster's resignation was not accepted and he continued as the seventh president of the college.

As the hostage crisis grew more dire, Dr. Mays wrote an essay titled "Prisoner in Harkness Hall," which described the situation and reflected his strong disapproval of the militant behavior by the student activists. His firsthand observations are revelatory. At 10 A.M., the Atlanta University board adjourned and the Morehouse Board meeting was supposed to begin. It never got started. The protesters refused to leave the Morehouse board meeting and presented certain demands. The teacher from Spelman obviously was in control of the group. Mays had come to the meeting at 9:30 that morning, April 18, and it was 3:30 A.M., April 19, when he wrote his account. They had been chained in for eighteen hours by this point.

The group outside the room, in the hall, numbered about fifty or sixty and a Morehouse professor. The doors were locked and chained. The students in the hall were presumed to be from several institutions associated with the center, but Mays surmised that "some of them are not students at all. Some of the group of students are most insulting, they curse and use vulgar language. We were permitted to go to the restroom one at a time, but after midnight, the trustees were not allowed to go to the restroom at all. If the methods and demands of this group are implemented, Dr. Mays argued, the black colleges will soon pass away. I have never met a more insulting group in all of my years."[12] Sidney R. Jones Jr., a lawyer from Chicago and 1928 graduate of Atlanta University, gave similar observations in a piece he wrote titled "Twenty-eight Hours of Torture and Imprisonment," revealing that "as the day wore on, sandwiches were provided for the hostages, and on Saturday morning, April 19th, breakfast was brought in between 8:00 and 9:00."

One of the concerns for all parties involved in the Morehouse lock-in was the role the Atlanta Police Department might or might not play in the tension-filled situation. It was rumored as early as Friday, April 18th, that the police, "referred to as 'pigs' by the McWhorter group," were coming. Preparing for this potentiality, the women began to cut large swaths from a bolt of white cloth to create homemade gas masks. But the

[12] Ibid.

Morehouse authorities were reluctant to call the police because they feared the situation would escalate into physical violence and serious injuries to the captors and hostages. Not knowing what decisions were being made on the outside about calling in the authorities (Elmer Tuttle was a federal judge), including if this would involve the Federal Bureau of Investigation or the US Marshals, the protesters chained the doors to Harkness Hall and to the third floor.

The Atlanta University security police did not act to end the lock-in and appeared to be in league with the protesters. By this time, dozens of protesters had filled the hallway outside the Harkness Hall conference room. They sat on the floor, they yelled Black Power slogans, they sang African songs and Negro spirituals, stomped their feet, clapped their hands, and marched up and down the hall. And, according to one of the hostages, those locked inside "were abused, insulted, threatened, intimidated, cursed and in every way insulted and degraded."[13] As midnight approached, the militants announced that because people do usually go the bathroom after retiring at night, no one would be allowed to use the restroom after twelve o'clock. They did not consider that many of the trustees were old and that urinary and alimentary conditions might require a more frequent use of the lavatory.

The protesters broke into Dr. Gloster's presidential office and made telephone calls. They demanded amnesty for their actions once the lock-in ended. Nelson Taylor, the Morehouse SGA president, Donald Hense, and three other students from the college who were not members of the "Concerned Students" were described in positive ways, including as "a very able leader" and "dressed in normal attire." These students represented a different level of consciousness in the minds of some Morehouse students, perhaps representing the majority of the students at the college. They were in favor of social and institutional change but by using traditional methods—talks, negotiations, consensus, and planning. But it was the militant consciousness of the activists that held sway during the lock-in.

The hostage situation continued throughout Saturday morning as the Morehouse trustees continued negotiations with the Concerned

---

[13] Sidney Jones Jr.

Students. The women members of the group, largely from Spelman and dressed in African attire or jeans, were as militant as the men. They took turns calling Dr. Mays and President Gloster "Uncle Toms." Charles Merrill, chairman of the Morehouse board, was the object of much of the scorn of the students. As a white man of wealth, he represented all that they viewed as paternalistic and oppressive. The Concerned Students issued a "Protester's Fact Sheet" after the Morehouse student hostages were allowed to leave to participate in a meeting of the Morehouse student body in Sale Hall. The fact sheet began with a preamble that said,

> Recognizing that Black People will never be free until they control their own destiny, the students of the former Atlanta University Center have taken it upon themselves to rename and reorganize the complex. We have taken this action in order to establish an educational institution relevant and consistent with the needs of Black People everywhere. Henceforth, the Atlanta University Center will be known as the Martin Luther King University.

The fact sheet then delineated the demands of the students: "A. End self-perpetuating board (no succeeding beyond one term). B. Existing board will appoint 10 new board members, students, faculty, alumni and community representatives will appoint 15 members. C. Immediate resignation of all white board members." They also demanded a signed commitment agreeing to work toward consolidating all six schools in the AUC into Martin Luther King Jr. University.

The lock-in finally came to an end at 1:30 P.M., Saturday, April 19, once the trustees agreed to the demands of the Concerned Students and amnesty agreements were signed. The Morehouse Board of Trustees had been incommoded for two days, but this was by no means the end of the story. The lock-in had captured the attention of the national press as well as Morehouse alumni and friends of the college around the country. This was just a few weeks before commencement and became a major source of conversation, debate, and argument both on and off the campus. Many people were asking, "Who is Gerald McWhorter, aka Abdul Alkalimat?" Mr. McWhorter, now Dr. Alkalimat, had been born Gerald Arthur McWhorter on November 21, 1942, in Chicago's Frances Cabrini housing project. He earned a bachelor's degree in sociology and philosophy at

Ottawa University and a master's degree in 1966 in sociology. He would later earn his doctorate in 1974, also in sociology, at the University of Chicago. Dr. Alkalimat became one of the founders, along with Vincent Harding, Stephen Henderson, Howard Dodson, A. B. Spellman, William Strickland, Council Taylor, and others, of the Institute of the Black World (IBW).

The lock-in ended on April 19, 1969, and on May 13, the Morehouse Board of Trustees held a "Special Session of the Annual Meeting of The Board of Trustees" at the Roosevelt Hotel in New York City. Charles Merrill, chairman of the board, convened the meeting at 10:05 in the morning, and prayer was given by Dr. Martin Luther King Sr. Mr. Merrill remarked that the special meeting was necessary because of the events that had taken place in Atlanta between April 17th and 19th. According to President Gloster, a group of dissident students had attempted to raise funds to travel to New York City to continue the protest, and to the alarm of the trustees, "Dr. Gloster also reported an attempt by unknown persons to set fire to Sale [Hall] Annex at five o'clock on the morning of May 13, 1969, at which time a gasoline bomb was placed in the building." The bomb was discovered and disassembled before it exploded. President Gloster said that he and Dr. Thomas Jarrett, his counterpart at Atlanta University, had been continually harassed by students and others with threatening calls and visits to their offices and homes (both on their respective campuses). The FBI and the Atlanta Police were kept informed of the actions of the militants and, as warranted, evidence was turned over to the proper authorities.

After the roll was called and as reports were being conveyed, Linus Griffin and Harold McKelton, two Morehouse students, abruptly entered the room carrying a petition that they wanted to read and present to the board. The board, however, unanimously agreed to move forward with its planned agenda and not amend it to allow the students to speak. Subsequently, the students left the room but remained outside the door in anticipation of the board's decision. After a brief discussion, T. M. Alexander moved and Chauncey Waddell seconded the following motion, which was adopted by the board:

> RESOLVED, That inasmuch as the duly elected officers of the Student Government have been invited to appear at the meeting,

> the two students from Morehouse College who came to the meeting of the board of trustees without adequate credentials from the Student Government Association, not to be heard at this time and that their document be tabled.[14]

As Griffin and McKelton continued to wait outside the meeting room, the board adopted another resolution that was moved by John Wheeler and seconded by Martin King Sr "that the Board of Trustees proceed with its planned agenda and not to honor the request of the two uninvited students who have asked to discuss the document left with the board at the beginning of the meeting."[15] The students were given no opportunity to make their presentation to the board, but several interesting decisions were made in relation to the April lock-in and unrest. These decisions would change the Morehouse culture in profound and unexpected ways and help to usher in the "New Morehouse."

With the protest still on their minds and an awareness of which of the Morehouse teachers were involved, it was reported that one of the teachers would not be employed in the 1969 to 1970 academic year and that the other one had asked for a leave of absence for one year. However, the most significant decision that was made by the board with regard to the demands of the protesters was the report by President Gloster that the schools in the Atlanta University Center had "approved undergraduate majors and minors as well as a master's degree in Afro-American Studies." In "An Open Letter" to President Gloster, dated July 21, 1969, which put the protest in clear and concise perspective, Finley C. Campbell, a member of the Morehouse class of 1956 and a former faculty member in the Department of English at the college advised that

> Morehouse needs reconstruction. The self-study report revealed areas of weakness and strength in the structure of our beloved institution.... The over-thrust of power in the hand of those not directly related to the teaching process—bursar, dean, registrar, building and grounds people, and personnel office—needs to be remedied,

---

[14] Minutes of the Special Session of the annual board of trustees of Morehouse College. Roosevelt Hotel, New York, May 13, 1969, 3.

[15] Ibid., 4.

> the sense of harassment of students by people in secondary positions of power like Security Guards must be looked into.

With reference to the call for black studies, Campbell agreed that "the development of courses which deal with the needs of oppressed black people, ranging from social psychology to black studies need to be implemented immediately. A call is going out to involve Morehouse College more directly in the specific socio-political life of Atlanta, Georgia, and the Southeast." Additionally, he suggested that

> there should be joint student-faculty meetings. Students have been placed on all major committees. They should now be given a prominent voice in the A. U. Senate. Black-oriented arts, lecturers, and cultural programs needed to be given full enthusiastic financing. Part-time student programs should be developed for working students. A five-year program should be introduced: a program in which a student can elect to spend a year with full credit in the field working with a black liberation organization.

Finally, Campbell declared, "In a word, Morehouse needs radical Reconstruction from top to bottom."[16]

It was not just about the presidents and the trustees, it was about the system—a system that was a carryover from the days when the school was first under the authority of the American Baptist Home Mission Society and white paternalists. It could be argued that this had merit before the 1950s and the emergence of a new black consciousness. It might also be said that this system had value when there was a dearth of African Americans who were qualified to operate institutions of higher education. But this was now the 1960s, and black Americans had achieved much in all areas of life, yet historically black colleges and universities was conservative and slow to change. They could point to many success stories that came from the old system, and the leaders wondered why there was a need to change. This was certainly true at Morehouse, where many alumni had made their mark on the world stage, and it was on their accomplishments that the reputation of the college was predicated. These accomplishments were often recited. Why change now?

---

[16] "An Open Letter," Finley C. Campbell, July 29, 1969.

The psychological revolution that produced a new consciousness among African Americans during the Civil Rights Movement that saw the rise of the Black Power Movement also spawned the new behavior among black college students. The activists believed, as Dr. King Jr. believed, that "injustice anywhere is a threat to justice everywhere." The student activists believed that, in many ways, collegiate cultures mirrored the larger American culture in the ways they operated; they was authoritarian institutions. Nevertheless, once the lock-in ended, disciplinary actions were meted out. In his unpublished work on "The Morehouse Revolution," Dr. Trenton Bailey tells what happened.

> As a result of their participation in the lock-in, 28 Morehouse students were disciplined after hearings held on May 29th and 30th by the Advisory Committee, a faculty-student board which handles disciplinary problems at Morehouse College. After all petitions by some of those who were disciplined, thirteen students were dismissed, six were suspended for one semester, five were suspended for two semesters, and four were placed on probation.

Support for the actions taken by the advisory committee was widespread, from the alumni to the general public. "The Morehouse faculty went on record against the humiliations, insults, and terror tactics committed by the militants and recommended that the Advisory Committee take any disciplinary action it deemed necessary and proper."[17] Amnesty for the student protesters came from some of their schoolmates, twenty alumni, and a local newspaper columnist. And as the debate over the necessity, tactics, and merits of the lock-in continued, change came to the Morehouse culture.

At the May meeting of the Morehouse Board of Trustees in New York, about three weeks after the lock-in, the board accepted six of eight proposals presented to them by the Morehouse Student Government Association. And while the board chose not to vote on proposal number eight, which would have given amnesty to student protestors, it did agree to accept proposal number six, which called for adding nine new black members to its body. This was a major shift in the policy-making

[17] Trenton H. Bailey, "The Morehouse Revolution," unpublished paper.

organization in that three of the new members would be elected by the students (student representatives would serve on the board for the first time), three more would be faculty members (also a first), and three would be elected by the "community-at-large."

Changes were also coming to the curriculum. In fall 1969, curricular reforms were the primary agenda focus during a retreat at the Stone Mountain Inn in DeKalb County, Georgia. A faculty-student committee had been formed after the lock-in to consider the concerns of the demonstrators and others. At the September Stone Mountain retreat, which was held "to consider and approve proposed curricular reforms,"[18] it was decided that, among other changes in the curriculum, the proposal for an Afro-American Studies concentration would be approved and that this new course of study would be equivalent to a minor for majors in the humanities and the social sciences. In addition, the Atlanta University system's Council of Presidents approved the appointment of Dr. Tobe Johnson, professor of political science at Morehouse, as the director of the Afro-American Studies Program. A grant of $46,000 from the Ford Foundation was earmarked to pay Dr. Johnson's salary and that of the secretarial staff. By this time, courses on the African American experience had been added to the curriculums of the AUC schools, and it was thought that "the six Atlanta University Center institutions should become one of the national resources in the field of Afro-American Studies."[19] Further,

> the college received a Title III Government grant for a Critical Languages program which provided courses in Ibo and Swahili as well as Chinese and Russian. In addition, Atlanta University Center students were permitted to register for seminars offered by five senior research fellows in the Institute of the Black World, which, at that time, was a component of the Martin Luther King, Jr. Memorial Center.[20]

While it was controversial, uncomfortable, and unsettling, the confrontation with the Morehouse authority—the board of trustees, senior

[18] Semi-Annual Report of the President to the Board of Trustees of Morehouse College, Atlanta (November 1969) 8.

[19] Ibid., 17–18.

[20] Ibid.

leadership in the administration, and the student body—was not a quixotic exercise in futility. It was part of a larger national movement of social and cultural activism that would change black society and the nation in profound and lasting ways.

Speaking at the 1971 Founders' Day Convocation, Lerone Bennett Jr. emphasized the importance of self-worth, self-respect, and value in blackness. "Blackness is a truth which stands at the center of the human experience," Dr. Bennett said, "and...all who reflect the rays of that dazzling darkness reflect a truth which is close to the truth of man." And, waxing philosophical, Dr. Bennett said that "the black man is the truth or close to the truth, that blackness constitutes the truth of the truth, and that Black Studies is the revelation of that truth and the search for the true meaning of blackness." Describing the concept, he said blackness was "that universe of values and attitudes and orientations which rises, like dew, from the depth of our ancestral experience and pulls us toward the distant shores of our destiny."[21]

Dr. Vincent Harding, director of the Institute of the Black World in 1969, published "An Educator View: Black Students and the 'Impossible' Revolution" in the August 1969 issue of *Ebony* magazine. Laying the foundation for the students' activism in the struggles of the 1950s and early 1960s, he argued that "in some fiercely telescoped way, that *was* a generation ago, the beginning of our age of Blackness, and though we knew little of these things then, the students were indeed the vanguard of a movement which may one day—perhaps this day—rightly bear the name of revolution."[22] Morehouse students were an integral part of this "age of blackness," an age that "spoke of a newly found self-love and affirmation, saying what has long been known: no man can love another man unless he loves himself, no group can value the truth in others unless they perceive the essential value of their own truth." The Morehouse students "learned not only of personal self-love, therefore, but of love of the black community. They were pressed with a profound sense of that community's brokenness, its oppression, and its need. They were challenged

---

[21] *The Torch* (1971) 94.

[22] Vincent Harding, "An Educator's View: Black Studies and the Impossible Revolution," *Ebony* (August 1969): 141.

to see its life and its liberation as their first calling."[23] And while the majority of the Morehouse student body had not been on the side of the "revolutionaries" in the April 1969 lock-in, the consciousness of those involved was contagious and would soon infect the entire campus population. Bear witness to the transformative changes of the age of blackness at Morehouse College as seen in the outward behavior of the students: As the new age emerged, students began to speak in the language of the revolution. Addressing each other as "brother" became commonplace, and their schoolmates at Spelman were called "sisters." The words of Malcolm X, Marcus Garvey, Stokely Carmichael, and Nathan Hare, among others, were frequently quoted, and the 1971 *Torch* carried unattributed declarations such as "Lord, lord we done come far and still ain't nowhere near-even with long nappy hair and talk of rev'lution" and "God don't mean a thing baby when you got no bread or a bed and a bad head blinding you with black blues." Afro hairstyles, to one degree of fullness or another, were worn by most students, and dashikis and other forms of African attire were adopted. The women who represented the fraternities, classes, and other student organizations dressed in stylized versions of African clothing, and they wore matching hats, head wraps, or left their hair in the natural, or Afro, style. A Morehouse student is bare-chested, save for a string of African beads, and his hair is plaited in "Portrait of a Plait" in the yearbook, and the caption reads, "little plait, who made thee? doth thy know who made thee? nimble fingers and carved stick, called God's blessed AFRO PICK." This new public behavior was a sign of the radical changes at the college, changes that would not have been tolerated a decade earlier.

As the reforms in the culture were taking place at Morehouse, a new institution was being established that would involve Morehouse faculty and students and which would center around the college's must illustrious and celebrated alumnus—Dr. Martin Luther King Jr. Shortly after the obsequies for Dr. King Jr. had been completed, conversations about how to honor the slain martyr were taking place. The college received two grants to memorialize Dr. King Jr. "for the purpose of relating the college to the problems of the inner city of Atlanta." The first grant came from

[23] Ibid.

Charles Merrill, chairman of the Morehouse board, and was in the amount of $50,000, and the second grant was for $100,000 and came from the Field Foundation. Collectively, the grants' $150,000 supported two phases of College-Community Urban Relations Enterprises (CURE). The first phase took place in the summer of 1968, before the revolution, but was ramped up after the confrontation and "included projects in early childhood development and enrichment, youth development and enrichment, leadership training and development, basic and continuing adult education, and citizenship education." The second phase of Project CURE began in June 1969, after the lock-in, and provided resources information exchanges, "which provided resident of the inner city with knowledge about services offered by public and private agencies, and a community economic resources development component, which was concerned with the formulation and execution of a program to further consumer education in the inner city."[24] Dr. Anna Harvin Grant, professor of sociology, was appointed director of Project CURE.

The second way Morehouse planned to honor Dr. King Jr. was by erecting the Martin Luther King Jr. Memorial Hall, which was budgeted at $3 million in 1969. At the fall meeting of the board that year, a petition from a student committee to establish an Afro-American Hall of Fame in the memorial hall was approved. Around the same time, Mrs. Coretta Scott King, widow of the fallen leader, and others were planning a much more ambitious memorial to her husband. The college, through its president, had been collaborating with Mrs. King on "a memorial medal in honor of Dr. Martin Luther King Jr., with the income to be shared by Morehouse College and the Martin Luther King Jr. Memorial Center. It would take a decade before the dedication of the Martin Luther King Jr. International Chapel at Morehouse would take place.

When Morehouse commemorated its 103rd anniversary, Dr. Hugh M. Gloster was in the third year of his presidency. He had taken hold of the throttle of the Morehouse engine, and it was full speed ahead. The college began to expand by land and buildings, and King Memorial Hall was among the plans in the Gloster expansion of the college. A new period in the history of Morehouse College was at hand, but the administrators,

---

[24] *Morehouse Bulletin* (Spring 1971): 7.

faculty, staff, students, and alumni (more than any group) looked backward to move forward. A "new day was dawning, sunny and bright," but many of the traditions of the past were brought into the light. *Et Facta Est Lux*! This was the time of the "crowns of crowns"!

Chapter 15

"Burnishing the Crown": Revolution Is Reformation: Social, Cultural, and Physical Changes

The last class of "Bennie's Boys" were seniors in the fall of 1970. These Men of Morehouse, the class of 1971, were students at the college when Dr. Mays retired, when Dr. Gloster was elected and inaugurated as the school's seventh president, and when Dr. King Jr. was assassinated. They were there when the lock-in took place, signally the beginning of the revolution at the only institution of higher education in the world whose expressed mission, in part, was the education of black men. The members of the class of 1971 would experience, firsthand, the reformative changes taking place at the college due to the demands and concessions of the revolution of 1969. But what were these changes and how does social change happen?

Social forces have been defined as ideas that originate in individual motivations but coalesce in a collective manifestation of power. Social and cultural (behavioral) changes were evident at Morehouse as the college entered the 1970s in the aftermath of the lock-in. For the first time, three professors represented the faculty on the Morehouse Board of Trustees: Dr. James W. Mayo, professor physics, Dr. Charles W. Merideth, professor of chemistry, and Dr. Wendell P. Whalum, professor of music. The student body also had three representatives on the board, which was perhaps the more significant event. That year, Cecil H. Brim, a junior from Los Angeles; William C. Rudolph, a senior from Dothan, Alabama; and Malcolm H. Suber, a sophomore from Whitmire, South Carolina, were named to the board. Students also had seats on institutional committees, especially where student affairs were concerned. Other socio-cultural-political changes would take place at Morehouse in the next few years.

Lerone Bennett Jr., '49, was the keynote speaker at the February 18, 1971, Founders' Day Convocation. After the usual prelude, invocation, hymn, occasion, and musical performance by the Morehouse Quartet,

President Gloster introduced Dr. Bennett. His address was titled "The Time of the Whale," and he put much emphasis on the past years of the college with a nod to the present and future of this storied institution. The protest at his alma mater had occurred nearly two years ago at this time, and Bennett reminded the audience that "all over America, students are in revolt against the dogmas of the lesson plans of yesteryear." You did not have to agree with the tactics the "student soldiers" used to question the way American was educating its students, but you had to recognize the valuable service the activists performed by "raising dangerous and necessary questions about this longstanding education culture."[1] For the speaker, the social and cultural changes taking place in America did not negate the significance of Morehouse and other black institutions of higher education. "On the contrary," Dr. Bennett said, "the student challenge validates the experience we celebrate here and calls for the updating of that experience in a world that needs the light [the "candle"] Morehouse can give."[2]

Interestingly, and for unknown reasons, in his recitation of the traditional narrative of the history of Morehouse, Bennett failed to mention the first three leaders of the school—Presidents Robert, Graves and Sale—who were white men. He then addressed the controversy swirling around the emergence of black studies. Bennett was concerned that there had not been any "serious dialogue in the black community on this whole question of black studies and black education," but the issues raised by the activists could not be rejected so easily. He did not make the case in favor of black studies but thought that the "movement is serious and that it speaks to questions which have been raised repeatedly and never adequately answered."[3] Lerone Bennett was, in fact, an advocate for studying the black experience; he had published *Before the Mayflower: A History of the Negro in America, 1619–1962* almost ten year earlier, in 1962. This book became a staple in many black studies programs and departments at that time. Nevertheless, his speech validated the mission of the "student soldiers" at Morehouse who had taken extreme measures to get the board of

[1] Ibid.

[2] Ibid., 8–9.

[3] Ibid., 22.

trustees to hear them and to begin to understand why change was imperative.

Dr. Bennett ended his Founders' Day address calling for Morehouse students to "rise, Brothers, rise! Come...let us possess this land." Black studies came to Morehouse in the fall of 1971. But days after the convocation, the college community and the community of music and arts were saddened by the death of Professor William Kemper Harreld, Morehouse's legendary "Music Man." His funeral was held in Sale Hall Chapel on Saturday, February 27, 1971, at three o'clock in the afternoon. The college chaplain, Professor William V. Guy, '57, presided. Dr. Wendell Phillips Whalum had been in charge of the Department of Music and director of the Glee Club for more than a decade when his predecessor died, but Professor Harreld's spirit was still felt among Morehouse students and alumni, and with his death an important period in the history of the arts at the college came to an end. Professor Harreld and Dr. Whalum included the music of black composers in their repertoires, and black music became a part of the curriculum in black studies and black education. The timeline of the black experience in the United States coincides with the timeline of black music in this country.

For the first time in the history of the college, the Morehouse College catalogue for the academic year of 1971 to 1972 listed an "Afro-American Studies Program" in its academic curriculum. It was a minor in the Division of Social Sciences (a division separate from the humanities) but was also available to students whose majors were in the humanities and education. Dr. Tobe Johnson, director of the program, was a political scientist. Bolstering the traditional curriculum with these new courses and adding students and faculty members to the board of trustees and other college committees represented significant changes, demarking, in a sense, the New Morehouse from the Old Morehouse. Whether these changes were part of a revolution or reformative at the college is a matter of opinion. These dramatic changes, however, moved Morehouse into a new period in its history. Nonetheless, many of the traditions that had been enshrined at the college still remained. The young men who enrolled in Morehouse still attended "Chapel" in Sale Hall on Thursdays during their first year. (Enrollment was consistently more than one thousand young men at this time, so Chapel was not required for all students until King

Chapel was built.) And there was a continued emphasis on proper, or standard, speech and good etiquette, which were not only strongly recommended but required in some settings. In all majors, students were encouraged to do further study after graduating from Morehouse.

As the 1971 fall semester got under way, students moved into dormitories that had been dedicated during the 1970 commencement activities. Charles D. Hubert Hall, Howard Thurman Hall, and the Frederick Douglass Student Commons joined the other buildings on a seemingly ever-expanding campus physical plant. Benjamin G. Brawley Hall, an academic building, had been dedicated during Founders' Day, 1970 and became the home of the Departments of Economics and Business, English, History, Modern Foreign Languages, Music, Political Science, and Sociology. The hall also had a reading room on the lower level.

Morehouse was growing southward and, along with the other schools in the Atlanta University Center, had received a grant of $189,000 from the Ford Foundation to finance "a detailed study of the total educational, administrative, and financial structure of the Center and its member institutions by the Academy for Education Development, directed by Dr. Alvin C. Eurich." The academy submitted a proposal for future land use by Morehouse and her sister institutions on October 15, 1969. In the proposal, Morehouse requested property bounded on the east by Raymond Street, on the west by Ashby Street, on the south by Fair Street, and on the north by Parsons Street. The college also requested property bounded on the east and north by Westview Drive, on the west by Wellborn Street, and on the south by West End Avenue. At the time the Eurich proposal was made, Morehouse land ownership stood at 27.97 acres, upon which twenty-eight buildings stood. In making its bid for the land, the college reported that "in 1968–69 Morehouse had a total campus population of 1,184, including 1,031 students, 85 faculty members, 26 administrative personnel, and 42 staff members."[4] A decade and a half later, on the eve of his retirement, President Gloster projected that "for 1985–86, Morehouse would have a total campus population of 2,290, including 2,000 students, 160 faculty members, fifty administrative personnel, and eighty staff members." The land requested in the Eurich proposal was

[4] Semi-Annual Report to the Board of Trustees, 6–7.

eventually granted, and by the end of the 1970s, W. E. B. Du Bois Hall joined the dormitories on the "new campus," and Lane Dining Hall was expanded to include an additional eating room named for Professor Walter P. Chivers. John H. Wheeler Hall was completed in 1975 to alleviate the overcrowded Brawley Hall. Wheeler became the new home for the Departments of Business Administration and Economics, Computer Science, Political Science, Sociology, and an experimental psychology laboratory.

In 1978, the Martin Luther King Jr. Chapel, considered an auditorium at the time, was completed at a cost of $3.5 million. The auditorium had a seating capacity of 2,501, and its lobby featured marble walls with famous inscriptions from Dr. King's major speeches. The Hugh M. Gloster administration building was attached to the chapel.[5] Within a few years, the chapel was home to the Wendell Phillips Whalum Sr. Memorial Pipe Organ, a Wicks Organ Co. instrument that features 5,209 pipes and which was installed and dedicated on April 25, 1982, in honor of Dr. Whalum, Morehouse's Callaway Professor of Music, college organist, director of the Morehouse Glee Club, and chairman of the school's music department. Dr. Lawrence Edward Carter, who held a PhD from Boston University, was appointed by President Gloster as the founding dean of the Martin Luther King Jr. International Chapel. Dean Carter, as he is known, brought stature and recognition to the chapel through his choice of programing, ceremonies, and rituals, including the multiracial, international guests who are invited to speak from its pulpit.

Around the same time that the concept of the chapel was conceived, another idea was brought to the college that would enhance the prestige and brand of the institution immeasurably. In April 1971, President Hugh Gloster expressed an interest in establishing a medical school at Morehouse after the board of trustees for Atlanta University voted against the proposal for its own school. According to Dr. Louis Sullivan, the first dean and president of the future Morehouse School of Medicine, "Gloster had an advantage over Atlanta University in starting a medical school

[5] Morehouse Catalogue (1979–1981): 5.

because Morehouse College already had a strong premedical program"[6] Apparently the Morehouse Board of Trustees had authorized Dr. Gloster to establish a medical school, and while he believed historically white medical schools should continue to enroll black students, "he also understood that Blacks needed institutions dedicated to their own growth and education." The first obstacle facing the new venture was the agreement made in 1929 that established the Atlanta University Affiliation. In that arrangement between Morehouse, Spelman, and the new Atlanta University, graduate and professional education were assigned to the university, and affiliation bylaws forbade Morehouse from initiating graduate or professional education. The problem was solved on April 12, 1977, when the board of trustees for Atlanta University passed a resolution stating, in part, "that the Atlanta University Board of Trustees wishes to make it clear that whichever way the two-year medical school at Morehouse College is developing, the University does not feel itself aggrieved."[7]

At the founding of the Morehouse School of Medicine in 1975, there were only two medical schools associated with historically black institutions of education: Howard University's medical school in Washington, DC, and Meharry Medical College in Nashville, Tennessee. Seven historically black medical schools were established in the nineteenth century, but by 1923, five of them had closed, in part, due to the scathing *Flexner Report of 1910.*

The Morehouse School of Medicine became the first medical school founded at a historically black institution of higher education in the twentieth century. The fact that President Gloster and the Morehouse Board of Trustees had the vision and the fortitude to take on such an ambitious task speaks volumes about the New Morehouse. The first class of students at the Morehouse School of Medicine (MSM) was diverse along gender, racial, and ethnic lines, and women were once again students at the college. This New Morehouse College was built on the strong foundation of the Old Morehouse, and the development of the MSM by President Gloster and Dr. Sullivan and their colleagues is a study in confidence,

---

[6] Marybeth Gasman with Louis Sullivan, The Morehouse Mystique: Becoming a Doctor the Nation's Newest African American Medical School (Baltimore, MD: Johns Hopkins Press, 2012) 32.

[7] Ibid.

leadership, and vision.

Much of the credit for the creation of the medical school must be given to Dr. Louis Wade Sullivan, a 1954 Morehouse College graduate. The Morehouse College Medical Education Program (MCMEP), as the MSM was originally called, enrolled its charter class in 1978. It had been more than forty years since women had been enrolled at Morehouse, and provisions had to be made for their presence. "The first class at the medical school was integrated: 14 out of 24 students were Black, 6 were White, and 4 were South Asian."[8] And while the all-male Morehouse College student body was somewhat diverse along ethnic, geographic, and socioeconomic lines, the MCMEP was committed "to bringing in a class that boasted gender, racial, and ethnic diversity." As a Morehouse program, the first students enrolled in the MCMEP took their classes at the college. This caused "turmoil amid success." According to one account, the early turmoil had to do with the cumbersome bureaucracy of a fledgling medical school that was also a program at a college. Hugh Gloster was president of Morehouse College, but Lou Sullivan was the dean (soon to be president) of the medical school. In order to get things done, not only did Dr. Sullivan have to give his approval, Dr. Gloster's signature was needed as well. Dr. Sullivan recalled that "Hugh Gloster was a bit of a micromanager. He had to interview everyone, even secretaries. I told him that I could take care of all matters related to the medical school, but Hugh was afraid to fail. He had worked so hard to build Morehouse College and didn't want anything to interfere in its success."[9]

The Morehouse College Medical Education Program began with limited facilities. In addition to classroom space in the science buildings at the college used by students in science disciplines, two brown trailers were set up between Hope and Sale Halls for the new program. Dr. Sullivan's office was in Harkness Hall. Charles Stephens, a 1961 graduate of the college, was the med school's first fundraising officer, and soon the necessary funds were raised, albeit with some difficulty, to gain provisional accreditation from the Liaison Committee on Medical Education (LCME). "The school received that standing from the LCME in the

[8] Ibid., 68.
[9] Ibid., 69.

spring of 1978, which helped in its efforts to organize and develop the two-year medical school, with transfer agreements with four-year medical schools."[10] These transfer agreements were with Emory University, the Medical College of Georgia, Howard University, and the University of Alabama at Birmingham. It is interesting to note that no transfer agreement existed for Meharry Medical School.

Dr. Regina M. Benjamin, an MCMEP student and future recipient of the MacArthur "Genius" Award and surgeon general of the United States Public Health Service in the administration of President Barack Obama, completed her third and fourth years of medical education at the University of Alabama-Birmingham. Within four years, the MCMEP had evolved into the independent Morehouse School of Medicine, and when the med school graduated its first class of physicians on May 17, 1985, the MSM was fully accredited. Although the school was no longer at the college, its history would always be yoked to Morehouse. The independent MSM soon became affiliated with the Atlanta University Center.

In 1979, Dr. Hugh Morris Gloster was in the twelfth year of his administration. The college had more than doubled in acreage, and seven buildings had been erected to better serve the school's students, faculty, and staff. Administrative offices had been moved from Harkness Hall to Gloster Hall, and the decision to do so was not without controversy. The move was positive in that it provided more space for administrative operations than had been available in Harkness Hall, which was shared with Atlanta University. The offices that were relocated included those of the president, the academic dean, the dean of students, the business affairs department, and the registrar's office. But critics of the move cited the fact that the land where Harkness Hall stood had originally been property owned by Morehouse until the Atlanta University Affiliation was formed in 1929 (Harkness Hall was built in 1933). Leaving Harkness Hall meant that the Morehouse quadrangle was missing its eastern side. Critics also mentioned that fact that Gloster Hall detracted from the aesthetics of the Martin Luther King Jr. International Chapel by being an appendage, or wing, on its east side. Despite the controversy, the hall opened and served Morehouse constituents as the population of students, faculty, and staff

---

[10] Ibid., 58.

grew.

King Chapel played a crucial role for three major events that occurred in the years between 1984 and 1987: the death of Dr. Mays, the retirement of Dr. Gloster, and the death of Dr. Whalum, three important figures in the history of the college.

Dr. Benjamin Elijah Mays, the Great Schoolmaster, died at 7:20 A.M. on Wednesday, March 28, 1984, at Hughes Spalding Hospital in Atlanta. More than 2,500 students, alumni, faculty, staff, and friends participated in an emotional memorial service the next day in the Martin Luther King Jr. International Chapel. President Gloster presided at the campus memorial program. On the morning of Friday, March 30, Dr. Mays's remains were borne to Danforth Chapel, which had been erected during his administration and where his body lay in state. Later that afternoon, his remains were taken to Providence Baptist Church, just a few blocks from campus and where he had once preached. Hundreds paid their respects to the great man at the chapel and the church. Seller Brothers Funeral Home was in charge of the funeral arrangements, and on Saturday morning, March 31, 1984, the casket bearing the body of Dr. Benjamin Elijah Mays was brought to the Martin Luther King Jr. International Chapel on the Morehouse campus, a place he loved so deeply and where the public was allowed to view his body from 11 A.M. until 1 P.M., which marked the beginning of the final rite.

Mourners made their way to King Chapel early on that mild spring morning, and by one o'clock, every seat in the auditorium was filled. The Glee Club was in place on stage, as were the funeral program's participants. Floral arrangements sent by faculty, students, alumni, friends, and both nongovernmental and government organizations filled the area around the casket and the stage. The funeral service for the Great Schoolmaster was at times solemn, but it also represented a celebration of the life of this great man who had touched the lives of so many men and women throughout the world. Eleven tributes were delivered by old friends along with a eulogy, two hymns, two Scripture readings, and the performance of several musical selections.[11]

As Dr. Wendell Whalum played Walford Davies's "A Solemn

---

[11] Ibid., 5.

Melody," the Mays family processed down the aisle and friends entered the chapel. The full audience then stood and sang Isaac Watts's "O God, Our Help in Ages Past," one of Dr. Mays's favorite hymns. The prayer was invoked by Dr. William V. Guy, college minister and pastor of historic Friendship Baptist Church. Dr. Julius S. Scott, associate general secretary of the division of higher education of the United Methodists Church in Nashville, read the Old Testament Scripture, Psalms 8 and 23, and the New Testament Scripture, Matthew 25: 34–46, was read by Dr. Homer C. McEwen, retired pastor of the historic First Congregational Church in Atlanta. The Morehouse Glee Club then compassionately sang Duey's arrangement of the Hall Johnson Negro spiritual "Ain't Got Time to Die," which was followed by tributes from Dwight Powell, former chaplain of the Lorton Youth Service in Washington, DC; Dr. Gloster; Dr. Martin Luther King Sr.; Dr. Elmer Fowler, pastor of the Third Baptist Church in Chicago; and Dr. James E. Cheek, president of Howard University. After the audience sang "He Who Is Upright" (words by Horace), more tributes were given by Dr. Albert E. Manley, president emeritus of Spelman College; C. Shelby Rooks, executive vice president of the United Church Board for Homeland Ministries of New York City; Dr. Benjamin F. Payton, Dr. Mays's protégé and president of Tuskegee Institute (now University) in Alabama; Dr. Alonzo Crim, superintendent of the Atlanta public schools; and Dr. Jimmy E. Carter, thirty-ninth president of the United States of America.

The Glee Club then sang a moving arrangement of "The Impossible Dream" by Mitch Leigh with Oliver Sueing, class of 1972, as the tenor soloist. And after remarks were made by the Reverend Doctor Phillip Terry, pastor of the Providence Baptist Church where Dr. Mays had once preached, and baritone Uzee Brown Jr., also from the Morehouse class of 1972, sang Wendell Whalum's arrangement of "Sweet Home," the eulogy was delivered, with much emotion and power, by Dr. Samuel DuBois Cook, class of 1948, and president of Dillard University in New Orleans, one of Dr. Mays's many mentees. The audience was spellbound from his very first words.

> "It must be borne in mind," said a saint and prophet named Benjamin Elijah Mays, "that the tragedy in life doesn't lie in not reaching your goal. The tragedy lies in having no goal to reach."... Dr.

> Mays was a great soul. A giant has fallen. A mighty light has gone out. For decades, Dr. Mays has been a powerful and kind light in a world of tragic darkness and starless nights. No doubt about it, his death represents the end of an era. We will not see his like again.[12]

Dr. Cook was one of "Bennie's Boys," and, later in life, a personal friend of the Great Schoolmaster. He knew him well and loved him dearly. As he continued with the eulogy, what Dr. Cook said was telling: Benjamin Mays had lived a magnificent life, a "life of impossible possibilities." He had pursued the "unattainable ideal, the impossible dream" and was never satisfied with achievements because "high possibilities beckon." And while we might not reach perfection in anything we attempt, "we have a moral duty to strive for perfection in everything we do." Benjamin Mays "was a profound foe of complacency and self-satisfaction." He embraced high ethics and believed that "the heart of the ethical consciousness is the haunting and anguished cry of the human heart and soul for something better, higher, richer, nobler, fuller."[13] Dr. Cook emphasized the strong ethic that Dr. Mays practiced, saying, "I sometimes thought that it might be easier to please God than Dr. Mays." Referring to *Lord, the People Have Driven Me On*, one of Dr. Mays's books, Dr. Cook said he told the author that the title of the volume "was a great misnomer. The Lord knows that Bennie Mays drove the people on. And I told him that Bennie Mays drove the good Lord on." Respectful laughter filled the chapel. He continued, sharing that, as the mourners all knew, "Dr. Mays touched, enriched, inspired, educated, motivated, and transformed so many lives—black and white, rich and poor, male and female, learned and untutored, Gentile and Jew, Protestant and Catholic, Northerner and Southerner, religionist and secularist. So many owe him so much." Continuing in the honorific homiletic that was so richly deserved and appropriate for the funeral of the Great Schoolmaster, Dr. Cook's eulogy reached a ringing crescendo when he exalted, much to the audible approval of the audience, that Dr. Mays on his way to join the greatest contributors to human history and culture. In the oratorical, baritone voice and style unique to Dr.

---

[12] Ibid., 14.

[13] Ibid.

Cook, his words resounded through King Chapel. He ended his oration to his mentor by naming some of history's greatest people who were deceased—Socrates, Aristotle, Moses, Apostle Paul, Newton, Shakespeare, Handel, Frederick Douglass, Harriett Tubman, Gandhi, Langston Hughes, John Hope, Du Bois, Benjamin and Sadie Mays, and Martin Luther King Jr.—and telling "all the other great saints, prophets, intellectual giants, heroes, and wise and inspiring immortals—both the famous and the nameless, the unforgettable and the anonymous—of history, culture, and destiny, look out, make room, Bennie Mays is coming. Buck Bennie rides again. Hallelujah! Hallelujah! Hallelujah!"[14] Closing his eulogy, Dr. Cook reverently said, "So, our very special Dr. Mays, our beloved Bennie Mays, our 'Buck Bennie,' who has meant so much to so many, we mournfully, and yet with joy, say: Hail, thanks, love, and farewell." The thunderous applause of the audience signaled their absolute agreement. After Dr. Cook's brilliant, heartfelt, and poignant eulogy, Hosea Clay, '84, led the Glee Club in singing the traditional Negro spiritual "Guide My Feet (While I Run This Race)."

Dr. Cook had reminded the mourners, "I am one of Benny Mays' 'boys.' I have been one of his 'boys' since I was a kid on the red hills of Griffin, Georgia, and I will be one of his 'boys" until I die." Half of the mourners in the audience were also "Bennie's Boys," Morehouse Men, Men of Morehouse. And as the funeral came to an end, only those men were asked to stand while Dr. Whalum played "Dear Old Morehouse." It was a tearfully emotional moment. As the body of Dr. Mays, the great man, was removed from the chapel, the family, friends, Morehouse Men, and other mourners recessed to "For All the Saints," by Vaughn Williams. The funeral program read that final services would be held at South-View Cemetery, but history would eventually negate this: Dr. Mays's remains, and those of his beloved Sadie Gray Mays, would be returned to the Morehouse campus in 1995, where they are memorialized on the Century Campus in front of historic Graves Hall.

Tributes and condolences came from across the nation and included editorials in the *Atlanta Constitution* and the *New York Times.* The spring edition of *Black Family* also saluted the sixth president of Morehouse. At

---

[14] Ibid., 16.

the time of Dr. Mays's death in 1984, the movement to establish a federal holiday honoring Dr. King Jr. had realized its dream. On November 2, 1983, President Ronald Wilson Reagan signed into law legislation making the third Monday in January a national holiday in honor of the man who had graduated in the Morehouse class of 1948. Dr. Mays, in his final days, was pleased and proud that such an honor had come to one of his "Bennie's Boys." Benjamin Elijah Mays, sixth president of Morehouse, must be remembered into eternity. The Great Schoolmaster did much to carry forth the idea of the founders that black men could be educated and be of service to their people. He had done much more.

Hugh Morris Gloster, who had came under Dr. Mays's influence when he was a member of the faculty in the 1940s, continued to emphasize the ideals of the educated man who would be a steward in his community. In the 1970s, it took money to do this, so, in a letter dated November 28, 1986, President Gloster reminded his fellow alumni of his pending retirement on June 30, 1987, and asked for their generous support to complete two major initiatives at Morehouse: "The first is to complete the drive to raise funds for the construction of a $2.3 million Biology-Chemistry Building and a $1.7 million Humanities Building, and the second is to increase the endowment of the college from $15 million to $20 million." In the spring semester of 1987, the last semester of President Gloster's administration, plans were also being made for his retirement. The search for the eighth president of Morehouse eventually concluded with the election of Dr. Leroy Keith Jr., class of 1961.

In a 1986 survey sponsored by the Exxon Education Foundation, Hugh Gloster, "the grand old man of Morehouse College," was the only Georgia educator and president of a traditionally black college named as one of the 100 most effective college presidents in the United States. Among his peers on this list were the leaders of Harvard, Michigan State, University of North Carolina, University of Texas, Yale, University of Chicago, University of Illinois, University of Missouri, John Hopkins, and Boston University. Dr. Gloster was cited for "doubling the enrollment, the tripling of both endowment funds and scholarship money, and construction of 12 new buildings."

The recognition banquet that was held in honor of President Gloster was held at the Omni International Hotel in downtown Atlanta on Friday evening, April 24, 1987. The evening was a celebration of "two decades of progressive leadership," from 1967 to 1987, and it was clear that the main accomplishments of his administration came from a team effort of trustees, administrators, faculty, students, alumni, and friends. These accomplishments were numerous and included the development and establishment of the Morehouse School of Medicine, the establishment of eight new majors in the Department of Business, the establishment in 1968 of a dual-degree engineering program with Georgia Tech, the establishment of a major in international studies, the more than doubling the size and salaries of the faculty, an increase in the percentage of faculty PhDs to more than 65 percent, and the establishment of seven faculty chairs and fourteen new administrative offices. In addition, student enrollment had more than doubled during Dr. Gloster's tenure, and the quality of the student body had been enhanced thanks to upgraded standards in curriculum and instruction and the establishment of higher admission standards. By the time of his retirement, the Gloster administration had successfully completed a capital campaign for $20 million; quadrupled the college endowment to $20 million; acquired thirty acres of adjacent urban land, valued at $2 million; constructed twelve new buildings valued at $30 million, including an auditorium with a $360,000 pipe organ; and created an administration building, three classroom buildings, a dining hall, a student center, four dormitories, and a stadium that could accommodate 9,000 people and which included an Olympic track. Under Dr. Gloster's leadership, the college had raised funds for the construction of a new biology-chemistry building, acquired another classroom building, an apartment complex, and a president's home. Plus, Morehouse operated without a deficit during the 1970s and 1980s.[15]

Maynard H. Jackson was the toastmaster and Monica Kaufman (Pearson), a local ABC-affiliated news anchor, was the toastmistress at the Gloster Retirement Banquet. The event followed the "Morehouse style," and after those on the dais were introduced, Dr. Lawrence E. Cater, dean of King Chapel, gave the invocation. Dr. Calvin A. Brown Jr., vice chairman of the board of trustees and chairman of the presidential recognition

[15] Recognition banquet in honor of Hugh Morris Gloster, president of Morehouse College, 1967–1987. Biographical files, Robert W. Woodruff Library and Archives, Atlanta University Center.

committee, gave the occasion. After the Glee Club sang, dinner was served.

Following the dinner, Oliver Sueing sang and tributes were given by representatives from the White House, the United States Senate, the US House of Representatives, the Georgia governor's Office and the Georgia State Senate, the Fulton County Commission, the city of Atlanta, the Martin Luther King Jr. Center for Non-Violent Social Change, the Southern Christian Leadership Conference, the Ivan Allen Company, Citizens Trust Bank, and the Equitable Life Assurance Society. Uzee Brown then performed a solo, which was followed by tributes from Leon L. Allain, president of Allain and Associates; Christopher F. Edley, president and CEO of the United Negro College Fund; Dr. Samuel L. Myers, president of the National Association for Equal Opportunity in Higher Education; Dr. James T. Laney, president of Emory University and the Association of Private Colleges and Universities in Georgia; and the Reverend Doctor William S. Guy, pastor of historic Friendship Baptist Church. The Morehouse College Quartet sang, and then additional tributes were presented by those who had worked with Dr. Gloster or were members of his family, including Dr. Charles W. Merideth, chancellor of the Atlanta University Center; Wiley A. Perdue, vice president for business affairs at Morehouse; Archie Rich, president of the Morehouse Student Government Association; Charlie Moreland, president of the Morehouse National Alumni Association; Dr. Thomas Kilgore Jr., chairman of the Morehouse Board of Trustees; and, finally, Dr. Gloster's daughter, Mrs. Alice G. Burnett, who spoke for the Gloster family. The Glee Club performed again, and then the retiring president gave his penultimate valedictory address. Dr. Roswell F. Jackson, chairman of the Department of Philosophy and Religion, gave the benediction.

The crown had been burnished during the Gloster years, but as the attendees left the banquet with a great sense of pride in the accomplishments of the honoree, Dr. Hugh Morris Gloster, during his twenty years as president of Morehouse College, little did they know that less than two months later, sadness would envelope the campus as it mourned the death of one of the college's most exceptionally talented and iconic professors, the very embodiment of a Morehouse Man.

On June 9, 1987, as he was preparing for surgery at Crawford Long

Hospital (Emory Midtown Hospital), Dr. Wendell Phillips Whalum died. Morehouse students and alumni, especially current and former Glee Club members, faculty, staff, colleagues in the music discipline, and friends, were shocked at the untimely news of "P's" death: Dr. Whalum was only fifty-six years old. On Saturday, June 13, 1987, four days after he died, several thousand mourners solemnly filed into Martin Luther King Jr. International Chapel to participate in the last rites for this accomplished musician, teacher, composer, mentor, and the director of the internationally acclaimed Morehouse College Glee Club. The exterior of the chapel was shrouded in black cloth, and the day before the funeral, as the body lay in state, musicians performed from the stage of the facility.

Dr. Whalum's assistant David Morrow, class of 1980, took charge of the musical preparation for the funeral and invited former Glee Club members to join current members to form a mass chorus to sing at the funeral. Dr. William V. Guy, '57, officiated, and Dr. Joyce Finch Johnson, organist at Spelman College and a close friend of the decedent, provided the organ music. Dr. Johnson played R. Löffler's "Meditation" as a prelude to the processional . After the invocation, choirs from Allen Temple AME Church, Ebenezer Baptist Church, Friendship Baptist Church, Providence Baptist Church, and the multi-class representative Glee Club led the mourners in singing the hymn "All Hail the Power of Jesus' Name" (Diadem) by James Ellor. The sound of the hundreds of talented singers reverberated around the sanctuary of King Chapel like never before.

As quiet and dignified sobs filled the chapel, the Right Reverend Ernest Lawrence Hickman, retired bishop of the African Methodist Episcopal Church, moved to the podium and gave the lesson from the Old Testament, Psalm 46. The Reverend Roswell Francis Jackson, '47, pastor of Atlanta's Mount Calvary Baptist Church, read 1 Corinthian 15:50–58 as the lesson from the New Testament. Now under the direction of David Edward Morrow, '80, the mass Glee Club of more than 300 singers rose, and through many tears, performed a moving rendition of "The Welsh Choral" by Reese-Jones. Uzee Brown, '72, baritone, was the soloist. After the song, the Reverend Doctor Joseph L. Robert, pastor of historic Ebenezer Baptist Church, offer the prayer. Roland Carter's arrangement of James Weldon's and Rosamond Johnson's "Lift Ev'ry Voice and Sing" was performed by the Atlanta University Center Community Chorus, a very competent musical organization founded by Dr. Whalum. Remarks on the life and times of Dr. Whalum were given by President Gloster, '31; the Reverend Roderick Belin, '88, president of the Morehouse Glee Club; and Dr. Kenneth T. Whalum Sr., pastor of Olivet Baptist Church in Memphis. Sobbing continued, especially when the Glee Club sang Dr. Whalum's "I Got a New Name" with tenor Oliver Sueing, '72, as soloist.

The meditation was delivered by the Reverend William Vincent Guy, '57, pastor of the historic Friendship Baptist Church. The Glee Club, including other former members in the audience who could not make the rehearsals for the mass group, then sang the powerful Wagner-Mead arrangement of the "Prayer" from *Lohengrin.* And before the Reverend Doctor Benjamin Guy, pastor of the Allen Temple AME Church, gave the benediction, only the Morehouse Men in the audience silently stood as Lawrence Weaver, '55, played "The Morehouse College Hymn." Hundreds stood, some sobbing quietly, others audibly crying. The mourners said goodbye to Dr. Whalum by singing his version of "Fare Ye Well," and the audience recessed to "For All the Saints," by Vaughan Williams-Rosenberg.

Kemper Harreld, Benjamin Mays, Wendell Whalum, and many others profoundly influenced the culture at Morehouse College, but their most significant contributions were the countless Morehouse Men they advised and mentored. While only one of these visionary giants was an actual Morehouse graduate—Whalum—each internalized the ideals of the college, created traditions, and sent men from Morehouse to do further scholarship and be of service to people. The history of an institution cannot be separated from the people who are associated with it. Endowments, buildings, and grassy lawns notwithstanding, Morehouse is what it is because of the human factor. The history of Morehouse is founded in its people, all those in the Morehouse community who fostered the ideals of the school. "To old Morehouse, and her ideals, and in all things that we do."

Chapter 16

"Crowns at the Candle in the Dark": Reappraisal and Reform

The fall semester of 1987 began with the arrival of freshmen and transfer students on Thursday, August 20. New Student Orientation began the next day. After several days of seminars, workshops, speeches, visitations, receptions, and other meet-and-greets, new students registered for classes from August 27 to 28 and returning upper-class students registered from August 31 to September 1. Orientation represents the beginning of the process of imbuing the new Men of Morehouse with the ideals on which Morehouse stands, and it is a concentrated and intense period of time. Students must learn "Dear Old Morehouse," in which many of the school's ideals are enshrined, encouraging students "to give their lives to Morehouse," "give their lives in loyalty," and "to be true to Morehouse, and her ideals, and in all things that they do."

Classes for the new school year began on Wednesday, September 2, 1987, and for the first time in twenty years, a new president was at the head of the Morehouse administration. Dr. Leroy Keith Jr., a member of the class of 1961 and the second Morehouse Man to lead the school, was in place as the eighth president of the college. Dr. Weldon Jackson, '72, served as the vice president for academic affairs (there was no provost position in 1987); Wiley A. Perdue, '57, was vice president for business affairs; William "Bill" Dease Sr., '54, headed the Office of Records and Registration; and Dr. Raymon E. Crawford served as vice president for student affairs. Dr. Thomas Kilgore Jr. was the chairman of the Morehouse Board of Trustees that had elected Dr. Keith to the Morehouse presidency. The college had an enrollment of approximately 2,000 students from thirty-seven states, the District of Columbia, and fifteen foreign countries.[1] A Morehouse education, before, then, and now, "is designed to serve the three basic aspects of the well-rounded man: the

[1] Morehouse Catalog, 1987–1989.

personal, the social, and the professional." And it was in this context, and with these leaders, as well as a competent faculty, that the academic year 1987 to 1988 got underway. The quality Morehouse education was securely wrapped in the traditions and ideals that had graduated generations of Morehouse Men.

Dr. Keith assumed the office of president of the college at the beginning of the fiscal year in July 1987. An inaugural committee was formed to plan his inauguration ceremony, scheduled for Founders' Week 1988. In the meantime, academic and scholarly work and team, club, and organizational activities energized the campus. Dr. Keith, the-soon-to-be-installed eighth president, was complemented in his efforts by the president of the student government association, Calvin B. Johnson, a premed major. Together, these two men brought a new perspective to the way things should be done at the institution and, in the process, engendered a new attitude among staff, faculty, and students. What did they do? Reappraisal and reformation, the two actions constitute proper sequitur; they took stock of the situation and began to make changes. It is common for new leaders, such as presidents, governors, chancellors, or premiers, to reassess, reevaluate, or reexamine the quality, worth, or value of the nation, institution, or organization they are called to lead. Reappraisal involves reviewing past actions, evaluating them, and grading them anew. Reappraisal is usually done to make better an existing entity through reformational changes. Reformation often implies that something is wrong or unsatisfactory with the existing order of things and that change is sorely needed. But this is not always the case. "Reform is generally distinguished from revolution. The latter means basic or radical change, whereas reform may be no more than fine tuning, or at most, redressing serious wrongs without altering the fundamentals of the system. Reform seeks to improve the system as it stands, never to overthrow it wholesale."[2] When President Keith assumed the office of president of Morehouse College on July 1, 1987, he inherited a 120-year legacy that had led to the creation of one of America's finest institutions of higher education.

When Keith became president, the college was operating in the black when many other colleges had closed or were experiencing deficits.

---

[2] http://en.wikipedia.org

Morehouse had grown steadily and had five applicants for each vacancy in the freshman class. More than half of the students enrolled at the college ranked in the top fifth of their high school graduating class, and about half of the students came from outside the Southeastern states. Ninety-six percent of the students were full time, and about fifty percent were housed in college residence halls. In 1987, Morehouse was one of three historically black colleges, alongside Howard and Fisk Universities, and one of only four colleges in the state of Georgia—along with the University of Georgia, Emory University, and Agnes Scott College—to have a Phi Beta Kappa chapter. Morehouse led all predominantly black liberal arts college in the percentage of PhDs on the faculty, in the percentage of graduates proceeding to further study, and in the percentage of alumni who had become physicians, dentists, lawyers, and college teachers. The curriculum consisted of a general studies program—which sharpened skills in English and mathematics and provided a broad introduction to world history and cultures—and majors in nineteen departments. Morehouse was heeding the voice of the founders to educate black men for stewardship.

In 1987, there were 112 full-time and part-time faculty members, 67 to 75 percent of whom held earned doctorates. Twenty-two of the members of the faculty were Morehouse graduates at this time, as Dr. Keith became only the second alumnus to lead the college. In the academic year 1985 to 1986, enrollment stood at 2,160, of which 813 were business majors, 335 dual-degree majors, and 81 mass communication majors, totaling 1,229 students, or about sixty percent of the student population.[3] Clearly, the Morehouse of 1987, when Dr. Keith arrived, was not the Morehouse of 1967, when Dr. Gloster became president. The Morehouse that Keith inherited had a lot to do with the tireless work of President Gloster, who had wanted the college to be one of the best in the nation; if black men were going to be educated, let them study and learn at a quality school. A larger faculty and student body, however, posed more challenges and required different strategies and tactics. Paternalistic leadership was dying or dead by 1987, and President Keith knew this and acted accordingly. Although he was rightly respected, Dr. Keith was not

[3] Hugh M. Gloster, president, "A Proposal to the Ford Foundation for Morehouse College," August 20, 1986.

seen as a father figure.

As Dr. Keith greeted the new students, returning student, faculty, parents, and staff, his vision for the college was uppermost in his thoughts. The eighth president "envisioned a Morehouse that will compete with the finest liberal arts colleges in the country when measured by any of the indices of quality used in higher education."[4] He wanted "Morehouse to continue to be the most prolific producer of black male leadership in this nation. This would probably be one of the most significant contributions the college could make to society given the dismal outlook for black males based on most social indicators."[5] Although initially President Keith was not readily known to many in the Morehouse community, they quickly came to know him, first as a Morehouse Man and then as a successful leader in the world of education and business.

Leroy Keith Jr. was born on February 14, 1939, Valentine's Day and the same day Augusta Theological Institute was organized many years earlier. Educated in the public schools of Chattanooga, Tennessee, his hometown, Keith entered Morehouse in 1957 and graduated with the class of 1961. While at Morehouse, he made the dean's list and was on the Tiger Sharks swim team, along with such talented swimmers as Latimer Blount, Emory Jackson, and Bob Murphy. Leroy Keith Jr. and William Light were two of the best divers on the swim team when it competed in the Southern Intercollegiate Athletic Conference in the late 1950s.

After graduating from Morehouse, Keith continued his education at Indiana University in Bloomington, where he earned a master of science degree and his EdD degree. From 1970 to 1971, Dr. Keith worked as an assistant professor of education and urban studies and as director of the William Jewett Tucker Foundation Internship Program at Dartmouth College. He was promoted to the rank of associate professor at Dartmouth in 1971. In 1973, Dr. Keith was appointed associate vice president for university policy at the University of Massachusetts where he advised the president on the university's relations with various levels of government and other aspects of public education. This position led to his appointment as the chancellor of the Massachusetts Board of Higher Education

[4] Inaugural Address of Leroy Keith Jr., Morehouse College, February 20, 1988.

[5] Ibid.

in 1975. Dr. Keith was only thirty-six years old at the time, and he became the first African American to hold such a position in higher education in this country. In this capacity, he was responsible for planning and coordinating the thirty public colleges and universities in Massachusetts. He was also responsible for supervising the charters of more than sixty private colleges in the state, which included Harvard University and Radcliff College. As chancellor of the Massachusetts Board of Higher Education, Dr. Keith automatically served on the state's board of education, college board of trustees, and community college board of trustees. In 1978, after three years as chancellor, Dr. Keith became executive vice president of the University of the District of Columbia, with full administrative and managerial responsibility for institutional programs and the supervision of all other vice presidents. Just before elected as president of Morehouse, he served as vice president for policy and planning at the University of Maryland, College Park. In the job, "he was responsible for coordinating the development of long-range academic, fiscal and facilities planning for the five campuses in the University's system." At that time, the University of Maryland had an enrollment of 90,000 students and an operating budget of $800 million. From Maryland, Dr. Keith came to Morehouse.

As the fall 1987 semester began, plans for the spring 1988 inauguration were developed. The Glee Club started their rehearsals under the capable leadership of the group's new director, David Edward Morrow. The campus remained shocked and saddened by Dr. Whalum's death, but the transition was smooth. A Thanksgiving trip to Bennett College in Greensboro, North Carolina, and the annual Christmas Carol Concert were on the group's schedule, and just as they began to prepare, so did the players on the Maroon Tigers football team, the King Chapel Players, and the participants in the Miss Maroon and White coronation pageant.

Calvin B. Johnson, the SGA president, guided the student body during the 1987 to 1988 transitional year. As president of the student government association, Mr. Johnson was also a student representative to the Morehouse Board of Trustees. In addition, he served on the inaugural committee, which was chaired by Vice President for Academic Affairs Dr. Weldon Jackson. Dr. Thomas Kilgore, chair of the Morehouse Board of Trustees, was honorary chairman.

College life is often routine until something occurs to disturb the status quo. Routine, in and of itself, has historical value and is worth noting. At Morehouse, in the fall of 1987, the college community settled in to the tone and style of the Keith presidency.

Spring semester 1988 at Morehouse began uneventfully in January, and the Founders' Day Convocation, held on Thursday, February 18, 1987, marked the beginning of Dr. Keith's inauguration events. The Reverend Doctor Otis Moss Jr., '56, was the convocation speaker, and in his inimical style, he delighted the audience with his words of wisdom. Referring to black colleges as "Thank you Jesus" schools, Reverend Moss said, "There is no moment like the one when a young black graduate walks across the stage at a predominantly black institution to receive his degree. At the precise instant he shakes the president's hand and grasps hold of his degree with the left, then you hear, all the way from the balcony, the shout of a mother or grandmother saying, 'Thank you Jesus!'" On a more serious note, Reverend Moss called for more support of schools like Morehouse College. He entreated the audience by saying, "We have the responsibility of maintaining institutions like Morehouse that provide us with these precious moments of celebration. These institutions have survived through many years of struggle. They symbolize tradition, excellence. revitalization, leadership and liberation."[6] If Morehouse was going to survive, it would take money to sustain it. The audience gave Reverend Moss a standing ovation for his "soul-stirring message."

Honorary degrees were then conferred on Herman J. Russell (doctor of laws), chairman and CEO of H. J. Russell Construction Company, headquartered in Atlanta, and Dr. Donald Hopkins, '62 (doctor of science), senior consultant to the Task Force for Child Survival and Global 2000 at the Carter Center, also in Atlanta.

Convocations and assemblies are inextricably a part of Morehouse tradition, as they have been held since the early days of the school when a suitable space made it possible to hold them. These events help reinforce the mission of supporting college-educated black men and often showcase Morehouse graduates who are providing leadership in their professions and in other areas of life.

The "Inaugural Symposium," whose theme was "Educating

---

[6] *Alumnus*, Special Inauguration Issue (1988): 20.

Tomorrow's Leaders Today," was held on Friday, February 19, 1987, in the Martin Luther King Jr. International Chapel, with the morning session starting at ten o'clock. Dr. Anna Harvin Grant, professor of sociology and chair of the Department of Sociology, chaired the symposium. Notably, the symposium was funded by the Coca-Cola Foundation, the Ivan Allen Company, the Georgia Power Foundation, and Citizens and Southern National Bank. This was the first time such funding had been secured, and it demonstrated the new president's business acumen and connections.

The morning session was moderated by Dr. Louis Wade Sullivan, '54, president of the Morehouse School of Medicine, and the panelists were Dr. Bernard Harleston, president of the City College of the City University of New York; Dr. John Chandler, president of the Association of American Colleges; Dr. Blenda Wilson, executive director of the Colorado Commission on Higher Education; Dr. Elaine El-Khawas, vice president for policy analysis and research at the American Council on Education; and Dr. Charles Vert Willie, '48, professor at the Harvard Graduate School of Education. After a lunch break, Dr. Alton P. Hornsby Jr. professor of history and chair of the Department of History, gave opening remarks, and Dr. Dorcas Bowles, acting president of Atlanta University, moderated the session. Panelists for the afternoon session were Dr. Calvert Smith, president of Morris Brown College; Dr. John Turner, associate dean of the graduate school at the Massachusetts Institute of Technology; Mr. Trent Berry, a member of the junior class at Morehouse; Dr. Robert Brisbane, professor of political science; and Dr. Samuel Myers, president of the National Association for Equal Opportunity in Higher Education. The symposium closed with remarks from Dr. Grant and President Keith. As the symposium participants and audience left King Chapel for dinner and other social occasions, they prepared themselves for the inauguration program and ceremony the next day. The views expressed were the usual ideas about the state of educational standards and operations in the United States, highlighting areas in need of change as the country approached the twenty-first century.

At high noon on Saturday, February 20, 1988, Morehouse College inaugurated its eighth president. As the inaugural program and ceremony got underway, most of the audience could not help but be reminded of the death of Wendell Whalum. After many years as a fixture on the organ for Morehouse convocations and programs, he was not there. Michael Johnson, an accomplished musician in his own right, was the organist. After performing "Variations on an Austrian Hymn" by John Knowles Paine as the prelude, the processional began with Johnson's arrangement of George F. Handel's "Thanks Be to Thee." Then Johnson played the "Grand March" from Giuseppe Verdi's famous opera *Aida* as the processional began, which included marshals, bearers of the colors, delegates from various colleges and universities, delegates from learned societies and professional organizations, delegates from foundations, representatives from corporations and government agencies, the Morehouse faculty and administration, the Morehouse alumni, members of the Morehouse senior class, the board of trustees, and the eighth president's party. Once the members of the various units had taken their seats, the Reverend Doctor Thomas Kilgore Jr., chairman of the Morehouse Board of Trustees, moved to the podium to make opening remarks as the presiding official for the inauguration program and ceremony. Dr. James Costen, president of the Interdenominational Theological Center, offered the invocation, and Dr. Weldon Jackson, vice president for academic affairs gave the occasion.

The audience then stood and sang the hymn "Fight the Good Fight," composed by William Boyd. After the singing of the hymn, a succession of greetings were given, first by Mr. Calvin Johnson, president of the Morehouse student body. Dr. James Haines spoke for the faculty, and Mr. Charlie Moreland represented the Morehouse alumni. Dr. Charles Meredith gave greetings as chancellor of the Atlanta University Center Corporation; Dr. Johnnetta Cole represented Spelman College; Dr. Thomas Coles spoke for Clark College; Mr. Charles Bedford gave greetings on behalf of the University Center of Georgia; and Mrs. LeGree Daniels, assistant secretary of civil rights in the United States Department of Education, who represented the president of the United States and the secretary of the Department of Education. The Honorable Andrew Young, mayor of the city of Atlanta, gave greetings from the city and was the last to speak. Following the greeting, the inauguration of the eighth president of Morehouse College was at hand.

Dr. Hugh M. Gloster, president emeritus, passed the official

Morehouse medallion to Dr. Keith, after which Mr. Theodore M. Alexander, '31, presented him as the eighth president of the college and Dr. Kilgore, '35, conducted the "Act of Investiture." The Morehouse Glee Club then sang "Three Voices," composed for the inauguration by Dr. Uzee Brown Jr., '72, professor of music, with text by Dr. Anne Watts, professor of English. Tenor Theodore Debro III was the soloist as the Glee Club sang "A Prayer of Thanksgiving," "A Song of Celebration," and "A Pledge of Faithfulness." David Morrow directed the Glee Club, which was accompanied by organist Michael Johnson, pianist Johnathan Alvarado ('88), and Atlanta Brassworks. Following these performances, the new president gave his inaugural address, laying out his plans for Morehouse College.

President Keith opened his address with the usual recognitions and acknowledgments of those present, including the chairman of the board and other board members, Mayor Andrew Young, President Emeritus Gloster, the students, faculty, and staff, the alumni, the representatives of colleges and universities, and friends and relatives. He then reflected on his time as a student at Morehouse and the inspiring words of Dr. Benjamin Elijah Mays: "There is an air of expectancy at Morehouse College. It is expected that the student who enters here will do well. It is expected that once a man bears the insignia of a Morehouse graduate he will do exceptionally well. We expect nothing less." Dr. Keith reminded the audience that "The 'House' and the 'Morehouse Man' are held in high esteem in almost every part of the globe" and that the college was "truly a national treasure whose mission of producing outstanding black male leadership must be enhanced." He then reflected on the history and traditions of Morehouse.

> Most would agree that there is an illustrious history of accomplishment at this College. However, it will not suffice for Morehouse to live on past accomplishments. This administration is committed to maintaining the tradition of excellence already established. But, *maintaining* a tradition will be insufficient. What is required is the enhancement of an impressive legacy, our future bristles with possibilities. It is the goal of this administration to continue to cause the frontiers of ignorance to recede into nothingness.

To actualize this goal, President Keith envisioned a smaller student enrollment "but with increased quality in its academic programs, students, faculty, staff and facilities." He wanted the college to remain "exclusively an undergraduate institution" with "a more integrated core curriculum that will help students understand the interrelationships between the liberal arts disciplines." The eighth president of Morehouse spoke of the need for more Morehouse students to pursue PhDs and informed the audience of the Ford Foundation grant with matching funds from the Pew and Culpeper Foundations to support students interested in graduate school and teaching. This initiative was the Ford-Morehouse Scholars Program.

Dr. Keith made clear that the strengthening of the liberal arts did not mean that the science and business department programs would be forgotten. And for the first time, the Morehouse community heard of the plan to "make computers accessible in every classroom, building, dormitory, and office at the college."

Ethical and moral values, research on black male leadership, a higher quality of campus life, cooperative efforts with the other schools in the Atlanta University Center, faculty and staff development, more scholarship assistance, a diverse student body, and an improved physical plant were all in Dr. Keith's plans for Morehouse. The new president pointed out that achieving this "long and awesome agenda would require a herculean effort on the part of every constituent group at the college and increased support from outside sources." But in order to persuade outside sources to give to Morehouse, he rightly concluded that "the college must do a better job of helping itself." Alumni giving would be important to the continued success of Morehouse, but Dr. Keith knew that there was a "need to develop a formal structure for alumni fund-raising efforts and perhaps designate it as the Morehouse Annual Fund."

Recalling the history of the college, President Keith's closing words clearly registered with the audience when he said, "I urge you to join me in this effort to propel Morehouse into the twenty-first century [a mere twelve years away] with the competitive edge to be deemed one of America's foremost institutions of higher learning. The House will become a stronger House. With God's help, we will realize our goals." And with these words, President Leroy Keith Jr., the eighth president of Morehouse College, returned to his seat to enthusiastic applause and a standing ovation from the audience. A new era in the history of the college had begun—the Keith years.

Appropriately, following the inaugural address the Glee Club sang "I'm Building Me A Home," also arranged by Dr. Uzee Brown Jr., '72, and featuring baritone Ernest White as the soloist. After the singing of "Dear Old Morehouse," the benediction was bestowed by Dr. Lawrence Edward Carter, dean of the chapel. As organist Michael Johnson played Vaclav Nelhybel's "A Mighty Fortress" (based on Martin Luther's "*Ein feste Burg*"), the processional moved out of King Chapel and into the Beulah H. Gloster Conference Center adjacent to the chapel, where President and Mrs. Keith received the audience. William Jefferson and the other founders would have been pleased to hear Dr. Keith's vision and plans for Morehouse. As expected, the college had changed a great deal since its establishment in 1867, and the plans proposed by Keith would create significant change going forward. The new vision for the college was the talk of the evening at the Morehouse Inaugural Banquet, which was held at the Radisson Inn in downtown Atlanta. Maynard Jackson Jr., '56, was the toastmaster.

One of President Keith's plans for Morehouse did not come to fruition. Instead of becoming a smaller, more exclusive college, enrollment grew. The *1987–1989 Morehouse College Catalog* reported an enrollment at 2,000. By the time the 1989–1991 catalog was issued, enrollment had increased to 2,500. The school's enrollment continued to grow, and on May 22, 1988, 279 newly minted Morehouse Men received their baccalaureate degrees. Commencement 1988 was the first presided over by Dr. Keith.

Baccalaureate was held the day before commencement in the Martin Luther King Jr. International Chapel on Saturday, May 21, with Dr. Samuel Proctor, pastor of the historic Abyssinian Baptist Church in Harlem, New York, preaching the sermon. Rev. Proctor preached about "What Happens to Compassion in a Market Economy," which spoke to the rising standing of the market culture in America: ethics—compassion—must guide our way in such an economy. Closing his address, Rev. Proctor received the approval of the audience.

Commencement was held the next day, on Sunday, May 22. King Chapel was filled to capacity—standing room only. "President Keith challenged the Class of 1988 to leave Morehouse with a set of values that must successfully compete with the prevailing notion that wealth, power, and material things are ends which justify any means for acquiring them"[7] He also advised the graduates to pursue advanced degrees: the Morehouse Scholars Program, which had very recently been installed at the college, would assist in actualizing this vision.

Delivering the commencement address, Dr. John Slaughter, chancellor of the University of Maryland at College Park, encouraged graduates to "take intelligent risks to accomplish many of the things we deem worthwhile." He emphasized the fact that African Americans had lost valuable standing in the professional and educational arenas, and he emphasized that historically black institutions needed to play a major role in regaining that footing, aligning his views with the founding mission of the school. As Morehouse developed, the belief that her graduates would take on major leadership roles across all walks of life has been the driving force behind the successes that are frequently recited. "You can tell a Morehouse Man, but you can't tell him much."

Before the 279 men crossed the stage of King Chapel to receive their degrees—accompanied by thunderous celebratory applause and joyous shouts from parents, grandparents, other family members and friends—honorary degrees were awarded. Charlayne Hunter-Gault, who, along with former Morehouse student Hamilton Holmes, became one of the first two black students to graduate from the University of Georgia, and who was now a national correspondent for the McNeil-Leher New Hour, received an honorary Doctor of Laws degree, as did Herman Cain, a member of the Morehouse class of 1967 who was president and CEO of Godfather's Pizza. Cain would later make a bid for the office of president of the United States of America. Wole Soyinka, the Nigerian playwright, novelist, and poet who received the 1986 Nobel Prize for Literature, received the honorary doctor of humane letters degree. Both Albert Bowker, an educator and former chancellor of the City University of New York and the University of California at Berkeley, and John Slaughter, the first African American to serve as chancellor of the University of Maryland, were awarded honorary Doctor of Science degrees. To close the program,

---

[7] Ibid.

Artis White, a member of the class of 1951, responding to the call for alumni to give to the college, presented the college with a deferred gift of $1,500,000, which was the largest gift to Morehouse by a single individual in the 121-year history of the school. The fundraising campaign was off to a good start.

By the time his inauguration was held, Dr. Keith and his family had already moved into the president's residence on Flamingo Drive in southwest Atlanta. This house was the third official residence for the president of Morehouse, the first being the president's apartment in Graves Hall, and the second being the house just a few steps east and slightly north of Graves Hall. The Keiths did not live long in the Flamingo Drive home, though, and the move to a new house on West Wesley Drive, in the tony Buckhead section of northwest Atlanta, brought controversy to the Keith presidency.

Shortly after they took occupation of the Flamingo Drive residence, a storm severely damaged the home, and the Keith family sought housing elsewhere. Eventually, President Keith received approval from the Morehouse Board of Trustees to build a new house for the president in Buckhead, Atlanta's wealthiest neighborhood. The decision to locate the president's residence at a farther distance from the campus did not sit well with many students and alumni. Although the house had the approval of the board of trustees, its construction exceeded the allocated budget, raising eyebrows among many constituents of the college. Eventually, the house would become part of the controversy surrounding Dr. Keith that hastened his departure from the presidency at Morehouse.

One of the programs that blossomed during the Keith administration was the Morehouse/Ford Scholars Program, which admitted its first scholars in the fall of 1988. In May, the 1988 spring semester ended and summer programs began, meaning that most students were away from the campus participating in summer internships, gainfully employed, or enjoying enriching travel experiences. The Morehouse community was caught off guard on June 24, 1988, by the announcement of the merger between Atlanta University, a charter member of the Atlanta University Affiliation (along with Morehouse and Spelman) and Clark College. The merger, which fundamentally dismantled the affiliation, was effectuated based on a premise of financial responsibility and administrative efficiency. The disassembling of the affiliation had begun when Morehouse decided to establish a medical school, and now the merger created Clark-Atlanta University (CAU). Perhaps a more significant indicator of the dire future for historically black colleges was the closure of Bishop College in Dallas, on August 15, 1988. Over the next three decades, other black institutions of higher education would close or suffer financial setbacks, including Morehouse.

As the 1988 to 1989 academic year began, Leroy Keith Jr. was in the second year of his presidency and the Morehouse Scholars Program began its work with a grant from the Ford Foundation. The program was deemed necessary "because of the flight of competent individuals from the teaching profession during the past twenty years and the resulting urgent need for well-trained and highly motivated teachers in institutions of higher education throughout the United States."[8] Twenty-four students from the junior and senior classes would be selected to participate in the scholars program, each with a faculty mentor, and the Ford Foundation would provide $150,000 in support, with the understanding that the college would raise a matching $150,000. A total of $300,000 would be expended at the rate of $100,000 a year, beginning with the academic year 1986 to 1987.[9] For satisfactory performance, as determined by the faculty mentor and the program's director, each student participant received a yearly stipend of $1,500, which was paid in two installments of $750 each. The faculty mentor received a stipend of $1,000 per student for supervising and guiding the research and teaching efforts of the student scholars. There was a reciprocal relationship because, in addition to his own research project and writing, each student scholar served as a teaching assistant and research assistant working under the supervision of his faculty mentor.

The program and the Morehouse community rejoiced when a participant in the Ford Scholars Program became Morehouse College's first Rhodes Scholar. Nima Warfield, a member of the class of 1994, was among thirty-two students awarded the prestigious scholarship in 1993 to study at Oxford University in England. Dr. Melvin Rahming, a professor

---

[8] "Proposal to the Ford Foundation," 1.

[9] Ibid.

of English, was Warfield's mentor in the scholars program. Warfield, an English major from Plainfield, New Jersey, was not only the first Morehouse student to receive the honor, he was also the first American student from a historically black college or university to be awarded a Rhodes Scholarship. Nima, whose cumulative grade point average was 4.0, was twenty-one years old when he was selected from an applicant pool of 1,200, and he was a member of Phi Beta Kappa, the Sigma Tau Delta International English Society, the Golden Key National Honor Society, and the Morehouse Honor Society. Rhodes Scholarship winners are selected based on the applicant's academic transcript, letters of reference, essay, and personal interview. Nima Warfield attributed his win to the public schools he attended, to African American families, and to Morehouse, an HBCU. Subsequently, Morehouse was honored with four more students being awarded Rhodes Scholarships.

As the successful work in the early days of the Morehouse/Ford Foundation program continued, President Keith and his administration looked for other ways to leave their mark on the college. All new presidents of Morehouse, with the exception of President Archer, undertook building projects that left a legacy for the future. President Gloster was so prolific in constructing new buildings that some were heard to humorously say that he had an "edifice complex." As the eighth president of Morehouse, Dr. Keith began his construction legacy with the Thomas A. Kilgore Campus Center and Dormitory, which opened in 1992. There was some controversy surrounding the construction of this facility that fueled the rumor mills and myths. As the story went, Morehouse was to be the recipient of $10 million from Bill Cosby; the same amount was to be given to Spelman. There were stipulations on how the funds were to be used, though, and apparently President Keith did not follow these as they had been set forth in the agreement. Cosby, upset by the violation, gave Spelman the donation that was supposed to be given to Morehouse, and so Spelman ended up receiving a gift of $20 million. In hindsight, it may have been seen as fortunate when scandals rocked Bill Cosby and his image, forcing many institutions to return funds, negate honorary degrees, and take other actions to distance their institutions from Mr. Cosby; Morehouse removed him from its board of trustees. Before he was removed from the board, though, and while his relationship with

Morehouse was still good, Cosby gave substantial donations to the college. His son, Ennis William Cosby, graduated from Morehouse in 1992 while Dr. Keith was president.

The Ford Scholars Program had become a signature program at Morehouse, stimulating similar scholars programs in departments across the campus. One of these was the Dana Scholars Program, which was implemented in the early nineties and which also successfully recruited students who were interested in pursuing graduate degrees. In fact, there was some competition between the Ford Scholars Program and the Dana Scholars Program for the same students. Both programs were interdisciplinary in their missions, and, like the Ford program, the Dana program was part of a larger initiative to channel more college students into the professoriate. Additional scholars' programs were funded and implemented in other departments as more students considered graduate and professional school after earning their Morehouse undergraduate degrees. The invigorating scholarly climate at the college continued with the inauguration of the Benjamin E. Mays Lectures. Created to honor the sixth president of Morehouse, and President Keith's mentor, the first lecture was given Dr. Henry Louis "Skip" Gates, a Harvard professor, scholar, and intellectual extraordinaire.

In 1987, the year that Leroy Keith Jr. became the president of Morehouse, Billy Payne, an attorney and former University of Georgia football player, with support from Maynard Jackson and Andrew Young, conceived the idea of Atlanta hosting the 1996 Summer Olympic Games. Subsequently, the games were awarded to the city of Atlanta in September 1990, and Morehouse College benefitted from the international competition in many ways, including infrastructure enhancements, worldwide visibility, and financial gains.

In the meantime, at a November 1988 meeting of the Morehouse Board of Trustees a few short months after his inauguration, President Keith announced that the Founders' Day program would take place on February 16 and that a Founder's Day Banquet was being planned to recognize contributions of outstanding black male leaders from around the country. It was President Keith's hope that the event would draw as many as a thousand guests to the Peachtree Plaza Hotel and that this would become an annual affair "and develop into a major fund-raising activity."[10] Robert H. Bolton and Hardy R. Franklin, Morehouse alumni, made the idea a reality, and it became one of the most successful events in the history of the school. Bolton and Franklin were members of the college's development team in the Morehouse Office of Development, the precursor of the Office of Institutional Advancement. At that time, Richard A. Ammons, who had recently succeeded Dr. William Kearney as vice president for development, was assisted by Denise A. Whitely. Other members of the development office included Ronn Edmundson, director of public relations; Oliver R. Delk, director of government relations; Yvonne A. King, director of corporate relations; and Hardy Franklin, director of alumni affairs. Also working in development were Verna Bolton, Cassandra Carter, Sylvia A. McAfee, Patricia Sauls, and Martha Starks. The design for the gala was "to highlight the college's traditional mission of producing leaders, pay tribute to nationally acclaimed African American [male] leaders who were considered giants in their respective fields, and to showcase the talents and oratorical skills of Morehouse students." The name of the event, "A Candle in the Dark," paid homage to a book on the history of the college by the same name that had been written by Edward A. Jones, a member of the Morehouse class of 1926.

Hardy Franklin, director of alumni affairs, and Robert Bolton, assistant to the director of public relations cochaired the event. The first Candle in the Dark Gala was held at Atlanta's Peachtree Plaza Hotel on Saturday evening, February 18, 1989, during the college's Founders' Week commemoration and celebration. Two categories of award were created: The "Bennie" was named in honor of President Benjamin E. Mays and would be awarded each year to a Morehouse Man who demonstrated outstanding service, achievement, and trailblazing accomplishments. The Candle Award was created to honor other African American men for their accomplishments in a variety of professions and fields of endeavor.

These awards were regarded as prestigious from the very beginning, and the first Bennie awards were presented to Dr. Roderic Pettigrew, '72, physician and nuclear physicist, who received a Bennie Achievement Award; Dr. Otis Smith, '47, physician and president of the Atlanta

[10] Minutes of the meeting of the Morehouse College Board of Trustees, November 17–18, 1988, 16–17.

chapter of the National Association for the Advancement of Colored People, who was given a Bennie Service Award; and Dr. Louis W. Sullivan, '54, physician, founder, and first president of the Morehouse School of Medicine, who at the time was the secretary of the United States Department of Health and Human Services, who was awarded the Bennie Trailblazer Award. Eight "Candle" awards were presented: actor Danny Glover was honored for entertainment; professional athlete Vincent "Bo" Jackson was recognized in athletics; George R. Lewis, vice president and treasurer of the Phillip Morris Corporation, was selected for business; Henry Louis "Skip" Gates Jr., the W. E. B. Du Bois professor of literature at Cornell University, was honored in education; Kurt Schmoke, mayor of Baltimore, Maryland, was selected for law; Fred A. Gordon, commandant of cadets at the United States Military Academy at West Point, was selected for military; his Excellency, the Reverend Eugene A. Marino, archbishop of the Atlanta archdiocese of the Catholic Church, was chosen for religion; and Dr. Benjamin Carson, chief of pediatric neurosurgery at John Hopkins University Hospital, was given the award for science and technology. The inaugural Candle in the Dark Gala was a great success and enhanced the brand of the college.

Shortly after the beginning of the gala, "Reflections on Excellence" was added to the schedule of activities surrounding Founders' Week. "Reflections" presented the honorees for that year in King Chapel, where they inspired the audience with musings on their paths toward professional achievement and success. The chapel was nearly filled to capacity in 1990, the second year of the event, when Denzel Washington received a "Candle" for achievement in arts and entertainment. The year before, Washington had won the Academy Award (Oscar) for Best Supporting Actor for his portrayal of a confident and resistive ex-slave soldier in the acclaimed movie *Glory*. By 2021, the Candle in the Dark Gala celebrated thirty-two years of success and has become a signature event for Morehouse College. Over the years, hundreds of deserving men from various fields have received the awards.

The first Candle in the Dark awards dinner "was recognized as the most outstanding special event in Georgia [in 1989] and presented a 'Phoenix Award for Excellence' by the Public Relation Society of America,

Georgia Chapter."[11] The event was so successful and popular that its attendance, which started with several hundred guests, doubled, then tripled, and eventually grew to several thousand by its silver anniversary in 2014. Several hundred men and one woman, Ms. Oprah Winfrey (who was awarded the Lifetime Achievement in Humanitarian Service Award), have received a "Bennie" or "Candle" award. After several years at the Peachtree Plaza Hotel, the venue moved to the World Congress Center, and then to the Centennial Ballroom at the Hyatt Regency Hotel on Peachtree Street in downtown Atlanta, where it has remained to this day. Attire changed from business dress to formal wear during the Massey era; black tie and evening gowns became de rigueur.

The gala has become a well-staged, sophisticated event, notable for its purpose and the funds it raises for the Morehouse scholarship fund. It is one of the major events on the Atlanta social calendar and stands as a significant achievement of the Keith presidency. Nevertheless, a serious controversy soon surrounded Dr. Keith which would lead to his departure from Morehouse.

In its annual publication of selected salaries at colleges and universities in the spring 1994, *The Chronicle of Higher Education*, "using figures provided by Morehouse, put Dr. Keith's salary and benefits at $264,309, the third highest behind Wellesley and Barnard for small liberal arts schools. Overall, his salary ranked 25th in the country." Subsequent to the *Chronicle*'s report, the *Atlanta Journal-Constitution*, "citing the findings of a special audit, reported that board members were angered that the president received a compensation and salary that amounted to $428,00 and lived in a $700,000 ($1.3 million in 2014) college-owned house in Buckhead, a predominantly white section of the city several miles from the college's black neighborhood."[12] The disparity in the *Chronicle*'s salary number and the audit's figure might be due to a variety of things, according to the experts, such as "the mortgage payment on the presidential residence, the value of a car leased for the president's use and the maintenance of the home and the car." The accounting firm of KPMG Peat Marwick had conducted the special audit, which was ordered in 1993 by

[11] A Candle in the Dark Gala program (2011).

[12] www.nytimes.1994/09/28/us/morehouse-financial-questions-reach-board-chairman.

the Morehouse Board of Trustees. Dr. Benjamin Blackburn and James Hudson, classmates of Dr. Keith, announced that "the special audit was continuing and that the board was grappling with additional questions beyond the issue of the purchase of the president's residence and the compensation."[13] As the controversy surrounding Dr. Keith's compensation package exacerbated, the eighth president of Morehouse resigned on Friday, September 30, 1994.

At the same time that questions were asked about the fiduciary responsibility of President Keith, questions were also swirling around James Hudson, chairman of the Morehouse Board of Trustees. A group of fourteen trustees sent a letter to the chairman asking him "to step aside so that other board officers could oversee the continuing investigation into the findings of the audit." Mr. Hudson had no plans to step down, saying, "I have done nothing unethical."[14]

The audit at Morehouse was ordered in light of the highly publicized revelation of a $5 million deficit at Morris Brown College, another Atlanta University Center institution. At the time, Morris Brown had mounted a $2.5 million emergency drive to overcome its financial crisis. The "Independent Auditor's Report" by KPMG Peat Marwick LLP to the board of trustees of Morehouse College, September 16, 1994, "stood by its report that the financial statements in all material aspects, addressed the financial position of Morehouse College as of June 30, 1994, and the changes in fund balances and the current fund revenues, expenditures, and other changes for the years were in conformity with generally accepted accounting principles." The report was on point.

In his resignation letter, Dr. Keith argued that the audit was "filled with inaccuracies and misrepresentations," but he would leave Morehouse, where he had been president for seven years. Attorney James Hudson, chairman of the board, also resigned his position. Immediately after Keith's resignation, Wiley A. Perdue, vice president for business affairs, occupied the office of the president of Morehouse College. The board of trustees officially appointed him as acting president on October 1, 1994. The Reverend Doctor Otis Moss Jr., '56, was unanimously elected to

[13] Ibid.

[14] Ibid.

replace Hudson as chairman of the board. Dr. Moss, the pastor of Olivet Institutional Baptist Church in Cleveland, had been on the board since 1979, where he had been serving as vice chairman since 1992. In order to normalize the situation at the college, Acting President Perdue prioritized reaching out to the college's constituencies, including students, parents, faculty, staff, alumni, and supporters in the corporate and philanthropic communities. His message was that Morehouse was "built on a firm commitment of excellence undergirded by a 128-year tradition of serving the academic, moral and spiritual needs of [its] students and...society. That fact remains unchanged."

Shortly after he became acting president, Mr. Perdue was awarded an honorary doctorate at Dillard University in New Orleans, where Dr. Samuel DuBois Cook, '48, served as president. During the 1994 holiday season, Dr. Perdue visited ten cities nationwide to talk about issues facing the college. A dark cloud hung over the college yet the "candle in the dark" continued to burn brightly, illuminating the way for young men who made real the idea first conceived in 1867.

Wiley Perdue, a 1957 Morehouse graduate, had served as the vice president for business affairs in both the Gloster and Keith administrations before the board of trustees appointed him as acting president. Board chair Otis Moss Jr., commenting on Perdue's tenure, said, "Dr. Perdue [gave] exceptional leadership to our College at a critical moment of challenge and change. He lifted up the ideals of Morehouse in word, deed, and spirit, and earned our highest praise. In a decidedly limited period of time, Wiley accomplished much on behalf of Morehouse and her students."[15] Beyond maintaining a crucial sense of stability and continuity for the college after Dr. Keith's unexpected departure, some of Dr. Perdue's accomplishments during his ten-month tenure as acting president included the following: he obtained board approval to establish a leadership development center; obtained authorization for and oversaw the construction of memorials for Dr. and Mrs. Howard Thurman and Dr. and Mrs. Benjamin Mays; negotiated with the Atlanta Committee for the Olympic Games to build a 5,700-seat Olympic basketball arena on campus and to allow Olympic athletes the use of the Edwin Moses Track as a

---

[15] *Alumnus* (Summer 1995) 10.

practice facility; expanded the college's northern boundaries for the construction of a 200-bed student dormitory, which was initially used by guests visiting Atlanta during the 1996 Olympic Games; spearheaded an initiative that revamped and reemphasized college assemblies, including Crown Forum; initiated a management program for the college's information systems capabilities; launched a strategic planning, budgeting, and evaluation process to ensure reaccreditation by the Southern Association of Colleges and Schools; and established the Presidential Award of Distinction to honor individuals who made special contributions to Morehouse.[16]

Acting President Perdue was a "Bennie's Boy," having arrived at Morehouse from Jones County, Georgia, as a freshman in 1953. Graduating in 1957, he went on to earn a master's degree in business administration from Atlanta University in 1958 and accepted a position as an instructor of economics and business administration at Savannah State College (now University). At Savannah State, Perdue advanced through the system to become registrar, director of admissions, director and operator of the computer center, and a professor of business administration. In 1969, he came to Morehouse as registrar during President Gloster's administration and eventually became business manager and vice president for business affairs. Dr. Gloster said of Wiley Perdue, "For 18 of my 20 years as president of Morehouse College, Wiley and I worked closely together as an administrative team. I regard him not only as a first-class business executive but also as one of the best acting presidents I have ever known."[17] In this role, Dr. Perdue joined the ranks of Estes, Hope, Archer, and Hubert as one of the capable men who, by taking on the role of acting president during a time of need, ensured the college continued to operate.

---

[16] Ibid., 12.
[17] Ibid., 11.

Chapter 17

"The Glorious Crown": One of the Best Colleges Period!

The Morehouse community was in confusion and dismay when the news broke about Dr. Keith's resignation. There were as many opinions about the news as there were stories about what really happened. Dr. Keith had been seen as a good president of Morehouse, and its constituents were looking forward to many more years of growth and development in all areas of the college. Dr. Mays had served the college for twenty-seven years, and Dr. Gloster for twenty, and although college presidents no longer served for as long as they had in previous generations, it was assumed that President Keith would serve for at least ten or fifteen years. So his surprise resignation came as a tremendous shock to all. This had never happened at Morehouse. Regardless of where the blame belonged—whether with Keith, the board, or the treasurer—the image of the college was at risk. Morehouse College prided itself on the image of the Morehouse Man.

When more information reached the general public, it was revealed that no theft had taken place and that the exorbitant salary and perks had board approval. The board was left with a black eye as its chair resigned. As the controversy abated, Dr. Wiley Perdue kept the "candle in the dark" burning and made a valiant bid to become the ninth president of Morehouse, but his attempt fell short of its goal.

At an urgently called meeting of alumni in Sale Hall during Homecoming 1995, Dr. Perdue was grilled about his knowledge of the financial affairs of the college in relation to his role as both treasurer of the board of trustees and the vice president for business affairs for the college. By his own admission, he said he had been aware of Dr. Keith's expenditures but had not questioned the excessive outlay because "Keith was his boss."

After the spirited dialogue with Dr. Perdue, the discussion shifted to the question of who could assume the role of president and immediately boost stakeholder morale to refocus on prestige of the school—someone who could showcase "the glorious crown" that was above the heads of the sons of Morehouse, someone who would embody the "Idea" of what Morehouse was and could be. The words enshrined in the college's hymn, "To old Morehouse and her ideals, and in all things that we do," were sung with gusto at the end of the Sale Hall meeting. Very quickly, Dr. Walter Eugene Massey, class of 1958, became the unanimous choice of the alumni to be the ninth president of Morehouse College. Dr. Massey had recently been selected as chancellor of the California State University System, so his decision to accept the offer from Morehouse was met with mixed opinions in the Golden State.

Dr. Eugene and Mrs. Shirley Massey became the ninth president and first lady of Morehouse College on July 1, 1995, the beginning of the school's fiscal year. Dr. Massey brought with him an international reputation as a scientist, educator, aesthete, and humanitarian, and his track record drew him closer to the glorious crown that hovers over the heads of the sons of Morehouse. Nonetheless, controversy surrounded the Masseys at the outset, but one that would have a positive outcome: they refused to stay in the Morehouse-owned president's residence on West Wesley in Buckhead that had been built for the Keiths and took up residence instead in an apartment at the Georgian Terrace Hotel, at 659 Peachtree Street in Midtown Atlanta. This inspired the board of trustees to immediately make plans to build a new president's house on the Morehouse campus, and the Masseys vowed to remain at the Georgian Terrace until this was done. The new president's home was quickly constructed, and the Masseys moved in shortly thereafter. It was named Davidson House in honor of its most generous benefactors, Robert and Faye Davidson.

Early in the afternoon of Friday, February 16, 1996, at half past one o'clock, and as the sun filtered through snow flurries, the inauguration of Morehouse College's ninth president began. As the Howard Thurman bells rang, hundreds of delegates—including Morehouse students and faculty; representatives from other colleges, universities, and learned societies; alumni; and the Morehouse class of 1996—left Archer Hall, where they had been marshaled in the longest processional in the history of the college. The line of march moved east on Fair Street, turned onto the campus proper behind historic Graves Hall, walked down Brown Street to Westview Drive, and then into the Martin Luther King Jr.

International Chapel. They processed to "Triumphal March of Heritage," composed by Uzee Brown, '72, which was commissioned for the occasion. David F. Oliver was at the manuals of the Wendell Phillips Whalum Sr. Memorial Pipe Organ and played pre-ceremonial music that included Fred Swann's "Trumpet Tune," Johann Sebastian Bach's "Piece d'Orgue, BWV 572," Charles Marie Widor's popular "Toccata," and Oliver's own moving improvisation on "Dear Old Morehouse." Members of the African American Philharmonic Orchestra provided the music for the academic march.

After more than half an hour, the delegates, representatives, and platform party were seated, and the Reverend Emmett Thomas Martin Jr., pastor of the historic Springfield Baptist Church in Augusta (where Morehouse was first organized in 1867), signaled the call to order by the ringing of the bell. The Reverend William Vincent Guy, '57, pastor of historic Friendship Baptist Church (where the college first held classes when it moved to Atlanta), offered the invocation, and greetings were delivered by Dr. Vartan Gregorian, president of Brown University, where Dr. Massey had been a professor of physics and dean of the college; Dr. Arthur M. Sussman, chief legal officer at the University of Chicago, where the ninth president of Morehouse had been vice president for research; and Dr. Anna Harvin Grant, professor and chair of the Morehouse Department of Sociology.

The Morehouse Glee Club then performed Dr. Uzee Brown's "God, Give Us Men," based on words written by Dr. Martin Luther King Jr. and D. G. Holland. The anthem was accompanied by a brass quintet and timpani. Following the reading of the inaugural poem, titled "Massey's Ministry" by Michael S. Harper, a professor of English at Brown University, the investiture of the ninth president of Morehouse College was conferred. The Reverend Doctor Otis Moss Jr., '56, gave the charge, and Dr. Lerone Bennett Jr., '49, delivered the affirmation and charter. The keys and the seal were presented by Attorney Willie J. Davis, '56, the prayer was invoked by the Reverend Doctor Robert M. Franklin, '75, and the mace was handed to the new president by Dr. Moss. The investiture complete, the trumpet then sounded and the Glee Club rose and sang "In His Care-O," a spiritual by William Dawson.

As the Glee Club took their seats to the applause of the audience, Dr.

Walter Eugene Massey, the ninth president of Morehouse, came to the podium to give his inaugural address, "A Culture of Affirmative Excellence." Beginning, he exclaimed, "I have said it before. But I must say it again: It is good to be back at Morehouse." Speaking proudly as a Morehouse Man, he said, "I am honored to stand here today. Indeed, more than honored, I am humbled. The task of leading this marvelous institution into the twenty-first century is an enormous responsibility, a challenge I eagerly, but solemnly, embrace." He then spoke of the challenge of leadership and made a pledge to the college: "In meeting the responsibility of leadership entrusted to me, I pledge to draw on my career as an educator, my experience as an administrator, my skills as a scientist, and my uncompromising commitment, as a Morehouse Man, to the highest standards of excellence and integrity—to the standards embraced by all members of the Morehouse family, but best exemplified by our remarkable and beloved Benjamin E. Mays." The audience applauded. The new president reminded the audience of the contemporary social and economic issues "in these contentious times"—global warming, budget deficits, technological preparedness, rising crime rates, teen pregnancy, persistent poverty, rising intolerance, and the plight of black men. "There is no dearth of challenging issues on our horizon," he continued. "Indeed, I am reminded of the old Chinese curse: 'May you live in interesting times.' Well, these are interesting times. Yet when I consider this daunting array of issues—in the context of the heritage and rich tradition of education at Morehouse—another Chinese saying comes to mind, a proverb familiar to many members of our College family: 'It is better to light a candle in the dark than to curse the darkness.'" Briefly recalling the heritage of the college, he then referenced W. E. B. Du Bois when he declared that the mission of the university or college was "to be the organ of that fine adjustment between real life and the growing knowledge of life, an adjustment which forms the secret of civilization." The ninth president then addressed three of the challenges of the day as the college looked toward the twenty-first century.

The first of the three challenges Dr. Massey addressed was *cultural* challenge. As technology continued to shatter boundaries and barriers, "blurring divisions among cultures, religions, and races, and rendering the term 'minority' less and less meaningful," he asked his audience, "What kind of education is needed in a world where our careers, family structures, and intellectual and social development often require us to work and socialize with individuals from various cultures throughout our international community?"

The second challenge of the twenty-first century was the need to focus on *moral and ethical education.* "Indeed, higher education must instill in students a set of values appropriate to our international community. Within the international tapestry is a rich diversity of race, religion, culture, and language, a metropolis of neighborhoods with varied traditions and values."

The third challenge addressed by President Massey was the *intellectual* needs of the times. He argued that "one aspect of this challenge—and it bears directly on our competitiveness as a nation in the new global marketplace—is our need to produce more scientists, especially among African Americans." To accomplish our mission "to produce leaders for the global metropolis that the world will be in the next century," Dr. Massey posited that "the first thing we can do is to appreciate and harness the diversity within our own communities." He then said "a basic prerequisite for appreciating diversity is appreciating oneself." Concluding his inaugural address, the ninth president of Morehouse said, "Above all, we will prepare our students by continuing to engage them in an intellectual, moral and ethical dialogue that underscores our recommitment to a *culture of excellence*, a dialogue that will...establish Morehouse as one of the best undergraduate, liberal arts colleges in the nation, one of the best institutions of any historical tradition, one of the best—period." After the loud and sustained applause of the audience, which included hundreds of alumni, Dr. Massey asserted that "to do so, we dedicate ourselves to affirming excellence at Morehouse, to a recommitment to excellence in scholarship, leadership and service. This is our challenge. This is our goal. This is our commitment."[1] With these words, Dr. Massey returned to his seat to the ovations of the gathered throng. After the affirming applause, the Reverend Doctor Moss Jr. gave concluding remarks, the audience stood and sang the college hymn, and the Reverend Doctor Lawrence Edward Carter, dean of the chapel, gave the benediction. The dignitaries and

[1] Walter E. Massey, "Inaugural Speech" (February 16, 1996).

delegates recessed to the same music played for the processional—Brown's "Triumphal March of Heritage." Organist Oliver played "Fantasie on 'National Hymn'" as post-ceremonial music.

The reception for the new president took place in the Thomas Kilgore Jr. Campus Center, where guests engaged in conversations about how Morehouse was one of America's best colleges, not just one of the best black colleges. And while black colleges are American colleges, they are oftentimes set apart from other institutions of higher education and judged by different standards. The Higher Education Act of 1965 created the term "historically black colleges and university" (HBCU), and in 1996, that was the popular way to identify black colleges, including Morehouse. But President Massey wanted the same standards used to judge Morehouse to judge all liberal arts college. Period!

Early in the presidency of Dr. Walter E. Massey, which began in August 1995, Dr. Perdue returned to his previous position as vice president for business affairs. Other members of Massey's leadership team in the first years of his presidency were Yong J. Lee; executive assistant to the president; Weldon Jackson, vice president for academic affairs; William K. Dease, dean of admissions, financial aid, and records; Andre Pattillo, acting director of the Office of Admissions; Eddie Gaffney, acting vice president for student affairs; Oliver Delk, acting vice president for development; Dr. Bernard Smith, vice president for policy and planning; and Henry Goodgame, director of alumni affairs.

At the end of his first year as president, Dr. Massey presided at the May 19, 1996, commencement exercises. Late in the afternoon, at five o'clock, as the temperature reached a searing 96 degrees on the Century Campus, 508 Men of Morehouse became Morehouse Men when they received their baccalaureate degrees. The commencement program featured as its keynote speaker Attorney Johnnie L. Cochran Jr., who had recently garnered worldwide attention as the "If it doesn't fit, you must acquit" lawyer for O. J. Simpson. Impressed by the crowd of nearly 10,000 parents, friends, faculty, staff, alumni, and spectators, Mr. Cochran told the graduates and the audiences, "It is no exaggeration that the world benefits from Morehouse. As you leave today, the world will benefit from you, too, because the qualities and skills you have honed here for the past four years give you the makings of greatness. But becoming great is a process that takes a while." And reminiscent of the O. J. trial, Mr. Cochran advised the graduates, saying, "So wait to be great." He then reminded them, "You are not the first to leave here so honored, nor will you be the last. Try and make sure the tradition is ever strengthened."[2] Strengthen the Morehouse traditions to make the school one of the best colleges, period!

During the time Leroy Keith Jr. and Wiley Perdue led the college, there were discussions about the role Morehouse would play in the Centennial Olympics. As commencement exercises were taking place at Morehouse and the other colleges and universities around the metropolitan Atlanta area, plans were being finalized for the arrival of the athletes and the Olympic events. The 1996 games in Atlanta were officially known as the Games of the XXVI Olympiad (the Olympics Games are played every four years), and unofficially called the Centennial Olympics. Atlanta was selected to host the Olympics on September 18, 1990, in Tokyo, Japan, and the city erupted in unbridled jubilation when Juan Antonio Samaranch made the announcement. Maynard Holbrook Jackson Jr., '56, was serving his second stint and third term as mayor of Atlanta, and as the announcement was made that his city had won the games, he rose, smoothed his hair, and, with all of the regalness for which he was known, radiated pride and confidence. By his side were Andrew Young (honorary), the mayor of Atlanta when the bid for the games was first made, and William "Billy" Payne, the architect and chief administrator of the Atlanta Committee for the Olympic Games (ACOG). Once the games were awarded to Atlanta, planning and preparation got underway. Mayor Jackson accepted the Olympic flag at the closing ceremony for the games in Barcelona, Spain, on August 9, 1992.

Morehouse College played a pivotal role in the activities leading up to the opening of the games thanks, in part, to Andre Bertrand, the director of administrative service who was promoted to vice president for campus operations. Working with Wiley Perdue, then vice president for business affairs, the college was successful in getting a basketball arena constructed on campus. Now known as Forbes Arena, the venue was used for practice sessions and playoff games. Morehouse also gained a larger footprint with the acquisition of additional land, a new dormitory with

[2] *Alumnus* (Summer 1996) 14.

the construction of Perdue Hall, and became the host for hundreds of international security personnel.

Many Morehouse alumni were involved in the games. Morris Dillard, '60, served as managing director of operations for ACOG and was responsible for security, transportation, logistics, and medical services. Roy D. Terry, '66, and Rudolph Terry, '69, co-owners of Terry Manufacturing Company of Roanoke, Alabama, were licensed to make and sell shirts, pants, and shorts bearing the Olympic logo and were the sub-licensees for apparel made by the sports-clothing company Champion, for whom Terry Manufacturing screen-printed, embroidered, and sewed Olympic logos. Edwin Moses, '78, a hurdler who had won two Olympic gold medals (in Montreal in 1976 and Los Angeles in 1984) and the bronze medal (in Seoul, South Korea, in 1988), was chief spokesperson for the Olympic athletes, "representing their views and concerns on issues ranging from eligibility to transportation to accommodations."[3] And Kenneth Pressley, '87, thanks to his impressive volunteerism with Big Brothers/Big Sisters of Atlanta, was honored by that organization as one of the Olympic torchbearers.

The Centennial Choir included members of the Morehouse Glee Club, which sang an arrangement of "I Have a Dream" at the closing ceremonies on August 4, 1996. The legacy of the Olympics can still be seen at Morehouse today. Although planning for participation took place before President Massey became president, the execution of these plans occurred at the end of his first year in office.

In the second year of his presidency, Dr. Massey made changes to his leadership team. Dr. John H. Hopps Jr., '58, replaced Dr. Weldon Jackson and carried the new and more prominent title of provost (the first in the history of the college) and *senior* vice president for academic affairs. The inclusion of the word "senior" in the new title spoke to the controversy surrounding the recent succession of the vice president for business affairs, not the vice president for academic affairs, to the office of president when the president resigned. Phyllis M. Bentley became the executive assistant to the provost, Freddie Johnson replaced Perdue as the vice president for business affairs, John Baker Brown was vice president for college

[3] Ibid., 17.

relations, Dr. Sulayman Clark was appointed vice president for development, Eddie Gaffney continued as vice provost for student affairs, Sterling Hudson became vice provost for admissions and enrollment management, John Foster Brown was the vice provost for educational technologies and information resources, Dr. Obie Clayton was vice provost for research, and Dr. Anne W. Watts served as vice provost for special academic programs. The mission of the president was now underway and this was his team.

Dr. Massey's reputation was well established before he accepted the job as president of Morehouse. In explaining why he returned to his alma mater to serve as its ninth president, he said a number of things convinced him and Mrs. Massey that coming here was the right decision. First, and foremost, was the strong support and encouragement of the alumni, many of whom, of course, were the Masseys' friends and colleagues. He also had the encouragement of many people he knew and respected from higher education and from the foundation and corporate world who saw Morehouse as an important institution. President Massey believed "it became more and more obvious that I could make a bigger difference by helping Morehouse achieve its mission than I could at probably any other institution. When I came back to visit the campus and met the students, I really became convinced. I just knew I would enjoy being here."[4] More than any constituent group, it is the students who, over the years, have kept the 1867 idea alive and have made the college an "important institution." The "glorious crown" is over their heads and they work very hard to try to wear it. But the crown keeps moving higher and higher.

One of the greatest challenges facing Morehouse in the last years of the twentieth century was the effort "to create a culture of excellence that permeates the institution." Dr. Massey thought the college was doing very well in attracting good students and faculty, and that the endowment was strong, but his goal was not to remain "where we are, but...[to become] one of the best undergraduate colleges—period—in the United States." If Morehouse were to continue to play the role in the twenty-first century that it had played for more than a century, "creating a culture of excellence is required. The other challenge is to generate the necessary resources."

[4] Ibid., 16.

Preparing for the twenty-first century required some expansion, re-articulation, sharpening, and refocusing of the mission. Despite President Massey's belief that there was no need to grow the student body, the student population increased. By the turn of the century, enrollment had topped 3,000. Land was purchased to expand the footprint of the college, some as a result of the Olympics. New programs were added, including a major in computer science, because they were needed, not just for the sake of expanding the curriculum. Faculty and students began to have more global experiences and more international perspectives, which affected the curriculum. Further, Dr. Massey asserted that everything taught at Morehouse should include some component of the African American experience. The college moved to become more technologically able, not just in terms of the systems, but in how technology would be infused in and implemented throughout the curriculum."[5]

Computer Science had been available as a major for Morehouse students for more than five years, and faculty members were adjusting to having personal computers in their offices. Interestingly, a new-and-improved African American Studies Program was approved by the faculty and the board of trustees in the spring of 1996 and began offering courses as a major, minor, and concentrate in the Department of History. Technically, African American studies had existed as a minor at Morehouse since the 1970s, but there were no opportunities to major in the field, so there were no students officially enrolled in the discipline. Courses on the African American experience had been offered at Morehouse since the late 1960s, but renewed interest in the field emerged among students and faculty participating in the Morehouse Scholars Program in 1990.

Still basking in the afterglow of the college's involvement in the 1996 Olympics, the new administration, faculty, staff, alumni, and students got down to the business of moving Morehouse forward to the new millennium. Within the first two years of his presidency, Dr. Massey added the administrative role of vice president for human resources to reorganize, restaff, and revitalize the department of human resources in order to deliver better customer service to Morehouse employees. Archer Hall, the old gymnasium, was converted into a student activities center, Sale Hall

[5] Ibid., 16–17.

Annex was renovated, and Lane/Chivers Dining Hall was renovated and the kitchen completely renovated. Perhaps most stunning of all the new developments was the opening of the Executive Center in the fall of 1998, now known as Davidson House in honor of Robert and Faye Davidson, who generously contributed to the establishment of the facility. Davidson House is the official residence of the president of Morehouse, and, as discussed earlier, this is the home where Dr. and Mrs. Massey moved after temporarily residing in an apartment at the Georgian Terrace Hotel while the college fulfilled its commitment to build a house for the president "on campus." The Executive Center was erected on Fair Street at what was then the north end of the campus, across from Nabrit-Mapp-McBay Hall, which is on the site where the old president's residence stood until 1969. The lower level of the center contains office space and four meeting rooms. The public meeting space is on the main floor and provides a great room, kitchen, formal dining room, library, and living room. The second, or top, floor is where the presidential suite is located along with a guest suite and two additional bedrooms.

In order to accelerate fundraising for the college, Dr. Massey began "Morehouse on the Move" (MOM), which took the president and other members of the Morehouse community to strategic cities across the country where the greatest impact would be realized. The first MOM was hosted by famed author Bebe Moore Campbell and her husband, Ellis Gordon Jr., a Los Angeles banker, at their vacation home on Martha's Vineyard in Massachusetts. The event was cohosted by Robert "Bob" Davidson, president and CEO of Los Angeles-based Surface Protection Industries and a member of the Morehouse Board of Trustees, and his wife, Faye.

The second MOM was held at the elegant Chicago Club in the Windy City and was attended by 250 guests. The event was cohosted by Oprah Winfrey and John Bryan, CEO of the Sara Lee Corporation. Ms. Winfrey gave a second gift of $1 million to the college at the MOM social and fundraising occasion where the Morehouse Quartet serenaded the guests.

The third MOM was held in the grand hall of the Dorothy Chandler Pavilion in Los Angeles, and was cohosted by David Coulter, chairman and CEO of BankAmerica, and entertainment titan Quincy Jones. The event was attended by 400 "movers and shakers," among whom were Michael Ovitz, Hollywood super-agent; Dr. Joe Bailey II, '57; Dr. Artis White, '51; and Dr. Joe Adams, a pioneer for African Americans in the radio, television, stage, and film industries, and Emma, his wife. Dr. and Mrs. Adams donated $1.5 million to the Morehouse Community Service Program.

The next MOM was held on September 8, 1998, in the nation's capital. Morehouse on the Move was an amazing idea that gained traction as monetary contributions to the college increased. Morehouse was truly on the move, and President Massey believed the college was "on target for achieving our objective to make Morehouse one of the finest liberal arts colleges in the nation and the world."[6]

Shortly after the national inaugural season in 1997, President Clinton announced his choice for the vacant position of United States surgeon general. Saying "no one is better qualified to be America's doctor," the president of the United States announced that Dr. David Satcher, '63, was his choice to fill the position. Morehouse College rejoiced and the world took notice. Dr. Satcher had come to Morehouse in 1958 from the cotton fields of Anniston, Alabama, and was a premed/biology/chemistry major at the college. As a "Bennie's Boy," David Satcher soaked up the wisdom of Dr. Mays and was influenced by the prominent speakers he heard in morning chapel five days a week. Dr. Mays had said, "It is not your environment, it is you—the quality of your minds, the integrity of your souls, and the determination of your wills—that will decide your future and shape your lives." Satcher, who had completed his primary and secondary education in the segregated public schools in Anniston, excelled as a student at Morehouse and served as president of the Morehouse Student Government Association in his senior year. After graduating from Morehouse, he enrolled at Case Western University in Cleveland and became the first African American at the university to earn both an MD and a PhD concomitantly. Before becoming the sixteenth surgeon general of the United States and the tenth assistant secretary for health, Dr. Satcher was a professor and chair of the Department of Community Medicine and Family Practice at the Morehouse School of Medicine and served on the

[6] "From the President," *Alumnus* (Fall 1998).

faculty at the UCLA School of Medicine, the UCLA School of Public Health, and the King-Drew Medical Center; served as interim dean of the Charles R. Drew Postgraduate Medical School and as the director of the King-Drew Sickle Cell Research Center; served as president of Meharry Medical College and as director of the Centers for Disease Control and Prevention; and worked as an administrator at the Agency for Toxic Substances and Disease Registry. With a keen understanding that government was different from academia, Dr. Satcher said, "I want to be the surgeon general who reaches our citizens with cutting-edge technology and plain, old-fashioned straight talk. Whether we are talking about smoking or poor diets, I want to send messages of good health to our cities and our suburbs, our barrios and reservations and even our prisons."[7] The Morehouse community honored the new surgeon general and felt a great sense of pride in his accomplishments. Dr. Satcher is representative of the thousands of Morehouse Men who, over the years, have had accomplished careers in medicine and other professions, and these graduates have worn the insignia of Morehouse Men very well. The glorious crown still hovered over their heads.

As Dr. David Satcher began his service as surgeon general, the twenty-first century was just two years away. The Morehouse of the late twentieth century had dramatically changed in the 1990s. This was the age of hip-hop, and the students at the college were not immune to its influence. Hip-hop, as a culture, had been around for two decades by this time and was gaining in popularity. This was the era of Tupac Shakur (whose collection is housed at the Robert W. Woodruff Library along with the famed Martin Luther King Jr. collection) and Christopher Wallace, aka Notorious B.I.G. (or Biggie Smalls). Dr. Jeffrey O. G. Ogbar, '91, author of *Hip-Hop Revolution: The Culture and Politics of Rap*, asserts that the history of hip-hop had its beginnings among African Americans and Puerto Ricans in the South Bronx in New York. "In the early 1970s, as the Black Power movement and Puerto Rican nationalist activism began to wane, a convergence of factors gave rise to hip-hop in New York City."[8]

---

[7] *Alumnus* (Fall 1998): 2.

[8] Jeffrey O. G. Ogbar, *Hip-Hop Revolution: The Culture and Politics of Rap* (Lawrence: University of Kansas Press, 2007) 3.

But like all artistic movements, its origins are deep and built on many factors that preceded its blossoming. The most logical sequence is the evolution from soul to disco to hip-hop, all cultural leitmotifs among African Americans more than any other demographic group. Whether in the South Bronx or South Central, the powerful hip-hop movement had its origins among black folks. And by the end of the twentieth century, the movement influenced the students and faculty at Morehouse.

As the twentieth century was in its last months, Morehouse was thriving. Enrollment was up, the endowment was growing, and the college was on its way to becoming one of the best in the country—period! At the 131st Founders' Day commemoration and celebration, on February 12, 1998, Herman Cain, '67, chairman of the National Restaurant Association and former CEO of Godfather Pizza Company, was the keynote speaker. More than a decade later, Mr. Cain, a lifelong member of the Republican Party, would make a strong bid to be nominated to run for president of the United States against incumbent President Barack Obama in 2012.

In the late 1990s, "Creating a World House at Morehouse" was a call to action declared by Morehouse Men, the Men of Morehouse, faculty, staff, administrators, and friends of the institution. In his "Message from the President" piece that appeared in the fall 2000 issue of *The Alumnus*, President Massey spoke of the state of the college. He said, "Over the past five years since I returned to my alma mater to serve as its ninth president I have talked a great deal about my vision for Morehouse—that it will be among the finest liberal arts colleges in the world, that it will continue to focus on the development of leaders, and that it will continue to be the college of choice for African American men." He continued, "As I have shared this vision with our faculty and staff, with our students and parents, and with our alumni and friends, I have been excited by the fact that so many of you also see what I see for Morehouse—an excellent college that ranks with the best of the best institutions of higher learning of any kind, anywhere." Lastly, he added that "working together toward that vision, we have made a great deal of progress. We have recruited new faculty and launched new academic programs. We have upgraded the campus infrastructure and completely wired the campus. We have established new relationships in the community and, most important, continued to recruit and graduate some of the finest young men in the world."[9] Morehouse was a historically black college that was one of the best colleges in America, period!

Ten months later, at midnight on December 31, 1999, a new century and new millennium were ushered in on January 1, 2000, and much to the surprise of some those who had unwarranted fears, the college had survived. Not only had Morehouse welcomed the new century/millennium, it had survived for 133 years. The "Idea" that was conceived in Augusta in 1867 now stood with a "glorious crown" over its head as it aspired to be one of thew best colleges, period!

[9] *Alumnus* (Spring 2000): 24.

Chapter 18

"Crowning the Millennium": Morehouse and Massey

On January 1, 2000, as Emancipation Day programs were held across the nation to commemorate the signing of the Emancipation Proclamation by President Abraham Lincoln on January 1, 1863, Morehouse College, an institution founded in the aftermath of the Civil War—that great conflict for freedom—had existed in three centuries. The institution was founded in the nineteenth century on the idea that black men could be educated for scholarship and stewardship, an idea that blossomed and flourished in the twentieth century as the black men who attended the college manifested the idea, and now the college was a great world house of academic exceptionalism, scholarship, and stewardship in the twenty-first century. President Massey had been at the head of the college for five years by this time, and the school had grown in measurable and immeasurable ways due, in great part, to his wise and efficient leadership.

As the twenty-first century began, the Morehouse College National Alumni Association, under the capable leadership of Lonnie C. King Jr., '69, approved a resolution on June 3, 2000, that, among other recommendations, was meant to "encourage each Morehouse graduate and each former student to contribute in a significant way to the upcoming Capital Funds Campaign." The resolutions came out of the joint "Morehouse-Spelman Conference 2000" held in Washington, DC, that month. Meeting under the theme "New Heights for a New Era," the conference featured guest speakers, a fifty-company job fair that interviewed 2,000 candidates, a health forum, and tours and a gala hosted by actress, dance and television star Jasmine Guy. In addition to Mr. King, the conference was led by President Massey; Dr. Audrey Manley, president of Spelman; Dr. Louis Sullivan, president of the Morehouse School of Medicine; and Pearline Davis, president of the Spelman National Alumnae Association. Former Glee Club members from both schools performed at the ecumenical brunch on the last day of the meeting. So, as the new century began,

Morehouse was "striving for new heights in leadership" at a world house that was poised to be one of the best colleges—period!

The college and the world were shocked on September 11, 2001, when terrorists hijacked four planes, which resulted in two being flown into the twin towers of the World Trade Center in New York, one into the Pentagon in Washington, DC, and a fourth crashing into a field in Shanksville, Pennsylvania, after passengers attempted to retake control. Family members and friends of Morehouse were some of those who perished in the attacks. The September 11 attacks, or 9/11, was a defining moment in the history of the United States and the world, and the tragic events of that day had an impact on Morehouse directly (travel) and indirectly (homeland security).

Two years into the new century, two days after Founders' Day, and on the day of the Candle in the Dark Gala, the Morehouse community received the sad news that Dr. Hugh Morris Gloster, seventh president of the college, had died. President Emeritus Gloster passed away on Saturday, February 16, 2002, after a brief illness. He was ninety years old. The "Omega Service" (Alpha Phi Alpha Fraternity) for Dr. Gloster was held on Wednesday evening, February 20, in King Chapel at Morehouse, followed the next morning by the funeral rites in the chapel. The Reverend Doctor Otis Moss Jr., pastor of Olivet Institutional Baptist Church in Cleveland and chairman of the Morehouse board of trustees, officiated. The Morehouse Glee Club provided music for the service. The memory of the seventh president of Morehouse was on the minds of many of those who participated in or attended the 117th commencement exercises on Sunday, May 19, 2002. A memorial to President Gloster was established on the east side of the building that bears his name—Hugh M. Gloster Hall.

The class of 2006 began arriving on campus in August 2002 to begin New Student Orientation. New and returning students enrolled for classes on Friday, August 23rd, and on Monday and Tuesday, the 26th and 27th, and classes began on Wednesday, August 28, 2002. The usual first-semester activities energized the campus in September and October. Clubs and organizations met, athletic teams practiced and competed, musical groups rehearsed and performed, and, above all, classes were held and exams given. Homecoming, one of the big social events of the semester, was held on Saturday, October 26, and featured the traditional events: the coronation of Miss Maroon and White, balls and parties, a massive tailgate on the south side of campus, and, of course, the football game in B. T. Harvey Stadium. This was a "normal" college semester until a shocking incident occurred in the first week of November.

Among the several thousand students enrolled at Morehouse in the fall of 2002 were Gregory Love, a third-year student from Woodbury, New Jersey, and Aaron Price, a second-year student from Chicago. The paths of these two Men of Morehouse intersected on November 3, 2002, in Brazeal Hall. According to the report, the two students were in the shower area of the residential hall when Price interpreted a glance from Love as a homosexual advance, and he was offended. (Later, Love stated that he was not wearing his glasses and thought his roommate was in the next shower.) In a state of rage, Price returned to his room, retrieved a baseball bat, returned to the bathroom, and then viciously, with malice, beat Love, seriously injuring him. The beating was so severe that Love lost some of his teeth and was sent to the emergency room at the Atlanta Medical Center Hospital where he underwent surgery to repair a fractured skull. He received twenty stitches.

This tragic event reverberated around the campus and across the nation. The story was carried by the nation's electronic and print media, including *The Chronicle of Higher Education*, and prompted a conversation about homophobia at Morehouse and elsewhere. Eddie Gaffney, vice president for student services, imposed a moratorium on student activities shortly thereafter, but it was lifted by President Massey when he returned to the campus from a business trip not long after the disturbing event. The president called the imposition of the moratorium the result of gross miscommunication and stated, "There is no such thing as an off-limits topic at Morehouse."[1]

Price turned himself in to the police the day after the savage attack and was charged with one count of aggravated assault and one count of aggravated battery. His bond was set at $10,000. Eventually Price was found guilty of the charges and sentenced to ten years in prison. Love's

---

[1] "Beating at Morehouse Raises Debate Over Perceived Homophobia," *Chronicle of Higher Education* (November 29, 2002).

attempt to sue Morehouse was decided by the Georgia Court of Appeals against the complainant in *Love v. Morehouse College, Inc.* on October 5, 2007. The ruling said, "Applying the relevant law to these allegations, we cannot say with certainty that Love had failed to assert any cognizable claims against Morehouse and find that measuring the basis of those claims at this early stage of the proceedings is premature."[2] Although the court favored Morehouse, the college took no pleasure in it.

Still reeling from the challenges of November, the Morehouse community received a much-needed boost of good news on December 8, 2002, when it was announced that Christopher Elders, a senior political science major from Kansas City, had been selected as a Rhodes Scholar. Elders was the only African American among the thirty-two Americans chosen from a competitive applicant pool of 925 and the second Morehouse student to receive this prestigious scholarship; the college relished it. The twenty-one-year-old Elders, while elated with the honor, took it all in stride. He was a graduate of Raython South High School in Kansas City, and his parents were Judy, an elementary school teacher for gifted children, and Wesley Elders, a middle school principal. The scholarship winner said he was deeply inspired by his parents but also by the legacy of Nima Warfield, '94, the first Rhodes Scholar from Morehouse and an HBCU. Emboldened by his participation in the Student Scholarship/Fellowship Committee (SSFC), Elders was a tutor and mentor at schools in the Atlanta area and at a juvenile detention center. He also volunteered with AID Atlanta and with voter-registration projects. Christopher Elders also received several other honors and awards, including the Harry S. Truman Scholarship, the John Kenneth Galbraith Fellowship from the Kennedy School of Government at Harvard, the National Science Foundation Undergraduate Research Fellowship, and the Charles A. Merrill Travel and Study Abroad Scholarship. Elders had studied at the London School of Economics and Political Science, traveled through Western Europe, the Czech Republic, and Taipei, Taiwan, where he participated in anthropological field research among the Amis people, an aboriginal ethnic group, while studying at Shih Hsin University. Commenting on receiving the Rhodes, Elders said, "I didn't feel the pressure. Because it's such a crap-

---

[2] http://caselaw.findlaw.com/ga-court-of-appeals/1024644.html.

shoot, you can't get your hopes up too high. I was prepared to go on with my life if I didn't get it. But I'll take it."[3] Morehouse regarded this signal honor as recognition of the high quality of student who were admitted to the college, who were "crowning the millennium."

As Morehouse College continued to develop into one of the best institutions of higher education—period—on November 24, 2003, the college community was again delighted to hear that a yet another Man of Morehouse had been awarded a Rhodes Scholarship. Oluwabusayo "Topé" Folarin became the third Rhodes Scholar from Morehouse, which had produced more than any other HBCU. Topé, whose full name means "to God be the Glory," came to Morehouse in 2000, and, like many first-year college students, was not very happy. He remembered: "I actually went to Morehouse, because I thought I would find myself there, literally and figuratively. I thought I'd find a lot more Topés at Morehouse. I thought I'd become more comfortable with who I was after a sort of weird childhood. None of those few things happened, because I found a lot of people who were obsessed with what it meant to be black and acting out what they thought blackness was." He found that "unappealing initially," so he went to Bates College in Lewiston, Maine, for his sophomore year, and also studied in South Africa. When he arrived at Bates, Folarin recalled,

> I completely disengaged, and I think it was the best thing I could have done for myself. That's not to say I didn't have friends or didn't travel. During the week, for example, I dedicated a lot of time, if I wasn't reading, to just thinking about where this is all going and trying to come to terms with myself about leaving adolescence, leaving high school, struggling with my own identity. It was something I needed to do to resolve a lot of questions. I'm still on the journey, but at the end of that initial phase I learned a great deal about myself and other people.[4]

Folarin returned to Morehouse for his junior and senior years.

In addition to producing three Rhodes Scholars, Morehouse has also produced Fulbright Scholars, Luce Scholars, Watson Scholars, Luard

---

[3] *Alumnus* (Winter 2002): 3–5.

[4] http://rhodesholars.wordpress.com.2007.11/14/tope-folarin.

Scholars, and White House Fellows among the other fellowships, scholarships, and awards given to its students. Clearly, Morehouse was "crowning the millennium" and on the "road" to being one of the best colleges—period. In the meantime, in 2004 the college became concerned about its "human infrastructure."

In order to realize his vision to make Morehouse one of the best colleges—period!—the college began an intensive self-assessment, which led to the development of a strategic plan that would be implemented in five-year increments. The strategic plan laid out goals, time tables, and templates to measure progress. The process involved the college examining its size, programs, organizational structure, curriculum, and facilities. And so, on Valentine's Day, February 14, 2003, on the portico of Kilgore Hall, President Massey, with the strong support of the board of trustees, announced "The Campaign for a New Century," a capital campaign to raise $105,700,000, the most ambitious fundraising initiative in the history of the college. Rather than use the old, tired, "hat-in-hand" approach to fundraising, Massey told the Morehouse story with so much enthusiasm and conviction that "people came to understand Morehouse as important not just for the nation but maybe for their own companies, in terms of recruiting our students, having relationships with Morehouse faculty, and the like." The campaign officially ended at the close of the fiscal year, June 30, 2006, and the initial goal of $105.7 million was met and exceeded by $15 million. The capital campaign was successful because it was not just about facilities, but bold ideas predicated on the Morehouse mission, legacy, and legendary roster of luminaries, many more than are generally known.[5] This reflected the "crowning the millennium."

In 2004, as the college celebrated the announcement of its third Rhodes Scholar, the Institutional Values Project continued the work that began in 2001 and proclaimed that this would be the "Year of Responsibility." The motto "I work for Morehouse. *I take responsibility*" was the guiding principle of the project and for the Morehouse community. The overall goal was to equip students, faculty, and staff "with the ethical tools they needed to support the shared vision of making Morehouse one of the finest liberal arts colleges in the nation." All stakeholders were encouraged

[5] http://blackcollege.blogspot.com.2006/09/massey.to.retire.as.morehouse.html.

to take seriously their roles in promoting the best practices for the advancement of the school. As always, they were reminded of the founding idea of the school to educate black men, now all men, for scholarship and stewardship.

On Thursday, September 14, 2006, the college heard the bittersweet news that President Massey would retire at the end of the 2006/2007 academic year. He had begun a dialogue with the board of trustees about retiring in 2004, but "waited to do so until key leadership positions were filled and the school's ambitious capital campaign ($105,000,000) had come to a close." Commenting on the pending retirement, Marcus Edwards, president of the Morehouse Student Government Association, said that Dr. Massey "had done an amazing job and never tried to sweep anything under the rug. He's a great leader."[6]

President Massey and First Lady Shirley Massey were recognized at the 2007 Candle in the Dark Gala, and on Friday evening, April 13th of that year, at an evening "Celebrating the Legacy of Dr. Walter E. Massey, '58," was presented at the Atlanta History Center, in northwest Atlanta. It was a grand and festive occasion. Sponsored by some of Atlanta's, and the nation's, major corporations, including BP, the Coca-Cola Company, McDonald's Corporation, AT&T Georgia, Georgia Power, and Chick-fil-A, guests arriving at the history center were treated to valet parking and directed to a registration table where they were given their seat assignments for dinner and a flute of champagne. The cocktail reception was held on the main and lower levels of the center, where select pieces from the recently acquired Martin Luther King Jr. Collection were exhibited. As guests sipped champagne and other refreshing beverages, they marveled at the items from the King Collection. Perhaps more than any one item, a blue book examination that King took as a Morehouse student in the late 1940s was the talk of the evening. Considered by many to be the most important of all the King collections (others are at the King Center, Stanford University, and Yale University), under the strong leadership of the Honorable Shirley Franklin, mayor of Atlanta, the King Collection had been purchased by a quickly assembled group of Atlanta movers and shakers at a price tag of $32 million. And at the request of Mayor Franklin, it

[6] "Vision Realized. Period: The Massey Legacy, Morehouse College, 1995–2007."

was decided that the collection would be donated, free and simple, to Morehouse College. In short order, Dr. Vicki Crawford was hired as director of the collection, and its more than 10,000 items were named the Morehouse College King Collection. On the evening of the gala for Dr. and Mrs. Massey, the invitees viewed the partial collection in awe. As the beginning of the celebration was announced, guests made their way into the beautifully set tables and elegantly decorated ballroom.

The theme for the celebration was "Vision. Realized. *Period.* The Massey Legacy, 1995–2007." Willie "Flash" Davis, chairman of the Morehouse Board of Trustees, greeted the assemblage and introduced Ms. Fredricka Whitfield, CNN's award-winning news anchor, who was the mistress of ceremonies. Greetings were then given by John Rice, honorary chair of the legacy dinner, vice chairman of GE, and president of and CEO of GE Infrastructure. The invocation was delivered by the Reverend Doctor Otis Moss Jr., and Monica Hargrave, a talented and much-in-demand harpist, provided music during dinner. After the decadent dessert was eaten, guests were treated to a mini-concert by Oleta Adams, whose 1990 debut album "Circle of One" went platinum. As the beverages had taken effect, many of the guests sang along with Ms. Adams when she enthusiastically performed "Get Here," the Brenda Russell composition considered by some as the unofficial anthem of the 1991 Gulf War. The guests were in a convivial mood when the video presentation of the Massey legacy was shown. Tributes were then made by Christopher M. Jones, '99, assistant dean for graduate students at MIT; Willis "Butch" Sheftall, '64 professor of economics and business and administration, who had also served as senior vice president for academic affairs; the Honorable Shirley Franklin; and Joe Adams, president of Ray Charles Enterprises. After a special presentation was made by Chairman Davis, Mrs. Massey treated the guests with words in her engagingly delightful way. The celebration of Dr. Massey's legacy of concluded with words from the honoree. In four months, the tenure of the ninth president of Morehouse would come to an end and the tenth's would begin. But President Massy had two major official functions to perform before the end of his presidency: baccalaureate and commencement 2007.

When Dr. Walter Eugene Massey retired, Morehouse College was 140 years old, just ten years away from its sesquicentennial. The ninth president of Morehouse left a lasting legacy at the college, one that loomed large and powerful, with the most visible aspect being the expansion of the school's physical plant. In this regard, President Massey made a connection between the idea of the academic village at Morehouse and investing in facilities. "We wanted facilities that reflected this notion of being among the best—facilities that are state-of-the art or close to that. In each case, we wanted our buildings to be aesthetically pleasing. We were not going to build just a functional square box."[7] The growth of the physical facilities during the Massey administration included the 70,000-square-foot leadership center, now named the Walter E. Massey Leadership Center, with its attached Shirley Massey Conference Center. In addition, the John H. Hopps Jr. Technology Tower, which is situated between Hope and Merrill Halls, provided office space for faculty and computer laboratories. The addition of the Otis Moss Jr. Residential Suites added a new dimension to residential living at Morehouse in that the "suites" provided a 375-bed apartment-style living space on campus for the college's students. Davidson House, the on-campus president's residence, had been constructed at Dr. Massey's insistence during the early days of his administration. Also, plans for the Ray Charles Performing Arts Center (RAY-PAC), with its 575-seat concert hall, were made during the Massey years at Morehouse. The college's investment in facilities increased nearly fourfold during the Massey presidency, from approximately $43 million to almost $145 million.[8] But more than buildings, the ninth president saw the need to improve the appearance of the campus. The "curb appeal" of the college was important to President Massey and First Lady Shirley Massey, whom he appointed to cochair the Morehouse Campus Beautification Committee (a similar committee had existed during the Keith presidency). President Massey was so passionate about the appearance of the campus that he was not adverse to carry a stick to spear paper and other debris as he moved about the campus, which he often did as he frequently walked from Davidson House to his office in Gloster Hall. He did not subscribe to the notion that just because Morehouse was an all-male institution that it should not have beautiful plants and flowers and a well-

---

[7] Ibid.

[8] Ibid., 23.

maintained lawn. He knew, as did others, that an attractive campus would not only inspire the students who were matriculating there, but also be an advantage in recruiting new students. President Massey had a strong aesthetic sense, which, in part, led him to the presidency of the Art Institute of Chicago after retiring from Morehouse.

Described as a "man for all seasons," President Walter Eugene Massey was, and continues to be, scholarly, compassionate, polished, visionary, well-rounded, and cosmopolitan. The ninth president recalled, "I thought it was important for the students to see that the president is a human being. It can be hard for students to get to know a president no matter how much they speak with you or see you about. They can have this image of you as this austere, distant person, and might come to believe that's what it takes to be successful. We have to grow and learn. But as we do so, we don't have to sacrifice those human qualities about ourselves that we like."[9] With this mindset, and a love for Dear Old Morehouse, President Massey left the college with a living, evolving legacy for future administrations, faculties, staff, alumni, and students to pursue.

President Massey was the featured 2007 Morehouse Commencement speaker, and he used the occasion to accomplish two objectives: to explain in layman's terms his work as a physicist and how this related to human behavior, and to bid farewell to the school he had served for twelve years. Most of what the ninth president said about physics may have evaporated with time, but his final valedictory words will be remembered for years to come. He talked about the things he would miss after leaving Morehouse: colleagues, staff, trustees, his administrative team, and the close friends he had made.

> But I will miss most of all the students. And I will miss walking across the campus and having unplanned conversations and interactions. I will miss having students at Davidson House. I will miss playing tennis with members of our championship tennis team. I will miss my student office hours and many of you who stopped by simply to visit and tell me about the grand plans you're making or the challenges or the problems you're facing.

---

[9] *Maroon Tiger* (May 2, 2007): 12.

He would always be a Morehouse Man, he exclaimed. And with that, President Massey thanked the audience and returned to his seat to the adulation of the graduation crowd. The Massey era had ended, and the Franklin years lay ahead. The founding mission of Morehouse was enhanced and lifted up during the stewardship of President Massey and his team. But there was a perception, especially among some alumni, that something was going wrong at the House. They were concerned that the traditional standards that were signature of a Morehouse Man were being abrogated, signaling a decline in the reputation of the college. To wit, they saw this in the students' embrace of hip-hop culture, rap music, and the trend of wearing sagging pants. There was a crisis in behavior that besmirched the identity of Morehouse. The new president of the college would have to address this issue.

Chapter 19

"The Crown in Crisis": Franklin and the Renaissance

Several weeks before the 2007 Morehouse commencement season began, the college's board of trustees announced its unanimous selection of Dr. Robert Michael Franklin Jr., '75, as the tenth president of Morehouse College. Dr. Franklin was expected to embrace the idea that was expressed in 1867 that black men could be educated for scholarship and stewardship, and lift it up in a way that would continue the work and achievements of his predecessor.

In 2007, the culture at Morehouse mirrored that of the larger society, and the behavior of many students—reflected in their attire, language, and music—raised concerns among many in the broader Morehouse community. Dr. Franklin had recently published *Crisis in the Village: Restoring Hope in African American Communities* (2007), which addressed some of the issues that were the source of conversation among Morehouse Men and beyond. The chapter "Colleges: A Crisis of Moral Purpose" discussed the concerns of past leaders (such as Benjamin Mays, W. E. B. Du Bois, Lafayette Harris, and Mary McLeod Bethune), faculty, alumni, and students in relation to the current state of "a potentially embarrassing feature of black college life, namely the presence of 'purposeless' campus residents who appeared to waste the gift of college time with frivolities and negative behavior." This observation was held by many students who expressed a desire for President Franklin "to encourage morality, connect with the student body, and engage in successful fundraising."[1] Not since Mays era had the president of Morehouse been a preacher/pastor, and in making his bid for the presidency, Dr. Franklin had submitted a plan of action called "The Renaissance of Morehouse College: An Action Agenda for America's Most Important Academy." The plan called for the restoration of the Morehouse brand and to do this, he intended to launch a "national

[1] *Maroon Tiger* (May 2, 2007).

marketing-PR offensive to tell the Morehouse story."

Dr. Franklin planned to "project the twenty-first century image of the Morehouse Man as a symbol of hope" and to move the college to the top of the nation's institutions of research relevant to African American communities. The renaissance plan also called for the enhancement of the faculty by the "creation of a Center for Faculty Development and sending faculty members to media organizations to act as pundits and commentators on African American issues." The new president also wanted to improve faculty salaries and benefits in order to attract, retain, and appreciate faculty and staff "treasures." Julian DeShazier, Dr. Franklin's son and a 2005 graduate of Morehouse, said this about his father: "I am obviously quite proud of my father and honored that someone in my family—let alone 'Pops'—would have the opportunity to represent the next vein of leadership for Morehouse College. The House is my beloved alma mater and the greatest institution in the world, and this next generation of young leaders deserves a charismatic, brilliant, and profound man like Dr. Robert Franklin."[2] Julian's assessment of his father was the opinion held by many people who knew Dr. Franklin, who had graduated from the college thirty-two years earlier; his thoughts on student behavior then were similar to those held by many today.

During his freshman year at Morehouse, Robert Franklin was shocked to discover more than a few brothers who were not serious about learning and community service. "Weren't we all here, after all," he thought, "to take up and continue Dr. King's unfinished mission?" He said, "It did not take long to identify the smaller percentage of the student body which seemed to appreciate the privilege of this experience." This was "a time when many young men our age were being drafted into the military and shipped to Vietnam, and with the echo of the tumultuous decade of the '60s still ringing in our ears, here were Morehouse men behaving like the stereotypical frat boys of the leisure class." Franklin was critical of his classmates who "partied all night, smuggled women into the dormitories, consumed drugs, and engaged in fights against rival schools as well as young men in the surrounding neighborhood." And, "after uproarious weekends, these same young men would sleep late into Sunday

---

[2] Ibid.

afternoon. The small number of us who were up for Sunday worship services walked through the dorm halls that resembled deathly quiet catacombs, tombs of the purposeless." The "purposeless" behavior (then and in 2007) notwithstanding, alumni records show that many of these young men did have a purpose and achieved success in their chosen professions.

Dr. Franklin put the student culture at Morehouse in the early 1970s in context, saying that "it would not be fair to simply indict these students as purposeless without noting that their previous schools, the larger society, and its most visible leaders share in the failure to inspire and challenge young people to discover and embrace higher purposes." Furthermore, "at a time when the 'culture of narcissism' was and is corrupting and destroying a culture of civic virtue and public service, students may be up against much larger cultural forces than they can oppose without support. This is where the entire culture of black colleges must be mobilized to instill virtues like personal sacrifice for the greater good."[3] At a time when Morehouse students and those in the larger society were "bagging and sagging" their pants as they listened to "rap" music, many concluded there was a crisis in the Morehouse village and that someone was needed to instill these virtues of "personal sacrifice for the greater good." President Franklin was chosen to do this work, but any attempt to cultivate high moral values in twenty-first-century students seemed to be a return to the practices of the school at its founding, which were challenged in the 1969 revolution. Genuine in his belief that he could make a difference at Morehouse, President Franklin launched his plan for a renaissance at the college that would modify the behavior of the immediate Morehouse family, broaden their horizons, and make them more cosmopolitan.

President Franklin's first public address to members of the Morehouse community came at the "Welcome to Morehouse" assembly for new students held on August 15, 2007. In his opening remarks, the newly minted ninth president said, "Welcome to Morehouse College. My first words to this community are 'thank you.' As the new president, I must say to those faculty, staff, students, alumni and friends who have been here, thank you for welcoming me and my family. And thank you for

[3] Ibid.

making Morehouse the treasure that it is."[4] After more salutations, Dr. Franklin then told that marvelously moving story about his arrival at Morehouse, which resonated with the audience on many levels.

When Robert Franklin arrived at Morehouse thirty-six years earlier, he traveled by Greyhound bus with his mother. His father didn't make the trip, preferring to work so that he could pay for his tuition. The day of registration, Franklin and his mother took a taxi from Paschal's Hotel, located on Hunter Street, now Martin Luther King Jr. Drive, and when he saw the long line of brothers attempting to register at Graves Hall, he told his mother to leave him on Fair Street a short distance from the gate, so no one would see her escort him to the door. Young Franklin was wearing a shirt and tie and had a snazzy briefcase that had been given to him by the proud members of his church in Chicago. He said he felt that he was Mr. Morehouse, all set to dive into the Mystique. Years later, an uncle told him that his mother called him in tears as she returned home to Chicago alone. She had just left her baby at Morehouse. His uncle interrupted her and said, "Dorothy, listen to what you just said. You left him at Morehouse College. Some mothers are crying because they left their sons in jail. And some have left their sons in a morgue. But you have left your son at Morehouse." Those words made all the difference, and his mother's tears of grief transformed into joy and pride. "So, this is a word to parents. Leave your sons, grandsons and young men at Morehouse and be proud of what you have done. Although it may be difficult and painful to separate, do it for his sake. You're leaving him in good hands. He will continue to mature into a Morehouse Man, and we'll all be the better."[5] And then, for the first time, Dr. Franklin spoke about "the Morehouse Man as a Renaissance man with a social conscience." This would be the defining principle, motto, and mantra of his administration. He described a Renaissance man as "one who is a citizen of the world, acquainted with the great conversations in science and humanities, acquainted with the languages and cultures of the world, at home in every culture, widely read and widely traveled, capable of adapting to every environment, and always

---

[4] Robert Franklin, Crisis in the Village: Restoring Hope in African American Communities (Minneapolis, MS: Fortress Press, 2007) 198.

[5] www.morehouse.edu/about/franklinspeeches/atyourservice.html.

raises the level of class and sophistication of the company he keeps."[6] Soon after, the Morehouse community embraced the concept of the "Five Wells," conceived of and recommended by Dr. Robert Franklin: well-read, well-spoken, well-dressed, well-traveled, and well-balanced. A sixth "well," well-written, was added later.

A few weeks after Dr. Franklin addressed the new students, he was the featured speaker at the opening convocation on September 20, 2007. After the traditional greetings and performance by the Glee Club, the tenth president was introduced to the full Morehouse student body, faculty, and staff. And taking a line from Johnson and Johnson's "Lift Ev'ry Voice and Sing," the title of his address was "Facing the Rising Sun: A New Day Begun."

After saluting the men of senior class, Dr. Franklin began: "To the entire student body, let me say that you do not know how much I admire you. And, indeed, how much all of us appreciate your presence. As I travel about, I brag about you. And, when things are not right on this campus, my equilibrium is disturbed, and my impatience grows over every missed opportunity to achieve excellence." He complimented them, saying, "You, my brothers, are what Morehouse is all about. Many of you have come here against great odds, resisting every sort of obstacle and discouragement. You have defied the negative stereotypes and ignored all the odds. Now, we are privileged and obligated to provide a first-class education!" Clearly, this spoke to the idea that black men could be educated for scholarship and service. Morehouse in the twenty-first century was holding on to the cross and the candle as the crown appeared to be in crisis.

Standing on tradition, Dr. Franklin talked about the historical mission of Morehouse, about the need for careful planning and investment, and what the world looked like demographically. He then declared, "My vision is that Morehouse will become a global resource for educated and ethical leaders." Connecting educated and ethical leadership to Dr. Martin Luther King Jr., he stated that "our greatest and most generous alumnus...as he offered his life in service to others, was strongly convinced that we can and should pursue this course because it is in our institutional DNA." Franklin's vision was to "internationalize Morehouse" so that the

[6] Ibid.

college community would be "informed and concerned about global politics, world markets, scientific and technological advancements, cultural trends and ecological issues. I want people to say, 'You can tell a Morehouse Man, because his bags are packed, and he's headed out to offer hope and intelligent response where despair reigns.' We will go forth not simply as tourists, students, or employees—but also as ambassadors."

Arriving at the core of his address, the tenth president said, "In order to fulfill this vision, I am calling for the renaissance of Morehouse College." He called for a renaissance among Morehouse alumni that "must stretch and give beyond the reachable goals they imagined before." He wanted a renaissance among the Morehouse faculty—"smart and devoted teachers. We are strong and we must grow stronger." It was time for a renaissance among Morehouse staff as they continued their "professional development so that each year we can see and measure improvement in student and customer service." Finally, he called for the renaissance of the Men of Morehouse, saying, "I am energized to call for a renaissance of dignity and decorum on this campus. So many—have given so much—for you *few*—to learn and to give back in service to a global village in crisis." Dr. Franklin then gave a charge to the students:

> Brothers, we must show young boys and men in this community and beyond that we can resolve conflict without resorting to violence. We call for the renaissance of ethics and character, saying "yes" to personal class and community service. And saying "no" to plagiarism, "no" to petty theft, "no" to profanity in public spaces, "no" to disrespecting and abusing women, and "no" to the kind of personal dress that is inappropriate for an adult learning community.

As Dr. Franklin reached the end of his convocation address, he exhorted the Morehouse College motto *Et Facta Est Lux*—and then there was light (or, and light was made)—and closed with great optimism: "Together, we will *remake* Morehouse. We will make renewed light—bright light. While facing that rising sun of our new day begun, let us march on 'til victory is won." The convocation audience erupted in rapturous applause, truly believing that a new day had dawned at Dear Old Morehouse. The fall semester, 2007, was officially underway.

Residence halls were opened and New Student Orientation began on Tuesday, August 14th. All students finalized their class registrations on Monday and Tuesday (August 20–21), and classes began promptly at 8 A.M. on Wednesday, August 22, 2007. When the final registration numbers were counted, more than 2,500 students were enrolled at the college. While perhaps some in the Morehouse family—administrators, staff, faculty, students, or parents—had an inkling that a major economic crisis was looming that would have serious repercussions for the college, the nation, and the world, but most members were caught off guard. The Great Recession—the global financial crisis of 2007 and 2008—had already begun when the renaissance at Morehouse was still in its talking stages.

Twenty-four hours after Morehouse commemorated and celebrated its 141st Founders' Day, on Friday, February 15, 2008, at ten o'clock in the morning, the college inaugurated its tenth president. Robert Michael Franklin Jr., a member of the Morehouse class of 1975, had been on the job as the Morehouse CEO since succeeding President Walter Massey on July 1, 2007. But on this glorious morning, he was officially installed with the usual grand ceremony and memorable oratory in the Martin Luther King Jr. International Chapel.

Once the processional, with its traditional pomp and pageantry, concluded and the representatives had taken their seats, the "summons" was delivered by Dr. Willis Braswell Sheftall, '64, interim provost and senior vice president for academic affairs. The grand ceremony presented the expectation that all who studied or worked at the college should conduct themselves in an exceptional manner. The usual inaugural template was followed, and the call to order was delivered by the Reverend Emmett Thomas Martin Jr., pastor at historic Springfield Baptist Church, the place where the idea of educated black men was conceived. Then the Reverend Doctor Raphael Gamaliel Warnock, '91, senior pastor at Atlanta's historic Ebenezer Baptist Church, gave the evocation, which was followed by greetings delivered by several dignitaries: James T. Laney, Mae C. Jemison, Charles E. Blake, and Aaron L. Parker. The Morehouse Glee Club performed the inaugural anthem "And There Was Light," composed by Dr. Uzee Brown, chair of the Morehouse Department of Music, after which Dr. Robert Michael Franklin Jr. was invested with the symbols of authority of the office of president of Morehouse College by members of the board of trustees. The charge was delivered by Chairman Willie J. Davis, '56, and the "Affirmation of the Charter" was made by Dr. Benjamin A. Blackburn II, '61. The ceremonial keys were passed to the new president by Robert C. Davidson, '67, and the "robe" was presented by Dr. Walter E. Massey, '58. Mrs. Billye S. Aaron draped the medallion upon him, and the Revered Dr. Charles Gilchrist Adams, Hon. '84, presented a prayer. General James R. Hall, '57, delivered the mace to Dr. Franklin; John A. Wallace, Hon. '05, led him to the ceremonial chair; and the Glee Club sang the selected spiritual, Stacey Gibbs's "My Good Lord's A-Done-A Been Here." Impressive ceremonies and rituals, with pomp and circumstance, are public affirmations of the ideals of the college. Infused in all ceremonies at Morehouse is some sense of "the cross, the candle, the and crown," which represent the ideals of the college.

President Franklin's inaugural address was titled "Let Us Make Men...Morehouse Men." In the powerful and mellifluous oratorical style for which he is known, he exhorted,

> Let us make men. In order to complete creation, God declares 'Let us make something new, make something special.'... And so today, let us remember our traditions, our people, and our dreams. Let us reclaim our pledge, our plea, and our prayer.... Let us make men who understand that their strength is measured by the depth of their respect for women and their desire to nurture children.... [M]en who respect and celebrate diversity and are secure enough not to be intimidated by the presence of different sexual orientations but rather stand in solidarity with those who are in the minority.... [M]en who know how to dress for leadership and service and who will uphold the Morehouse mystique.... [M]en who replace profanity with uplifting discourse.... Let us make men.... Morehouse men...renaissance men. Up you mighty men. You can accomplish what you will. Up you mighty men. Let us create a brave new world.

Excited about what President Franklin had said, they gave him a standing ovation.

The inauguration of Dr. Robert Michael Franklin Jr. as the tenth president of Morehouse College concluded with words from Chairman

Davis, the singing of "Dear Old Morehouse," and the benediction, which was delivered by the Reverend Doctor Lawrence Edward Carter, dean of the chapel. The gathering recessed to Dr. Oliver's "O God, Our Help in Ages Past." A reception for the president and first lady, Dr. Cheryl Goffney Franklin, was held in the Frank Forbes Arena immediately after the inauguration. But as hundreds of well-wishers and stakeholders in Morehouse congratulated the new president and his family, dark clouds of financial ruin gathered on the horizon that would soon prove ominous for the school and have a lasting impact on the presidency of Robert M. Franklin and the history of the college.

Considered by many to be the worst financial crisis since the Great Depression of the 1930s, the global financial crisis that began in 2007, the year Robert Franklin took office as Morehouse president, hit the college hard. According to the Federal Reserve Bank, the "crisis" began on February 27, 2007, less than two weeks after Morehouse commemorated its 140th anniversary. On that date, the Federal Home Loan Mortgage Corporation, also known as Freddie Mac, announced that it would "no longer buy the most risky subprime mortgages and mortgage-related securities." The economic catastrophe that unfurled over the next two years affected people and institutions around the world, including Morehouse. As administrators, students, parents, faculty, staff, and alumni nervously monitored the developing crisis, recently installed United States President Barak Obama signed into law the American Recovery and Reinvestment Act of 2009, "which included a variety of spending measures and tax cuts designed to promote economic recovery." President Obama also announced the Homeowner Affordability and Stability Plan which would, among other things, "permit the refinancing of conforming home mortgages owned or guaranteed by Fannie Mae or Freddie Mac that currently exceed 80 percent of the underlying home." But while corporate giants were given a lifeline, American workers and the middle class were drowning in a vortex of rising unemployment (13 percent), decreasing home values (beginning in 2007), and a jump in inflation that was fueled by gasoline prices that peaked in 2008.

In an article titled "Historically Black Colleges and Universities in a Time of Economic Crisis," Marybeth Gasman, noted scholar of higher education, gave a convincing explanation that was applicable to

Morehouse. She said that there were "two main reasons why the current economic crisis has hit HBCUs so hard. First, these institutions serve a student population that is disproportionately low income where 90 percent of HBCU students received financial aid. Reflecting the institutions' commitment to educating low-income students, HBCU tuition rates tend to be 50 percent lower than those of their historically white counterparts." Gasman pointed out that "HBCUs cannot afford to alienate potential students, [since] a drop in enrollment can have dire consequences. Low-income African Americans might decide to attend community colleges or historically white state institutions, both of which boast relatively low tuition. For the 2008 to 2009 academic year many HBCUs experienced decreases in their enrollments."[7] Specifically, Professor Gasman stated that Morehouse College "garners roughly 80 percent of its revenue from tuition and fees" and revealed that the college "took a $40,000,000 loss in endowment" between 2008 and 2009. As a result, adjunct faculty were not hired, senior faculty were asked to teach more classes, and department and program budgets were slashed. These were difficult times for Morehouse.

As the financial crisis continued unabated, on April 14, 2009, Ben S. Bernanke, chairman of the board of governors of the Federal Reserve System, gave an address at Morehouse College. The title of the address was "Four Questions about the Financial Crisis," and he gave an answer for each. Question one, "How Did We Get Here?," was explained, in part, by "declining stock values, a teetering financial system, and difficulties in obtaining credit [that] triggered a remarkably rapid and deep contraction in global economic activity and employment." For question two, "What Is the Fed Doing to Address the Situation?," the chairman stated that "the Fed has...taken a number of steps to help the economy by unclogging the flow of credit to households and businesses." Question three was "Does the Fed's Aggressive Response Risk Inflation Down the Road?" Bernanke replied,

> Although inflation seems to be low for a while, the time will come when the economy has begun to strengthen, financial markets are

---

[7] www.asup.org/article/historically black-colleges-and-universities-time-economic-crisis.

> healing, and the demand for goods and services, which is currently very weak, begins to increase again. At that point, the liquidity that the Fed has put into the system could begin to pose an inflationary threat unless the FOMC (Federal Open Market Committee) acts to remove some of that liquidity and raise the federal funds rate.

In response to question four—"Why Did the Fed and the Treasury Act to Prevent the Bankruptcy of Some Major Financial Firms?"—Bernanke argued that because "large, complex financial institutions tend to be highly interconnected with other firms and markets,...waves of panic and fear washed over the markets, [and] the Fed and the Treasury became very concerned about the stability of a number of other financial firms." After acknowledging that "the current crisis has been one of the most difficult financial and economic episodes in modern history," he concluded, "I am fundamentally optimistic about our economy. Among its many intrinsic strengths are universities and colleges like Morehouse, which help talented students gain not only a command of a body of knowledge but also the capacity to think creatively and independently. Institutions like this one train the professionals, entrepreneurs, and leaders who will shape our economy in the future."[8] This represented a "Crisis in the Village" and a "Crisis in the Country," for sure.

The 2009 Morehouse commencement season came and went with its usual convening, conviviality, convocations, and ceremony. Four months later, as the 2009 fall semester began, on September 23rd, President Franklin issued "The Morehouse Model: Dressing the Part." This edict engendered acrimonious debate among members of the Morehouse community and beyond. The debate centered on the new "urban" dress worn by many Morehouse students that was the cause for criticism by some staff members and alumni along with the feminine attire and accessories a few student chose to wear. The controversy over dress at Morehouse overshadowed the financial health of the college, which became abundantly apparent when *VIBE*, the popular contemporary hip-hop magazine, published "The Mean Girls of Morehouse" the following year.

---

[8] "Four Questions about the Financial Crisis," remarks by Ben S. Bernanke, chairman, Board of Governors of the Federal Reserve System (Atlanta, Morehouse College, April 14, 2009) 15.

The October 11, 2010, issue of the magazine focused on a community of gay students at the college who were called "gender benders who rock makeup, Marc Jacob tote bags, sky-high heels and Beyoncé style hair weaves."[9] The "Mean Girls" were brought to the attention of the public by the students who were sagging their pants, who were of the opinion that the feminine dress of the "Mean Girls" was more offensive to the traditions of Morehouse than their pants were.

The heightened attention on "Dressing the Part" at Morehouse caused a national debate and undue attention to the college. Perhaps this was because Morehouse is an all-male, predominantly African American school where feminine dress is more obvious than it would be at a coeducational college, where the attire could blend in with that of the women on campus. Speculation notwithstanding, the issue of dress at Morehouse continued unabated until a radical change occurred in young male fashion: the advent of the slim fit or skinny pants. In the meantime, President Franklin moved forward with his vision of renaissance at Morehouse.

During Founders' Week 2011, President Franklin called together a large group of alumni and supporters to create the Renaissance Commission. Informally called RenCom, members were organized into two complementary groups: fundraising and thought leadership. RenCom was tasked with conducting its work through a combination of meetings as well as online and/or teleconference work sessions. Commission members were to meet as a group twice each year, and at least one of those meetings would be held in Atlanta or on the Morehouse campus. The RenCom fundraising group was charged with helping the college meet its goal of raising $125 million by 2017, the year of the Morehouse sesquicentennial. The goals of the thought leadership group were to examine three areas associated with the college: financial viability, academic enterprise, and fundraising. Projections indicated that the responsibilities of the thought leadership team would conclude in 2013 and the work of the fundraising committee would end by the sesquicentennial.

The first Renaissance Commission meeting was held on February 17, 2011, at the Ritz-Carlton Hotel in downtown Atlanta and attended by more than one hundred participating members and members of the

---

[9] www.vibe.com/article/mean-girls-morehouse.

Morehouse administrative staff. The commission was chaired by Muhtar Kent, chairman and chief executive officer of the Coca-Cola Company. Cochairs were Dale E. Jones, '82, vice chairman at Heidrick & Struggles; Charles D. Moody, '78, chairman and chief executive officer of C. D. Moody Construction Company; and Ralph de la Vega, president and chief executive officer of AT&T Mobility. The gathering of the RenCom members at the Ritz-Carlton was essentially a meet-and-greet and photo session, with the real work to take place the next day on the Morehouse campus.

The next morning, RenCom members convened in what is now known as the Shirley Massey Conference Center to explore the theme of "The Morehouse Distinction." After a continental breakfast, the morning plenary session got underway at 9 A.M. with the usual welcoming and opening remarks before the charge to the commission was reiterated and the work sessions briefly explained: "'Futuring' the College: Morehouse at Its Sesquicentennial," "The Higher Education Model," and "The Morehouse Operating Model." The latter theme captured most of the morning session with presentations from the Morehouse administrative staff. During the working lunch, members met in designated seminar rooms in what is now named the Walter E. Massey Leadership Center. The session on the sesquicentennial discussed the future of the college at its 150th anniversary with the anticipation that the Franklin model would be well-established by then.

The afternoon session of the RenCom was devoted to discussions about the academic enterprise at Morehouse, especially admissions, enrollment, curriculum, and faculty, with the usual questions and dialogue about the standing of the college among other HBCUs. Also discussed was the financial viability of the college and ideas and plans for funding the renaissance. Leading the RenCom were men of high finance, and others, who committed to supporting the financial viability of the enterprise. The first commission meeting ended with closing remarks at 3 P.M. The next meeting was planned for Washington, DC, and coincided with the return of the eighty-eight-year-old football rivalry between Morehouse College and Howard University. An actual working meeting of the commission did not take place, but a few of the members gathered for a cocktail reception where brief reports were made. It was a useful confab at which, once again, commitments were made to support all aspects of the RenCom's work. But the renewed football contest was more than a game, it was, as the commemorative program stated, "The HBC Experience."

The presidential symposium sponsored by Morehouse and Howard, as one aspect of the HBCU experience, began on Thursday morning, September 8, 2011, at ten o'clock in Cramton Auditorium on the Howard University campus. Scores of members of the Morehouse community had arrived in the nation's capital to be a part of this special event, and in a joint statement issued by Presidents Robert M. Franklin of Morehouse and Sidney A. Ribeau of Howard, the purpose of the symposium was presented. The presidential symposium took advantage of the national platform provided by the inaugural AT&T Nation's Football Classic, which was the centerpiece of the event. It was designed to permit HBCU presidents and leading scholars to engage in a moderated discussion of public policy issues affecting the development of the black community. The goal was for policymakers in Washington to become aware of the discussions. Additionally, the symposium aimed to provide a platform for scholars, sports columnists, and cultural artists to challenge stereotypes about black males in athletics, the sports industry, and entertainment. It also sought to present the perspective of student leaders from Morehouse and Howard, highlighting their diverse experiences as college students.[10] As two of the nation's top schools, the event captured the attention of prospective students, parents, and philanthropists. The event was held in Washington, and not in Atlanta, despite the lamentations of some Morehouse Men, because DC is the center of public policymaking and power in the United States. Both schools received federal funding, so spotlighting the schools was good for their image. Howard University has the largest endowment of all HBCUs due in large part because of the multimillion dollar outlay it annually receives from the federal government.

Perhaps the most anticipated event of the weekend, besides the football contest itself, was the inaugural Mordecai Wyatt Johnson-Benjamin E. Mays student debate that took place in Cramton Auditorium to a packed house on Friday afternoon. It is interesting to note that the debate

---

[10] "The HBCU Experience Is More Than a Game," 2011 Commemorative Program (September 8–11, 2011) 1.

was named for two giants in the field of education with close ties to Morehouse. Johnson was a 1911 graduate of the college and the first African American president of Howard, and Mays was the Great Schoolmaster at Morehouse.

The debate was embedded within a full program. Dubbed "the game before the game," the debate opened with an invocation delivered by Dr. Bernard L. Richardson, dean of the Howard University Chapel. After welcoming remarks were delivered by Dr. James Wyche, provost and chief academic officer at Howard; harpist Jeff Major, a television and radio personality, presented a musical selection. Dr. Thornton made statements, a musical selection was rendered by a Morehouse Glee Club Alumni Ensemble, and Presidents Franklin and Ribeau dedicated the event, after which the Howard University Gospel Choir delivered a performance.

After the debate teams were introduced by Dr. Terry Mills, dean of research and sponsored programs at Morehouse, and Dr. Barbara Griffin, vice president for student affairs at Howard, Angela D. Minor, Esq., the director and coach of Howard's Martin Luther King Jr. Forensic Program, introduced the debate. Ms. Minor moderated the debate.

There two subjects to be debated were "Resolved: Student athletes should be paid" and "Resolved: Cyber-bullying should be a criminal offense." Ably coached by Kenneth A. Newby, Esq., the Morehouse debaters were Christopher Fortson-Gaines, Kevin Porter, Franklin Kwame Weldon, and Austin Williams. The debaters from Howard were Marquis Barnett, Allen Reynolds, Gavette Richardson, Abraham Williamson, and Yosef Wise. In the end, and by the decision of the judges, the Howard debaters reigned victorious. Now "the game after the game"—football—was set to begin.

The Fighting Maroon Tigers football team, the Morehouse band, and the cheerleaders had arrived in the nation's capital by Friday morning as the HBCU College Showcase and Recruitment Fair/UNCF Empower Me Tour got underway at the Walter E. Washington Convention Center. Also on Friday, AT&T hosted an impressive kickoff rally, and that evening, an HBCU alumni networking reception was held at the DC Renaissance Hotel. Saturday morning at ten o'clock, the Pepsi MAX Fan Festival commenced on the grounds of RFK Stadium, the site of the Nation's Football Classic, but for Morehouse folk, the highlight of the weekend was the gathering of Morehouse Men, the Men of Morehouse, and Friends of Morehouse at the recently opened Dr. Martin Luther King Jr. Memorial.

Hundreds made the pilgrimage to the shrine that weekend in 2011 to pay homage to the college's most illustrious and celebrated graduate from the class of 1948. It was a warm but glorious September morning as the group assembled around the granite memorial at 1964 Independence Avenue, an address chosen to commemorate the Civil Rights Act of 1964, the bill Dr. King Jr. had fought so tirelessly to pass into law.

The King Memorial, known as the "Stone of Hope," is located in West Potomac Park at the northwest corner of the National Mall's tidal basin near the memorials to Presidents Thomas Jefferson, Abraham Lincoln, and Franklin Roosevelt. Its grounds cover four acres that were opened to the public on August 22, 2011. The dedicatory ceremony for the King Memorial was originally planned for Sunday, August 28, 2011, forty-eight years after Dr. King Jr. delivered the "speech of the twentieth century," his famous "I Have a Dream" speech, but Hurricane Irene caused a postponement of the event until October 16, 2011, which marked the sixteenth anniversary of the 1995 Million Man March on the nation's capital and the National Mall. Administered by the National Park Service, the memorial dedicated to the Morehouse Man from the class of 1948 is the first monument dedicated to an African American on or near the Mall, and Dr. King is only the fourth non-president of the United States to be honored in this way. The thirty-foot statue, which is the centerpiece of the memorial, is imposing, impressive, and awe-inspiring.

As the Morehouse family gathered to pay tribute to Dr. King Jr. during that weekend in 2011, other visitors to the memorial could sense that there was something uncommon or distinctive about the group, especially the alumni, many of whom were wearing the college's beloved colors—maroon and white. But it was much more than the tint in the shirts and hats, it was the behavior of these men who had gathered under a bright and warm sun. Whenever Morehouse Men and Men of Morehouse gather, a reunion always takes place. This is apparent at the major events and convocations at the college—Homecoming, Founders' Week, the Candle in the Dark Gala (the men's lounge almost takes on the air of a gentlemen's club), and commencement weekend. After tributary remarks were made by President Franklin and a few others, the Morehouse family crossed their arms, each holding the hands of the brother on his left and right, and sang the beloved Morehouse hymn—"Dear Old Morehouse." And on this occasion, it was sung with a certain poignancy, a peculiar air that gave it a spiritual quality. It was a moving scene, to say the very least. But after the robust singing of the last two lines of the last verse, "To old Morehouse and her ideals, and in all things that we do," the locked hands were shaken, hugs were exchanged once more, and the group left the memorial to prepare for the football contest that afternoon. Another Morehouse gathering was impending, so the meet-and-greets, brags-and-boasts continued. In the end, after all downs were played, the Morehouse Fighting Tigers lost to the Howard Bison 27–30, but, much like Homecoming, this game was more than a game. The financial benefits accrued and the increased enrollment numbers are unknown, but the event was special in every way as it allowed the candle and the crown to be on display in a different venue: the nation's capital. The members of the Morehouse community who participated in or witnessed the event were riding a crest of exhilaration when they returned to Atlanta. Nevertheless, in a little more than four months, the school would receive surprising, if not shocking, news. On the evening of January 30, 2012, Morehouse family and friends were stunned by the news that Dr. Robert Michael Franklin Jr. was stepping down as the tenth president of the college.

President Franklin had served his alma mater for five years by this time, but many expected his presidency to last at least until the sesquicentennial in 2017. At the 150th anniversary of Morehouse, Dr. Franklin would have served the institution for ten years, a tenure record for many college CEOs. In his resignation letter to alumni, Dr. Franklin said, "Every leader serves for a season and for a reason. My season as president of Morehouse College began five years ago when I was honored to be named the 10th president to our alma mater. My reason for leading this remarkable institution has been to fulfill the Board of Trustees' charge to restore and reenergize the intellectual and moral dimension of the college's mission and mystique." President Franklin asserted that he had "achieved these goals through my vision and our collective efforts to bring about a

Morehouse Renaissance."[11] His official day of resignation was slated for June 30, 2012.

A campuswide assembly was held in the Martin Luther King Jr. International Chapel at 11 A.M. on Tuesday, January 31, 2012, the day after the unexpected announcement of Dr. Franklin's resignation. Since President Franklin's resignation was a fait accompli, the question on everyone's mind was, Who will be the next president of Morehouse College? One rumor said the announcement would come before the end of the spring semester, while another had it that President Franklin's successor would be made known over the summer. But as all Morehouse stakeholders waited anxiously, the announcement of the selection of the eleventh president of Morehouse College did not come until November 2012. And while the Morehouse community and others waited, it is important to note that the "Five Wells" were well-established by this time. This is the lasting legacy of the Franklin presidency at Morehouse College. The "crown in crisis" was avoided, and the crown continued to remain in place above the heads of Morehouse Men. While some members of the Morehouse community feared that some students were not living up to the high standards generally expected of them and had strayed from the values that had guided the school since it was founded in 1867, the achievements of the men who proudly bore the insignia of Morehouse Men proved otherwise, dispelling any doubts. What earlier generations did not understand is that the times had changed, leading students to dress and talk differently. Their minds, however, were still set on the crown. They still had their eyes on the prize.

[11] http://www.morehouse.edu/communicatiions/releases/index.html.

Chapter 20

"The Crown and the Dream": The World and Wilson

Shortly after the startling announcement that Dr. Robert Michael Franklin Jr. would be transitioning from the presidency of Morehouse, the college's board of trustees began its search for the eleventh president of the school. A robust nationwide search was undertaken with the professional services of the recruitment firm Heidrick & Struggles, and on November 12, 2012, the board announced that Dr. John Silvanus Wilson Jr., a member of the Morehouse class of 1979, had been chosen as the next president of the college. Board chairman Robert C. Davidson Jr. thanked the board and the search consultants for their thorough evaluation of the excellent pool of candidates, which was not made public, and commended all on their outstanding recommendations.

Dr. Wilson was considered to have the vision, experience, and passion to ensure that Morehouse would continue to produce global leaders who could make a difference in the world. He was selected because his record of "academic excellence and public service" was consistent with that of Morehouse Men, and his leadership would mean "Morehouse would be well-positioned to continue delivering the educational environment that prepares our students for lives of leadership and service."[1] The announcement reached the office of the president of the United States, the highest office in the land, and President Barack Obama opined that John Wilson, who had been a trusted voice in his administration, had done good work in helping his team follow through on his commitment to strengthen historically black colleges and universities. President Obama wished "John the best as he takes on this important new role as the president of Morehouse College and as he continues to inspire more of our

---

[1] www.morehouse.edu/communications/releases/idex/html.

nation's youth to pursue higher education."[2] Dr. Wilson had worked as the executive director of the White House Initiative on Historically Black Colleges and Universities before he was tapped to return to his alma mater as the school's CEO. He officially assumed his new duties as the eleventh president of Morehouse at the end of January 2013. Before his inauguration, Dr. Willis B. Sheftall Jr., interim provost and senior vice president for academic affairs, served as the sixth acting president of Morehouse in the meantime.

At the twenty-fifth anniversary of the Candle in the Dark Gala, held two weeks after his inauguration, President Wilson made an announcement that registered with the audience in a deep and profound way. In measured speech, Dr. Wilson announced that President Barack Obama would be the 2013 commencement speaker. Hearing the announcement, the gala guests, students, alumni, and friends exploded in jubilation. And so, from the outset of the Wilson administration, the Morehouse name was spotlighted around the world. The worldwide media prepared to come to the college to cover the president's visit. But controversy soon surfaced over the visit by President Obama, who had very recently been elected and inaugurated for a second term in office. The first issue had to do with the selection of the Reverend Doctor Kevin Johnson, '96, as the 2013 baccalaureate speaker. Reverend Johnson was the senior pastor at Bright Hope Baptist Church in Philadelphia and had been critical of the dearth of black appointees in President Obama's cabinet during his first term in office. The Reverend Doctor Johnson had written an opinion piece that appeared in the *Philadelphia Tribune* on April 14, 2012, arguing that "as President Barack Obama begins his second term, there is something noticeably different about his new cabinet—the absence of African American leaders and advisors." Furthermore, the op-ed piece continued, "in sum, when one compares the first African American president to his recent predecessors, the number of African Americans in senior cabinet positions is very disappointing: Clinton (7), Bush (4), and Obama (1). Obama has not moved African American leadership forward, but backwards." Johnson then said, "Moreover, while having African

---

[2] http://www.bizpacreview.com/2013.05/01/prominent.black-pastors-speaking-invitation-revoke.

Americans in senior cabinet positions does not guarantee an economic agenda that will advance Black people, it at least is a starting point and puts us in the driver's seat. With President Obama, we are not in the driver's seat—or even in the car." As you can imagine, this editorial was not well-received by Wilson, an Obama friend.

As the result of Johnson's opinion piece, President Wilson apparently moved to have the Reverend Doctor Johnson disinvited to speak at baccalaureate, which prompted a group of Morehouse alumni who had formed an organization called "Citizens for Change" to denounce this decision, calling it "quite disturbing." The Reverend Delman Coates, '95, senior pastor of the Mt. Ennon Baptist Church in Clinton, Maryland, supported his fellow minister in the controversy, pointing out that the views Reverend Johnson shared had been "expressed in his monthly columns and national media appearances." Johnson had a right to an opinion. Further, the Reverend Doctor Amos Brown, '64, senior pastor of Third Baptist Church in San Francisco, said that "if President Wilson turns his back on one of our most distinguished alums because of an exercise of free speech and political commentary, he will have set Morehouse on a dangerous course and departed from the great tradition bequeathed to us."[3] When all was said and done, the Reverend Doctor Johnson did speak at the baccalaureate service, but so did two other Morehouse preachers: the Reverend Anthony Miller, CEO of Giant Steps Leadership Academy in Philadelphia, and the Reverend Olusesgun Abayomi, a master of divinity-degree student at Boston University's School of Theology. Both Reverend Miller and Reverend Abayomi were recent graduates of Morehouse. So, while on the one hand, the controversy was unsavory, on the other hand, it was interesting to see an all-Morehouse Men public debate on the issue at hand. The preaching by the three ministers at the 2013 baccalaureate, as you might imagine, was as good as it could get. Such fire and high rhetoric, such articulation and exhortation. They "tore the chapel church up," to paraphrase a saying from the black Baptist church tradition. Great oration has been a part of the Morehouse tradition since the idea was conceived that black men could be educated for scholarship and stewardship in 1867. Learned and articulate preaching was a part of

---

[3] Commencement 2013 Commemorative Issue, *Morehouse Magazine*, 8–18.

the original mission of the school, and this practice continues to this day. Dr. Martin Luther King Jr. was one of the best examples of Morehouse oratory.

The next morning, Sunday, May 19, 2013, after the Saturday baccalaureate service, it rained as Air Force One carried the president of the United States from Washington, DC, to Atlanta and to Morehouse College. The rain was drenching at times while security was extremely tight, prompting some commencement participants, parents, alumni, friends, and guests to begin arriving as early as 4 A.M. Secret Service personnel had been on campus for nearly two weeks and had created a "bubble" around the central part of the campus bounded by Fair Street, Ashby Street, West End Avenue, and Lee Street. A temporary security fence was erected around the perimeter and magnetometers were installed for security clearance. Everyone attending the 2013 commencement exercises inside the bubble had to have a ticket to enter the grounds. If you were to be seated within arms reach of the president, commonly referred to as ARP, you had to submit to a background check for the Federal Bureau of Investigation (FBI). A few members of the faculty who would normally have been seated on the stage, and, therefore, in ARP, refused to be investigated and, as a result, did not participate in the commencement program. But despite the heavy security and inclement weather, President Obama arrived at Hartsfield-Jackson International Airport and the presidential motorcade made its way to the campus.

The motorcade ended behind Hope Hall, John Hope Tech Tower, and Merrill Hall. Merrill Hall was the robing site for the president and his party, and at the appointed hour, after the rain-dampened commencement processional, President Barack Obama came out of the north doors of Merrill Hall to the applause and ovation of the audience. President John Wilson was with him. It was somewhat otherworldly to see thousands of people in the audience wearing clear plastic parkas as the commencement program proceeded in its usual way, with the ringing of the bell by the Reverend Doctor Woodrow Miller Jr., pastor of historic Harmony Baptist Church in Augusta, the former home of Augusta Theological Institute. This was followed by the evocation by the Reverend Raphael Warnock of Ebenezer Baptist Church, the presentation of the colors by the Reserve Officers' Training Corps (ROTC), and the singing of "The

Star-Spangled Banner," which was followed by the singing of "Lift Ev'ry Voice and Sing." Greetings were brought by Robert Davidson, chairman of the Morehouse Board or Trustees, and special presentations were made to salutatorian Ernest James Nelson Jr. and valedictorian Betsgaw Tadele by President Wilson and Dr. Willis Sheftall. Mr. Tadele then delivered his valedictory address, which was followed by the anthem, an exhortation delivered by David Conte, and the singing of Gerhard Krapf's "The 150th Psalm" by the Glee Club. The forty-fourth president of the United States then moved to the podium and began his commencement address to the Morehouse class of 2013. The rain continued, but heavier. President Obama opened his commencement address with a little levity, saying, "I also have to say that you all are going to get wet. And I'd be out there with you if I could. But Secret Service gets nervous. So, I'm going to have to stay here, dry. But know that I'm there with you in spirit." He then recognized that some of the women in the audience were upset by the rainy weather and commented that "[First Lady] Michelle would not be sitting in the rain. She has taught me about hair." After the usual anecdotes of a natural raconteur, with references to the icons in the history of Morehouse, and after reminding the audience that his job as president "is to advocate for policies that generate more opportunity for everybody—policies that strengthen the middle class and give more people the chance to climb their way into the middle class. Policies that create more good jobs and reduce poverty, and educate more children, and give more families the security of health care, and protect more of our children from the horrors of gun violence," President Obama told the graduates the following: "There are some things, as black men, we can only do for ourselves. There are some things, as Morehouse Men, that you are obliged to do for those still left behind. As Morehouse Men, you now wield something even more powerful than the diploma you're about to collect—and that's the power of your example."[4]

The president of the United States reminded the graduates that some of them had come from communities where "life was about keeping your head down and looking out for yourself." He continued, saying that as Morehouse Men, some of the graduates may have come to believe they

---

[4] Ibid.

had escaped. But Mr. Obama admonished them, declaring, "But I will say it betrays a poverty of ambition if all you think about is what goods you can buy instead of what good you can do." He admitted that he made a few mistakes as a young man, as many young men make, and said, "Sometimes I wrote off my failing as just another example of the world trying to keep a black man down. I had a tendency sometimes to make excuses for me not doing the right thing. But one of the things that all you have learned over the last four years is there's no longer any room for excuses." The forty-fourth president talked about the Affordable Care Act (informally called Obamacare) and the hyperconnected, hypercompetitive world that they were living in, the world in which they, the members of the class of 2013, would have to make their way. Mentioning Dr. Mays's name several times, President Obama reminded the audience that he himself had been "raised by a heroic single mom [and] wonderful grandparents [who] made incredible sacrifices for me." His message resonated and registered with the audience when he declared, "As Morehouse Men, many of you know what it's like to be an outsider, know what it's like to be marginalized, know what it's like to feel the sting of discrimination. And that's an experience that a lot of Americans share." After giving more encouraging words to the graduates, Mr. Obama closed his address with a caveat, saying,

> Success may not come quickly or easily. But if you strive to do what's right, if you work harder and dream bigger, if you set an example in your own lives and do your part to help meet the challenges of our time, then I'm confident that, together, we will continue the never-ending task of perfecting our union. Congratulations, Class of 2013. God bless you. God bless Morehouse. and God bless the United States of America.[5]

A standing ovation followed President Obama's address, with the loudest applause coming from members of the graduating class.

Following the president's address, the commencement program continued with the singing of the spiritual "Joshua Fit de Battle of Jericho," by Colin Lett. And then, with the help of President Wilson, Provost Sheftall, and Chairman Davidson, Mr. Barack Hussein Obama officially

---

[5] Ibid.

became a Morehouse Man when he received the honorary degree of doctor of laws. Despite the rain that continued to fall, the moment everyone had been waiting for arrived as baccalaureate degrees were conferred on the members of the class of 2013. ROTC officers were commissioned by Captain Mario Mifsud, and the class of 2013 was inducted into the Morehouse National Alumni Association by President Kevin R. McGee, '93. The Glee Club and former members sang "Prayer" from the opera *Lohengrin*, which had been composed by Richard Wagner and arranged by George Mead. After the singing of the college hymn, the benediction was delivered by Rev. Dr. Lawrence Edward Carter, dean of King Chapel, and "Fare Ye Well" was sung with gusto, the recessional took the graduates, as a class, from the Century Campus for the very last time. By this time, the rain had stopped and a bright, sunny afternoon was a welcome sight to all. The historic day at Morehouse College had ended, but the conversations about the day would last for years.

President Obama had been inaugurated for his second term just a few months before he delivered his Morehouse Commencement address. Dr. John Silvanus Wilson was still eight months away from his own inauguration as the eleventh president of Morehouse, and many changes took place at the college in those intervening months. Two weeks before the 2014 Founders' Week and Wilson's inauguration, on January 28, Atlanta was hit with a freak ice- and snowstorm that paralyzed the city. Many members of the Morehouse community were among those who had been caught off guard and stranded on freeways, highways, and thoroughfares for hours. Another storm brought more ice than snow the week of the inauguration, but this time, the citizens of metropolitan Atlanta had fair warning and stayed off the thoroughfares by the millions. Classes were canceled, and by Thursday, February 13, 2014, conditions had not improved, so the Founders' Day Convocation was canceled. Nevertheless, on Friday, February 14, 2014, a slightly modified inauguration took place at one o'clock in the afternoon (it had been scheduled for 11 A.M. in the morning) in the Martin Luther King Jr. International Chapel. The template created for the inauguration of Dr. Hugh Morris Gloster, the seventh president of Morehouse, was followed with a few changes. After all of the people in the processional had taken their places, Dr. Garikai Campbell, the recently appointed provost and vice president for academic affairs, summonsed all to witness the inauguration of Dr. John Silvanus Wilson as the eleventh president of Morehouse College. The Reverend Hardy Spurgeon Bennings III, pastor of the historic Springfield Baptist Church, where Morehouse had been organized in Augusta, rang the ceremonial bell. The evocation was delivered by the Reverend William Vincent Guy, '57, pastor emeritus of historic Friendship Baptist Church, the first home for the college in Atlanta. Phillip L. Clay, former chancellor of MIT; Dr. Clarissa Myrick-Harris, dean of the division of humanities and social sciences; Eugene V. Wade Jr., '92, founder and CEO of University Now in San Francisco; Jeh Charles Johnson, '79, United States Secretary of Homeland Security and a former classmate of the eleventh president; and William H. Cosby, honorary '87, whose salutation was prerecorded and projected on the large screen in the chapel, delivered greetings. Then the Morehouse Glee Club sang "My Strength and My Song," composed by Dr. Robert Tanner, associate professor of music at Morehouse.

The investiture of the new president continued with the conferring of the symbols of the office by the following individuals: the charge was delivered by Robert C. Davidson, '67, chairman of the board; the affirmation and charter were presented by the Honorable Andrew Young, honorary '75; the keys and seal were given to the president by Dale E. Jones, '82; the rules of order were presented by Avery A. Munnings, '86; the robe was given by Valerie Ervin; the medallion and hoof were presented by Charles H. James III, '81; the prayer was said by the Reverend Otis Moss Jr., '56; the mace was presented by Jim Moss, '70; and the convocation chair was pointed out by C. David Moody, '78. "And then the trumpets sounded." Before the eleventh president delivered his inaugural address, the Glee Club rose and sang "Let Go, Let God," by P. J. Morton. Cliff Slay, of Olive Branch Community Church in Sandy Spring, Maryland, was the guest soloist.

The title of President Wilson's inaugural address was "The World of Our Dreams," which would become the central theme of his presidency. The newly inaugurated president addressed the current challenging economic and political climate and made the argument that "even in the midst of this dramatic uncertainty, expectations remain sky-high for today's college presidents. At once, we are expected to ensure institutional affordability, accountability and agility. We are expected to decrease tuition, discount it, and at the same time increase net-tuition revenue and overall quality." The new president asserted that new college presidents must modernize facilities, monetize research, and optimize governance. They were expected to enhance on-campus education, integrate online education, and investigate on-site education. And they had to break all fundraising records, all while continually enriching the campus experience so well that each and every student became thoroughly brilliant, ambitious, ethical, and employable. After talking about the high expectations associated with the job of college president, Dr. Wilson moved to the core of his address, which was divided into seven parts: "Capital and Character Preeminence," "The Freedom Imperative," "The Identity Imperative," "The Dream Imperative," "Recovering the Morehouse Embrace," "Morehouse Universal," and "It's Up to Us!" After discussing the need for Morehouse to have a first-rate campus in order to produce first-rate men, Wilson then said, "I need you to know that Morehouse College is not just for Morehouse Men. In fact, it is my dream that Morehouse will be to all men and especially to all African American men, what Israel is to all Jews—the homeland, the definitive base for what it means to be a man in this world, the place where our identity as men and men-in-the-making is at its best." President Wilson closed his inaugural address with these words: "Ladies and gentlemen, I am quite certain that realizing the world of our dreams on this campus and on this earth, is, in God's name, *up to us!* Thank you! God bless you! And God bless Morehouse College!"[6] After receiving the applause of the audience, the program ended in the usual way, and President Wilson led the platform party and all attendees to a reception in the Shirley Massey Conference Center. Morehouse had been educating African American men since 1867, and while it attracted men of other races and ethnicities, its core mission remained focused on the school's founding idea of educating black men for scholarship and service.

The eleventh president of Morehouse vigorously set about improving the financial health of the college and ramping up the character capital of the school's constituents. As his administration continued to form, President Wilson challenged each member of the class of 2018, and, by inference, all Morehouse students, to "Determine yourself, Sharpen yourself,

---

[6] Ibid.

Deepen yourself, Ground yourself, and Distinguish yourself."[7] As the chief academic administrator and his "right hand man," President Wilson appointed Dr. Garikai Campbell, former associate vice president for strategic planning and special assistant to the president at Swarthmore College, as Morehouse's new provost and senior vice president. Within a few months, Dr. Campbell made significant changes in the academic administrative structure at Morehouse by dismantling the "deanery" and implementing an associate and assistant provost structure. The new academic officials were appointed from Morehouse faculty: Jann Adams, associate provost for faculty affairs; Keith Howard, assistant provost for faculty affairs; Clarissa Myrick-Harris, associate provost for pedagogical and curricular initiatives; Michael Hodge, associate provost for faculty research, scholarship, and creative production; Vickie Cox Edmondson, associate provost for student success; and David Wall Rice, assistant provost for student success. The new academic structure was the source of much discussion.

For the faculty and staff members working on the inside of the Wilson administration, things were going well. The president moved the Office of Communications and Public Relations directly under his authority in order to control information coming from the college. Any member of the college's faculty or staff had to get approval to speak to the media and/or bring speakers to the campus. Some of these changes were perceived as attempts to resurrect outdated nineteenth- and twentieth-century paternalistic and authoritarian administration styles in a twenty-first century academic culture. The "Five Qualities of a Morehouse Man" were introduced as a replacement for the "Five Wells of a Morehouse Man," which had been the hallmark of President Franklin's administration, and which had been embraced by students and alumni—well-read, well-spoken, well-dressed, well-traveled, and well-balanced. The new qualities described the Morehouse Man as demonstrating acuity, integrity, agency, brotherhood, and consequential lives. These noble ideals were meant to be guideposts for the Wilson presidency, but dark clouds began to form on the college's horizon, and by fall 2015, the first clap of thunder was heard: the Morehouse Board of Trustees, under the chairmanship of

---

[7] Ibid.

Robert Davidson, voted to extend president John Wilson's contract for only one year beyond his original three-year contract. This meant that his tenure at the college would end June 30, 2017. The news of this decision reverberated around the country, among Morehouse Men and others. It was clear to all that something was wrong at the House.

President Wilson practiced a "transactional" style of leadership that had elements of the authoritarian leader. "Transactional leaders focus their leadership on motivating followers through a system of rewards and punishments. This type of leader identifies the needs of their followers and give rewards [or punishments] to satisfy those needs in exchange for certain levels of performance."[8] The fissure among faculty members revealed in the months leading up to the termination of Dr. John Silvanus Wilson was a clear indication of this idea: Those faculty who supported Dr. Wilson were rewarded materially, psychologically, and/or situationally, and those who did not support the president were not so rewarded. The overarching leadership style of Morehouse presidents should be transformational. Leaders that follow the transformational style of leading can challenge and inspire their followers with a sense of purpose and excitement. Transformational leaders also create a vision of what they aspire to be and are able to communicate this idea to their followers.[9]

Never in the history of Morehouse College had there been such a great divide among faculty, staff, students, and alumni as there was during the Wilson administration. The chasm rapidly opened after the controversial board of trustees decided not to extend his contract beyond June 30, 2017, which was met with both criticism and praise from stakeholders in the college. Those who supported President Wilson thought the board's decision was a travesty and that it was insulting to humiliate him by publicly announcing the unusual decision. Those who did not support Wilson's presidency thought the decision showed a lack of fiduciary responsibility by keeping him on as head of the college beyond the original three-year contract: they wanted him out in 2016.

When news of the board's decision was made public in a letter from Chairman Robert Davidson and then picked up by the media, the oral

---

[8] "Leadership Styles," Wikipedia.

[9] Ibid.

and written arguments over the board's action began to shake the foundation of the House. For the next year and a half, the controversy gain momentum unlike anything seen at the college before, culminating in the termination of the eleventh president of Morehouse College in April 2017. Here is how it unfurled.

The first sign that there was a leadership problem was when the Association of Governing Boards Consulting (AGB) was contracted to look into the work of and relationship between President John Wilson and board chair Bob Davidson. In a lengthy report written by AGB's Rick Legon and Alvin Schexnider dated May 14, 2014 (updated September 2014), under the subject "A Summary of Reflections and Recommendations Resulting from AGB's Assessment (Self-Study) of Morehouse Leadership and Board Governance," a concern was raised "that important steps are still awaiting action at the college, and we feel obligated to submit a final summary of our work." For context, it must be remembered that John Silvanus Wilson had just been inaugurated as the eleventh president of Morehouse just a few months prior, in February 2014.

AGB Consulting, according to its website, "is your best source for experts on advancing the work of your board and institution." It asserts that they "provide individualized solutions for board members and campus leaders to respond to governance challenges and crises, and to successfully lead higher education systems, institutions, and affiliated foundations."

In its report to Wilson and Davidson, AGB stated that their "conclusions indicate that it is time to take action and, it is our hope that these recommendations can serve as a road map to a healthier governance structure and a more productive board structure." AGB stated that the report was conducted using a "careful review of policy documents, as well as interviews with board members, president and chair, and several senior staff members. In addition, a number of meetings were held leading to the board self-study workshop to review those inputs. Our recommendations are informed by current best practices in institution governance." AGB strongly encouraged "recognition that most of these recommendations are linked—that is, they lose impact if only selectively implemented. Governance should tell a 'story' about institution mission and mutual expectation, and commitment to the future—it must hold together in ways that work holistically and that are supported by all institution stakeholders."[10]

The AGB report was presented in three parts: "President's Relation with the board," "Governance Policies," and "President-Board Chair Relationship." Under the first topic, it was revealed that the "president at Morehouse College has expressed some specific views about his expectations of governing boards—some of those views seems to have created tensions with board members and administration." Apparently, some members of the board had taken "extreme and unrelenting positions about presidential communications (and trust)," and the report recommended "the president should rethink his outreach and communications with all members of the Morehouse College board." The actions of President Wilson should be "intentional about sharing information" and the board should not be "surprised" by his actions. The report emphasized that "trust and advocacy on behalf of the president should define this relationship, yet currently those criteria appear to be missing from this most essential of relationships." The consultants observed that the relationship between President Wilson and Chairman Davidson was "untenable." This relationship resulted in Davidson's decision to stop participating in major convocations while Wilson was president, only to return when Wilson's tenure at Morehouse ended in April 2017; Davidson participated in the college's sesquicentennial commencement.

The consultants argued that there were problems with the make-up of the board and its structure. In order to be positioned to do "thought partner" work, the board needed to redraft its bylaws "in order to be consistent with best practice." In doing so, it needed to look at the role assignments of board officers and the executive committee. AGB recommended that the name of the "Governance Oversight" committee be changed simply to "Governance Committee." Further, the report concluded that the terms of board members needed updating to allow for "new and fresh expertise," honorary and emeritus board status should not be automatic, there were too many alumni on the board, and in relation to looking forward, it was noted that "alumni dominated boards often look out the rear-view mirror." So, while the Morehouse Board of

[10] Association of Governing Boards (AGB) Memo to John Wilson and Bob Davidson, May 14, 2014.

Trustees was not falling apart, it needed to do some soul-searching and make hard decisions about internal changes going forward.

As the remainder of the fall semester 2015 stretched to its conclusion, the climate at Morehouse seemed to have calmed. But seething just beneath the surface was a virus that would soon infect the college's constituents. The conversations among members of the Morehouse community for the first nine months of 2016 had much to do with the employment status of President Wilson. As the board prepared to meet in October of that year, two developments took place: faculty on both sides of the issue submitted petitions to board chair Robert Davidson, and dissatisfied alumni started a petition on change.org calling for the firing of President John Wilson. This is when "The War at Morehouse" began.[11] The theaters of this war were numerous and varied. Pro-Wilson, anti-Davidson students, led by Johnathan Hill, president of the Morehouse Student Government Association, fought from its offices and from the law office of its legal counsel, and the faculty's pro-Wilson, anti-Davidson forces were led by Derrick Bryan. Anti-Wilson faculty, students, and staff were amorphous, for the most part, and the Morehouse alumni on both sides of the controversy weighed in at sites around Atlanta and across the country. A fierce exchange of words ensued in January 2017 when board chairman Davidson committed a faux pas and inaccurately announced that President Wilson had been discharged and that William "Bill" Taggart, chief operating officer at Morehouse, had been appointed interim president. What happened next is the stuff of Shakespearean drama.

Controversy had surrounded president John Silvan Wilson from the beginning of his administration. His first meeting with students, early in the spring semester of 2013, had not gone well, and some students left the assembly in King Chapel taken aback by the eleventh president's abrasive and strident attitude. Without equivocation, it was Wilson's autocratic style of leadership that destroyed the foundation of his presidency and led to his firing four years later. The precursors to the War at Morehouse, hereafter referenced simply as the "War," began in fall 2016 on the eve of a meeting of the board of trustees. A dissatisfied group of faculty members sent a letter to Robert ("Bob") Davidson: "We, a group of tenured faculty

---

[11] https://www.theroot.com/the-war-at-morehouse-1793541413.

member at Morehouse College, respectfully submit this letter of deep concern with the leadership of the current President and Provost. Their leadership of the college has proven to be in direct contradiction to the historical institutional ethos of the college and its many publics, resulting in our inability to work positively any longer with the current President and Provost." The letter outlined, in bulleted statements, the areas where the president and provost had failed: "Policies and Procedures" and "Leadership."

The first area of concern was in relation to faculty governance and faculty bylaws, which gave an entity known as the Faculty Welfare Committee (FWC) the responsibility "to examine College policies and make recommendations with respect to tenure and promotions, examine fringe benefits and make recommendations, and develop policies concerning the evaluation of faculty members." Tenured faculty members stated that "the administration failed to consult with the FWC, which had review and recommendation purview over faculty matters, about changes of the health benefits before its adoption. [The] FWC was consulted only after decisions to change the plan coverage and cost were made."

The next point of contention by the concerned tenured faculty was the failure of the provost to view the "student evaluation of faculty form" that the FWC was tasked to create, and deciding, instead, to purchase an online instrument from the IDEA Company. The letter revealed how "the Academic Affairs Office justified this costly adoption as adhering to supposed national standard assessment measures." But, according to the missive, "the FWC-designed evaluation form included standard measures as well as questions that address the unique values and needs of Morehouse College."

Faculty governance through the FWC was abandoned when the Office of Academic Affairs proposed a new plan for evaluating the performance of faculty without its input. The FWC had "recommended several changes to implement checks and balances in the assessment process and to remove the excessive time and paperwork demands on the faculty, which can obstruct what we do best: teaching and mentoring." And although recommendations from the FWC were acknowledged at a faculty meeting, the provost, as the chief academic officer, ordered his preferred plan implemented and ignored major parts of the FWC's recommendations. Further, with regard to strategic planning at Morehouse, tenured faculty members stated that a "Strategic Plan booklet" was given to the faculty that contained "no time parameters or baseline data and it [did] not lend itself to the procedures described by the Office of Strategic Planning." The letter to Chairman Davidson and the board revealed that although regular assessment was required by the Southern Association of Colleges and Schools Committee on Colleges, the Office of Academic Affairs had conducted its last formal assessment in the 2013 to 2014 academic year, and it pointed out that the provost had ignored the Quality Enhancement Plan (QEP) document, "deflecting questions about the document and whether it continued to guide the college."

The letter raised questions about the effectiveness of the Office of Human Resources and the Office of Ethics and Compliance in addressing complaints made by faculty members: both offices were slow to respond to reports of incidents considered detrimental to the physical and mental well-being of staff members. Faculty and staff members were also left in a state of confusion about their status at the college as the provost failed to send out letters of appointment and reappointment in 2015, which he admitted was his failure on September 26, 2015. Provost Garikai Campbell also failed to follow the schedule for tenure and promotion, according to the faculty handbook, as faculty members were not notified of successful tenure and promotion until after commencement in May 2015.

Troubled by the leadership of President Wilson and Provost Campbell, the letter pointed to issues of transparency, communication, and campus safety. "The lack of shared governance has, in less than four years, created a hostile work environment in which employees fear retaliation if they disagree and/or report unethical behavior that takes place." With reference to Campbell and the Office of Academic Affairs, the missive stated that with "the large number of associate and assistant provosts that he has appointed, the provost has become removed from the faculty. He has lost direct communication with the faculty and is unable to respond directly to faculty queries." The report stated that

> the firing, movement, and hiring of support staff across campus has not been communicated promptly and efficiently. The lack of communication creates anxiety for all personnel and interruption in services. Terminations across campus have left us with staff that

> knows nothing about Morehouse and its culture, nor does that staff appear interested in learning. Indeed, one walks into an office and is greeted by the question, "Who are you?" Or even worse, in some academic departments, there is no staff person or secretary.

The authors of the letter believed the campus was unsafe and informed the chairman that "the number of police persons has for some time shrunken to four, too small a number to secure the campus and protect the students. Without sufficient police officers, our campus is open to people walking on who have no reason to be or should not be on campus. Security people...are different from police officers."

The most scathing part of the letter was its assessment of the effectiveness of Provost Campbell. In very direct words, the tenured faculty said that "the provost has not shown upper-level management and leadership abilities. He starts too many initiatives, and because of his failure to follow through, most projects remain unfinished or unresolved. Consequently, there is an air of doubt about the future and a sense of 'unfulfillment' among faculty and staff." Furthermore, Provost Campbell was "grossly ineffective in leading the faculty. Although required by the Faculty By-Laws (Article V.1), a regular secretary has not been appointed to take minutes at faculty meetings, hence, the faculty has no record of faculty decisions. Rarely are we provided an agenda before meetings (Article V.1), and rarely does the provost complete an agenda before the end of the allotted time [for faculty meetings]."

Continuing its blistering evaluation of Provost Campbell, the letter stated that "the provost has shown during his tenure at the college an inability to meet the needs of timely decision-making about the affairs of the college. He has repeatedly failed to follow through on promises that he has made at meetings to resolve issues raised by the faculty." It noted that "the Office of Academic Affairs has yet to be settled into a definitive structure. The personnel keep changing, and their roles are not properly defined or communicated to the faculty."

The anti-Wilson/Campbell camp argued that one root cause of a lack of shared governance arose from an imbalance in the distribution of roles. It pointed to the chief of staff, who also served as the general counsel, director of the Office of Ethics and compliance officer, and the Title III grant principal investigator/director. They feared an absence of checks and balances could "compromise the financial standing, legal status, or communal reputation of the college."

Referencing the glorious history of Morehouse College, the letter from the concerned tenured faculty ended with a statement about their belief in the good intentions of President Wilson and Provost Campbell, but that they were nevertheless greatly concerned about the school's present situation and future trajectory. Wilson and Campbell had not inspired a sense of confidence or community on campus or sustained support among the alumni. The letter was unsigned, which was its major shortcoming, but the "tenured faculty" feared retribution if the president and provost were not "separated from the college," and even if terminated, they feared they might face retaliation during the balance of their terms in office.

The battlelines were drawn when Provost Campbell distributed the "resolution" letter from twenty-two faculty members from the Division of Humanities and Social Sciences and the "Concerned Morehouse Faculty Members" letter addressed to Bob Davidson to the faculty. Campbell told the faculty that these two letters were the only faculty opinion the board had, "but if you are of a different opinion, it may also be worthwhile to add that different perspective to the board's understanding."[12] He said he had complete faith in anything faculty would send to the board, at least to Robert Davidson and Dorothy Cowser Yancy, chair of the Education Policy Committee. Provost Campbell concluded his memorandum to the faculty by stating that he was "very proud of the work that we have been able to do and am not in any way naïve about what work remains. I am grateful to those with whom I have worked and will continue to work until I am no longer Provost, just as I am grateful to the voices who challenge us and then help us to make Morehouse an even stronger place, all in service to developing our students in the best ways possible."[13]

Another volley was fired in the War when a group of Morehouse alumni signed an appeal on the online petition-writing website change.org calling for President Wilson's dismissal. Dated October 6, 2016, the

---

[12] "Regarding the President and Provost of Morehouse College," Garikai Campbell, October 7, 2016.

[13] Ibid.

subject line read "Alums Call for the Firing of Morehouse President." The petition read, "With the history and future of Morehouse College on the line, it is with the deepest regrets, but the most urgent call to action, that we call for the nonrenewal of the contracts of President John Wilson and members of his senior team, and for the formation of a search committee to commence surveying for a permanent replacement for the position of President of Morehouse College." Hundreds of Morehouse Men signed the petition, which was brought to the attention of the board. By this time, the board had voted to extended President Wilson's contract through June 2017, but the petition called for his immediate removal from office. The petition also revealed the names of the signing alumni, some of whom were tenured faculty at the college. The board did not extend Wilson's contract, and it delayed a vote on his employment until later. And so the waiting began amid growing tensions and loaded missives. Bob Davidson had given the impression that Wilson's tenure was secure when he publicly stated, in October 2016, that the president had the full support of the board. The pro-Wilsonians were comforted, the anti-Wilsonians disheartened.

On October 25, 2016, President Wilson sent invitations to several faculty members to "A Dinner to Listen" at Davidson House. The opening lines shared why he wanted to "listen":

> On several occasions in my life when I have been asked to share my own personal "secrets of success," I have invariably emphasized the power of empathy. At the very heart of empathy is listening, and I have always prided myself on being a great listener. As a beneficial consequence of that, whenever there has been any kind of discord in my professional experiences, a good dose of listening, followed by a set of healthy remedial steps has always brought me and others to the higher echelon where we all deserve to function. Accordingly, in light of what I have been hearing for the last several months, I want to do a kind of listening tour, which will include several dinners at my home for focused sessions where those special people who are gathered can be more open and candid.[14]

The dinner was held on November 2, 2016, and President Wilson

[14] "A Dinner to Listen," Davidson House, Morehouse, October 25, 2016.

once again revealed why he wanted to have the listening dinner party. "I want to just listen to you." This "listening" was supposed to be done with the knowledge that the views and concerns among the faculty were good and bad, and President Wilson said he was "committed to figuring out how to be more responsive, sensitive and sensible about ensuring that we have a more shared view of our certain destiny—something for which all Morehouse presidents have had to handle, and which I happen to call, 'the world of our dreams!'" The invitation closed with Wilson acknowledging his "temporary station as the Morehouse president, as in my permanent station as a Morehouse alumnus." Then, introspectively, he shared,

> I care deeply about this place. I truly love this institution, and I am honored to be in a privileged position to make her better. Any yet, I am well aware that I cannot do that by myself. I regard faculty as the primary beneficiaries of my most important work. I believe that when I make things better for you, then we can all make things better for our young men. That is, we can optimize our ability to make them world-class Morehouse Men! Nothing more is required of us. And nothing less will do.[15]

Several faculty members who were invited to the dinner did not attend. But others did, so the dinner was held at Davidson House on Wednesday evening, November 2, 2016. But despite efforts by President Wilson to quiet the sounds of War at Morehouse, the battle between the anti-Wilson and pro-Wilson, and, by extension, the related Provost Campbell constituencies, grew louder. They were tempered by the coming holidays—Thanksgiving and Christmas—but would erupt in a pitched battle in January 2017.

The fall semester of 2016 ended as usual: the famous Christmas Carol Concert performed by the Morehouse Glee Club, the Spelman Glee Club, and the Morehouse Spelman Chorus was presented on the first weekend in December. This was the ninetieth Christmas Carol Concert, and Dr. David Morrow directed the Morehouse singers and Dr. Kevin Johnson directed the Spelman carolers. The much-beloved Dr. Joyce Finch Johnson served as organist, as she had done for more than sixty

[15] Ibid.

years. For many campus and community members, this concert marks the beginning of their Christmas holiday season. The wonderful performances by the well-rehearsed singers tend to put the audience in a good mood and prepare them for the weeks ahead. But the philosophical and political struggle among the constituents of the college did not go away, as these tensions were a topic of conversation even among concertgoers.

Final examinations began on Monday, December 5, 2016, as the sesquicentennial class anticipated its last semester as Men of Morehouse. The coveted nomenclature of "Morehouse Man" was just a few months away for the Men of Morehouse in this class: commencement was scheduled for May 21, 2017.

A course on the Social and Cultural history of Morehouse College was offered in the second semester of 2017, and what a class it turned out to be. Many of the school's top student leaders enrolled in the class, and these students (some of whose names are recorded below), along with the other students who took this course during the four years it was taught, are bearers of the college's formal history. They represent the ideals of the college and are the manifestation of the 1867 idea that black men can be educated for scholarship and stewardship. This "power class," composed of academically exceptional students engaged in a variety of leadership roles and activities, well represents the many outstanding students who have embraced the 1867 idea. These are just a few of their members:

Je'lon Alexander, junior, History Major, Concert/Marching Band, Mellon-Mays Fellow

Blake Benyard, senior, Math Major, Cross Country, Track, Phi Beta Kappa

Douglas Bowen, senior, Valedictorian, Economics Major, Investment Club, Ambassador

Ryan George, senior, Political Science Major, SGA Vice President, Ambassador

Kaj Gumb, senior, Political Science Major, Phi Alpha Delta, NAACP

Johnathan Hill, senior, Political Science Major, SGA President, Board of Trustees

Darius Johnson, junior, English Major, Sigma Tau Delta, Baseball, Bands, the Torch

Rashad Jones, junior, Political Science Major, SGA, Collegiate 100 Black Men

Lewis Miles, junior, Sociology Major, Mellon-Mays Fellow, Ambassador

Xavier Milton, freshman, Finance Major, Glee Club, Ambassador

Makhai Moore, sophomore, Biology Major, Toastmasters Club

Christopher Polston, senior, Biology/Religion Majors, SGA, Band, Chapel Assistant

Juwan Pulliam, senior, Business Major, Morehouse Management Group President

Taylor Pullen, senior, English Major, Pre-Law Society, TRIO Program

Ryan Russell, junior, Political Science Major, SGA, Oprah Winfrey Scholar, Soccer

Corbin Sanders, senior, Music Major, AUC Symphony Orchestra

Sean Sheppherd, senior, Finance Major, Project House, Ambassador

Purvis Stafford, senior, Political Science Major, Phi Alpha Delta, Living Green Club

Christopher Sumlin, senior, CTEMS Major, Published Writer

Perry Washington, senior, Religion Major, SGA, Peer Leaders, Chapel Assistant

The leadership positions at the college held by the members of this exceptional class, coupled with their accomplishments, speak to the quality of the students that Morehouse continued to enroll at its 150th anniversary. Several of these students were later inducted into the Phi Beta Kappa Society. Half of the students enrolled in the course were members of the Morehouse Sesquicentennial Class—the class of 2017. As would be expected, these student leaders immersed themselves in the debate over the future of President Wilson at Morehouse.

As if to presage the coming intensity of the War, on January 9, 2017, Chairman Davidson sent out an email message saying that the board would meet in "Executive Session for Elected Trustees and Visitors" only. The purpose of the session was to complete the discussion on President Wilson's employment agreement that had begun in October 2016. Just before the meeting started, Davidson met with Johnathan Hill, the president of the Morehouse Student Government Association who was also a student member of the board, and informed him "that he would not be able to attend or participate in the meeting unless he disclosed to him how he and the other two student trustees would vote on the matter of the renewal of President Wilson's employment agreement. Mr. Hill declined to disclose that information to Chairman Davidson."[16] Subsequently, the three student members and three faculty members of the board were not allowed to participate in the discussion on Wilson's contract renewal. Later that day, January 13, 2017, a Temporary Restraining Order (TRO) was filed on behalf of the student trustees to prevent the board from holding its meeting without the full participation of the student trustees. Ominous clouds gathered over the Morehouse landscape, and the legal, political, and personal conflict between Davidson and Hill flared. The board of trustees met in executive session without the student and faculty trustees and made the decision not to renew Dr. Wilson's contract beyond the June 30, 2017, reiterating the employment agreement that had been made in 2015.

In a movement meant to garner support for his continued employment at Morehouse, President Wilson delivered a PowerPoint presentation to the faculty on Tuesday, January 17, 2017. Almost every slide featured the "Emancipation Proclamation" stamp that had been issued by the United States Postal Service and which had been unveiled in the lobby of King Chapel in 2013.

The title of Wilson's presentation was "Morehouse College Freedom Agenda in Pursuit of the World of Our Dreams." He stated that he

[16] "Timeline Updated," February 8, 2017.

wanted "to position Morehouse College students, faculty, staff, and trustees to finally be free enough to do our very best work!" and evoked Dr. Martin Luther King Jr.'s "Strides toward Freedom," citing some of the successes of faculty and students. Except for Wilson's role in helping secure President Obama as the 2013 commencement speaker, all of the other achievements were made, primarily, independent of the president. Under "Capital Preeminence Highlights," which is directly impacted by the president, Wilson cited the following: "Annual fundraising up 41%, all-time alumni giving was up in 2015 and 2016, alumni donor count was up in 2013, alumni cash giving up 100 %, use of financial consultants down 97%, capital expenditures up 14%, athletic scholarships up 66%, advancement office staff up 175%, gifts from three new billionaires, initiated Task Force on new Revenue Streams, and repaired broken endowment systems ($12M)."

In addition, according to Wilson, there was a lot of "unfinished business" at Morehouse, including the following: Morehouse and the Southern Association of Colleges and Schools Commission on Colleges; Morehouse and the 2017 Budget; Morehouse and a Campus Investigation Underway; Morehouse and Advancement; Morehouse and Its Physical Plant; Morehouse and Trustee Giving; and Morehouse and Campus/Board Relations: A New Narrative. The presentation ended with "Morehouse Needs Time!," including time to move four key metrics associated with refining and stabilizing enrollment, mastering cash/financial/operational management, enhancing fundraising effort, and growing the endowment. In consideration of these goals, though, these things do not have a fixed ending, as Wilson suggested, but rather will continue ad infinitum. And if Morehouse needed time, was that time dependent on any one person? The Morehouse Board of Trustees did not think it was dependent on John Silvanus Wilson.

Amid this turmoil, President Wilson attended a meeting of leader from HBCUs that was associated with a photo opportunity for President Donald Trump. The gathering was held in the Oval Office and as a preface to the Trump administration's announcement of a "New Deal for Black America." For the most part, the "fly-in," as it was dubbed, did not sit well with many black Americans. President John Wilson was one of them, and he later said, "Many had high hopes about this meeting.... But instead of the long-awaited executive order containing or signaling any outcomes, the key change is a symbolic shift of the White House HBCU Initiative from the Department of Education to the White House. It is not possible to measure the impact of this gesture anytime soon, if ever."[17] Often called the "We Got Played Speech," this meeting generated much debate and argument among Morehouse people and others. The meeting with President Trump was nothing more than a photo opportunity that had no substance whatsoever. It was part of the propaganda of the president's administration, and this is what Wilson meant when he said "we were played."

It is the nature of human beings to propagandize but, in relation to President Wilson's presidency, never in the history of the college had Morehouse been so divided. The propaganda from both sides of the controversy was vile, vituperative, vitriolic, and vehement. Most of the arguments that went public came from the pro-Wilson camp.

In relation to one issue in particular, it was asked by what authority did Chairman Davidson excuse student members from the session where President Wilson's employment agreement was discussed? In section 2.5, paragraph two of the Morehouse College Board of Trustees' bylaws, it states that "Student Trustees are bound by the confidentiality and conflict of interest guidelines that apply to Elected Members and should declare any conflict and excuse themselves from discussions that may lead to a conflict of interest. Student Trustees must excuse themselves from participation and voting on matters of the appointment, promotion and dismissal of faculty members or the president."[18] This meant, according to the bylaws, that Chairman Davidson did have the authority to excuse the student trustees from the session and to get their input before they were excused. At the temporary restraining order hearing, however, the three student trustees argued their right, without legal standing, to participate in the session where Wilson's contract with the college was discussed. In the meantime, Bob Davidson moved forward with the discussion and voting on the renewal of Wilson's employment agreement, and the student

[17] "Morehouse College President Issues Statement on Trump Meeting with HBCUs," *Rolling Out*, https://rollingout.com/2017/03/02/morehouse-college-president-issues-statement-trumps-meeting-hbcus/

[18] www.morehouse.edu.

trustees fully participated in the deliberations of the board the next day, January 14, 2017. But the story did not end there. The student trustees brought civil action against Robert C. Davidson Jr., chairman of the Morehouse College Board of Trustees. File number 2017CV284794 was filed by Catherine Robinson, clerk of the Fulton County Superior Court, at 10:57 A.M. on February 8, 2017.[19]

What was the "relief requested" by the students' civil action?

> That the Court enter a preliminary and permanent injunction ordering the Defendant to: rescind all action taken by the Morehouse Board of Trustees on January 13 2017 while the three student trustees were excused from its meeting on said date, reschedule and provide due notice of a substitute meeting of the full Morehouse College Board of Trustees so that the matters taken up during the January 13, 2017, meeting may be taken up anew as if never addressed ("substitute meeting"), permit student trustees to attend and participate in the substitute meeting and exercise the full powers and duties of the Morehouse Board of Trustees as set forth in Article I of the Morehouse College [Board of Trustees] Amended and Restated By-laws ("By-laws").

The court issued a preliminary injunction against Chairman Davidson, "ordering and adjudging" that he was required to rescind all actions taken by board on January 13, 2017, while the three student trustees were excused from the meeting. Further,

> Chairman Davidson is required to reschedule and provide due notice of a substitute meeting so that matters taken up during the January 13, 2017, meeting may be taken up anew as if never addressed, Chairman Davidson is required to permit the student trustees to attend and participate fully in the substitute meeting and exercise the full powers and duties of the Morehouse College Board of Trustees, Chairman Davidson is required to permit the student trustees to attend and participate fully in the substitute meeting, including relating to the matter involving the renewal of the president's employment agreement, Chairman Davidson is required to cease and desist from enforcing the provision in the By-laws giving

[19] Ibid.

> himself the power to excuse student trustee from any meeting, The order shall remain in force and effect until further order of the Court, and This order shall be binding upon the parties who receive notice of this order.

The TRO was short-lived: on February 14, 2017—the birthdate of the college—Fulton County Superior Court Judge Robert McBurney ruled that the board's bylaws allowed its chairman to exclude student and faculty trustees from board meetings. But while Chairman Davidson was pleased with the ruling, Harold W. Spence, of Cuffie Law Firm, and a member of the Morehouse class of 1977, was not pleased, although he opined that Judge McBurney had followed the law in making his decision.

In the midst of the War, the Morehouse College Sesquicentennial season got underway with the Founders' Week Convocation "Celebrating Our Sesquicentennial Anniversary, 1867–2017," held on Thursday, February 14, 2017. The event began with the processional at 10:45 that morning. Dr. Garikai Campbell, provost and senior vice president, presided. Dr. Joyce Finch Johnson, Spelman College professor emerita and college organist, performed the pre-ceremonial music: Johann Sebastian Bach's "Fantasia in G Minor, BWV 542" and Louis Vierne's "Carillon Westminster."

The student, faculty, and platform party entered King Chapel processing to "Trumpet Tune" by D. Johnson, J. Stanley, et. al. The Reverend Doctor Lawrence Edward Carter, Dean of the Martin Luther King Jr. Chapel, invited the Reverend Doctor Raphael Gamaliel Warnock, '91, fifth senior pastor of historic Ebenezer Baptist Church in Atlanta, to come forward to do the "Lighting of the Candle of the Mystique." Dean Carter then gave the evocation, followed by the presentation of the colors, "The Star-Spangled Banner," and one verse of "Lift Ev'ry Voice and Sing."

As the convocation continued, Provost Campbell offered the "occasion," including an oft-told version of the history of Morehouse. Campbell recognized VIPs in the audience, including Dr. Crystal Morehouse, the great-grandniece of Dr. Henry Lyman Morehouse, and other ancestors of early stakeholders in the school: William Jefferson White's descendants were present. Robert Davidson, however, was not present, and F. Euclid Walker, '95, a member of the Morehouse Board of Trustees, brought greetings on behalf of the board. Following the announcement of the winners of the Otis Moss Oratorical Contest, the Morehouse College Glee Club sang the anthem and "Unity," a commissioned world premiere arrangement by Carlos Simon, a 2008 graduate of the college. Dr. David Morrow directed the singers, who were accompanied by Jerrell Melton II on piano, David Oliver on organ, Melvin Jones, '01, on trumpet, and Edward William III, also on trumpet.

One was struck by two elements of the anthem "Unity": its pathos was overwhelming as it did not present an uplifting, celebratory mood, and the words that the Glee Club sang were plaintive and prayerful: "How good is it when God's people live in unity" was a refrain. A house united in love was a petition submitted to a disunited Morehouse. When the anthem was sung and President John Silvanus Wilson moved to the rostrum to introduce the Founders' Day speaker, he described the anthem as being spectacular, and added that "now is the right time to say this—unity."

Cedric Richmond received a citation by Wilson, which also served as his introduction. The Honorable Congressman Cedric Richmond, a member of the Morehouse class of 1995, represented the 2nd Congressional District of Louisiana. He was a Democrat and chairman of the Congressional Black Caucus (CBC). After the usual gracious recognitions, including some of his Morehouse baseball buddies who were present, Representative Richmond invited the audience to join the Twitter feed for the CBC. The theme of his brief address was "Leadership, Purpose, and Focus." He, too, for the third time in the program, recited the mythical founding of the college in the basement of Springfield Baptist Church. Calling attention to President Donald Trump's mantra "Make America Great Again," Richmond said Morehouse Men helped make this country great in the first place; the expected names were mentioned. The audience was moved to chuckles when Congressman Richmond said, "Never argue with a fool, because at a distance you can't tell who is who."

As the Founders' Day speaker continued, he reminded the audience, especially the Men of Morehouse, that "you are here to serve others" and that he learned a lot from his mother, a graduate of Southern University whose husband—his father—died when Richmond was seven years old. His mother was a giver, he said. Then he challenged the graduates by asking, "What will you do with all your knowledge and talent?" Interestingly, he juxtaposed a quote from the Bible with lyrics from rapper T. I.'s song "Live Your Life": As long as you have financial aid and exams, you will have prayer. Richmond encouraged the graduates to not listen to the chatter of those not focused on moving forward. It was an interesting, if not rousing, call to order, to embolden Morehouse Men for the near and distant future. While his message was not the typical elegant, rousing oratory, it felt like a Morehouse Brother "talking" to his Morehouse Brothers.

Following Representative Richmond's talk, proclamations were made by the Honorable John H. Eaves, '84, chairman of the Fulton County Board of Commissions, and the Honorable Congressman Sanford D. Bishop, '68, United States House of Representatives from the 2nd Congressional District of Georgia. The sobering hymn, "Dear Old Morehouse," the beloved alma mater was sung, and the recessional was played by Dr. James Abbington, '83, FHS, organist and associate professor of church music and worship at Emory University. He played "Sortie" by Healey Willan. And thus did the 150th Morehouse anniversary convocation come to an end: it was not an "Ode to Joy"!

In the weeks that followed, circumstances would become dire at the college. While the days went by after the tumult of January, some members of the faculty mounted a campaign to remove Bob Davidson as chairman of the board and to support John Wilson's presidency. A letter was sent to the trustees on March 5, 2017, citing a January 17th request to Chairman Davidson for a meeting with the faculty to explain why Wilson's contract was not renewed. Apparently, Davidson had not "given the faculty any explanation for why an administrative change is necessary at this critical moment in the history of the college, during the reaffirmation of our reaccreditation and at a time when administrative stability is needed to attract investment in the institution." The petition requested that Davidson and any other interested trustees meet with the entire faculty at the next regularly scheduled faculty meeting, which was scheduled for Tuesday, March 21, 2017, at 11 A.M. The board was instructed to void the decision not to renew President Wilson's contract and to conduct both additional deliberations and a revote that would include full participation from student and faculty trustees at the regularly scheduled board meeting in April.[20]

Two days later, Chairman Davidson, in a March 7 letter to the alumni, suggested that Wilson was being stripped of much of his authority and that a transfer of power to William Taggart was underway. As the constituents of the college and the general public wondered "what the hell was going on at Morehouse," Aileen Dodd, a spokesperson for the college, told the *Atlanta Journal-Constitution* that the report that Wilson had been fired was "erroneous." Dodd stated, "Dr. John Wilson is still the president of Morehouse College." Dr. Wilson also made statements to the media stating the same.

The next day, Davidson issued another statement clarifying his earlier one:

> President Wilson will begin to transition the day-to-day responsibilities to William "Bill" Taggart, Morehouse College Chief Operating Officer, in order to ensure a smooth transition of leadership when President Wilson's contract expires this June. Davidson said the board would meet in April to consider its decision regarding the appointment of an Interim President. Until then, Dr. John Wilson and Bill Taggart will continue to work together while serving their respective roles as President of Morehouse College and Chief Operating Officer.[21]

While the War at Morehouse escalated, academic, cocurricular, and extracurricular work and activities of the college continued. Midterm exam were given during the week of March 6th to the 10th, and spring break provided a respite from the campus turmoil the next week, March 13th to March 17th. When the faculty and students returned to the campus on March 20th, though, so did the controversy and debate. The Morehouse faculty, at least many of them, were concerned about "governance practices and the governance culture at Morehouse." The pro-Wilson, anti-Davidson forces argued that the faculty was "concerned primarily with the board's lack of transparency and accountability and its unwillingness to work collaboratively with the faculty and students. We believe that the

---

[20] "Why We Have No Confidence in Our Board Chairman: An Open Letter from Concerned Faculty at Morehouse College," 1.

[21] Ibid.

erratic behavior of the board under the leadership of Chairman Davidson is threatening to imperil the long-term viability of the institution as well as the college's ability to carry out its extraordinary mission and to serve her exceptional students."[22] With this perspective in mind, the pro-Wilson camp passed a vote of no confidence in Davidson's leadership on Tuesday, March 21, 2017. As the pro-Wilson faculty voted against the chairman of the board, the anti-Wilson/Campbell faculty fell silent. As a matter of fact, nothing from this camp had been made public except that one faculty member had expressed no confidence in President Wilson and Provost Campbell by signing the change.org petition in October 2016. The general public only heard the voices of complaint and protest against Davidson and the board of trustees. The silence on the part of the anti-Wilson/Campbell camp could be interpreted in several ways. Were they afraid of retaliation if Wilson prevailed and was given an employment agreement extension? Or were they satisfied with the detailed missive they had delivered to Chairman Davidson in the fall of 2016, seeing no need to wage a contest against the president and provost in the public arena. Whatever the reason, the War at Morehouse appeared lopsided.

By the end of March 2017, the relationship between President Wilson and Johnathan Hill, SGA president, had deteriorated. Wilson summoned Hill to a meeting after his "accusations of laughter and disrespect at a student leaders conference," so Hill sought the advice and counsel of Dean Kevin Booker and COO Bill Taggart. With some trepidation, Hill stated, "Quite honestly, I do not want to meet with the president. I am looking to put our toxic relationship behind me and focus on graduating and completing a few more solid projects for the SGA."[23] Around this same time, the faculty called a meeting in the Shirley A. Massey Conference Center with Dr. Keith Eigel. A professional training coach and co-founder of the Leaders Lyceum, Eigel had served as counsel to the president and chairman of the board at Morehouse for more than twenty months before he submitted a report on the relationship between the Morehouse administration and its board. In his September 12, 2015,

[22] "Why We Have No Confidence in Our Board Chairman."

[23] Email from Jonathan Hill, president of the Student Government Association, to William Taggart and Kevin Booker, March 28, 2017.

report, Eigel had been critical of the board and especially direct about the chairman.

> I believe the board needs to be led by someone not so principally at odds with the president. With status quo Board leadership in place, the only way to realize alignment is for the president to take 100% of the responsibility to change. This scenario is unrealistic. There is no functional relationship of any kind that works this way. Even if the president could singlehandedly take 100% of the responsibility, the required acquiescence would actually work against what is ultimately required to appropriately lead the change necessary at Morehouse.

Eigel further claimed "that there is an in-group and an out-group on the board. This clique culture, more than any other factor, contributed to the dysfunction in key relationships that puts Morehouse realizing her potential at risk." The "in-group" was characterized as the "old guard," who, I suppose, were wedded to the glorious traditions that had brought Morehouse "thus far along the way." Eigel argued that this group was resistant to change and tended "to micromanage tactics and the president's leadership style in an almost parental way."

Perhaps the reason the pro-Wilson, anti-Davidson faculty wanted to meet Eigel was due to this seventeen-month-old assessment of the board and Dr. Wilson. Of Wilson, the report was laudatory: "I believe President Wilson is a highly effective, mature, capable and principled leader. It is my assessment that his rare and unique strengths are a great fit for Morehouse at this time. He has assembled a strong, talented, and independent team and shows humility and transparency in his collaboration with them." Furthermore, "his knowledge of higher education, his connectedness politically, academically, and in business circles, his ability to communicate both publicly and in writing, his fortitude in the face of internal criticism, his commitment to Morehouse in specific are a special combination of knowledge, skills, and abilities, not easily found in the Academy." In summation, the report supported Wilson, concluding that "the board would be hard-pressed to find anyone more capable of leading the change required for Morehouse to become one of the leading higher education institutions in the world, thereby honoring the legacy of her past."

Why Eigel found it necessary to describe Wilson as "mature" is a mystery, and the lack of respect for Morehouse inherent in his comment about the "change[s] required" for it to become "a leading higher education institution in the world" is striking. Eigel's report was written as the board was about to decide Wilson's fate as a continuing employee of Morehouse through June 30, 2017.

Nine days after the faculty meeting with Dr. Eigel, amid the percolating turmoil at the college, the board of trustees met on April 7th and officially decided to remove President John Silvanus Wilson from office. "Dear Morehouse Community," the letter began.

> Today, the Morehouse College Board of Trustees voted unanimously to make several major leadership changes within the board and Administration of the college. While some of these actions were planned, the Board of Trustees voted today to immediately turn the page and begin the investment in a new future for Morehouse. With today's actions, the board acknowledges that it has heard the voices of students, faculty, alumni and many of the key members of the Morehouse family who have called upon all of those who love this historic institution to put aside our differences and put Morehouse and our mission first.

Then the bombshell was dropped: "Effective today, John Wilson will step down as president of Morehouse College, and William Taggart will immediately assume the role of Interim President. We would like to take this time to thank President Wilson for serving Morehouse over the past four years and wish him ongoing success. The Presidential Search Committee will continue its efforts to identify a permanent new leader who can bring a renewed vision to the college." Robert Davidson had voluntarily agreed to step down as chairman of the board and end his tenure on that governing body on June 30, 2017. Willie Woods, a member of the Morehouse class of 1985 and president and managing director of ICV Partners in New York, became the new chairman of the board. Twelve days later, on April 19, 2017, Dr. Garikai Campbell resigned from his position as provost and senior vice president, and chief academic officer. And while there was some residual rancor and dissatisfaction, the War at Morehouse began to subside. Woods and Taggart began an informational lap among Morehouse constituents and stakeholders, coupled with "meet and greets." Some semblances of normalcy returned to the college as its end-of-the year activities began, which would culminate in the commencement exercises of the sesquicentennial class of 2017.

As seniors posed for their class photographs in B. T. Harvey Stadium and participated in rehearsal in King Chapel, Dr. Howard Willis, '76, presided over the general body meeting of the National Alumni Association in Nabrit-Mapp-McBay Hall. At approximately 3:40 that afternoon, the alumni began the procession from the Benjamin E. Mays memorial to King Chapel. Once they were in the chapel, the alumni rite of passage and the "lighting of the candle" ceremony took place, reflecting a moving ceremony, indeed. Among the speakers who emboldened the graduates was William "Bill" Nix, '68. The seniors participated in the "parent pinning" ceremony and a reception was held in the Emma and Joe Adams Concert Hall of the Ray Charles Performing Arts Center. Following this event, it was on to the social occasions of the evening. Baccalaureate, which was held on Saturday, May 20th, began with pleasant weather. Once the processional was completed, Demarius Vedall Brinkley, a member of the sesquicentennial class, gave the evocation. Willie E. Woods, '85, the recently named chairman of the Morehouse Board of Trustees, spoke on the occasion, and Robert C. Davidson Jr., chairman emeritus of the board, gave memorial tributes to Benjamin Elijah Mays and Hugh Morris Gloster. As the order of worship followed its particular presentations, the audience stood and sang "God of Our Fathers," text by Daniel C. Roberts and performed to the national hymn tune.

As the ceremony continued, Ja'Lon R. Smith, a member of the sesquicentennial class of 2017, read the Scripture, which was Psalm 139:1–18. The widely acclaimed Morehouse College Glee Club sang the anthem and "Great Is He, the Lord Eternal," an arrangement by Bryan Davies. Mr. William J. Taggart, interim president, introduced the preachers for the worship service. An electric energy began to move through the several thousand worshipers as the Reverend Doctor Otis Moss Jr., class of 1956 and pastor emeritus of Mt. Olivet Institutional Baptist Church in Cleveland, and his son, the Reverend Doctor Otis Moss III, a member of the class of 1992 and senior pastor at Trinity United Church of Christ in Chicago, rose from their seats on the dais and moved to the pulpits arranged for their sermons. The audience was captivated by the presence of the two men, standing reverential and tall, as they began to speak.

Reverend Moss Jr. was chairman emeritus of the Morehouse Board of Trustees, and Reverend Moss III was a member of the board. The father spoke first, and in his signature voice and style, set the mood of the encouraging sermonic exhortations. Embodied in these two graduates of Morehouse was the very essence of what the founders had in mind when they established Augusta Theological Institute in 1867, a school that would educate black men for scholarship and stewardship. They were men of erudition and elocution, and they were men who worked to improve the well-being of African Americans and people in general. After 150 years, the idea on which the school was predicated could be seen in the Reverends Moss, the graduating class, and the thousands of Morehouse Men around the world.

Following the powerful and impactful religious discourse delivered by the two preaching giants and social activists, the Glee Club performed Richard Jackson's arrangement of "Rock My Soul," with Joshua Troutman, tenor and a member of the sesquicentennial class of 2017, as the soloist. As soon as the Glee Club took their seats, the Reverend Doctor Dean Carter began the ceremony for the unveiling of three oil portraits. After sharing remarks about the individuals being honored, three exquisite portraits by artist Dwayne Mitchell were revealed. Two of the portraits that would hang in the galleries of King Chapel were of retiring professors: the first was of Dr. Marcellus Chandler Barksdale, '65, professor of history and founding director of the African American Studies program, and the second was of Dr. Tobe Johnson, '54, chairman of the political science department and Avalon Professor of Political Science. The last portrait unveiled was a pictorial representation of two important stakeholders in the Morehouse system—Dr. Robert C. Davidson, '67, and Mrs. Alice Faye Davidson, a Morehouse power couple. "Then Shall the Trumpets Sound" was performed by organist Dr. Oliver, after which the audience stood to sing "Dear Old Morehouse," by J. O. B. Moseley, '29. Before the benediction by the Reverend Doctor Keith Norman, class of 1987, Dean Carter made closing remarks and announcements and shared that because of the very good chance of thunderstorms the next day, for the first time in almost three decades, graduation exercises would return to the Martin Luther King Jr. International Chapel, with overflow at the Shirley A. Massey Conference Center and the Ray Charles Performing Arts Center. With disappointment in the air, all were resigned to the immutable laws of nature. Rather than enduring a soaking rain, the college would prepare King Chapel for commencement. "Trumpet Voluntary," the well-known composition by Henry Purcell, served as the baccalaureate recessional music. That evening and into the night, graduation celebrations and alumni activities abounded.

Thunderstorms and heavy rain began around midnight on May 21st. By 6 A.M., as the graduates, their families, faculty, staff, and dignitaries began to arrive, the skies were mostly cloudy with a light rain. Undaunted, the ceremony was delayed by an hour in order to allow the CCTV staff and other technicians to set up in King Chapel for viewing in the other locations around the campus. At 9 A.M., rain and fog descended on the campus and any reservations people had about the change in venue turned to gratitude. All lines of march were formed in Gloster Hall and King Chapel.

Around 9 A.M., organist Dr. David Francis Oliver began the august ceremony by playing his arrangement "Improvisation on Doxology" as the pre-ceremonial music. Dr. Anne Wimbush Watts, retired associate vice president for academic affairs and president of Powerful Presentation, Inc., approached the rostrum to give her signature "The Crowning Moment." Dr. Anne Wimbush Watts, an institution at Morehouse, usually gave her emblematic exhortation when commencement was held on the Century Campus, but here she was, extemporaneously giving the raison d'étre in King Chapel; it just was not the same. There was no Brown Street procession through the alumni and faculty, with the platform party saluting the graduates from the portico of Thomas Kilgore Hall. There was no symbolic emergence of the sesquicentennial class of 2017 from the north side of Graves Hall and down the green carpet of grass covering the red clay hill on which the old campus was built. There was no sight of the rising sun over Harkness Hall (built on land once owned by Morehouse and where the college's administration offices were once housed), *Et Facta, Est Lux*! But there *was* the Morehouse Brotherhood, binding "each son the other." A new class of several hundred black men were about to be anointed with the insignia of Morehouse Men, men who had been imbued with the idea that they had been academically prepared to do well in their chosen careers, but that they should also be of service to humankind.

There was a Spirit, "A Holy Spirit," permeating the air as the processional began. Felix Mendelssohn's "War March of the Priests" from *Athalia* was magnificently performed by Dr. Oliver, and the "Sesquicentennial Torch of Excellence" was brought into the chapel, hoisted into the air by Edwin Moses, internationally acclaimed track athlete and member of the class of 1978. "The Torch" was the result of a collaboration between Morehouse College and Georgia Tech, led by Morehouse's Willie Rockward, chairman of the Department of Physics, and Kathrine Fu, professor of mechanical engineering at Tech. The specially designed torches—five were constructed—featured a GPS unit and camera "along with a unique fuel gel that allows the flame to burn continuously." The vision behind the torch relay belonged to Dr. Keith Hollingsworth of the Department of Business and Finance. The torch was designed to be carried outdoors, but because it would be borne into the chapel this day, its flame was not lit. The effect was flat, to say the least. The audience applauded more for Moses than for the torch. But the Sesquicentennial Commencement Convocation was officially underway, with William James Taggart, interim president, presiding.

The call to order at the 2017 commencement exercises was made by Willie E. Woods, '85, chairman of the Morehouse Board of Directors. The Reverend Doctor Woodrow Miller Jr., pastor of Harmony Baptist Church, the second home of Morehouse in Augusta, did the "ringing of the bell" as the founders' representative. The Reverend Doctor J. Wendell Mapson, '67, senior pastor at Monumental Baptist Church in Philadelphia, gave the sesquicentennial evocation, followed the presentation of the colors by members of the Reserved Officers' Training Corps. "The Star-Spangled Banner" and "Lift Ev'ry Voice and Sing" were sung, and greetings and commemorative presentations were made by Mr. Woods to Robert C. Davidson '69, Otis Moss Jr., '56, Willie James Davis, '56, and James Hudson, '61. All of these Morehouse Men had served as chairman of the Morehouse Board of Trustees at one time or another in the last three decades. Dr. Michael L. Hodge, interim provost, presented the Vulcan Materials Company Award for Excellence in Teaching to Dr. Tobe Johnson. Special recognitions were given to Gerard Randolph Vanloo, salutatorian; Douglas Alexander Bowen, valedictorian; and Michael Christopher Scott, valedictorian. Interim President Taggart and Interim

Provost Hodge gave the recognitions, and the co-valedictorians addressed the audience.

Dr. Michael Lomax, president and CEO of the United Negro College Fund, headquartered in Washington, DC, gave tribute to the "50th Anniversary of the Delta of Georgia Chapter of the Phi Beta Kappa Society." Dr. Lomax had been one of the first Morehouse students inducted into the chapter. About an hour and a half into the ceremony, the Morehouse Glee Club performed "Unity," by Carlo Simon, '08. The composition had been commissioned for the 150th anniversary of the founding of the college, and the performance, directed by Dr. David Edward Morrow, was accompanied by Jerrell Melton III, '18, on piano; David Oliver, organ; Melvin Jones, '01, trumpet; and James Seda, trumpet. (Unfortunately, the full artistic effect of Mr. Simon's composition was not experienced due to an organ malfunction.)

Following the performance of the anthem, Interim President Taggart introduced CNN political commentator Van Jones as the sesquicentennial commencement speaker. Perhaps it was lost on the Sesquicentennial Committee that a more symbolic speaker could have come from the ranks of Morehouse graduates, but Mr. Jones it was. "Van Jones Tells Morehouse College Class of 2017 to Shrink Their Egos" was the title of an article that appeared online in the e-version of Rolling Out. He talked about four power centers: democracy (Washington, DC), plutocracy (Wall Street), technocracy (Silicon Valley), and mediaocracy (Hollywood). Closing his address to the sesquicentennial class, Jones gave the graduates and the audience three strategies for how they might influence the four power centers.

> Your destiny is more important than your fate. Everybody has a fate, and everybody has a destiny. They are not the same thing. Your fate is the stuff you can't do anything about. For example, I can never be a good-looking, 23-year-old Asian guy. I was born at a certain time, a certain place, and a certain body. The most miserable people you will ever meet are the people who sit and bemoan their fate. There are only a few people who recognize there is something else. Your destiny is the call to greatness inside you.

Jones continued, saying, "Your soul is more important than your ego. 'You' is plural.... You don't need a big ego. A big ego presents a big target and gets very little done. You need a small, strong ego. Let your soul shine beautifully. Let your connection to God, your people and your purpose play a huge role. You can change the world." Finally, the speaker emphasized the brotherhood of Morehouse Men. "'We' is more important than 'me.' As a professional or within your profession, if you feel you have the ability to be a world class communicator of your values...you have each other, a power network that will help you change the world."[24] After Van Jones received the respect of the audience, the Glee Club sang "My Soul's Been Anchored in the Lord," arranged by Moses Hogan, edited by Peter Eklund.

The conferring of baccalaureate degrees, the main reason for the convocation, was next. About two and a half hours had transpired by this time, as the noon hour approached. Interim Provost Hodge, with Interim President Taggart, presided over this ritual, and Dr. Uzee Brown, '72, chairman and professor of the Department of Music, in his eloquent and elegant voice and persona, announced each candidate's name. Dr. Melvin Fowler Foster, chair of the Division of Humanities and Social Sciences; Dr. Julie Elu, cochair of the Division of Business Administration and Economics; and Dr. Duane M. Jackson, '74, chair of the Division of Science and Mathematics, conferred the degrees on 317 graduates.

In the fall of 2013, the Morehouse Sesquicentennial Class of 2017 enrolled in the college. Out of 2,690 applicants to the school, 1,798 were admitted, or 68 percent. Of the 1,798 men admitted to Morehouse in 2013, only 488 actually enrolled, or 33 percent. Full-time students numbered 486, and two were part-time. By contrast, in 2008, 2,279 applicants applied, 1,645 men were admitted (72 percent), and 715 enrolled (43 percent). Full-time students in 2008 numbered 695, while twenty were part-time Men of Morehouse.[25] Clearly, the first-time student enrollment was in decline as the sesquicentennial class entered the college. This created one of the smallest graduating classes in the twenty-first century, the class of 2017: only 317 students graduated from Morehouse that year, a

---

[24] *Rolling Out* (May 22, 2017).

[25] "Morehouse Facts 2014," www.morehouse.edu.

noticeable drop from an average of 500 graduates in recent years.

More than three hours had passed by the time Admiral Stephen C. Evans, commander of the Naval Service Training Command in Atlanta, gave the oath of office to the new officers in the United States Military units. Dr. Howard C. Willis, '76, president of the Morehouse College National Alumni Association, inducted the Morehouse Sesquicentennial Class into the National Alumni Association, waiving their first year's membership dues. As Glee Club alumni made their way to the stage (some of whom were already seated, due to the need to get as many people into King Chapel as possible), Interim President Taggart prepared his charge to the class of 2017. After the Glee Club and alumni members sang "Prayer" from *Lohengrin* the George Mead arrangement of Richard Wagner's composition, Taggart said, "We charge you to hold out a bright beacon of light so that your brother or sister, who is lost at sea, may find their way back home. Through the trials and tribulation of life, Mother Morehouse and her teachings will always be your safe haven."[26] The Morehouse Sesquicentennial Commencement Convocation ended with the singing of "Dear Old Morehouse," which was followed by the benediction by the inimitable Reverend Doctor Lawrence Edward Carter Sr., dean of the Martin Luther King Jr. International Chapel. The spiritual "Fare Ye Well," arranged by Wendell P. Whalum, '52, was sung, and the well-known "Pomp and Circumstance, Military March No. 1," by British composer Sir Edward Elgar, provided music for the recessional. Dr. David Oliver, organist, played the composition on a Steinway Brothers piano.

The skies were clear and sunny, when the four-hour sesquicentennial commencement came to an end. The crowd gathered, en masse, around the campus, and those who had invitations to the reception in the Shirley A. Massey Conference Center made their way to the facility next door to the chapel, while many others simply left the campus for lunch at private homes and restaurants around Atlanta and its environs. The formal ceremonies of the Morehouse Sesquicentennial had ended. Academic achievement and community service, the founding idea for the school, had survived and expanded for 150 years. "But he dreamed a dream, then it all

---

[26] Ibid.

went wrong."[27] Within a few hours, the celebratory mood would fall silent, and the commemoration would be left for the intellectuals and laypersons to dissect.

[27] Les Miserables.

Chapter 21

"Whither the Crown?"
Taggart, Martin, and Thomas

By the time the sesquicentennial celebration ended early in the afternoon on Sunday, May 21, 2017, the rain had come to an end, the clouds had disappeared, and the sun was brightly shining. In the mindset of the Morehouse family, the "leadership cloud" that had hovered over the college earlier that year had also disappeared. Interim President William Taggart had deftly handled the college's sesquicentennial baccalaureate and commencement ceremonial duties expected of the leader of Morehouse College, and he was expected by many to be elected the twelfth president of Morehouse by the board of trustees. And although Taggart did not hold a doctoral degree, something all Morehouse presidents had since Dr. Mays, he was a graduate of Howard University and the Harvard Business School. He was a tall man, standing well over six feet in height, and made a striking presence as he stood at the podium during the college's assemblies and convocations. He was amiable and well-liked by the stakeholders of the institution. Taggart spoke with certainty but not in a condescending manner, and he walked with the stride of the basketball player he once was. And as the former president and chief executive officer of the Atlanta Life Financial Group, a black company founded by Alonzo Herndon in 1905, Taggart had the business acumen that Morehouse needed at this crossroads in its history. Taggart was forward-looking, and that was just what the school needed. Although he was not a Morehouse graduate, he acted like a Morehouse Man, and his obvious intelligence mollified those who thought the head of the college should have a doctoral degree. The month of May 2017 was the month of William Taggart at Morehouse College. The Morehouse community breathed a sigh of relief and looked to the future with the college train back on track. And then the college lost one of its beloved and renowned brothers, Dr. Samuel DuBois Cook.

Several days after the commemoration and celebration of the Morehouse Sesquicentennial, "A Service in Witness to the Resurrection of Dr.

Samuel DuBois Cook" was conducted in King Chapel. Dr. Cook died on May 29, 2017, at the age of eighty-nine, one of Morehouse's shining lights in the metaphorical dark. Morehouse Men never wear the crown as we continue to learn, grow, and develop, but Martin Luther King Jr, a classmate of Sam Cook's, came the closest of any alum to wearing it, and Dr. Cook was in the league with Marty, as Dr. King was affectionately known by his classmates.

Dean Carter served as the officiant at the Cook funeral, and the Reverend Doctor Robert Michael Franklin Jr. gave the eulogy. Although he did not have a role in Dr. Cook's funeral, Interim President Taggart attended the service. Days later, on June 8, 2017, the Morehouse family, the city of Atlanta, the state of Georgia, and people across the nation were stunned by the news that William Taggart had died from an aneurysm. A sense of helplessness was felt by many, and they were left asking, Where do we go from here? What should we do now? The Morehouse Board of Trustees appointed Dr. Michael Hodge, recently appointed provost, acting president of the college. Meanwhile, arrangements were being made for a high convocation final rites ceremony for Interim President Taggart.

Condolences poured in from students, faculty, alumni, Morehouse staff and trustees, politicians, Howard and Harvard Universities, and friends. Willie Woods, a 1965 Morehouse graduate and chairman of the Morehouse board, described Taggart as "smart, gracious, passionate, well-connected and well-liked by everyone." Further, Woods said, "He was full of energy and a person who decided to get out of the business world and do something more purposeful"[1] Chris Lemmie, a lifelong friend, said Taggart "could have chased...bigger dollars, but he wanted to give back to more people than what a corporate executive's job might do."[2] In a statement from the office of the mayor of Atlanta, Kasim Reed, a Howard alum, expressed the sentiments of many when he said,

> I am saddened by the passing of Morehouse Interim President Taggart. Bill was a respected businessman, a devoted father and husband, and a civic leader dedicated to our city. He has served Morehouse with distinction for the past two years, providing steady

[1] "Interim President Dies at Age 55," FOX 5, June 8, 2017.

[2] Ibid.

> leadership for one of the nation's best HBCUs and one of the most important institutions in the City of Atlanta. My thoughts and prayers are with Bill's family and with the entire Morehouse community. For all his accomplishments, I know Bill had so much still to give. This is a loss we will feel for generations.[3]

And from the Morehouse Board of Trustees, the following statement was issued:

> We are deeply saddened by the sudden passing of interim President William J. "Bill" Taggart, a beloved colleague, father and friend. For the past two years, Bill devoted himself wholeheartedly to Morehouse College. We are eternally grateful for his loyal support, counsel, and the leadership he provided to students, faculty, and alumni. Throughout his tenure, Bill had a positive impact on Morehouse College and the greater Atlanta business community. He leaves behind a long legacy of compassion, integrity and devotion. Our thoughts and prayers are with his family at this time.[4]

While condolences continued to pour in to Taggart's family, students were concerned about the future of their school. Garrett Miller, a political science major from Landover, Maryland, was "worried for incoming freshman, sophomores and juniors because the state of Morehouse is now more in flux than it has ever been." It seemed that students were concerned about the direction the school was taking and the need for more transparency from the leaders of the college. Justin Henderson, a senior political science major from Lithonia, Georgia, was concerned about "the upperclassmen talking about the disfunction that exists within the school" and its impact on the freshmen.[5] Whether there was disfunction at Morehouse in 2017 is a matter of opinion. But the idea that was envisioned in Augusta in 1867 had been kept alive in the minds and action of thousands of black men for 150 years. It transcends death and is not imbued in a person or a group; it is timeless. But in 2017, the college was at a serious crossroads and had to decide which direction it would take.

---

[3] Ibid.

[4] Maria Saporta, "Morehouse Moving Forward Despite Loss of Interim President—Bill Taggart (saportareport.com, June 16, 2017).

[5] Ibid.

Acting President Hodge presented a sense of stability in an effort to allay the concerns and reservations of the school's stakeholders. In the midst of deep grief, Morehouse had to move forward. And as the college prepared to hold the funeral for Interim Present Taggart, Willie Woods, chairman of the Morehouse Board of Trustees, announced that the board would conduct two searches simultaneously: one for another interim president to serve until the position was filled by a permanent president. The search for a permanent president had been underway since April. Woods believed that "situations like these always bring healing. We have got to get over our petty differences and rise above them. We have got to think about the future because we might not be here tomorrow."[6] Hodge agreed and felt that Bill had "left a real impression in a short period of time on the [college's] culture" and that Morehouse must move forward preparing young men for their lives ahead.[7]

On the day of William Taggart's last rite, Harold Martin, secretary of the board of trustees, was deeply saddened, and, referring to the Morehouse family, said, "This was a tough day. We named Bill Taggart as interim president 67 days ago. We got that exactly right. Bill was excited about being interim president.... Whenever you lose a leader, it's painful. It rocks you to your core."[8] Although Taggart was not a Morehouse Man, he was mentored by Morehouse Men. In fact, Robert Franklin, class of 1975 and tenth Morehouse president, had a mentoring dinner with Taggart the night of his death. Taggart was quick to point out that, like him, Dr. Mays, the Great Schoolmaster, hadn't attended Morehouse. According to Ron Thomas, director of the Morehouse journalism program, "We didn't get to see the fruits of his labor"; the staff of the Office of Institutional Development had tripled in the two years he was its chief operations officer. Thomas recalled that Taggart had a vision of creating an egalitarian campus—faculty, staff, and students.[9] Dale Jones, class of 1972, a member of the board and CEO of Diversified Search, chaired the search committee, and Isaacson Miller, the Boston-based search firm, was retained to help in the search. But the difficult task of laying Taggart to rest

---

[6] Ibid.

[7] Ibid.

[8] Ibid.

[9] Ibid.

was at hand as his body lay in repose in King Chapel.

On Friday morning, June 16, 2017, several thousand mourners—including students, faculty, and staff of the college—gathered in the Martin Luther King Jr. International Chapel to celebrate the life and legacy of William "Bill" James Taggart. Morehouse staff, the Reverend Doctor Lawrence Carter Sr., the dean of King Chapel, the officiant, and Gus Leverett & Sons Funeral Home planned the service. As college organist Dr. David Francis Oliver performed the prelude—"How Great Thou Art" by Abin Wentworth, "Fantasie in G Major BWV 572" by Johann Sabastian Bach, and "Praise God from Whom All Blessings Flow" by Fred Bock—the mourners positioned themselves for the processional and call to celebration by the Reverend Doctor Carter, dean of the chapel. Timothy Miller sang Douglas Miller's "My Soul's Been Anchored" before the eulogy was delivered by the Honorable Andrew Young Jr., '75 (honorary). A former ambassador to the United Nations, Young was chairman of the Andrew J. Young Foundation, a member of the Morehouse Board of Trustees, former mayor the city of Atlanta, and an alumnus of Howard University.

William "Bill" James Taggart was born at Grady Memorial Hospital in Atlanta on December 15, 1961, the son of Marian Howard Taggart and James Taggart. He was the oldest of three children who grew up in the Adamsville community on the west side of Atlanta, not far from Martin Luther King Jr. Drive. His maternal grandfather, Henry, had a passion for sports, especially for Atlanta teams. Bill Taggart attended Leonora P. Miles Elementary School on Bakers Ferry Road in southwest Atlanta and Northside High School on Northside Drive in northwest Atlanta. Taggart had been an honor student who excelled in soccer and track, and after high school, he left Atlanta to enroll at Howard University, where he engaged in "Bison Life," both academic and social. He was a member of the New York DJ crews, Delta Sigma Pi business fraternity, and Beta Gamma Sigma honor society. It was at Howard that Bill pledged Kappa Alpha Psi, Xi Chapter, in 1982, and he interned in the administration of President Ronald Reagan. After Howard, Bill continued his studies at the Harvard Business School in Cambridge, Massachusetts, where he earned an MBA. His business acumen and leadership skills earned him the sobriquet "Dollar Bill."

Still in a state of disbelief, the Morehouse Board of Trustees appointed Harold Martin Jr., secretary to the board, as the new interim president of Morehouse as the search for a permanent leader continued. Martin, a 2002 summa cum laude graduate of Morehouse who had been his class's valedictorian, went on to earn his MBA from Harvard Business School before receiving his JD from Yale Law School. His record in the business community was accomplished, but it was his work as an associate partner with McKinsey and Company, the prestigious management consulting firm, that best prepared Martin for the job of leading Morehouse. At McKinsey and Company, Martin "helped academic institutions solve complex strategic, financial, and organizational challenges," initiatives much needed at Morehouse at that time. He was "also a leader in the firm's Higher Education Practice, which studied trends transforming the landscape of higher education and best practices exemplified by leading colleges and universities."[10]

Interim President Martin had worked closely with Taggart and supported his plans for Morehouse, saying, "I will continue to execute the plan in the days and weeks ahead and look forward to working with Morehouse's Board, students, parents, faculty, staff, alumni and donors to solidify Morehouse's position as an academic leader during this pivotal time in our College's history."[11] As a Morehouse Man, Martin intimately knew the often vaunted culture of the school, and this was good for the college at the time. Interim President Martin was young, intellectually capable, and a twenty-first century Morehouse Man. He was imbued with the Morehouse Mystique, and would, as Board Chairman Woods said, "deliver on our promise of putting the college and its students first, and working toward delivering the highest levels of academic excellence."[12]

During the summer of 2017, the search for the twelfth president of Morehouse College ramped up. The candle burned brightly as the shining crown hovered above Harold Martin's head. He well represented the vision held by the founders of the college: he was intelligent, well-educated, and a steward in the community. Whither Morehouse? Whither the

---

[10] Uncf.org, "Harold L. Martin, Jr., Interim President of Morehouse College."

[11] Ibid.

[12] Alexis Taylor, AFR/The Black Media Authority, "Morehouse College Names Harold Martin, Jr. New Interim President" (July 17, 2017).

crown? Martin was the answer.

The fall semester of 2017 began two months after Martin assumed the responsibilities of interim president of Morehouse, and by mid-August, the college was ready to welcome the class of 2021. New Student Orientation was informative and emotional, but for many parents, the question uppermost on their minds was, Who would be the twelfth president of Morehouse? Who would lead the college as it approached the third decade of the twenty-first century? Who would be the head of the college when their sons graduated in four years? In the midst of the uncertainty about the leadership at Morehouse, the semester began with challenging academic work, artistic and athletic practices, and the social life of the school.

At the first gathering of the Morehouse family in B. T. Harvey Stadium for the first home football game—which was played against Lane College, and which the Maroon Tigers won 24 to 10—the chatter between cheers was "Who?" At the first rehearsal of the Glee Club, the talk centered on "Who?" When the History Major Club met, the question was "Who?" When the Martin Luther King Jr. chapel assistants congregated, they wondered "Who?" When the Health Careers Society, the English Major Club, the William Tucker Society: The African American Majors and Minors Club, the staffs of *The Maroon Tiger* and *The Torch*, and all of the other student organizations convened, the question of who would be chosen as the next president of the institution was discussed. Over coffee in faculty offices, the question was "Who?" At dinner parties and religious services, "Who?" Telephone conversations, "Who?" Emails and texts between alumni and friends, "Who?" And while dozens of applications were made for the coveted job, it was not until October 2017 that the answer finally came: David Anthony Thomas, whose credentials were top drawer, was elected by the board of trustees as the twelfth president of Morehouse College. For many in the Morehouse family, the question they now asked was, Who's David A. Thomas?

November is a short month in the semester, with the term ending after the Thanksgiving holidays. But in the days leading up to the last full week in November in 2017, students from Morehouse and Spelman protested allegations made by a Spelman student who said she was raped by a Morehouse student. Protesters voiced their concerns that other students were subjected to a toxic sexual environment, and they criticized the schools for failing to take active or proactive measures when allegations were reported, viewing this inaction as a sign of indifference. The schools were under a two-year Title IX investigation by the United States Department of Education to determine whether or not they duly reported incidences of sexual misconduct. Protesters called attention to their complaint by spray painting the Martin Luther King Jr. Chapel at Morehouse. There is no evidence that the stately Sisters Chapel at Spelman was defaced. Members of the Morehouse Police Department removed the signs the protesters installed on the grounds of King Chapel that read "Practice what you preach Morehouse & end rape culture." A brown tarp was used to cover up the spray-painted graffiti. A protesting student created a Twitter account called #WeKnowWhatYouDid, where Morehouse students were anonymously accused of rape; individual names of students and even entire lists of Morehouse Men were posted on the account without evidence.

Morehouse responded to the protest in a swift and forthright way. In a statement released to the media and the public, the college emphasized its policy of investing "all claims of sexual harassment, sexual assault, violence, and discrimination filed with our Title IX coordinator." Additionally, Morehouse stated, "We have programs in place to educate students about sexual misconduct, including the Not In My House campaign, launched to communicate that violence, discrimination, and disrespect will not be tolerated at Morehouse College."[13] Interim President Martin, in a Crown Forum speech to the Morehouse community, revealed that he had read the information on the Twitter account and thought "Underlying the hashtag #WeKnowWhatYouDid is clearly a belief that there is a population that does not feel heard on this very important issue in the AUC and on our campus." Bothered about the defacing of King Chapel, Martin firmly made it clear that this would not happen again, but tackling serious issues like allegations of rape, sexual violence, and sexual discrimination is an American problem that requires national attention. In 2015, then vice president Joe Biden visited Morehouse to talk about the efforts

---

[13] Catherine Park, "WeKnowWhatYouDid: Flyers Accuse Atlanta College of 'Protecting Rapists'" (13WMAZ. November 10, 2017).

the White House was taking to fight campus assault. Martin, in November 2017, pointed out that the college would fully investigate all reports of sexual misconduct, but added that the college would give "due respect and compassion" to the accused and not jump to conclusions "before having all the facts."[14]

The "sibling relationship" between Morehouse and Spelman was still very strong, even amidst the controversy, and the annual Christmas Carol Concert that featured both the Morehouse and Spelman glee clubs performed that year, just as they had for ninety-one years. The concert was held in King Chapel on the evenings of December 1st and 3rd, and at Spelman's Sisters Chapel on December 2nd, 2017. As finals week ended on December 8th, the campus fell silent with the exception of those who remained, including a few international students, those who worked in the records and registration departments who were responsible for getting grades out, and the Morehouse Police Department. Over the 2017 holidays, the Morehouse community looked toward the arrival of its new leader, Dr. David A. Thomas, who did not assume the office of president until February 1, 2018. Harold Martin's appointment ended December 31, 2017, so Acting Provost Michael Hodge once again held the office of president, this time during the month of January 2018.

The J-Mester at Morehouse began on January 8, 2018. By this time, members of the Morehouse community had mined information from the internet about Dr. David Anthony Thomas, and they knew that he had been born in Kansas City, Missouri, and had graduated the Paseo Academy of Fine and Performing Arts, a school in the Kansas City Public Schools System. And while Thomas had been accepted to Morehouse as an undergraduate in 1974, he did not receive the level of financial support offered by Yale University in New Haven, Connecticut, so he chose the Ivy League school, which he graduated from in 1978 with a bachelor of arts degree in administrative science. After earning a master's degree in organizational psychology from Columbia University, another Ivy League institution, in 1981, Thomas returned to his undergraduate alma mater, where he earned another master of arts degree, this time in philosophy, in

[14] Sarah Brown and Julia Martinez, "Signs Naming Students Accused of Sexual Assault Reopen Wounds at Atlanta Colleges," *Chronicle of Higher Education* (November 9, 2017).

1984, and his PhD in 1986. Dr. Thomas's first job after earning his doctorate at Yale was at the Wharton School at the University of Pennsylvania, yet another Ivy. At Wharton, Dr. Thomas held two positions: assistant professor of management and Atlantic Richfield Foundation Term Assistant Professor of human resource management. His work was exemplary, so much so that Harvard offered him a position at its business school.

Dr. Thomas began his work at the Harvard School of Business as an assistant professor in 1990, and by 1993 was tenured as an associate professor of business administration. After his promotion to professor, he was named the H. Naylor Fitzhugh Professor of Business Administration in 2000. Once again, his work received notice, and in 2011, Dr. Thomas accepted the position of dean of the McDonough School of Business at Georgetown University, the Jesuit school in Washington, DC. He returned to Harvard in 2016 and was about to accept the deanship of the business school at the University of Michigan when he was elected the twelfth president of Morehouse. Morehouse Men (Gloster, '31, Keith, '61, Massey, '58, Franklin, '75, and Wilson, '79) had led the college for fifty years, so the choice of a non-graduate of the storied school, with its celebrated traditions, gave pause to some alums and others in the Morehouse community. Others welcomed the appointment, though, and reminded the skeptics that Dr. Mays, the Great Schoolmaster, was not a graduate of Morehouse. And as all waited to see if Dr. Thomas was a good fit for the college, in January 2018, preparations were well underway for the thirtieth anniversary of the Candle in the Dark Gala that supported the school's scholarship program.

Spring semester 2018 began, and Morehouse College's new president arrived on February 1st. The first time most members of the Morehouse community saw Dr. Thomas was at the Founders' Day Convocation on February 15th (the actual birthdate of the school is February 14). Finally, the much-anticipated time had arrived for Dr. David Anthony Thomas to approach the podium and introduce himself to the Morehouse community. He was now the college's twelfth president, and first impressions were mixed. Thomas did not possess the oratory presence of Benjamin Mays or Robert Franklin or the general confidence that comes from a deep knowledge of Morehouse traditions. He appeared to be an "everyman," a regular guy. There was nothing fundamentally impressive about his demeanor, and he even appeared a bit overwhelmed by the moment. But first impressions often belie what lies beneath the initial image. Time would tell the true story about the new president's competence, intellectual and scholarly depth, organizational and leadership skills, and likeability. You can't judge a book by its cover. Idioms and metaphors, notwithstanding, the Morehouse community was anxious to see how the idea of educating black men—and by 2017, men of other colors—would be actualized under the leadership of Dr. Thomas. It was all about the 1867 idea.

The Founders' Day program continued with the announcement of the winners of the 2018 Otis Moss Oratorical Contest by Dr. Leah Creque, chair of the Department of English and director of the honors program; along with Caleb Henderson, the 2017 winner; and Mr. Munnings. Malachi Walden, '21, was the first-place winner. After the singing of the spiritual "Got a Mind to Do Right," arranged by Dr. David Morrow, by the Glee Club, Dr. Thomas introduced Dr. Gary Dorrien, Reinhold Niebuhr Professor of Ethics at Union Theological Seminary and professor of religion at New York's Columbia University. The author of eighteen books on subjects germane to his intellectual bent, Dr. Dorrien was a member of the Religion and Socialism Commission of the Democratic Socialists of America. *The New Abolition: W. E. B. Du Bois and the Black Social Gospel* (2017) and *Breaking White Supremacy: Martin Luther King Jr. and the Black Social Gospel* (2018) are two of his works relevant to the occasion and of interest to the Morehouse community.

After the traditional salutations and recognitions, Dr. Dorrien gave a talk that was appropriate for the occasion. He put the college squarely in the center of the black Civil Rights Movement, positing that no other institution has come close to providing as many leaders in the social gospel and black freedom movements as Morehouse has. Dr. Dorrien cited Mordecai Wyatt Johnson, Howard Thurmond, Benjamin Mays, and Martin Luther King Jr. as exemplars of this extraordinary tradition. Acknowledging its agreement with this declaration, the audience applauded. Dr. Dorrien continued his speech by stating that the story of Martin Luther King Jr. is America's greatest treasure. He explained how King and the Civil Rights Movement he led were a revelation to his own upbringing in a white, lower-class community in Michigan. He had been taught that America was the greatest nation the world had ever seen, but the Civil Rights Movement proved otherwise.

Civil rights activists and scholars of the movement know that the movement made King, not the other way around, and this was emphasized by Dr. Dorrien. It was the activism of the Student Nonviolent Coordinating Committee (SNCC) that pushed King into Gandhian action, and King became increasingly "radical" from 1960, the year SNCC was organized, to the end of his life. Dorrien pointed out that the presidency of Barack Obama exposed the widespread existence of white racism, which Donald John Trump seized upon, leading to his "whitelash presidency." Dr. Dorrien closed by arguing that today, more than ever, we need the witness of Martin Luther King Jr.: love with the call for justice, moderation with militant action, tools of moderation with powers of coercion, and ethical idealism as well as power politics. In the grand scheme of things, Dorrien reiterated Morehouse's long-standing tradition of involvement in social justice activism, a truth embedded in the college's history. The Founders' Day audience gave Dr. Dorrien a standing applause. After final comments by Provost Hodge and the singing of "Dear Old Morehouse, the stage dignitaries, Glee Club, faculty, and students recessed through the Wellborn Street exit of the chapel. The 151st Founders' Day Convocation was concluded. But more celebration and conviviality was yet to come: the Candle in the Dark Gala was two days away.

Following tradition, on Saturday morning, February 17, 2018, students, faculty, alumni, and the general public gathered in the Emma and Joe Adams Concert Hall in the Ray Charles Performing Arts Center (Ray-Pac) to hear "Reflections of Excellence" by the "Candle" and "Bennie" honorees who would be formally introduced and given their awards at the gala that evening. The Candle in the Dark Gala, a mega-event on the social calendar of the Morehouse community and other Atlantans, was held two days after Founders' Day. This year's event represented the thirtieth anniversary of the gala and was held at the Hyatt Regency Hotel in downtown Atlanta. Several thousand guests attended.

As it had done over the years, the gala was held to honor black leaders in two categories: Bennie Awards honor the achievements of Morehouse Men while the Candle Awards honor the accomplishment of black men in general. Bennie Awards were bestowed on Dr. Emmett D. Carson, '81; Dr. William Lewis Jr. of Lazard Freres & Co. LLC; Oz Scott, producer and director of *The Jeffersons* and *The Cosby Show*; and Robert F. Smith, founder of Vista Equity Partners, who donated $1 million to the Morehouse General Scholarship Fund. Roderick Diamond II, a Morehouse junior, captured the essence of the thirty-year-old event in precise words when he wrote that "the experience of the gala is unique because of the ceremonial details the college holds. The music, food, Brotherhood, along with networking with alumni from decades ago make the experience unique. This all happens while being your best dressed at the black-tie affair. You gain a deeper love for Morehouse and its possibilities. Being steadfast, honest true with dear old Morehouse and her ideals in all things that we do."[15] Founders' Week now over, students returned to their regular routine of taking classes across the disciplines and attending and participating in organizational meetings and activities. Commencement 2018 was just a few weeks away.

When graduation day arrived, on a glorious Sunday morning, the traditional program presentations were held. The grand processional was followed by the ringing of the historic bell, the presentation of colors, the singing of both "The Star-Spangled Banner" and "Lift Ev'ry Voice and Sing," and the delivering of the evocation and "occasion." After welcoming remarks were shared and the salutatorian introduced, the valedictorian gave his speech.

President Thomas then introduced the speaker, the Honorable Sanford Dixon Bishop, '68, United States congressman (D-GA, 2nd District). After the usual greetings, salutations, and recognitions, Representative Bishop reached the heart of his address: "Today, you are joining the ranks of generations of men spanning 151 years who have been molded and shaped into Morehouse Men by an institution with a rich history and deep commitment to developing Black men, so as to empower them to change the world." The congressman knew the founding mission of Morehouse to educate black men for scholarship and stewardship. After referencing President Franklin's model of the Morehouse Man as a

---

[15] Roderick Diamond II, "On the 30th Anniversary of Its Famous Gala, Morehouse Receives Generous Gifts" (Morehouse Advance News Writing, February 23, 2018).

Renaissance man, President Mays's concept of an "Air of Expectancy" for Morehouse graduates, and Howard Thurmond's idea of a "crown over the heads of Morehouse Men," Congressman Bishop recalled his entrance into the college fifty-four years earlier, in 1964. Four years later, and two months before his commencement, he shared with the graduates and the audience his experiences of shock and anger during that time in 1968. In the end, he said, "that Morehouse experience caused me and countless others of my generation to commit our lives to keeping Dr. King's dream alive and making it a reality." Quoting E. L. Sharp and Josiah G. Holland, Representative Bishop charged the class of 2018 to "go forth and change the world!"[16] And by doing so, he repeated the idea of the founders that black men can be educated for stewardship and service that would change the world. "Whither the crown?"

Following the well-received address by Congressman Bishop, the divisional deans gave the charges to the graduates in humanities, mathematics and science, and business administration and economics. With a cadence reflective of his musical talents, Dr. Uzee Brown, chairman of the Department of Music, called each graduate's name as he came to the platform to receive his diploma. At that moment in time, each young graduate was transformed from a Man of Morehouse to the highly regarded Morehouse Man, and the crowd of thousands recognized his achievement with raucous applause and cheers. The president of the national alumni association inducted the graduates into the organization, reminding them of their obligations to the association and to the college. After the singing of "Prayer" from *Lohengrin*, the traditional petition offered each year by the Glee Club and alumni members of the celebrated performing arts group, the president and provost offered some final words. These were followed by the singing of "Dear Old Morehouse" before delivered by Dean Carter delivered the benediction. And for the last time, the class of 2018—these newly minted Morehouse Men—recessed out of the Century Campus toward stately old Graves Hall. And so, the end of the 2017 to 2018 academic year came to an end.

Summer came and went, and the 2018 fall semester at Morehouse

---

[16] "Congressman Bishop Delivers 2018 Commencement Address at Morehouse College," press release, May 22, 2018, bishop.house.gov

began with the arrival of more than six hundred first-time, degree-seeking students—freshmen. The well-organized and carefully orchestrated New Student Orientation (NSO) began on August 6, 2018. The class of 2022 consisted of 571 black or African American, non-Hispanic students, with the remainder including one white, non-Hispanic student, one American Indian student, nineteen who identified as mixed-race, non-Hispanic, and six students whose race or ethnicity was unknown.[17] When classes began on August 15, 2018, 1,497 returning degree-seeking students had retuned, making the fall enrollment at the college 2,145, a comfortable number for a school of its physical size and mission.

As the first full academic year of Dr. Thomas's presidency began, and after orientation, the men of "Thomas's Team" were in place when classes began on Wednesday, August 15th. A week prior to that, Dr. Thomas did something few college administrators are willing to do: on August 7th, he moved into Graves Hall, the dormitory reserved for freshman honor students and others. Explaining why he did this, President Thomas stated, "For two days, I turned back the clock and lived like a freshman at Graves Hall, the oldest dorm on the campus of Morehouse College. It was a social experiment that allowed me to bond with a group of young men from across the world who were experiencing their first taste of independence."[18] The room he occupied was a modest one on the first floor of stately Graves Hall, which stands on the highest elevation on campus. As he surveyed the room, which had a poster of Martin Luther King Jr. on the wall, as the young men and their parents were busy preparing their "nest," he wondered "who they would become when they finished their Morehouse journey." He recalled how the dorm's residence advisor told him that there should be no loud noise during study hours, and no visitors were allowed until October, "not even if that visitor happens to be your wife of 34 years." Like thousands of Morehouse students before, the new students in Graves Hall in 2018 had dreams and aspirations that the college would help them make real in a few years. As educated men, they would be encouraged to be stewards in service to their communities. Not

[17] "Common Fact Data 2018–2019," www.morehouse.edu.

[18] David A. Thomas, "Moving into the Freshman Dorm 44 Years Later: The New President of Morehouse Dives into College Life, *Washington Post* (September 11, 2018).

unlike bygone years, in 2018, the world was changing, some for good, some for bad. It would be up to the Graves Hall students, and those in the other dorms across the campus and across the world, to carry "the Torch," the Morehouse emblem, as they continued to grow tall enough to wear the crown that represented their achievements and accomplishments. "Whither the crown?"

President Thomas remembered how popular he was on his final experiential night in Graves Hall. His wife, Willetta Lewis, "had packed a care package of snacks—oranges, candy bars, lollipops, potato chips"—that he shared with twenty students in the common area of the dorm. As they ate the "comfort food" late in the evening, around 11 P.M., the president and the students swapped stories. He told the students how he had been accepted to study at Morehouse forty-four year earlier, and that while Morehouse had been his first choice, he could not afford to attend. Forty-four year later, living in a freshman dormitory at Morehouse simulated his entrance into the school. Now, as a Man of Morehouse, he was beginning his journey toward becoming a Morehouse Man. The experiment had a lasting impact on his recommendations and actions as president and drew him closer to students. After he moved out of Graves Hall and back into Davidson House, the upscale president's residence across the street from the dorm, Dr. Thomas continued the work for the college he had started the prior spring—and he promised to get new televisions for the gathering rooms in the dorm. The experiment received wide coverage in the media and captured the attention of potential donors to the college. Dr. Thomas, an organizational psychologist, worked this experiment to the advantage of the college that he was now leading. A few days later, Dr. David Anthony Thomas was presented to the college community in a formal way during the 2018 Morehouse College Opening Convocation in King Chapel.

President Thomas posted an announcement of his dorm experience on his Twitter account, @ProfThomas, something that might be expected of a twenty-first-century college president. He illustrated his experience with pictures of the dorm room and his first interaction with the residence advisors, who read him the rules. The reactions to President Thomas's strategic act was positive among alumni. C. P. Moore said, "If this is a new direction of leadership, I'm all for it. It's small gestures like this that will leave a positive mark in these young men's lives. Long live the House!" Similarly, another member of the Morehouse community said, "And he brought the Five wells back. This will help the public (all ages and backgrounds) better articulate the characteristics of a man of Morehouse/Morehouse Man." Calvin Harris thought it was "fantastic" that the president was staying in his old dorm room (Room 304), and Janie Douglas thought Dr. Thomas was "bonding in ways that the students will remember for a lifetime." Senator Marion Kimpson, District 42 in South Carolina and a Morehouse graduate, expressed the sentiment of many when he said that he thought the act was "awesome!"

For 150 years, the institution had gathered in the sanctuaries of Springfield, Harmony, and Friendship Baptist Churches, in the Graves Hall Chapel, Sales Hall Chapel, Archer Hall gymnasium, and King Chapel. These assemblies, religious services, and convocations featured speakers who edified the student body with their insightful lectures, preachers who mesmerized them with their electrifying oratory, and artists who stirred their minds and souls. So it was only fitting that, on September 13, 2018, students, faculty, staff, administrators, and guests once again convened in King Chapel to officially mark the 2018 to 2019 academic year, thus beginning the next 150 years in the history of Morehouse College. The program adhered to the format that had been followed for nearly three decades. Dr. Michael Hodge, provost and senior vice president, presided, and after the prelude, processional, opening declaration, Dean Carter's prayer, the presentation of the colors and the singing of "The Star-Spangled Banner" and "Lift Ev'ry Voice and Sing," he introduced the members of the platform party and special guests in the audience. When he delivered the "occasion," Provost Hodge spoke of the college's commitment to excellence, and, with the past in mind, he said the new academic year would be about rebirth and renewal. The theme for the year was "The Morehouse Journey: Reaffirming Values of Excellence through Hope, Faith and Resilience." To put it another way, the Morehouse journey would continue to validate the idea that black men, and men of other hues, could be educated for stewardship and service. This would require a partnership between faculty, staff, and students, the provost challenged as he ended his remarks. After the Glee Club sang Ludwig van Beethoven's "Hallelujah" from *Christ on the Mount of Olives*, the provost introduced

President Thomas, the keynote speaker for them occasion.

Unlike when he made his presentation in February, when he was not the featured speaker, Dr. Thomas was now the focus of the occasion. After ceremoniously and respectfully applauding, the audience waited anxiously and with rapt attention to hear what the new president had to say and how he would say it. After the usual greetings and salutations, President Thomas yoked himself to the class of 2019 by pledging to make it their best year. Little did he know how historic this class would become.

President Thomas talked about how this was a time of reflection, particularly on the fact that 391 men graduated in 2018. Excellence is a habit, he said, in all that we do—academically, athletically, administratively, and more. He mentioned money that had been raised, including $1 million from Aaron's Inc. to support scholarships for twenty students through 2022, and the $1.5 million-dollar donation made by 2018 Candle Award-winner Robert Smith.

President Thomas briefly spoke about the capital funds campaign to raise between $250 to $500 million for an endowment to secure the college for the future. He mentioned the "Sixth Well" of the Morehouse Man—"well-written" And he challenged students to take charge of their lives: "Don't let your future be in someone else's pocket. Strive to be the best, there is already a package in the universe with your name on it."

The theme of Thomas's address was "Morehouse: The Global Power of an Idea in the 21st Century,"[19] and while he introduced the theme of his administration at this convocation, he said he would more fully address it at his inauguration in February 2019. But he did describe the school's 2,000+ students as young men defying gravity, in a reference to President Benjamin Mays, saying "we expect you to do well." Reaffirming the founding mission of the college, President Thomas believed the Morehouse idea was in tune with the idea that they could change the world. In a statement that might find refrain, Thomas said that "challenge is not hard but heavy." He called the audience's attention to what some were calling the VUCA times they were currently living in—Volatile, Uncertain, Complex, and Ambiguous. Morehouse, therefore, must build a

---

[19] David A. Thomas, "Inauguration Speech," Morehouse College (YouTube, February 15, 2019).

greater Morehouse, an idea that President John Hope had more than a century earlier. Unlike Dr. Mays, who had been in the business of "building Men," Dr. Thomas was building an institution. As expected, the new president called on all to join him on this journey.

Inspired by Langston Hughes's famous poem "I Dream a World" (1941), President Thomas, like President Wilson before him, "Dreamed a Morehouse." A Morehouse as a premier institution, defined by excellent customer service. A Morehouse where black men could come and just be black men. Thomas dreamed a Morehouse where a capital campaign might reach a half billion dollars, and a Morehouse whose grand concept would be fulfilled every day. In order to make his dream for Morehouse, all must work together. "How do you dream a Morehouse?," President Thomas asked. How do you envision the enduring idea of educated men in service to humankind? The assemblage of Morehouse constituents gave the new president an honest standing applause, impressed most of all by his dream of a $500 million capital campaign. Appropriately, the Glee Club sang "Good News." After closing remarks by Provost Hodge, the audience crossed their arms and held hands of Brotherhood and sang the college's hymn, "Dear Old Morehouse." Then the 2018 opening convocation ended with a recessional through the Wellborn Street exit of the chapel. The impressions of President Thomas were mixed, as expected from the "our kind of people"[20] attitude of Men of Morehouse and Morehouse Men. Whatever they thought of the new president in September 2018, though, would morph into an almost uniform song of praise within just a few months. Nonetheless, the college was being led by a non-Morehouse Man, something it had not seen in fifty years, and that was a reason for disquiet among some in the community. They took comfort in remembering that the first six presidents of Morehouse were not graduates of the school, and the great success Dr. Mays had.

Classes for the fall semester of 2018 began a week before the opening convocation. The football team was on a winning streak, having defeated the University of Arkansas-Pine Bluff 34–30 on September 1st, and Lane College 42–20 on September 8th. Hometown fans would not be

[20] Lawrence Otis, Our Kind of People: Inside America's Black Upper Class (New York, Harper Perennial, 1999).

disappointed two days after the convocation when, on September 15th, the Maroon Tigers beat Central State University at B. T. Harvey Stadium on campus. The wins kept coming as the team played against Miles College (23–21), Kentucky State University (23–21), and Tuskegee University (30–24), where the "classic" game was played in Columbus, GA. The Tigers were finally defeated by the Rams of Albany State University (19–41) on October 14th, in Atlanta, before a hometown crowd of exuberant fans. Morehouse loyalists sang "whether in defeat or victory we are loyal just the same." The team returned to its winning ways the next week when it defeated Benedict College (14–10) but lost a heartbreaker on Homecoming Day, October 27th, against Fort Valley University (22–27). Somewhat dispirited, but still fighting, the Maroon Tigers were beaten by their archrival, the Panthers of Clark-Atlanta University (13–30), on the CAU stadium just a few blocks away.

The Maroon Tigers basketball team began its season on a high note when they defeated Winston-Salem State University (66–61) in mid-November, and the team ended its season with a record of 20–5 to move forward in the Southern Intercollegiate Athletic Conference Tournament, which was played in Birmingham, Alabama, in March 2019. The team was eventually defeated by Claflin College (69–77) in the semifinals on March 2nd. "They took it on the chin."

By November 2018, the semester was at its halfway mark, and, as usual, papers were written and edited, clubs and fraternities met and actualized their agendas, and the Glee Club prepared for the group's 92nd Christmas Carol Concert, November 30th to December 2nd, which would be held at King Chapel at Morehouse and Sisters Chapel at Spelman. As always, the concert featured the Spelman Glee Club and a chorus comprised of singers from both musical groups. The concert heralded the beginning of the Christmas season for many alumni and other Atlantans, and it also signaled the beginning of final exams, scheduled for the Monday following the last of the three concerts. Weeks before the end of the fall semester in 2018, the Inaugural Steering Committee had begun its work for the installation of the twelfth president of Morehouse College, Dr. David Anthony Thomas, in February 2019. Willie E. Woods, '85, was the honorary chair of the committee; Lawrence E. Carter Sr. was the executive chair; Willetta Lewis, served ex-officio; Henry M. Goodgame

Jr., '84, as the planning vice chair; Anne W. Watts, served as chief of staff for the inauguration; Judy D. Carroll, as inaugural consultant; and Kimberly Moore, served as inaugural administrator. Of the thirty-eight persons who constituted the committee, nine were Morehouse alumni.

By January 2019, a little more than a month before his inauguration, President Thomas had been on the job for one year. Classes for the spring semester began on January 16th, and after the observance of Martin Luther King Jr.'s birthday on January 21st, classes organized and the work of the steering committee began in earnest. Temperatures in Atlanta that February were above normal by about nine degrees.

After commencement, Founders' Day is the second most important convocation at Morehouse. The 152nd Founders' Convocation had added significance because it was also inauguration day for the twelfth president of the college. The momentous event took place in the Martin Luther King Jr. International Chapel on February 15, 2019, and was witnessed by nearly two thousand students, faculty, staff, alumni, and friends of the school. The weather was pleasant as President-Elect Thomas, Willetta Lewis, his wife, their children, and extended family had breakfast at Davidson House and prepared for the important event that would take place later that morning. Dr. Thomas had had a restless night as he fretted over the content of his inaugural address and how he would deliver it. He knew his speech to the Morehouse community would afford him an opportunity to present his strategic vision for the school, setting the tone for his administration; he knew that this would be one of the most important speeches he would make as president. As the hour for the convocation drew closer, the Thomas family left Davidson House for the chapel and the staging area for the platform party. Following the grand processional and the expected ceremonial activities, the Glee Club sang the inaugural anthem "Expect a Miracle," a song commissioned for the inauguration and composed by Dr. Uzee Brown, '72, chairman of the Department of Music. The texts of the anthem were written by Edwin Lewis Cole, who had been inspired by Dr. Thomas's 2018 opening convocation speech, "The Morehouse Journey: Reaffirming Values of Excellence through Hope, Faith and Resilience." The anthem was also inspired by Dr. Thomas's dream of a half-billion-dollar capital campaign. That would be a miracle on Westview Drive.

The investiture of the twelfth president of Morehouse College and the conferring of the symbols of the office were part of, as they should have been, a solemn ceremony. It began with the "summons," which was given by Lawrence E. Carter Sr., dean of the chapel, and which was followed by the sanction and charge, delivered by Willie E. Woods, chairman of the board. John L. Thornton gave the affirmation and charter; Dorothy Cowser Yancy, former president of Johnson C. Smith and Shaw Universities of North Carolina, and a member of the Morehouse Board of Trustees, presented the keys and seal; Avery A. Manning, '86, gave the rules of order; former interim president Harold L. Martin Jr. presented Dr. Thomas with the robe; and F. Euclid Walker, '94, delivered the medallion and hoof to him. Otis Moss III, '92, offered the prayer, and finally, the mace and the chair were presented by Richard Thaler Jr. and Dale E. Jones, '82, respectively.

Then the trumpets sounded, heralding the election of Dr. David Anthony Thomas, twelfth president of Morehouse College. After the Glee Club sang "Got a Mind to Do Right," arranged by Dr. Morrow, the twelfth president came to the podium to present his inaugural address, "Morehouse: The Global Power of an Idea for 152 Years." The audience listened with rapt attention.

At the moment of his installation as the twelfth president of Morehouse, it is important to remember that Dr. Thomas was preceded by eleven presidents and seven acting, probationary, or interim presidents of the college. Hundreds of faculty and staff personnel had given sacrifice and service to the idea and the ideals that serve as the bedrock of the institution, to which tens of thousands of young men, and two dozen women, had subscribed, steadfast, honest, true. Boards of trustees had guided the college through good times and bad years, and many prayers had been offered for succor and thanksgiving. Some supporters might even remember the words from the gospel song "We've come this far by faith, leaning on the Lord..." But a new day, a new era in the history of Morehouse College, was about to begin as President David Anthony Thomas prepared to present his vision of leadership that would carry the college forward. As he began his address, one could sense the tension in the new president's voice, but he pressed on into his prefatory remarks. He said it was "a great gettin' up morning," echoing the words from a

Mahalia Jackson song that used to play in the home of his youth.

After the usual platitudinous and gratuitous opening remarks were made, Dr. Thomas thanked all who were participants in his inauguration, with special thanks extended to the Morehouse faculty and staff and the men of the class of 2019, his second graduating class. He seemed somewhat confused when he said, "I stand on the shoulders...of the nine other men who have experienced the awesome responsibility to lead Morehouse College." There were a total of nineteen, fulltime or otherwise, who had led the college before him, but perhaps the meaning of his statement came from the oft-repeated but erroneous narrative that neglected to speak of the important role the first three presidents of the school had played—Robert, Graves, and Sale.

As the newly minted president pressed on with his address, he delivered some important ideas about the direction his administration would take. Dr. Thomas talked about the things that distinguish Morehouse as an institution—loyal alumni and the somewhat insularity the college provides—and stated that Morehouse was "an idea that the world needs to have the imagination about and what it can and should be.... The narrative of black men.... They want to lead, and they want to serve.... We believe they can change the world." He thought the Morehouse idea was not perfect, like the American idea, "but we are working to perfect it." The heart of what President Thomas wanted for Morehouse was not too different from that of his predecessors. "Our mission," he said, "is to develop men with disciplined minds, to lead lives of leadership and service. And we must pursue this mission focused on a clear vision of excellence and impact, to be the premier liberal arts college in the world, attracting and educating black men and other men who identify with our mission and share our values." Under his leadership, Dr. Thomas foresaw the school as "the global voice on the education and development of men of color and in doing so, [Morehouse would] be an exemplar of excellence." Toward that end, four themes would guide his work: "The first is realizing the innate excellence in every Morehouse learner. The second is elevating our mission, the sustainability of Morehouse now and into the future. The third is Morehouse beyond borders. And the fourth theme...requires us to exercise stewardship over our resources effectively and efficiently."

Perhaps what the audience wanted most to hear was President

Thomas's ideas about the school's capital campaign, an endeavor that would have four pillars: endowment for scholarships, building a campus for the future (as he noted, Morehouse could not educate for the twenty-first century on a mid-twentieth century campus), supporting centers of excellence and innovation, and supporting research and professorships. This announcement captured the attention of the audience. Where do we go from here? The capital campaign "would be historic and dwarf any previous campaign effort in the school's history. The greatest challenge is not the charting of a greater Morehouse, rather, it is the belief and courage to invest and pursue it." This dream, this vision for Morehouse, was not something that could be achieved by President Thomas alone, but instead required all in the Morehouse family, "powered and sustained by the guiding spirit of our mission and its core values as we give life to new aspirations, to blaze new trails for new paths of service, and move forward with renewed energy to formulate viable plans to engage an exciting future." It would not be easy, as it would require everyone—faculty, staff, students, alumni, and friends—to examine what we do to make a distinctive and unique impact on the world. All stakeholders should as the question, "'Does the world need Morehouse?' And then commit accordingly with time, with talent, and with treasure." Clearly, this vision for Morehouse in 2019 was in line with the vision of the founders, in supporting a school that would educate black men for service to their communities and now the world. This wonderful vision notwithstanding, it was the scope of the impressive capital campaign that grabbed the attention of most in the Morehouse community.

President Thomas closed his inaugural address by vowing "today, and most especially to my students who will be here during my tenure, and to all members of this audience, that I will do the very, very best I can every day that I am president of Morehouse College." With that, and to a standing applause, the twelfth president of Morehouse thanked the audience and returned to his seat.

Board chairman Woods concluded the program, which ended with the singing of the college hymn, an offering of the benediction prayer by the Reverend Doctor Edward L. Wheeler (president of the Interdenominational Theological Center), and the recessional, which was guided by David German's "Trumpet Tune." Events marking and celebrating

President Thomas's inauguration and the 152nd commemoration of Founders' Week, however, were just getting started.

On Friday, February 16th, a presidential symposium on "The Morehouse Idea: Opportunities, Complexities, and Challenges for the Global Black Community in the Twenty-First Century" was held in the Ray Charles Performing Arts Center (Raypac). The symposium began at 10 A.M. and was moderated by Bakari Sellers, a 2005 African American Studies alumnus of the college. That afternoon, beginning at two o'clock, and held in the same venue, Dr. Henry Louis "Skip" Gates, the Alphonse Fletcher University Professor at Harvard University, shared excerpts from his documentary, "Reconstruction: America after the Civil War," which was later aired in its entirety on PBS stations across the country.

A concert was presented on Friday evening, and "Reflections of Excellence," the traditional panel of "Bennie" and "Candle" awardees, was held on Saturday morning, also in Raypac. The Candle in the Dark Gala/Inaugural Ball followed a lavish cocktail hour just across from the main ballroom.

The week of inaugural and founders' activities ended with a worship service featuring the Aeolian Choir from Oakwood University in Huntsville, Alabama, and a concert by the Morehouse Glee Club. As the campus returned to the academic and administrative work of the college, reflections on the traditional and new things that were happening at Morehouse were topics of conversation for weeks. The school was moving in the right direction as March and April were busy with exams, club activities, SGA elections, and end-of-the-year social events. But as normal school work and activities continued, on April 13th, the board of trustees announced a "Gender Identity Policy and Matriculation Policy," which sparked controversy and discussion within the Morehouse community. Following a similar policy instituted at Spellman in 2017, the Morehouse gender identity policy would "allow individuals who self-identify as men, regardless of the sex assigned to them at birth, to be considered for admission in the nation's black school for men." The new policy would go into effect in the 2020 fall semester, but would not impact students currently enrolled. Bennett College, the traditionally black college for women located in Greensboro, North Carolina, preceded Spelman in admitting transgender women for matriculation. Other traditionally black colleges, such as

Howard University in Washington, DC, Morgan State University in Baltimore, and Southern University in Baton Rouge, Louisiana, had implemented gender identity policies. Many traditionally white colleges and universities had established transgender admissions policies as well, and the Morehouse policy was a continuation of this trend toward gender equity.

Terrance Dixon, Morehouse's vice president for enrollment management, spoke for the president and his administration when he said, "In a rapidly changing world that includes a better understanding of gender identity, we're proud to expand our admission policy to consider trans men who want to be a part of an institution that has produced some of the greatest leaders in social justice, politics, business, and the arts for 150 years." In addition, he stated that "the ratification of this policy affirms the college's commitment to develop men with disciplined minds who will lead lives of leadership and service." The policy only applied to trans men, not trans women "or individuals who identify as women regardless of the sex assigned to them at birth," who would not be considered for admission to Morehouse.

In order to clarify the new policy and clear up any misunderstanding, President Thomas met with about fifty students, although all were invited to attend, where he answered questions and explained the origin of the policy and the need for the change. He revealed that a survey had been sent to approximately 17,000 students, alumni, parents, faculty, and staff asking questions about the proposed policy. The Gender Identity and Matriculation Policy was developed nearly ten years after the college had issued its "Appropriate Attire and General Behavioral Expectations Policy," which, among other things, banned students from wearing women's clothing, sagging pants, and walking barefoot on campus.[21] Regardless of the importantance of gender equity, the new policy did not meet with approval from some in the Morehouse family. However, the conversation about the new policy had quieted by commencement, as the class of 2019 graduated.

The traditional programs and activities leading up to a Morehouse

[21] Tucker Toole, "Morehouse President Faces Questions about College's New Gender Admissions Policy," *HBCU Education* (May 8, 2019).

Commencement are rich and memorable. After final grades were tabulated, Senior Week afforded the class of nearly 400 graduates all sorts of social and cultural opportunities—family dinners, clubbing, golfing, short trips back home or to other destinations, and/or pool parties. They were also participants in the very solemn and emotion-packed "Rite of Passage" service held on Friday, May 17th, and baccalaureate the next day, at 3 P.M. in King Chapel. Induction into Phi Beta Kappa for qualified students was also held on Friday. The baccalaureate preacher was Dr. E. Dewey Smith, class of 1986 and pastor of House of Hope in Macon, Georgia. The fiery oratory and declamation expected by the speaker at the service was demonstrated by Pastor Smith. As always, at the conclusion, Dean Carter gave directives and a weather forecast for the next morning, commencement day.

Commencement day has not always been pleasant at Morehouse. Since the 1990s, when the tradition of holding the convocation on the Century Campus began, the weather has been a concern for all involved—planners, administrators, parents, and students. The Morehouse community remembered the 2013 commencement when President Barack Obama was the speaker and how both the graduates and the crowd were drenched by a steady rain. But on the morning of May 19, 2019, the day dawned with clear skies and moderate temperatures. As thousands of parents, families, and friends of the college made their way to the Century Campus, the class of 2019 prepared for the procession. At the appointed time, they processed from King Chapel on Westview Drive, through the gate onto Brown Street into the campus, where they passed the platform party arrayed on the portico of Kilgore Hall, around historic Graves Hall and the memorial to President and Mrs. Mays, and down the grassy aisle to their seats. Once the gate was closed and the alumni, faculty, and platform members were seated, the program began. The 2019 Morehouse College Commencement program followed the traditional format established decades ago, with its opening remarks, the ringing of the bells, the prayer, the presentation of colors, and the singing of "The Star-Spangled Banner" and "Lift Ev'ry Voice and Sing." After the "occasion" was given and the salutatorian introduced, the valedictorian delivered his speech to his fellow classmates. At this point, President Thomas introduced billionaire philanthropist Robert F. Smith, the commencement speaker chosen for the class of 2019.

Robert Frederick Smith was born in Denver, Colorado, in 1962, and graduated from Cornell University (BA) and Columbia University (MBA). He is the chairman and CEO of Vista Equity Partners, a private equity firm that invests in software, data, and technology-enabled businesses. The company was founded in 2000 and has offices in several cities, including New York and San Francisco. Smith has registered two US and two European patents and is a chemical engineer. By 2019 Vista Equity, had more than $46 billion in funding. Mr. Smith's philanthropic and charity is broad and deep.[22] After introducing Mr. Smith to the assemblage, President Thomas took his seat.

At the podium, Robert Smith was at ease and appeared honored to be a part of the momentous occasion. The faces of the hundreds of black men seated in front of the platform and its podium, and the thousands of parents and others filling the sacred space of the Century Campus, with venerable old Graves Hall standing stately as a sentinel, made a brilliant scene as Mr. Smith stood at the podium. Morehouse programs, convocations, and other events are notoriously long, and the 2019 commencement was no exception. The program was nearly two hours long by the time Mr. Smith began his address, following, as it did, the awarding of honorary degrees to him and the celebrated actress Angela Bassett. Smith engaged the graduates when he asked them to stand and stretch and then jokingly said, that they were in for a long program. Mr. Smith opened by recognizing his mother and by mentioning his family that included a third generation of college graduates. He recalled the luminaries who had graduated from Morehouse and his two-decades-long friendship with Willie Woods, chairman of the board of trustees. He recalled his early education in Denver and how he had been influenced by the men and women of achievement in his community, and how the students on bus number 13 were bused to a high-achievement school. It made a difference in his life. The importance of intellectual capital is a strong value today. He argued that we must continue to fight against racism, and he stated that a successful career required hard work. These graduates must put in the "grind!" He encouraged them to take thoughtful risks and to evaluate their

---

[22] www.wikipedia.org, "Robert F. Smith, Investor."

options. He told the gathering to be intentional about the words they used and how they defined themselves. Always know you are enough. Demand respect from others and from yourself. He then reminded them to help liberate others along the way and to think about how they could contribute to the people around them. Smith challenged the class of 2019 to be the changemakers and told them that people would observe their actions every time they were in public. Communities thrived based on the smallest of gestures, he told them, and all people needed to be treated with dignity. Smith then asked the graduates to stand up again and this time to give each other a hug. Then he said, "This is my class, and my family is making a grant to eliminate their student loans." The surprise and elation on the faces of those standing behind him, especially President Thomas, was palpable. Glad-handing was seen, and the seniors roared, shouting, "MVP!" Some of them exhorted, others looked dazed, and some parents looked to the sky with a prayerful countenance on their faces. Within hours, news about the generous act, eventually estimated to be worth about $34 million, spread around the country and the world. The sun shone bright, as bright as it ever had. Returning to the podium, the provost said, "You are graduating debt free." There was an electricity in the air, a sense of great joy. A jubilee!

By Monday morning, May 20, as the national media reported the stunning gift to the Morehouse class of 2019, the campus had emptied of its students and their loved ones. President Thomas had been president of the college for two years and had overseen some significant developments at the school. He had demonstrated strong leadership and proven his mettle, even to the skeptics. He was on his way to becoming a Morehouse Man, by default, and he took pride in the Rhodes Trust Scholarship Committee's selection of Franck Nijimbere for membership in the International Rhodes Scholars 2019 Class at Oxford University. Nijimbere would begin his studies at the prestigious school in the United Kingdom in October, and he would also represent his home country of Burundi. Nijimbere graduated from Morehouse summa cum laude with a 3.86 grade point average and was inducted into Beta Kappa Chi and Phi Beta Kappa. A computer science and mathematics major, he went on to study artificial intelligence and machine learning at Oxford. On the selection of the college's fifth Rhodes Scholar, President Thomas said, "The Rhodes Scholar recognition is an endorsement of the academic excellence of Morehouse students and the quality of instruction offered in science, technology, engineering, and mathematics at the college. It places Morehouse among the best liberal arts colleges in the country." The vision of a $500 million capital campaign, the class of 2019 graduating debt free, and now another Rhodes Scholar from Morehouse all made for an excellent reflection on both the college and its new president. This was "feel good" news.

Morehouse continued to bask in these positive developments, but a negative story about the college surfaced in July 2019 when two students shared videos accusing a staff member of sexual harassment. In the videos, which were widely shared on Twitter, the staff member was accused of being sexually inappropriate with the students and of making inappropriate comments about their sexuality. As an investigation got underway, the college took a serious look at the operations of its Title IX office and its sexual harassment policies and procedures. Morehouse addressed the issue of inappropriate sexual behavior on campus by holding dialogues and other activities on masculinity, training students to organize and lead conversations about sexual misconduct, and conducting recurring campus surveys on the serious issue of inappropriate sexual behavior.

The 2019 fall semester at the college got underway in mid-August with the arrival of more than six hundred new students who were ready to experience the famous Morehouse New Student Orientation and begin classes. The semester unfolded as it had done for decades as students created a sense of brotherhood in and out of the dorms, adjusted to class routines, learned to navigate the Atlanta scene, hunkered down over study hours (sometimes "burning the midnight oil" or enduring all-nighters), and learned how to order food and have it delivered to the campus security gate. And then there was the return of nearly 1,500 upperclassmen, with whom the new students would soon form friendships and enjoy the social and cultural life of the college and the Atlanta University Center, especially Spelman. There was the opening convocation, where President Thomas delivered his second address at the beginning of the new academic year. The football games, especially the one with Clark-Atlanta University and Tuskegee University, the "classic" game played in Columbus. The Glee Club prepared for the Christmas Carol Concert and its annual spring tour, and the various cocurricular and social clubs met and planned their agendas. It was a normal semester in every way until Oprah Winfrey gave $13 million to Morehouse to continue the support for the scholars program that was in her name.

The Oprah Winfrey Scholars Program at Morehouse started thirty years earlier and had been successful in helping graduate Morehouse students who had demonstrated the founders idea that black men, who were often misunderstood, could be educated for stewardship in their communities and beyond. Whether black men are an "endangered species" or not, as Ms. Winfrey believed, they are certainly marginalized. The image of the black man needed to change, and Morehouse was doing that work. "This is who we really are."[23] The generous gift from Oprah Winfrey in 2019 was newsworthy and was carried by the media. Such a gift as this was not only good for the financial health of Morehouse, it was good publicity for the college as well. The extent of the public relations value of the gift from Ms. Winfrey and Robert Smith's gift to the class of 2019 is immeasurable. Suffice it to say, additional donations of various sizes from philanthropists and alumni arrived in the coming months.

The fall semester 2019 ended as previous semesters had done for many years, with final papers, the Christmas Carol Concert, and final exams. Students departed the campus the second week in December for home and parts unknown. The winter break was more than five weeks long, and the campus would not come alive again until just before Martin Luther King Jr. Day. The King holiday is always celebrated on the third Monday in January, and in 2020, the observance of the great civil rights leader fell on January 20th. The holiday commemorates Dr. King's birthday, and in 2020, it honored what would have been his ninety-first birthday.

At this time, as commemorative programs and activities around the country were held to honor the life and legacy of Dr. King, Morehouse's most illustrious graduate, a Washington State resident became the first person in the United States diagnosed with a confirmed case of the 2019 novel coronavirus. SARS-CoV-2, the virus responsible for COVID-19, was first identified in Wuhan, China, in December 2019. The

[23] "Oprah Winfrey Announces $13 Million Gift to Morehouse College for Scholars," www.morehouse.edu.

coronavirus, as the infectious disease was commonly called, is an acute respiratory illness whose symptoms include a dry cough, headache, muscle aches, and difficulty breathing. On January 19, 2020, a thirty-five-year-old man who had returned from a family visit to Wuhan went to an urgent-care clinic in Snohomish County, Washington, and reported that he had a persistent cough and a "subjective" fever. The man survived the disease after spending days in the hospital, but it was not until there was an outbreak of the disease at a nursing home in Kirkland, Washington, that the Centers for Disease Control and Prevention (CDC) held a teleconference with the staff at the facility to get an understanding of what was happening. At that time, it was reported that twenty-seven of the 108 residents and twenty-five of the 180 staff had some symptoms of COVID-19.[24] The first reported official death was a man in his fifties (who was not at the nursing facility), but as time passed, it was thought that others had perhaps died earlier, unbeknownst to medical professionals. By March 1' 2020, eight deaths were "confirmed and probable," but by April 1, 2020, the number of deaths had increased exponentially to 5,337. By this time, following spring break, Morehouse decided to evacuate the campus as diagnosed cases and deaths due to COVID-19 increased. At this time, Fulton County, Georgia, where the college is located, had only twenty cases of the dreaded disease, but by late July, there were nearly 14,000 cases of the coronavirus.[25]

Working with all leadership constituencies, President Thomas decided to suspend all in-person teaching and learning at Morehouse and implement a virtual, or distance learning, model. A pass/fail grading system was implemented, and commencement, usually held two months after spring break, was canceled. Reunion classes—the ones ending in 0 and 5—were also canceled. All of the solemn rituals and festive activities associated with a Morehouse graduation week were canceled. The Morehouse Torch flickered but did not extinguish. Educating black men for service to their communities was put on hold, but it was hoped that the disease

[24] Eric Boodman and Helen Branswell, "First Covid-19 Outbreak in a U.S. Nursing Home Raises Concerns," February 29, 2020.

[25] Lonnae O'Neal, "Morehouse College decided to open but is now closing based on the science," July 24, 2020. https://andscape.com/features/morehouse-college-decided-to-open-but-is-now-closing-based-on-the-science/

would die out or subside over the summer of 2020 so classes could resume as normal. If classes could not be fully in-person, perhaps a hybrid of in-person and distance classes. However, on August 19, 2020, Morehouse decided to close the campus and move all classes to an online platform. This meant there would be no New Student Orientation (a highly anticipated series of activities), no opening convocation (which sets the tone for the academic year), no Homecoming (which speaks for itself), and no Christmas Carol Concert. But above all, there would be no in-person classes where the traits are imbued for which Men of Morehouse are made into Morehouse Men utilizing the Six Wells. There would be no opportunity to hone leadership skills through the student government association or one of the many other campus organizations. There would be no chance to refine their social skills by interacting with each other and other students in the AUC and beyond. Except for the continuation of the academic excellence for which Morehouse is best known, the traditional college life was suspended. The action taken by the leadership at Morehouse corresponded with leadership decisions at the other schools in the Atlanta University Center and around the country. As fear gripped the nation, people began to get inoculated and wear masks.

On May 25, 2020, shortly after the end of the spring semester, and while Morehouse College was closed and its students were preparing for summer courses, George Perry Floyd Jr., a forty-six-year-old security guard, was murdered by Derek Chauvin, a Minneapolis policeman, during an arrest. A clerk at the Cups Foods store had accused Floyd of trying to pass a counterfeit $20 bill, and as the police tussled with Floyd, he fell to the ground, where Chauvin compressed his neck, causing cardiopulmonary arrest. Using her cellphone, Darnella Frazier, a black teenager, had the presence of mind to record the last few minutes of Floyd's life as he lay dying, pinned under the knee of the policeman for more than nine minutes, begging for relief, crying "I can't breathe," and calling for his mama. Frazier's video went viral and was viewed by millions of people around the world, including thousands of Morehouse students, faculty, staff, and alumni in Atlanta and across the country. Millions of people were shocked and outraged by what they saw, and many took to the streets. Protests were mobilized all over the United States and in cities in Europe, South America, Canada, Africa, and Asia. The repercussive outrage following the death of George Floyd ushered in a new period of "racial reckoning."

What became known as George Floyd protests took place all across Georgia, from Rome to Savannah, and from Athens to Columbus. In Atlanta, George Floyd protests were mobilized for eleven consecutive days. Some of the protest marches were in the area of the Georgia State Capitol, but many of them took place in and around Centennial Olympic Park and the CNN Center on Marietta Street in downtown Atlanta. As protests reached a highly charged and confrontational level, a Morehouse student and his friend from Spelman were arrested around 9:30 P.M. on Saturday night, May 30th, after attempting to drive through an area on Marietta Street that had been blocked by Atlanta police. When Messiah Young, the Morehouse student who was driving the car, refused to get out of his car, Officers Mark Gardner and Ivory Streeter yanked both college students from the car, roughing them up in the process. President Thomas issued a statement shortly after the arrest that was published in *The Washington Post* on June 22, 2020. In the rather long but powerful statement, Thomas said, in part, "Today, protesters lift their voices to expose institutionalized racism that has worked against minorities in the United States for far too long. Their cries for justice have echoed across the world. Yet they, and our society more broadly, still have much to accomplish." President Thomas referred to the deaths of George Floyd and Rayshard Brooks, who was killed at a Wendy's restaurant by an Atlanta policeman as he tried to run away, and he described the "terror of two Morehouse and Spelman College students at being yanked from their car, Tasered and dragged across broken glass." Thomas, in essence, summarized what would later be described as "racial reckoning" when he wrote,

> Through peaceful protests, diverse voices of the anti-racism movement are asking for what their fathers [and mothers] before them asked. They want solidarity to bring about change. They want equal justice under the law. They want to reimagine community policing, to reform the educational system so it is equitable and excellent for all students, and to develop policy strategies that bring jobs, investment, revitalized housing and ultimately, hope into low-income neighborhoods. Surely, more Americans can now empathize with this plight.

President Thomas worried about the safety of his daughter and two sons and the 2,200 students at Morehouse, for whom he was the caretaker, when they took part in peaceful protest. He had recently participated in a march with his sons and "felt encouraged that black and brown children entering K-12 classrooms would benefit [from the protest marches]. Now anti-racists would be slower to judge their abilities to achieve greatness." Certainly, President Thomas's sentiments were shared by many Americans, signifying, in the words of the song made famous by the legendary Sam Cooke, that "a change [was] gonna come." Pandemic and protests coexisted and changed Morehouse in obvious ways.

Because of the unrelenting pandemic, Morehouse College remained closed for in-person teaching and learning, but the administration continued to operate as the academic program remained strong and the endowment continued to grow. On May 16, 2021, Morehouse College held its 2021 commencement on the Century Campus and beyond. The "Idea" on which the school had existed for more than 150 years showed itself to be resilient and strong. Having weathered the crisis brought on by the COVID-19 pandemic, Morehouse never lost sight of its 154-year-old mission—the "Idea"—to train, teach, and educate men—primarily African American men—to have disciplined minds for lives of sacrifice and service. This is the esprit de corps, the Brotherhood, the Mystique, the Men of Morehouse, and the Morehouse Men, the zeitgeist for 150 years: "Holy Spirit, Holy Spirit, make us steadfast, honest, true. To old Morehouse, and her ideals, and in all things that we do."

Coda

The narrative history of Morehouse College is a story of how the founders' idea of establishing a school in Augusta, Georgia, which would educate black men for stewardship in their communities as preachers and teachers developed into one of America's most prestigious schools for black men and others by the twenty-first century. The school struggled to survive at times, but nevertheless, the idea, the vision, of the men who established Augusta Theological Institute in 1867 survived and is celebrated in many ways today. The cross, candle, and crown are emblematic of Morehouse over its 157 years of scholarship and stewardship. One hundred years from now, Morehouse College will still be recognized as one of America's best institutions of higher educations, period! Along the way, there will be good times and bad ones, but the resilience of Morehouse will stand the test of time and develop into Morehouse University. The story of the college I have told here will serve as a starting point for future narrators of the history of Morehouse. As I end my narrative, the Morehouse story continues.

Na matakwa bora. (Best wishes.)

Bibliography

INTERVIEWS

Kelley, Robin D. G. Interview by the Reverend Thomas A. Kilgore Jr. (www.oac.cdlib.org)

McKinney, Rev. Samuel Berry, '49. Greater Seattle Alumni Association.

Ross II, Glenwood, '71. Interview by Christopher Owoyemi.

Wheeler, Herbert, '68. Interview by Elbert Byron Green.

DOCUMENTS

Angus, David L. *ECF Education Brief: Issues in Public Education: Research Analysis.* Arlington, VA: Education Consumers Foundation, 2001.

Association of Governing Board to John Wilson and Bob Davidson, Memo, May 14, 2014.

"Atlanta University in Affiliation with Morehouse College and Spelman College for Women." Leadership in the Heart of the Race Problem. Atlanta, 1931. Washington, DC: Library of Congress.

Barnes, Mo. "Morehouse College President Issues Statement on Trump Meeting with HBCUs." *Rolling Out* (March 2, 2017).

Belcher, Edwin. "Teacher Monthly Report," February 1867. Richmond County, Georgia. Superintendent of Schools, Freedmen's Bureau. Georgia Archives, Morrow, GA.

"Biographical Sketch of Wendell Phillips Whalum." Biographical Files, Robert W. Woodruff Library and Archives, Atlanta University Center.

"Black Institutions of Higher Education: Their Development and Status, 1860–1982." National Center for Educational Statistics. Washington, DC.

Blake, Elias, Linda Jackson Lambert, and Joseph L. Martin. "Degrees Granted and Enrollment Trends in Historically Black Colleges: An Eight-Year Study." Washington, DC: Institution for Service to Education, 1974.

Bookman, Eric and Helen Branswell. "First Covid-19 outbreak in a U. S. nursing home raises concerns," February 29, 2020.

Brawley, Benjamin G. to John Hope, February 3, 1917. John Hope Collection, Robert W. Woodruff Library and Archives, Atlanta University Center.

Brisbane Jr., Robert H., ed. *A Working Conference on Cooperative Programs among Universities and Predominantly Negro Colleges.* Washington, DC, Office of Education, 1965.

Brown, Charles I. "The White Presence at Traditionally Black Public Colleges and Universities: A Synopsis, 1838–1980." Report ED 224 379, North

Carolina.
Burt, Sarah M. to Rev. E. P. Smith, April 6, 1867. American Missionary Association Archives, Auburn Avenue Research Library and Archives.
A Candle in the Dark Gala program (2011).
Carter, James. "Harmony Baptist Church." Augusta Historical Society.
Cheek, James. "The Future of Black Colleges." Address before the National Association for Equal Opportunity in Higher Education, 1985.
The Chicago Defender, September 1964, 5–11.
"Chronology: The King Holiday." MLK Vertical File, Box 12. Robert W. Woodruff Library and Archives, Atlanta University Center.
The Colored American, Archives, University of Georgia, December 30, 1865.
"Common Fact Data 2018–2019." https://morehouse.edu.
"Congressman Bishop Delivers 2018 Commencement Address at Morehouse College." Press Release, May 22, 2018.
"A Dinner to Listen." Invitation from President John Wilson, Morehouse College, October 25, 2016.
"Equal Opportunity for Blacks in Higher Education: An Assessment." Institute for the Study of Educational Policy, Washington, DC, 1976.
"Four Questions about the Financial Crisis." Morehouse College. Remarks by Ben S. Bernanke, chair of governors of the Federal Reserve System, April 14, 2009.
"From the President." Morehouse *Alumnus* (Fall 1998).
Gilbertson, Eric R. "The Supreme Court and Academe: The Evolution of Constitutional Doctrines for Higher Education." Association for the Study of Higher Education Annual Meeting, Chicago, 1985.
Gloster, Hugh M. "Dear Alumnus," November 28, 1986. Biographical File, Robert W. Woodruff Library and Archives, Atlanta University Center.
———. "A Proposal to the Ford Foundation for Morehouse College," August 20, 1986.
Goldman, F. H. "Integration and the Negro College." Center of Liberal Education for Adults, 1963.
Harris, John J. "Impact of Desegregation: A Historical and Legal Analysis." American Educational Research Association's Annual Meeting. Toronto, Canada, 1978.
"Harold Martin, Jr., Interim President of Morehouse." Uncf.org.
"The HBCU Experience Is More Than a Game." Commemorative Program, September 8–11, 2011.
Hill, Jonathan, Morehouse Student Government Association president, email message to William Taggart and Kevin Booker, March 28, 2017.
"The Historically Black Colleges: Prospect and Options for Federal Support."

Library of Congress Congressional Research Service, Education and Public Welfare Division, Washington, DC, 1977.
Holleran, C. J. "Know Your Georgia," *Atlanta Constitution,* January 21, 1952.
Hope, John to Mrs. F. M. Wilson, March 18, 1909. John Hope Collection, Robert W. Woodruff Library and Archives, Atlanta University Center.
Hope, John to Mordecai W. Johnson, March 4, 1918. Mordecai W. Johnson Papers, Moorland-Spingarn Collection, Howard University, Washington, DC.
"Independent Minority Colleges and Universities: National Models of Educational Pluralism." National Alliance of Independent Colleges and Universities. Washington, DC: Educational Resource Information Center, 1991.
"Instructions for the Funeral of John Hope, and the Memorial Service." John Hope Collection, Robert W. Woodruff Library and Archives, Atlanta University Center.
"Interim President of Morehouse Dies at Age 55." FOX 5, June 8, 2017.
Jacobs, Frederick and Tyler Tingley. "The Evolution of Eligibility Criteria for Title III of the Higher Education Act of 1965." Harvard Graduate School of Education, 1977.
Johnson, Rev. Kevin R. to Dr. John Wilson Jr., April 27, 2013.
Johnson, Mordecai W. to John Hope. Mordecai W. Johnson Papers, Moorland-Spingarn Collection, Howard University, Washington, DC.
Jones, J. C. "Differences in Perceived Sources of Academic Difficulties: Blacks in Predominantly Black and Predominantly White Colleges." Educational Resource Information Center, Washington, DC, 1970.
Jones, Jesse T. "Negro Education: A Study of the Private and Higher Schools for Colored People in the United States." *Bulletin* 28 (1917).
Keith Jr., Leroy. "Inaugural Address of Leroy Keith." Morehouse College, February 20, 1988.
Klein, Arthur Jay. "Survey of Negro Colleges and Universities." *Bulletin* 7 (1928).
Lartey, Jamiles. "Atlanta protest takes on importance after trump insults civil rights leader." *Atlanta,* January 21, 2017.
MacVicar, Malcolm, superintendent of education at the American Baptist Home Mission Board, to John Hope, professor at Roger Williams University (Nashville, TN), June 14, 1898. John Hope Collection, Robert W. Woodruff Library and Archives, Atlanta University Center.
The Maroon Tiger, Morehouse College, May 2, 2007: 12.
Massey, Walter E. "Inaugural Address." *Alumnus* (1996).
———. "Vision Realized. Period: The Massey Legacy, Morehouse College, 1995–2007."

Minutes of the Fall Meeting of the Board of Trustees, Morehouse College, November 17–18, 1988: 16–17.

Minutes of Middle Georgia Baptist Association Meeting, September 2–5, 1881. Office of the President, Missionary Baptist Convention of Georgia: Hawkinsville, GA.

Minutes of the Morehouse Board of Trustees, November 17–18, 1988.

Minutes of the Special Session of the Annual Meeting of the Board of Trustees of Morehouse College, Roosevelt Hotel, New York, May 13, 1969.

Morehouse *Alumnus* (February 1941); 15 (1942); (July 1957); (Summer 1967); Special Inauguration Issue (1988); Commencement Issue (1988); (Spring 1994); (Summer 1995); (Spring 1996); (Summer 1996); (Fall 1998); (Spring 2000); (Fall 2000); (Winter 2002).

Morehouse College Bulletin (Spring 1971); (Spring 1967); (Summer 1967); (Summer 1968); (May 1968); (Spring 1969); (Summer 1969); (Winter 1984).

Morehouse College Bulletin Collection, Catalogue 1940–1941. Robert W. Woodruff Library and Research Center, Atlanta University.

Morehouse College Catalogue (1965–1966); (1967–1968); (1979–1981).

"Morehouse Facts 2014." https://morehouse.edu.

Morehouse Football Schedule: 2018. https://thesiac.com/schedule.aspx?schedule=1354

Morehouse, Henry Lyman to John D. Rockefeller, June 13, 1890. Sleepy Hollow, NY: Rockefeller Archive Center, Box 28, Folder 2.

Morehouse Magazine Commemorative Issue (2014).

"Morehouse Strategic Plan," June 19, 2017. https://morehouse.edu.

Morehouse University online: https://morehouse.edu.

National Register of Historic Places, NPS Form 10-900a, United States Department of the Interior, National Park Service, Atlanta History Center Collections.

National Survey of the Higher Education of Negroes. United States Office of Education, Washington, DC, 1942–1943.

"Number of new cases of coronavirus (COVID-19) in the United from January 20, 2020, to August 12, 2021, by day." Ststista.com.

O'Neal, Lonnae. "Morehouse College decides to open but is now closing based on the science," July 24, 2020. https://andscape.com/features/morehouse-college-decided-to-open-but-is-now-closing-based-on-the-science/

Opening Chapel Service, September 18, 1940. Speaker President Benjamin E. Mays. *Alumnus* 15 (1941): 6–8.

"Oprah Winfrey Announce $13 Million Gift to Morehouse College for Scholars," Morehouse College, October 7, 2019.

Order of Service for the funeral of John Hope. *Atlanta University Bulletin* 15 (1936): 6. Hope Collection, Woodruff Library and Archives, Atlanta University.

"Our Baptist Ministers." American Baptist Historical Papers, Mercer University Collections.

Park, Catherine. "We Know What You Did." Flyer. 13WMAZ, November 10, 2017.

Proclamation in Recognition of Harmony Baptist Church. Office of the Mayor, Deke Copenhaver, May 11, 2008.

Recognition Banquet in Honor of Hugh Morris Gloster, President of Morehouse College, 1967–1987. Biographical Files, Robert W. Woodruff Library and Archives, Atlanta University Center.

"Regarding the President and Provost of Morehouse College," Garikai Campbell, October 7, 2016.

Report of the Board 1884, American Baptist Home Mission Society. Sleepy Hollow, NY, Rockefeller Archive Center, Henry Lyman Morehouse Collection, Record Group 1, Box 28, Folder 1.

Rockefeller, John D. to Henry Lyman Morehouse, July 19, 1890. Rockefeller Letter Book, Sleepy Hollow, NY: Rockefeller Archive Center.

Roy, Joseph E. "The Higher Education of the Negro, No Mistake." The First and Second Mohonk Conference on the Negro Question, New York: Negro Universities Press, 1969.

Saporta, Maria. "Morehouse Moving Forward Despite Loss of Interim President—Bill Taggart," June 16, 2017. https://saportareport.com/morehouse-moving-forward-despite-loss-interim-president-bill-taggart/sections/reports/maria_saporta/

"Saving the African-American Child: A Report of the Task Force on Black Academic and Cultural Excellence." National Alliance of Black Educators. Educational Resource Information Center, Washington, DC, 1984.

"School Report," May 1966, Augusta, GA, Freedmen's Bureau Papers, Georgia Archives, Morrow, GA.

Self-Study Report on the African-American Studies Program in the Department of History at Morehouse College (Fall 2000): 13.

Semi-Annual Report to the President of the Board of Trustees of Morehouse College, Atlanta, November 1969.

"Small Change: A Report on Federal Support for Black Colleges." Southern Education Foundation, Atlanta, 1972.

Smelser, Neil J. *Theory of Collective Behavior.* New York: Free Press, 1971.

"Still a Lifetime: The Status of Historically Black Colleges and Universities." National Advisory Committee on Black Higher Education. Washington,

DC: Government Printing Office, 1980.
"Student Life at Morehouse College." Sleepy Hollow, NY, Rockefeller Archive Center, 1951, 1952.
Taylor, Alexis. "Morehouse College Names Harold Martin, Jr., New Interim President." AFR/The Black Media Authority, July 17, 2017.
Thomas, David A. "Inaugural Speech." Morehouse College, February 15, 2019, YouTube.
"Timeline Updated," February 8, 2017.
"Traditionally Black Institutions of Higher Education: Their Development and Status, 1860 to 1982." National Center for Educational Statistics, Washington, DC.
United States Census Publication
"Why We Have No Confidence in Our Board Chairman: An Open Letter from Concerned Faculty at Morehouse College," March 30, 2017. https://medium.com.
Wright, S. "The Black College I Historical Perspective: Historical Perspectives on the Development of Equal Opportunity in Higher Education." ACT Special Report No. 22, Iowa City, 1976.

THESES

Bailey, Trenton H. "The Morehouse Revolution." Unpublished manuscript.
Benson, Alexa Wynelle. "Race Relations in Atlanta, As Seen in a Critical Analysis of the City Council Proceedings and Other Works, 1865–1877." Master's thesis, Atlanta University, 1966.

BOOKS

Abernathy, Ralph David. *And the Wall Came Tumbling Down.* New York: Harper & Row, 1989.
Adams, Myron W. *A History of Atlanta University, 1865–1929.* Atlanta: Atlanta University Press.
Albright, Robert L. and George Neeley Jr. *Challenges for the Traditionally Black Colleges: A New Look.* ED Report 114024, 1975.
Alexander, Phillip. *A Widening Sphere: Evolving Cultures at MIT.* Boston: MIT Press, 2021.
Allen, Walter L., Edgar G. Epps, and Nasha Z. Haniff. *Colleges in Black and White.* New York: State University of New York, 1991.
Ashley, Dwayne with Shawn Rhea. *I'll Find a Way or Make One: A Tribute to Historically Black Colleges and Universities.*
Atlanta Baptist College Catalog, 1899–1900.
Atlanta in 1890: The Gate City. Atlanta Historical Society. Macon, GA: Mercer

University Press, 1986.
Bacote, Clarence A. *The Story of Atlanta University: A Century of Service, 1865–1965.* Atlanta: Atlanta University, 1969.
Bell, Derrick. *Confronting Authority: Reflections of an Ardent Protester.* Boston: Beacon Press, 1994.
Bennett Jr., Lerone. *Before the Mayflower: A History of the Nero in America, 1619–1962.* Chicago: Johnson Publishing Co., 1962.
———. *The Negro Mood and Other Essays.* Chicago: Johnson Publishing, 1964.
Berkhofer Jr., Robert F. *A Behavioral Approach to Historical Analysis.* New York: Free Press, 1969.
Billingsley, Andrew. "The Black Presence in American Higher Education." In *What Blacks Are Saying.* New York: Hawthorn Books, 1970.
Bond, Horace Mann. *The Education of the Negro in American Social Order.* Englewood Cliffs, NJ: Prentice Hall, 1934.
Bowles, F. and F. A. DeCosta. *Between Two Worlds: A Profile of Negro Higher Education.* New York: McGraw Hill, 1971.
Brawley, Benjamin G. *A History of Morehouse College.* Atlanta.
Brawley, J. *The Clark College Legacy: An Interpretive History of Relevant Education, 1869–1975.* Princeton, NJ: Princeton University Press, 1977.
Brazziel, W. *Quality Education for All Americans: An Assessment of Gains of Black Americans with Proposals for Progressive Development in American Schools and Colleges for the Next Century.* Washington, DC: Howard University Press, 1974.
Brinton, Crane. *The Anatomy of Revolution.* New York: W. W. Norton, 1938.
Brisbane, Robert H. *Black Activism: Racial Revolution in the United States, 1954–1970.* King of Prussia, PA: Judson Press, 1974.
———. *The Black Vanguard: Origins of the Negro Social Revolution, 1900–1960.* Valley Forge, PA: Judson Press, 1960.
Brown, Hugh Victor. *A History of Negro Education in North Carolina.* Goldsboro, NC: Irving Swain Press, 1961.
Bullock, H. *A History of Negro Education in the South, 1619 to the Present.* Cambridge: Howard University Press, 1967.
Butler, Addie Louise Joyner. *The Distinctive Black College: Talladega, Tuskegee, and Morehouse.* Metuchen, NJ: Scarecrow Press, 1977.
Caliver, A. *A Background Study of Negro College Students.* Washington, DC: United States Government Printing Office, 1933.
Campbell, Clarice. *Mississippi: A View from Tugaloo.* Jackson: University Press of Mississippi, 1979.
Cashin, Edward J. *Old Springfield: Race and Religion in Augusta.* Augusta, GA:

Springfield Park Foundation, 1995.

Cheek, James. *Higher Education's Responsibility for Advancing Equality of Opportunity and Justice.* Washington, DC: Institute for the Study of Educational Policy, 1977.

Clift, Virgil A. *Appropriate Goals and Plans for the Future of Negro Education in America.* New York: Harper & Row, 1962.

Clowse, Barbara Barksdale. *Ralph McGill: A Biography*. Macon, GA: Mercer University Press, 1998.

Coleman, J. F. B. *Tuskegee to Vorhees: The Booker T. Washington Idea by Elizabeth Evelyn Wright.* Columbia, SC: R. L Bryan, 1922.

Coleman, J. S. et. al. *Equality of Educational Opportunity.* Washington, DC: US Office of Education, 1966.

Coleman, Kenneth, ed. *A History of Georgia*. Athens: University of Georgia Press, 1991.

Cook, S. D. *The Socio-Ethical Role and Responsibility of the Black College Graduate.* New York: Teacher College Press, 1978.

Cook, Samuel DuBois. *Benjamin E. Mays: His Life, Contribution and Legacy.* Franklin, TN: Providence House Publishers, 2009.

———. *Quotable Quotes of Benjamin E. Mays.* New York: Vantage Press, 1993.

Cowan, Tom and Jack Maguire. *Timeline of African History: 500 Years of Black Achievement*. New York: Perigee Books, 1994.

Cozart, John W. *A History of the Association of Colleges and Secondary Schools, 1934–1965.* Charlotte, NC: Heritage Press, 1967.

Crandall, Latham A. *Henry Lyman Morehouse: A Biography.* New York: American Baptist Society, 1919.

Cruise, Harold. *The Crisis of the Negro Intellectual.* New York: Harper & Row, 1967.

Davis, Leroy. *A Clashing of the Soul: John Hope and the Dilemma of African American Leadership and Higher Education in the Early Twentieth Century.* Athens: University of Georgia Press, 1998.

Derbingy, Irving A. *General Education in the Negro College.* Palo Alto, CA: Stanford University Press, 1947.

Du Bois, W. E. B. *Dusk of Dawn: An Essay Toward an Autobiography of a Race Concept.* New Brunswick, NJ: Transaction Publishers, 1940.

———. *The College-bred Negro.* Atlanta: Atlanta University Publications, Atlanta University Press, 1920.

———. *The Talented Tenth: The Negro Problem.* New York: James Pott & Company, 1903.

The Early Efforts for Industrial Education 22. New York: John F. Slater Fund, 1923

Eaves, John H. *The Morehouse Mystique: Lessons to Develop Black Men.* Fruitvale, CT: African American Images, 2009.
Edward, Harry. *Black Students.* New York: MacMillan, 1970.
Ellison, Ralph. *Invisible.* New York: Random House, 1947, 1952.
Farber, David. *The Sixties Chronicle.* Lincolnwood, IL: Legacy Publishing, 2004.
Favors, Jelani Manu-Gowon. *Shelter in the Time of Storm: How Black Colleges Foster Generations of Leadership and Activism.*
Fiore, Douglas J. and W. Weldon Hill. *Creating Personal Success on the Historically Black College and University Campus.* 2011.
Fleming, Jacqueline. *Blacks in College.* San Francisco, CA: Josey-Bass, 1984.
Fleming, J. E., ed. *Black Students in Higher Education: Conditions and Experiences in the 1970s.* Westport, CT: Greenwood Press, 1981.
Forbes, Frank L. *History of Athletics at Morehouse College, 1896–1966.* Atlanta: 1966.
Fosdick, Raymond B. *Adventure in Giving: The Story of the General Education Board. A Foundation Established by John D. Rockefeller.* New York: Harper & Row, 1962.
Franklin, John H. *Soon One Morning.* New York: Alfred Knopf, 1963.
Franklin, Robert M. *Crisis in the Village: Restoring Hope in African American Communities.* Minneapolis, MN: Fortress Press, 2007.
Fredrickson, George M. *The Black Image in the White Mind: The Debate on Afro-American Character and Destiny, 1817–1914.* New York: Harper & Row, 1971.
Gallagher, Buell. *American Caste and the Negro College.* New York: Columbia University Press, 1938.
Garibaldi, A., ed. *Black Colleges and Universities: Challenges for the Future.* New York: Praeger, 1984.
Gasman, Marybeth. *Envisioning Black Colleges: A History of the United Negro College Fund.* Baltimore, MD: Johns Hopkin Press, 2007.
Gasman Marybeth with Louis Sullivan. *The Morehouse Mystique: Becoming a Doctor at the Nation's Newest African American Medical School.* Baltimore, MD: Johns Hopkin Press, 2012.
Gayle Jr., Addison. *The Black Aesthetic.* Garden City, NY: Doubleday, 1972.
Goodson, Martha Gram, ed. *Chronicles of Faith: The Autobiography of Frederick D. Patterson.* Tuscaloosa: University of Alabama Press, 1991.
Goodwin, B. *The Emergence of Black Colleges.* Pittsburgh, PA: Good-Patrick Publishers, 1974.
Grant, Donald L., ed. *The Way It Was in the South: The Black Experience in Georgia.* New York: Carol Publishing Group, 1993.

Grier, William H. and Price M. Cobbs. *Black Rage.* New York: Basic Books, 1968.

Gurin, Patricia. *Black Consciousness, Identity, and Achievement: A Study of Students in Historically Black Colleges.* New York: John Wiley & Sons, 1975.

Guy-Sheftall, Beverly and Jo Moore Stewart. *Spelman Centennial Celebration, 1881–1981.* Atlanta: Spelman College, 1981.

Hale Jr., Frank, ed. *Black Colleges Empower Students: Lessons for Higher Education.*

Harris, Adam. *The State Must Provide: Why America's Colleges Have Always Been Unequal—And How to Set Them Right.* Ecco, 2021.

Harris, William T. *Normal School Training for Negroes: The First and Second Mohonk Conference on the Negro Question, 1890–91.* New York: Negro Universities Press, 1969.

Heintze, Michael R. *Private Black Colleges in Texas, 1865–1954.* College Station: Texas A&M Press, 1985.

Hicks, Terrence and Lemuel Watson, eds. *Black Administrators in Higher Education.* 2018.

Hill, S. *The Traditionally Black Institutions of Higher Education, 1860–1962.* Washington, DC: National Center for Education Statistics, 1984.

Hine, Darlene C. et al. *African Americans: A Concise History.* New York: Pearson, 2012.

Historically Black Colleges and Universities Fact Book. Volumes 1, 2, and 3. Silver Springs, MD: Marco Systems, 1983.

Holmes, Dwight Oliver. *The Evolution of the Negro College.* College Park, MD: McGrath, 1934.

Horne, Gerald and May Young. *W. E. B. Du Bois: An Encyclopedia.* Westport, CT: Greenwood Press, 2001.

Hornsby Jr., Alton. *A Short History of Black Atlanta.* Atlanta: Apex Museum, 2003.

Huggins, Nathan I. *Harlem Renaissance.* Oxford, UK: Oxford University Press, 1971.

Jaffe, A. J. *Negro Higher Education in the 1960s.* New York: Praeger, 1968.

Johnson, Charles S. *The Negro College Graduate.* New York: Negro Universities Press, 1938.

Jones, Edward. A. *A Candle in the Dark: A History of Morehouse College.* Valley Forge, PA: Judson Press, 1967.

Jones, Lance G. E. *The Jeanes Teacher in the United States, 1908–1933.* Chapel Hill: University of North Carolina Press, 1937.

Jones, Maxine D. *Talladega College: The First Century.* Tuscaloosa: University of Alabama Press, 1990.

Jones, S. J. and G. B. Weathersby. *Financing the Black College.* New York: Teachers College Press, 1978.

Karenga, Maulana. *Introduction to Black Studies.* Los Angeles: University of Sankore Press, 2010.

Katz, Michael B., ed. *Education in American History.* New York: Praeger, 1973.

Kull, Irving S. and Nell M. Kull. *Encyclopedia of American History in Chronological Order.* New York: Popular Library, 1965.

Leavell, Ullin Whitney. *Philanthropy in Negro Education, 1930.* New York: Negro Universities Press, 1970.

Lee, Gordon. *The Struggle for Federal Aid.* New York: Columbia University Press, 1949.

LeMelle, T. J. and W. J. LeMelle. *The Black College: Strategy for Achieving Relevancy.* New York: Praeger, 1969.

Logan, Rayford W. *Howard University: The First Hundred Years, 18867–1967.* New York: New York University Press, 1969.

———. *The Negro in American Life and Thought—The Nadir, 1877–1901.* New York: Dial Press, 1954.

Lovett, Bobby L. *America's Black Colleges and Universities.* Macon, GA, Mercer University Press, 2015.

Luker, Ralph E. *Historical Dictionary of the Civil Rights Movement.* Latham, MD: Scarecrow Press, 1997.

Martin, Robert E. *Negro Education in America.* New York: Harper & Row, 1962.

Mays, Benjamin E. *Born to Rebel: An Autobiography.* New York: Scribner's Sons, 1971.

McGrath, E. J. *The Predominantly Negro College and Universities in Transition.* New York: Columbia University Press, 1965.

McKenzie, Fayette A. *Ideals of Fisk.* Nashville, TN: Fisk University Press, 1915.

McKinney, Richard I. *Religion in Higher Education among Negroes.* New Haven, CT: Yale University Press, 1945.

McKinney, T. E., ed. *Higher Education among Negroes.* Johnson C. Smith University, 1932.

Meier, August. *Negro Thought in America, 1880–1915.* Ann Arbor: University of Michigan Press, 1963.

Mingle, J. R. *Black Enrollment in Higher Education: Trends in the Nation and the South.* Atlanta: Southern Regional Education Board, 1978.

Mohr, P., ed. *Black Colleges and Equal Opportunity in Higher Education: A Variety of Papers Advocating the Retention of Black Colleges and Universities.* Lincoln: University of Nebraska Press, 1975.

Morais, Herbert M. *The History of the Negro in Medicine.* New York: Publishers

Co., 1968.

Morris, J. *Elusive Equality: The Status of Black Americans in Higher Education.* Washington, DC: Howard University Press, 1979.

The Negro and Higher Education in the South. Commission on Higher Education Opportunity in the South, Southern Regional Education Board, Atlanta, 1967.

Nevins, Allen. *Study in Power: John D. Rockefeller, Industrialist and Philanthropist.* New York: Scribner's Sons, 1953.

Neyland, Leedwill W. *The History of Florida Agricultural and Mechanical University.* Gainesville: University of Florida Press, 1963.

Ogbar, Jeffrey O. G. *Hip-Hop Revolution: The Culture and Politics of Rap.* Lawrence: University of Kansas Press, 2007.

Oltman, Adele. *Sacred Mission, Worldly Ambition: Black Christian Nationalism in the Age of Jim Crow.* Athens: University of Georgia Press, 2012.

Patterson, Zella. *Langston University: A History.* Norman: University of Oklahoma Press, 1979.

Peabody, Francis G. *Education for Life: The Story of Hampton Institute.* Garden City, NY: Doubleday, 1918.

Peare, Catherine O. *Mary McLeod Bethune..* New York: Vanguard Press, 1951.

Range, Willard. *The Rise and Progress of Negro Colleges in Georgia, 1865–1949.* Athens: University of Georgia Press, 1949.

Read, Florence Matilda. *The Story of Spelman College.* Princeton, NJ: Princeton University Press, 1961.

Richardson, Joe M. *The American Missionary Association and Southern Blacks, 1861–1890.* Athens: University of Georgia Press, 1986.

———. *A History of Fisk University, 1865–1946.* Tuscaloosa: University of Alabama Press, 2002.

Ridgely, Torrence. *The Story of John Hope.* New York: McMillan, 1948.

Rouse, Jacqueline A. *Lugenia Burns Hope: Black Southern Reformer.* Athens: University of Georgia Press, 1989.

Rovaris Sr., Dereck J. *Mays and Morehouse: How Benjamin E. Mays Developed Morehouse College, 1940–1967.* Silver Spring, M D: Beckham House, 2006.

Selden, William K. *Accreditation: A Struggle over Standards in Higher Education.* New York: Harper & Brothers, 1960.

Sheer, Robert G. *Subordination or Liberation? The Development of Conflicting Theories of Black Education in Nineteenth Century Alabama.* Tuscaloosa: University of Alabama Press, 1977.

Spofford, Tim. *Lynch Street: The May 1970 Slaying at Jackson State.* Kent, OH: Kent State University Press, 1988.

Stearns, Charles. *The Black Man of the South and the Rebels, or the Characteristics of the Former and the Recent Outrages of the Latter.* New York: American News Company, 1872.

Stodghill, Ron. *Where Everybody Looks Like Me: At the Crossroads of American Black Colleges and Culture.*

Talty, Stephan. *Mulatto America: At the Crossroads of Black and White Culture—A Social History.* New York: HarperCollins, 2003.

Thomas, G. E. "Black College Students and Their Major Fields of Choice." In *In Pursuit of Equality in Higher Education.* Edited by Anne S. Pruitt. Dix Hills, NY: General Hall, 1987.

Thomas, G. E., ed. *Black Students in Higher Education: Conditions and Experiences in the 1970s.* Westport, CT: Greenwood Press, 1981, 1988.

Thomas, G. E. and J. Braddock. *Determining the College Destination of Black Students.* Atlanta: Southern Education Foundation, 1981.

Thompson, Daniel C. *Black Elite: A Profile of Graduates of UNCF Colleges.* Westport, CT: Greenwood Press, 1986.

———. *Private Black Colleges at the Crossroads.* Westport, CT: Greenwood Press, 1973.

Thornbrough, Emma L., ed. *Booker T. Washington.* Englewood Cliffs, NJ: Prentice-Hall, 1969.

The Torch. Yearbook. Morehouse College, Atlanta, 1961.

Turner, W. H. and J. A. Michael. *Traditionally Black Institution of Higher Education: Their Identification and Selected Characteristics.* Washington, DC: National Center for Educational Statistics, 1979.

Washington, Booker T. *Working with the Hands.* New York: Doubleday, Page and Co., 1904.

White, Walter. *Rope and Faggot: A Biography of Judge Lynch.* New York: Alfred A. Knopf, 1929.

Whiting, Albert N. *Guardian of the Flame: Historically, Black Colleges Yesterday, Today, and Tomorrow.* Washington, DC: American Association of State Colleges, 1991.

Willie, Charles V., and R. R. Edmonds, eds. *Black Colleges in America.* New York: Columbia University Press, 1978.

Withrow, Dolly. *West Virginia State College, 1891–1919: From the Grove to the Stars.* Charleston, WV: Trans Allegheny Publishers, 1991.

Wolters, Raymond. *The New Negro on Campus: Black College Rebellions on Campus in the 1920s.* Princeton, NJ: Princeton University Press, 1975.

Woodson, Carter G. *The Education of the Negro prior to 1861.* New York: G. P. Putnam's Sons, 1915.

ARTICLES AND BOOK ENTRIES

"The American Negro College." *Crisis* 70.

"American Missionary." *American Missionary Association* 1 (1876).

Anderson, E. and F. Hrabowski. "Graduate School Success of Black Student from White Colleges and Black Colleges." *Journal of Higher Education* 48: 197, 294–303.

Aptheker, Herbert. "The Negro College Student in the 1920s—Years of Preparation and Protest: An Introduction." *Science and Society* 33 (1969): 150–67.

Atwood, Rufus B. "The Origin and Development of Negro Public College, with Special Reference to the Land-Grant College." *The Journal of Negro Education* 31 (1962): 240–50.

Bacote, Clarence A. "The Negro in Atlanta Politics." *Phylon* 4 (1955): 333.

———. "Some Aspects of Negro Life in Georgia, 1880–1908." *The Journal of Negro History* 43 (1958): 188.

Badertscher, Nancy. *Education* (June 16, 2017).

Badger, Henry C. "Negro Colleges and Universities, 1900–1950." *Change* 5 (1973): 27–33.

Barbour, Russell Conwell. "A Tribute to My Teacher—Dr. Joh Hope." *National Baptist Voice* 15 (1936): 6.

Barrett, L. G. "Jackson College." *American Baptist Home Mission Monthly* 16 (1989).

"Beating at Morehouse Raises Debate Over Perceived Homophobia." *Chronicle of Higher Education* (November 29, 2002).

Bell Jr., Derrick A. "Black Colleges and the Desegregation Dilemma." *Emory Law Journal* 28 (1979): 949–84.

Bellamy, Donnie D. and Diane E. Walker. "Slaveholding in Antebellum Augusta and Richmond County, Georgia." *Phylon* 2 (1987).

Blackmon, Douglas A. "Mayor's Freaknik decision draws criticism, tepid praise." *Atlanta Journal-Constitution* (September 23, 1994): D-3.

Blake Jr., Elias. "The Black Protest Tradition of Historically Black Colleges: A Comparative Analysis of Historically Black and Historically White Institutions." *Debate and Understanding: A Journal for the Study of Minority Americans' Economic, Political and Social Development* (1978): 228–39.

Bokelman. Robert W. and Louis D'Amico A. "Changes in Faculty Salaries and Basic Student Charges in Negro College." *The Journal of Negro Education* 18 (1962): 561–67.

Bond, Horace Mann. "The Origin and Development of the Negro Church-Related College." *The Journal of Negro Education* 29 (1960): 217–26.

Barbour, Russell Conwell. "A Tribute to My Teacher—Dr. John Hope."

National Baptist Voice (February 29, 1936): 1.

Bottoms, L. W. "The Policies and Rationale Underlying the Support of Negro College and Schools Maintained by the Presbyterian Church in the United States." *The Journal of Negro Education* 29 (1960): 264–73.

Boykins, L. L. "Trends in American Higher Education with Implications form the Higher Education of Negroes." *The Journal of Negro Education* (1957): 193–99.

Bracey, Meier, and Rudwick. *Black Nationalism in America.* Indianapolis, IN: Bobbs-Merrill Co., 1970.

Brawley, Benjamin G. "Every Race Had a Peculiar Genuis."

Brazell, Johnetta Cross. "Bricks without Straw: Missionary-Sponsored Black Higher Education in the Post-Emancipation Era." *Journal of Higher Education* 63 (1992): 26–49.

Brimmer, Andrew. "The Economic Outlook and the Future of the Negro College." *Daedelus* 100 (1971): 539–72.

Brown, Aaron. "The Negro Graduate, 1950–1960." *Negro Educational Review* 11 (1960): 71–81.

Brown, Herman. "Black Studies at Predominantly Black Colleges and Universities." *Negro History Bulletin* 36 (1973): 24–36.

Brown, Sarah and Julia Martinez. "Signs Naming Students Accused of Sexual Assault Reopen Wounds at Atlanta Colleges." *Chronicle of Higher Education* (November 9, 2017).

Brown, T. "Black Colleges Fight to Make It." *New World Forum* (September 1979).

Brownlee, Frederick L. "The Negro Church-Related College: A Critical Summary." *The Journal of Negro Education* 29 (1960) 401–407.

Bryant, Lawrence C. "Graduate Degree Programs in Negro Colleges, 1927–1960." *Negro Educational Review* 11 (1961): 177–84.

Calloway, Thomas J. "Booker T. Washington and the Tuskegee Institute." *New England Magazine* 17 (1897): 131–46.

Carter, Donald L. "Myth and Realities about Historically Black Colleges in Higher Education." *Debate and Understanding: A Journal for the Study of Minority Americans' Economic, Political, and Social Development* 4 (1978).

Cashin, Edward J. "Cities and Counties: Augusta." *New Georgia Encyclopedia.*

The Chicago Defender (September 5–11, 1964).

Clement, Rufus E. "The Church School as a Social Factor in Negro Life." *The Journal of Negro History* 12 (1927): 5–12.

Collins, Ernest M. "Integration in the State-Supported Colleges and Universities in the South." *The Journal of Negro Education* 32 (1961): 239–46.

D'Amico, Louis A. and Reed M. Maeylie. "A Comparison of Tuition and Fees

Charged in Negro Institutions in the Southeast and the Nation." *The Journal of Negro Education* 33 (1964) 186–90.

Daniel, Walter H. "Liberal Arts and Teacher Education in the Negro Public College." *The Journal of Negro Education* 34 (1962) 404–13.

Davis, John W. "The Future of the Negro Public College." *The Journal of Negro Education* 31 (1962): 421–28.

Davis, Thomas E. "Some Racial Attitudes of Negro College and Grade School Students." *The Journal of Negro Education* (April 1937): 157–65.

Davis, Thomas E. "A Study of Fisk University Freshmen from 1928 to 1930." *The Journal of Negro Education* 2 (1933): 477–83.

Dease, Barbara C. "Looking through the Looking Glass: A Historical and Factual Perspective on Black Higher 'Book' Learning." *ADFL Bulletin* 14 (1982) 18–24.

DeFrost, Henry S. "Does Higher Education Benefit the Negro?" *American Missionary* 48 (1887): 71–73.

DeLeon, Robert. "Living Memorial to King Takes Shape." *The Atlanta Journal-Constitution* (November 9, 1969): 3D.

Diamond II, Roderick. "On the 30th Anniversary of Its Famous Gala, Morehouse Receives Generous Gifts." Morehouse Advance News Writing.

Doody, Hurley H. "The Progress, of the Negro in Higher Education." *The Journal of Negro Education* 32 (1962): 485–92.

Du Bois, William E. B. "The College-Bred Negro." *Atlanta University Publication*. New York: Russell & Russell, 1910.

———. "Criteria for Negro Art." *The Crisis* 32 (October 1926).

———. "Economic Co-Operation among Negro Americans." *Atlanta University Publications* 12. New York: Russell & Russell, 1907.

Dunne, William. "The Roman Catholic Church: The Rationale and Policies Underlying the Maintenance of Higher Institutions for Negroes." *The Journal of Negro Education* (1960): 307–14.

Enck, Henry S. "Black Self-Help in the Progressive Era: The Northern Campaigns of Smaller Black Industrial Schools, 1900–1915." *The Journal of Negro History* 61 (1976): 73–87.

———. "Tuskegee Institute and Northern White Philanthropy: A Case Study in Fund Raising, 1900–1915." *Journal of Rural Education* 3 (1980): 133–34.

Fen, Sing-Nan. "Liberal Education for Negroes." *The Journal of Negro Education* 30 (1961): 17–24.

Fleming, Cynthia Griggs. "The Effects of Higher Education on Black Tennesseans after the Civil War." *Phylon* 44 (1983): 204–16.

———. "A Survey of the Beginnings of Tennessee's Black Colleges and

Universities, 1865–1920." *Tennessee Historical Quarterly* 39 (1980): 195–207.

Foster, E. C. "Carter G. Woodson's 'The Mis-Education of the Negro' Revisited: Black Colleges, Black Studies." *Freedomways* 13 (1973): 28–38.

Franklin, V. P. "Whatever Happened to the College-Bred Negro." *History of Education Quarterly* 24 (1984): 411–18.

"Future of Private Negro Colleges." *Ebony* 16 (1961): 88–90.

Gist, Noel P. "Aspirations of Negro and White Students." *Social Forces* 42 (1963): 40–80.

Golden, Harry. "The American Negro in Higher Education: *Crisis* 70 (1963): 405–409.

Graham, Edward K. "The Hampton Institute Strike of 1927: A Case Study in Student Protest." *American Scholar* 38 (1969): 668–83.

Green, Harry Washington. "Higher Standards for the Negro College." *Opportunity* 9 (1931): 8–11.

Gurin, P. and C. Gaylord. "Educational and Occupational Goals of Men and Women at Black Colleges." *Monthly Labor Review* 99 (1976): 10–16.

Harding, Vincent. "And Educator's View of Black Students and the Impossible Revolution." *Ebony* (August 1969).

Harris, John J. et. al. "A Historical Perspective of the Emergence of Higher Education in Black Colleges." *Journal of Black Studies* 6 (1976): 55–68.

Henderson, T. H. "The Future of the Non-Land Grant Negro Public College." *The Journal of Negro Education* 27 (1958): 397.

Henderson, V. "Negro Colleges Face the Future." *Daedalus* (1971): 630–48.

Holmes, D. O. W. "Beginnings of the Negro College." *The Journal of Negro Education* 3 (1934): 168–93.

———. "The Negro College Faces the Depression: *The Journal of Negro Education* 2 (1933): 16–25)

Holsendolph, Ernest. "Black Colleges Are Worth Saving." *Fortune* 84 (1971): 106–107.

Hope II, John. "The Negro College Student Protest and the Future." *The Journal of Negro Education* 30 (1961): 368–76.

Hornsby Jr., Alton. "Historical Overview of Black Colleges in the Unites States." *Western Journal of Black Studies* (Fall 1978): 162–66.

Jackson, Luther Porter. "The Origin of Hampton Institute." *The Journal of Negro History* 10 (1925): 131–49.

Jenkins, Martin D. "Enrollment in Negro Colleges and Universities, 1937–1938." *The Journal of Negro Education* 7 (1938): 118–23.

Jet (March 10, 1960): 30.

Johnson, G. E. "Desegregation and the Future of the Negro College: A Critical

Summary." *The Journal of Negro Education* 27 (1958): 430–35.

Jones, M. "The Responsibility of the Black College to the Black Community: Then and Now." *Daedalus* 100 (1971): 732–44.

Jordan Jr., V. E. "Blacks in Higher Education: Some Reflections." *Daedalus* 104 (1975): 160–65.

Kelly, Don Quinn. "Ideology and Education: Uplifting the Masses in Nineteenth Century Alabama." *Phylon* 40 (1979): 147–58.

Lamon, Lester C. "The Black Community in Nashville and the Fisk University Strike of 1924–1925." *The Journal of Southern History* 40 (1974): 224–44.

Laukaitia, William E. "Problems and Progress in the Desegregation of the Predominantly Public University of North Carolina A&T University." *Negro Educational Review* 31 (1980): 60–69.

Lindsey, Beverly et. al. "Progressive Education and the Black College." *The Journal of Black Studies* 7 (1977): 341–57.

Little, Monroe R. "The Extra-Curricular Activities of Black College Students, 1868–1940." *The Journal of Negro History* 65 (1980): 135–48.

Logan, Rayford W. "The Evolution of Private Colleges for Negroes." *The Journal of Negro Education* 27 (1958): 213–20.

Marable, Manning. "Tuskegee Institute in the 1920s." *Negro History Bulletin* 40 (1978): 764–68.

Martin, Sandy Dwayne. "The American Baptist Home Mission Society and Black Education in the South, 1865–1920." *Foundations: A Journal of History Theology and Ministry* 44 (1981): 310–27.

Mathews, Marcia M. "The Difference between Black and White." *The Saturday Evening Post* 232 (1960): 13–15.

Mays, Benjamin E. "The Black Colleges in Higher Education." in C. V. Willis and R. R. Edmonds, eds., *Black Colleges in America*. New York: Columbia University, Teachers' College Press, 1978, 24–31.

———. "What is the Future of Negro Colleges." *Southern School News* (1961)

———. "The Future of Negro Colleges." *Saturday Review* (1961): 53–54.

McKay, Rich. "Post-Slavery South Chained to Hard Labor." *Atlanta Journal-Constitution* (July 25, 2011).

McWhorter, Gerald A. "Struggle, Ideology and the Black University." *Negro Digest* 18 (1970): 89–90.

Miller, Kelly. "The Past, Present and Future of the Negro College." *The Journal of Negro Education* 2 (1933): 411–22.

Mills, James A. "Changes in the Faculties of Negro Colleges." *The Quality Review of Higher Education Among Negroes* 30 (1962): 153–57.

Mitchell, E. C. "Higher Education and the Negro." *American Baptist Home Mission Monthly* 18 (1896).

Mitchell, James J. "Negro Higher Education: Years of Crises." *The Quarterly Review of Higher Education among Negroes* 30 (1962): 18–21.

Mitchell, Theodore R. "From Black to White: The Transformation of Educational Reform in the New South, 1890–1910." *Educational Theory* 39 (1989): 337–50.

Moreland, Marc. "Samuel Howard Archer: Portrait of a Teacher." *Phylon* 4 (1949): 351–55.

Morgan, Thomas J. "Defects of Industrial Education." *American Baptist Home Mission Monthly* 22 (1900).

Morris, E. W. "The Contemporary Negro College and the Brain Drain." *The Journal of Negro Education* (1972).

Morrow, David. "The Morehouse College Glee Club: History and Recent Highlights." *Western Journal of Black Studies* 11 (1987): 181–84.

"Negro Higher and Professional Education in the United States." *The Journal of Negro Education Yearbook* 17 (1948).

"The Negro Private and Church-Related College." *The Journal Negro Education Yearbook* 29 (1960).

Newby, Robert G. and David B. Tyack. "Victims without Crimes: Some Historical Perspectives on Black Education." *The Journal of Negro Education* 40 (1971): 192–206.

The New York Times (March 29, 1984).

Noble, Jeanne. "The Black Student Movement: A Search for Identity." *The Journal of the National Association of Women Deans & Counselors* 32 (1969): 49–54.

Oak, Vishnu V. "Higher Education and the Negro." *Education* 53: 132, 176–81.

Oppenheimer, Martin. "Institutions of Higher Learning and the 1960 Sit Ins: Some Clues for Social Action." *The Journal of Negro Education* 32 (1963): 286–88.

Our Baptist Ministers. American Baptist Historical Papers, Mercer University, 531–32.

Patterson, Frederick D. "College for Negro Youth and the Future." *The Journal of Negro Education* 27 (1958): 110–11.

Rafky, D. M. "The Black Professor and Academic Freedom." *Negro Education Review* (1971).

Ray, Louis. "Revisiting Charles H. Thompson's Proposal for Educating Gifted African American Students. 1933–1961." *The Journal of Negro Education* 81 (2012): 190–99.

Reed, J. "Increasing Opportunities for Black Students min Higher Education." *The Journal of Negro Education* 48 (1978): 18–24.

Rosser, J. M. "Higher Education and the Black American: An Overview." *The Journal of Negro Education* 47 (1972): 143–50.

Roth, Robert M. "A Self-Selection Process by Southern Negroes Existing in a Southern Negro College." *The Journal of Negro Education* 28 (1959): 185–86.

Roy, Joseph E. "The Higher Education of the Negro, No Mistake." *First and Second Conference on the Negro Question.* New York: Negro Universities Press, 1969.

Saunders Jr., R. Klein, and Arthur Jay. "Survey of Negro Colleges and Universities." *Bulletin* 7 (1928).

Saunders, R. Frank and George A. Rogers. "Joseph Thomas Robert and the Wages of Conscience." *Georgia Historical Quarterly* 1 (2004): 1–24.

Scott, Emmett J. "Twenty Years After: An Appraisal of Booker T. Washington." *The Journal of Negro Education* 5 (1936): 543–45.

Simms, William E, ed. "Black College Bicentennial Offers Little Hope." *The Journal of Negro Education* 45 (1977): 219–24.

Singh, Harbans. "A Proposal for a College for Gifted Negro Students." *The Quarterly Review of Higher Education Among Negroes* 30 (1962): 158–59.

Sisk, Glen. "Morehouse College." *The Journal of Negro Education* 27 (1958): 201.

———. "The Negro Colleges in Atlanta." *The Journal of Negro Education* 33 (1964): 131–35.

Streator, George. "Negro College Radicals." *Crisis* 42 (1934).

Taylor, Dalmas A. "The Relationship between Authoritarianism and Ethnocentrism in Negro College Students." *The Journal of Negro Education* 31 (1962): 455–59.

Thomas, David A. "Moving Into the Freshman Dorm 44 Years Later: The New President Dives into College Life." *The Washington Post*, September 11, 2018.

Thompson, Charles H. "The Education of the Negro in the United States." *School and Society* 42 (1935): 625–33.

———. "The Negro College: In Retrospect and in Prospect." *The Journal of Negro Education* 27 (1958): 127–31.

———. "The Present Status of the Negro Private and Church-Related College." *The Journal of Negro Education* 29 (1960): 227–44.

———. "The Socio-Economic Status of the Negro in the United States." *The Journal of Negro Education* 2 (1933): 26–37.

Thompson, D. C. "Black College Faculty and Students: The Nature of Their Interaction." In *Black Colleges in America: Challenges and Development.* Edited by Charles V. Willie and R. R. Edmonds. New York: Columbia

University Teachers' College Press, 1978, 37–45.
Toole, Tucker. "Morehouse President Faces Questions about College's New Gender Admissions Policy" *HBCU EDUCATION* (May 8, 2019).
Trent Jr., W. J. "The Future of the Negro College and Its Financing." *Daedalus* 100 (1871): 647–59.
Tribble, Israel. "Black Choice in the Higher Education Marketplace." *Negro Educational Review* 30 (1979): 233–41.
Urban Wayne J. "Philanthropy and the Black Scholar: The Case of Horace Mann Bond." *The Journal of Negro Education* 58 (1989): 478–93.
Vernon, Carlos H. "A Current History of Black Colleges." *Black World* 22 (1973): 26–33.
Viorst, Milton. "Howard University: Campus and Cause." *Harper's* (1961): 51–60.
Walters, Hubert. "Black Music and the Black University." *Black Scholar* 3 (1972): 14–21.
Ward, William Hayes. "Higher Education." *American Baptist Home Mission Monthly* 22 (1900).
Ware, Edward T. "Higher Education of Negroes in the United States." *Annals of the American Academy of Political Social Science* 49 (1913).
Watkins, William H. "Teaching and Learning in the Black College: A 130-Year Retrospective." *Teaching Education* 3 (1990): 10–25.
Weaver, George L. "The New Challenge to Negro Colleges." *Negro Digest* 11 (1962): 33–37.
We Are Morehouse Magazine (June 2019).
Webster, David S. "Black Student Elite: Enrollment Shifts of High Achieving, High Socio-Economic Status Black Students from Black to White Colleges during the 1970s." *College and University* 56 (1981): 283–91.
White, William J. "The Founding of the Atlanta Baptist College." Atlanta University Presidential Records, John Hope, Box 72. Archive Research Center, Robert W. Woodruff Library.
Williams, Clyde C. "Myth and Realities Concerning Black Colleges in Higher Education: A Lodestar for a Historical Analysis." *Debate and Understanding: A Journal for the Study of Minority Americans' Economic, Political and Social Development* (1979): 221–27.
Williams, Lea E. "Public Policies and Financial Exigencies: Black Colleges Twenty Years Later, 1965–1985." *Journal of Black Studies* 19 (1988): 135–49.
———. "The United Negro College Fund in Retrospect: A Search for Its True Meaning." *The Journal of Negro Education* 49 (1980): 363–72.
Willie, Charles V. "The Educational Goals of Black Colleges." *The Journal of*

Higher Education 50 (1979): 89–96.

Wilson, Reginald. "Can Black Colleges Solve the Problem of Access for Black Students?" *American Journal of Education* 98 (1990): 443–57.

Wingard, Edward. "The Experience of Historically Black Colleges in Serving Diversely Prepared Students." *New Directions in Experiential Learning* 17 (1982): 29–36.

Winston, Michael R. "Through the Back Door: Academic Racism and the Negro Scholar in Historical Perspective." *Daedalus* 100 (1971): 678–719.

Wright, Stephen J. "The Development of the Hampton-Tuskegee Pattern of Higher Education." *Phylon* (1949): 334–42.

Young, Carlene. "The Struggle and Dreams of Black Studies." *The Journal of Negro Education* 53 (1984): 368–78.

WEBSITES

https://www.aaup.org/article/historically-black-Colleges-and-universities-time-economic-crisis

https://abogond.workpress.com/2009/05/29/the_clark_doll_experiment

https://www.active.cm/page22630.aspx?PageMode=Print

https://www.africa-upenn.edu

https://askville/amazon.co./funeral-home-prepared-Dr-Martin-Luther-King-Jr-'s-body.vie.

https://www.atlantamagazine.com.Channels/bestofatlantapro-files/story.aspx?ID=116970.

https://www.biography.com/articles/Booker-T-Washington-9524663?print

https://www.bizpareview.com/2013.05/01/prominent.black-pastors=speak-ing=invitatioin.revoke.

https://blackcollege.blogspot.com/2006/09/massey-to-retire-as-morehouse

https://www.buckhead.com/neighborhoods/tuxedo-park/

https://books.google.com.books/about/Rob-ert_A_M_Stern.html?id=keB1CpZp3-8C

https://books.google.com/books?pg=PA116&dq=Wallace%20Buttrick%20

https://caselaw.findlaw.com/ga-court-of-appeals/1024644.html

https://education.stateuniversity.com/pages/1855/College-ExtrscurricularActiv-ities.html.

https://encyclopedia.jrank.org

https://www.georgiaencyclopedia.org/nga/Article.isp?id=h-880.

https://georgiainfo.galileo.usg.edu/gahistmarkers/centralcityhistmarker.html

https://www.thehabarinetwork.com

https://harvardmagazine.com

https://www.history.navy.mil/faqa57-4/html

https://jolomo.net/atlanta/trolley/html
https://www.majoritylorassociatiion.org/moses_bio.html.
www.migenweb.net/kent/baxter1891/31churches.hmtl
https://www.mlk-kpp01.stanford.edu
https://www.morehouse.edu/about/franklinspeeches/atyourservice.html
https://www.morehouse.edu/aboiut/franklinspeeches/atyourservice.html
https://www.morehouse.edu/communicatioins/releases/index.html
https://www.nald.ca/library/research/adlitus/p19,html
https://naswdc.org/diversity/black_history/2005/hope/asp
https://www.newworldencyclopedia.org/entry/Normal_school
https://www.nytimes.com/1994/09/28/us/morehouse-financial-questions-reach-board-chairman.html
https://www.nytimes.com./2007/05/02/education
https://www.pbk.org
https://www.pbs.org/wgbh/pages/frontline/show/sats/where/history/html
https://www.questia/com/library/journal
https://www.quotecounterquote.com/2009/11
https://wwspartacus.schoolnet.co.uk/USA/Acivil64.html
https://tennesseeencyclopedia.net/entry.php?=1147
https://www.wcrhuibert.com/tribute_to_Dr_Hope_html
https://www.enwikipedia.org/wiki/Civil_Rights_Act_of_1964.
https://en.wikipedia.org/wiki/Cotton_States_and_Internatinal_Exposition
https //en.wikipedia.org/wiki/Academic_major
https://wikipedia.org/wiki/assassination_of_martin_luther_king-Jt
https://wikipedia.org/wiki/Donn_Clendenon
https://www.southviewcementery.com
https://www.time.com/time/magazine/article/0,9171.181039.00.html
https://www.vibe.com/features/editorial/mean-girls-morehouse-40456/
https://en.wikipedia.org
https://en.wikipedia.org/wiki/African_Americans_in_Atlanta
https://en.wikipedia.org/wiki/Attack_on_Pearl_Harbor
https://en.wikipedia.org/wiki/Civil_Rights_Act_of_1964
https://en.wikipedia.org/wiki/Early_entrance_to_college
https://en.wikipedia.org/wiki/Robert_F._Smith_(investor)
https://www.worldwar1.com

Index